mosiac floor

reservoir

cave of John the Baptist

baptizing pool

well

Church of John Paul II

water system

mosaic floor

JORDAN TOURISM BOARD

THE MONASTERY COMPLEX at Tell el-Kharrar contains several Byzantine-era churches as well as an elaborate water system that incorporated reservoirs, springs, wells and pools. A key focus of the site was a cave (upper left in photo) that was alleged to have been used by John the Baptist to conduct baptisms. Excavators here also uncovered numerous remains indicating settlement during the Roman era and as far back as the late Hellenistic period (second century B.C.). In the plan above, the monastery is at right.

The Cave of
John the Baptist

THE MOSAIC FLOOR (top photo) of the main church in
the monastery complex bears a five-line Greek inscription that
reads, "By the help of the grace of Christ our God the whole
monastery was constructed in the time of Rhotorios, the most
God-beloved presbyter and abbot. May God the savior give
him mercy." The primary focus of the site in ancient times
was the church built around a cave (bottom photo), which
uses the cave as its apse. Christian tradition identified the cave
as the dwelling place of John the Baptist.

ALSO BY SHIMON GIBSON

Archaeological Encyclopedia of the Holy Land
(New York, 2001)
Jerusalem in Original Photographs 1850–1920
(London, 2003)

Many pilgrims apparently preferred manmade
pools to the river currents; the steps leading into the pool
indicate that it was used for baptisms.

The Cave of
John the Baptist

The Stunning Archaeological Discovery
That Has Redefined Christian History

Shimon Gibson

DOUBLEDAY

New York   London   Toronto   Sydney   Auckland

PUBLISHED BY DOUBLEDAY
a division of Random House, Inc.
1745 Broadway, New York, New York 10019

DOUBLEDAY and the portrayal of an anchor with a dolphin are registered
trademarks of Doubleday, a division of Random House, Inc.

This edition of THE CAVE OF JOHN THE BAPTIST is published by special
arrangement with Century, a division of The Random House Group Limited
20 Vauxhall Bridge Road, London SW1V 2SA.

Cataloging-in-Publication Data
is on file with the Library of Congress.

ISBN 0-385-50347-4

PRINTED IN THE UNITED STATES OF AMERICA

September 2004
First Edition

10   9   8   7   6   5   4   3   2   1

Dedicated to Anne Whitehead, Sheila Bishop,
and the late Joseph Peeples
for all their enthusiasm
in the project

Acknowledgements

The cave was discovered during an archaeological survey of Suba and its environs which was conducted in 1999 in collaboration with Shimon Dar of Bar Ilan University. Excavations were subsequently conducted at the site of the cave from 2000 to 2003 by Shimon Gibson (Director) and James Tabor (Associate Director) on behalf of the University of North Carolina at Charlotte and with the sponsorship of the Jerusalem Historical Society (directed by the late Joseph Peeples) and the Foundation for Biblical Archaeology (directed by Sheila Bishop). The project was largely funded through the generosity of the John C. Whitehead and the Altman-Kaziekes Foundations, to whom I am most grateful. I am especially grateful to Anne Whitehead and Roger C. Altman for their generous support. Principal team members consisted of Egon Lass (Field Director), Rafi Lewis (Site Manager and Assistant Field Supervisor), Fadi Amirah (Surveyor and Draughtsman), Reuven Kalifon (Assistant Field Supervisor and Kibbutz Liaison) and Anna de Vincenz (Administrator). Additional staff and specialists working with us included Nick Slope (Field Director), Alexandra Drenka (Finds Curator), Mahmud Salami (Foreman), Neil Munro (Geomorphologist), Noël Siver (Pottery Conservation), Edward Maher (Fauna), Aryeh Shimron (Geologist and Plaster Expert), Mira Matthews (thorium-uranium tests), and Elisabetta Boeretto (radiocarbon determinations). I wish to thank the Kibbutz Tzova authorities for their support of the project, and particularly to Ya'aqov Ha-Tsubai, Amnon Shifman, Eyal Mutzan and Yisrael Karni.

During the writing of this book I was able to benefit from the advice and help of numerous people: Claudine Dauphin, Leah Di

Segni, Joan Taylor, Anna de Vincenz, M. Piccirrillo, Fanny Vitto, Rupert Chapman, Felicity Cobbing, Tal Ilan, Jonathan Price, Hans Konrad Koch, C. P. Thiede, Zbigniew T. Fiema, James H. Charlesworth, Katy Galor, Joe Zias, Émile Puech, Nikos Kokkinos, Magen Broshi, Maatje Dekker, Rami G. Khouri, Mohammed Waheeb, Jo Clarke, Habeeb Habash, and Boaz Zissu.

My profound thanks to my literary agent, Jonathan G. Harris (Luxton Harris Ltd), for his unstinting support during the writing of this book. I am also grateful to Mark Booth and Hannah Black at Century for their goodwill and patience on the bumpy road to publication. My thanks also to Pascal Cariss for excellent copy-editing.

S.G.

Contents

List of Illustrations

3.4: Comparative chart showing Byzantine period representations of secular, military and religious figures (different scales): (1) Suba cave; (2) Nazareth; (3) Avdat; (4) Avdat; (5) Nessana; (6) Nessana; (7) el-Amarna; (8) Beth Alpha; (9) Umm al-Rasas.

3.5: Suba cave: reconstruction of the interior of the cave in the Byzantine period.

3.6: Lead souvenir badge from the L. Wolfe collection, with the Nativity scene (left) and the Baptism scene (right).

3.7: Rome: baptism scenes from Catacomb of Callixtus (left) and from Catacomb of St Peter and St Marcellinus (right).

3.8: Ravenna: baptism scenes from the Neoniano Baptistery (left) and from the Arian Baptistery (right).

3.9: Baptism scenes on ivory plaque in British Museum (left) and on a wooden reliquary box in Vatican (right).

CHAPTER FOUR

4.1: The Bobbio *eulogia* depicting the flight of Elizabeth (left) and the Temple Mount *eulogia* fragment (right).

4.2: Nineteenth-century engraving depicting a typical shepherd.

4.3: Assyrian relief depicting men holding skewers with locusts.

4.4: Ain el-Habis: view of the monastery (above) and the entrance to the Cave of John the Baptist, in an engraving from 1681 made by Reyzen van Cornelius de Bruyn.

4.5: Ain el-Habis: (a) new plan of the Cave of John the Baptist; (b) section through cave with 'bed' of John the Baptist on far right; (c) section through cave and 'veranda' on the right.

4.6: Ain el-Habis: Zuallardo's engraving of the area from 1586 (version by Sandys): (a) 'wilderness'; (b) cave; (c) fountains; (d) monastery.

4.7: Ain el-Habis: the Chapel or Tomb of Elizabeth: (a) plan of building complex; (b) elevation of the western façade.

4.8: Ain el-Habis: the Chapel or Tomb of Elizabeth: (1) the *tabula ansata* lintel over the main entrance to the building and (below) the threshold of the entrance; (2) stone with incised Latin cross; (3) lintel with cross flanked by incised letters.

CHAPTER SIX

6.1: Reconstruction of vessel assemblage from the cave dating from the time of John the Baptist.

6.2: The so-called 'Altar' stone.

6.3: Drawing of the top of the 'Footstep' stone and a section through it.

6.4: Reconstruction showing how the 'Footstep' stone was used.

6.5: Reconstruction drawing of the cave as it would have appeared at the time of John the Baptist.

6.6: Plans of stepped ritual baths (*miqwa'ot*) (1) at Ain Karim: next to the traditional birthplace of John (St Johns); (2) Khallat Abu Sud; (3) Beit Jimal; (4) Qumran No. 71.

CHAPTER SEVEN

7.1: An axiometric drawing of the Suba cave: (1) stepped entrance; (2) basin; (3) basin; (4) alcove in east wall; (5) cave. The position of the Byzantine period drawings on the east are also shown here.

7.2: An axiometric drawing of the Suba cave and the valley outside: (1) valley floor; (2) pond (the *gbi*); (3) barrier wall; (4) basin; (5) entrance porch; (6) cave; (7) 'trough' area above cave.

7.3: Section through the cave showing the amounts of soil which accumulated during the different periods.

CHAPTER EIGHT:

8.1: Map of the Lower Jordan River showing the location of the sites mentioned in the text.

8.2: Portion of the Lower Jordan River on the Madaba Map showing the baptism sites (second half of the sixth century).

8.3: Tell el-Kharrar: dedicatory inscription in Greek mentioning Rhetorius.

8.4: Machaerus: general plan with the first-century-buildings marked in grey: (1) paved courtyard; (2) storerooms; (3) *miqweh*; (4) bath-house.

8.5: Machaerus: reconstruction of the courtyard as it might have looked at the time of John the Baptist.

8.6: Machaerus: one of the Roman siege-camps near Machaerus: (1-2) doorways; (3) building for the Roman commander.

CHAPTER NINE

9.1: Map of the ancient city of Samaria/Sebaste (based on Hamilton 1961 and a map of the village provided courtesy of the Municipality of Sebaste): (1) Cathedral of St John; (2-4) Roman tombs; (5) aqueduct from the spring of Ain Nakoura; (6) water fountain north of square; (7) village of Sabastiyeh; (8) Church of the Invention of the Head of John the Baptist; (9) Roman city wall; (10) altar?; (11) city gate (area of Betty Murray's excavations); (12) acropolis of site; (13) Roman forum; (14) stadium; (15) theatre; (16) temple; (17) columned street.

9.2: Plan of the Church of the Invention of the Head of John the Baptist and the adjacent remains of the monastery (based on Crowfoot 1937, Plate 12): (1) narthex; (2) church; (3) mosaic floor with Greek inscription; (4) apse; (5) chapel; (6) mosaic floor; (7) main north external wall; (8-9) graves; (10) main south external wall.

9.3: Greek inscription in mosaic floor in southern aisle of church (based on Crowfoot 1937, Plate 17c).

9.4: Painting in the east wall of the crypt of the Church of the Invention of the Head of John the Baptist: (1) soldier; (2) John the Baptist; (3) prison opening?; (4) adoring angels; (5) diggers; (6) head of John the Baptist being dug up from cavity; (7) onlookers – monks; (8) onlookers – pagans; (9) aperture in ceiling of crypt; (10) pavement (now destroyed); (11) white plaster fill; (12) covering slab for tomb; 13) tomb.

9.5: Plan of the underground Tomb of John the Baptist: (4) small domed structure; (15) doorway leading to steps; (22) original entrance to tomb chamber; (23) steps; (24) basalt panelled door; (25) arched alcove which was probably the place of the tomb of John the Baptist; (26) raised floor; (27) lower floor; (28) blocked loculus?; (29) Muslim prayer niche (*mihrab*); (30) *loculi*; (32) bone-collecting chamber; (33) arched alcove which was probably the place of the tombs of Elisha and Obadiah; (34) arched alcove; (35) arched alcove; (36) built pier.

9.6: Plan of the underground Tomb of John the Baptist as it would have appeared in the first century AD.

9.7: Sebaste ('Sebastis') on a mosaic floor from Umm al-Rasas (based on Piccirillo and Alliata 1994, Plate XII).

9.8: Plan of the Crusader Cathedral of St John at Sebaste: (1) main entrance; (2) chapel (*maqam*) above the Tomb of John the Baptist; (3) pier of Crusader church; (4) small domed structure; (5) pulpit (*minbar*) in mosque; (6) entrance to mosque; (7) minaret (*mithaneh*); (8) Muslim prayer niche (*mihrab*); (9) hall; (10) structure; (11) west wall of cathedral; (12) north-west tower (belfry?); (13) Roman defensive tower; (14) sunken paved courtyard in front of church; (15) entrance leading to underground Tomb of John the Baptist; (16) elevated platform; (17) elevated platform; (18) pier of church (not visible); (19) Muslim prayer niche (*mihrab*); (21) pier of Crusader church; (42) pier of Crusader church; (43) south wall of church; (44) window; (45) window; (46) large marble column; (47) west wall of chapel (*maqam*); (49) west wall of chapel; (51) east wall of chapel; (54) chapel (*maqam*); (55) extension

CREDITS

All the illustrations and plates in this book are held in copyright by the author (and the Jerusalem Archaeological Field Unit), except for a small number of illustrations and plates (4b, 7a, 15b) provided courtesy of the Palestine Exploration Fund, London; and one plate (13c) reproduced courtesy of Boaz Zissu and the Israel Antiquities Authority, Jerusalem.

Introduction

Brushing away the soil covering the lower part of the wall of the cave, I could not believe my eyes. 'Come and have a look at this,' I shouted to Arthur, the teenager assisting me with the archaeological surveying. 'What do you make of this?' We crawled closer to the wall of the cave, wriggling past boulders with the tops of our heads brushing against the ceiling, until our faces came close to the clammy yellow cave wall. I held the torch forwards at an oblique angle to help highlight an incised image I thought I could make out on the side wall of the cave. It seemed to be that of a large figure holding a staff or spear in one hand. Was this a drawing of a Roman soldier? I sensed I was on the verge of making a major archaeological discovery – I could feel tingling in my hands.

It was a cloudy November day on that morning of the discovery in 1999, and crawling about in a damp cave taking archaeological measurements was the last thing I felt inclined to do. I am now glad that I persevered. The cave was located on the edge of a hilly slope near the bottom of a deep valley and the entrance was almost totally obscured by a profusion of dank vegetation and unrelenting thorn bushes. The only way to get into the cave was by sliding in feet first with one's bags in one hand and the measuring equipment in the other. I had another look at the drawing of the figure – this was indeed an amazing discovery. Waving my torch from side to side I could now make out other drawings: the outline of an arm with the fingers of the hand outstretched as if in greeting and next to it a large cross. I began checking the other cave walls. On the opposite wall I could make out some more incised drawings, including one that seemed to be of a cross within a circle – or was it a representation of a head? The tingling in my hands continued and I instinctively knew I was going to be spending a lot more time doing research in this cave. Gazing at a row of incised crosses further along the wall it flashed into my mind that it was inconceivable that the large figure was of a Roman soldier and I could now see the spear was actually a representation of a shepherd's staff. The drawing of the crosses also had to be the work of a Christian. It suddenly occurred to me that the large figure might be a representation of John the Baptist himself.

Three years have now passed since this cave was discovered. Not coincidentally, as we shall see, the cave is located close to Ain Karim – the traditional birthplace of John the Baptist – west of Jerusalem. Much has changed during these years, almost two thirds of the cave have now been excavated and an enormous amount of soil and debris (more than four metres deep) has been removed. I owe all of this to the tremendous effort made by a dedicated and skilled staff of archaeologists and specialists working with me. The Associate Director of the expedition was James Tabor, a senior lecturer at the University of North Carolina at Charlotte, and groups of his students attended various stages of the excavation. Together we achieved a lot. I am now quite certain that this cave was connected with the ancient cult of John the Baptist. Indeed, this may very well be *the* cave of the early years of John's life, the place where he sought his first solitude in the 'wilderness' and the place where he first practised his baptism procedures. This may even be the place where Jesus brought his disciples for baptism. But, as you can see, I am already jumping well ahead of my story.

What sort of person was John the Baptist? We shall probably never know with absolute certainty. No memoirs or personal writings about him have survived, if indeed they ever existed, and the written information that we do have about him is extremely hazy and indirect, so much so that these texts probably say more about the commentators themselves than about John. And so he has remained a fairly shadowy and one-dimensional character, with an indistinct, almost aloof, persona. One could infer from this that John was nothing more than a literary invention, but modern scholarship does unequivocally accept that two thousand years ago there was indeed an historical person living in Palestine named John the Baptist. This is largely because we possess a brief mention of John outside the Gospels, in the writings of Josephus, a Jewish historian of the first century. He was, according to this account, a down-to-earth Jewish prophet and baptiser, with a unique public message regarding sin and repentance, which ultimately made him a popular leader among his fellow Jews. This John was a man of the people who was ultimately executed because he was seen to be a potential threat to the regime of a local ruler, Herod Antipas. A different – though not entirely inconsistent – depiction of John appears in the Gospel writings – a man with a unique childhood and an ascetic lifestyle, who withdrew into the desert dressed in animal skins and with a strange diet, whose mission was to prepare his followers for the coming of Jesus, a man who died on the whim of a female and not because he necessarily posed any ostensible threat to Antipas. One wonders therefore to what degree parts of the material in the Gospels (notably Mark 1:4–6; 6:14–29; Matthew 3:1–6; 11:2–6; Luke 1:5–25, 39–45, 57–80; 3:1–6, 19–20; 7:18–23; John 1:6–8, 19–42; 3: 22–30) were legendary or based only loosely on the actual historical figure? The circumstances of John's life were only deemed important for the Gospel writers in so far as it related to the central story about the mission and subsequent martyrdom of Jesus Christ. Hence, some of the 'facts' about John's life may well have been literary inventions, as some scholars have suggested. The John of the Gospels may in some way be a composite symbol of the many ascetics, prophets and revolutionaries who were prevalent in ancient Palestine during different stages of the first century AD.

As an archaeologist, I am constantly being asked whether the purpose of my work is to seek proof of the stories and events as they appear in the Old and New Testaments. My answer is emphatically that this is not possible, as the Bible is not an historical document to be proved or disproved, albeit there are numerous strands of historical information of varying quality that may actually be teased out of the texts. More importantly, however, the archaeologist is able to supply the archaeological *context* for the Biblical stories and events, by excavating ancient towns and places (the fortifications, gates, palaces and domestic houses), by examining contemporary inscriptions, as well as by looking at a myriad of other material cultural remains, such as pottery, weapons, jewellery and so forth. Of course, one must not infer from this that archaeologists are passionately hunting for the likes of Bathsheba's bath-tub or searching for fragments of tablets with the Ten Commandments inscribed on them. This would be patently absurd. However, at the same time, archaeologists are able to point quite confidently to general types of water-ablution installations and inscribed plaques (stelae) as *illustrations* of what might have been in the minds of those compiling the Bathsheba or Ten Commandment stories.

In regard to specific events and places relating to the Jesus and John

stories in the New Testament, an enormous amount of new archaeological data has emerged in recent years, but not enough of this
material has been absorbed by scholars investigating the historical
processes of that time – if one is to judge by existing publications. There
are a good number of sites associated with John the Baptist in Israel/
Palestine and Jordan, notably Ain Karim, Ain el-Habis, various places in
the Jordan Valley region, Machaerus and Sebaste, all of which have
exciting archaeological features which I shall deal with later on in this
book. While many of these sites have remains dating back to the time
of John the Baptist, none of these could be connected *directly* to the
actual belief systems of John and his followers. At least not until our
discovery in 1999 of a cave dedicated to John the Baptist in the hills west
of Jerusalem. When we subsequently excavated there, we discovered
beneath the Christian levels of the Byzantine period much earlier
remains dating back to the first century AD. As we gradually excavated
the lower parts of this cave we were quite astonished to find remains of
ritual activities relating to the practice of baptism dating back to the time
of John the Baptist and that of his followers. Could John the Baptist
himself have used this cave? This book is about the story of the
discoveries in the cave and the significance of the finds made there.

They say that a story is worthwhile hearing if you know who is telling
it, so perhaps I should say a few words about myself. My relationship
with the archaeology of Israel/Palestine is an intimate one, spanning
more than three decades. The Negev Desert is where it all began when
I was still a child and in my mind's eye I can still conjure up the bright
yellow and brown landscapes absorbed into the sharp glare (the sort that
makes a person want to squint) and can still feel the intense hovering
heat – especially around noon – as it would beat down on the rocks and
upon my neck, suffocating the air in the process. As a small boy from
London, used to being hemmed in on all sides by brick houses blocking
out even short distances, I was enthralled by the vast grandeur of this
landscape with its endless low hills spreading out in every direction
towards fluctuating bands of a purple horizon; eventually I trained my
eyes so that I could focus in on even minute details great distances away.
I enjoyed sitting and watching the ever-moving desert in much the same
way as someone will watch television: monitoring the odd way that
spiralling gusts of wind would skip and turn across the desert floor like
fingers from the sky; observing the special gait of camels threading their
way carefully along dusty trails, and keeping check on the slow pace of
the bleating goats shepherded along by dark Bedouin swathed in black.

The desert was my playground, and together with my twin brother I was forever hunting for wild donkeys, wandering along its paths, catching snakes and scorpions, picking up fossils. All of the desert's secrets lay in front of us and we wanted to explore every last bit of it. It was here that archaeology grabbed me – the ruined farmhouses from the Byzantine and Umayyad periods, water cisterns, broken pieces of pottery (some with geometric and moulded designs), and numerous examples of rock art with drawings of humans and animals, crosses, and Greek and Arabic letters. There were even scatters of prehistoric flint tools lying about, dating back many hundreds of thousands of years. Sometimes I wandered about the desert barefoot, dreaming – as a child sometimes will – that I was an ancient nomadic warrior striding through the wilderness, swinging my sword in the sky and uttering blood-curdling howls, sending shivers up the backs of my opponents. This was a potent fantasy, but as I grew older I wanted to know much more about the archaeological remains littering the desert floor and what they all meant, and I did this through reading as many books as I could get hold of, which was quite difficult, living, as I was, in the middle of a desert.

Moving to Jerusalem in the 1970s gave me my first taste of a city steeped in the cult of the past and in the architectural celebration of some of the major religions of the world. The great antiquity of the place is manifested at almost every corner in the Old City by numerous churches, mosques and synagogues, and especially by a number of very unique places: namely, the incense-choked Church of the Holy Sepulchre, containing within it the traditional Tomb of Jesus, and the magnificent Haram al-Sharif enclosure (also known as the Temple Mount), surmounted by the breathtaking Dome of the Rock, and on its western side by a wall built of enormous squared blocks of stone weighing many tons dating back to the time of Herod the Great. There are also the wonderful crenellated fortifications surrounding the city itself, built by Süleyman the Magnificent at the time of Ottoman rule in the 1540s, as well as schools, houses, markets, pools and narrow streets, and all of these I gradually came to explore, visiting shops, striking up friendships with the inhabitants, eating sweetmeats and hot pitta bread straight out of the oven. There was one shop I remember called Rittas in the Christian Quarter, full of interesting rubbish and bric-a-brac, where one could buy postcards of General Allenby riding through the Jaffa Gate in 1917. It was here in Jerusalem that I began appreciating the complexity of urban archaeology as opposed to desert archaeology, and although I was still only a teenager, I managed to get work on a major archaeological excavation that was being done on Mount Zion. For the first time I came to grips with the logistics of large-scale digging, excavating large chunks of fortification walls, houses and tombs, and being able to handle museum objects such as ceramic female idols, coins, inscribed potsherds (broken fragments of pottery vessels), decorated lamps, and so forth. It was here that many thousands of potsherds passed through my hands, and slowly I learnt how to differentiate between the many different types and forms of vessels, and how to date them.

My formal studies were undertaken in London, at the Institute of Archaeology in Gordon Square, a building with a rather austere appearance, but inside it my eyes were opened to the more theoretical and methodological aspects of the discipline, as well as allowing me to acquire a much broader perspective of Near Eastern archaeology through the study of the ancient past of countries such as Turkey, Syria, Iraq and Iran. Since my desert days I had always been fascinated by landscapes, and so it was quite natural that I should eventually write my doctorate on the development of the ancient agricultural field systems of the Israel/Palestine region. And it was this research that brought me one step closer to the subject of John the Baptist. It happened in the late 1980s during fieldwork for my dissertation on a remarkable system of agricultural terraces on the slope of a village site called Sataf with springs of water west of Jerusalem. Opposite this site, on the other side of the Soreq Valley, was the traditional Monastery of St John in the Wilderness (Ain el-Habis), which was reached along a path leading from the direction of the next village, Ain Karim, which also happened to be the traditional birthplace of John the Baptist. I was hooked on the archaeology of this region and over the next decade, although I continued conducting archaeological projects in many other parts of the country, I kept coming back there to further my researches, culminating in an archaeological survey that I made around Suba, just across the hill from Sataf, which resulted in the eventual discovery of the Cave of John the Baptist.

This is the story of the circumstances connected with the discovery and excavation of the Cave of John the Baptist, and the personal quest that I subsequently made to find out more about the life and times of John the Baptist from archaeological sites in the Near East and from historical sources. It is an honest tale of patience and deduction, disappointment and exhilaration. Archaeology is about very demanding physical and mental work. It can be mind-bogglingly boring at times and one needs to have the ability to fit together thousands of clues in a sensible and logical fashion, and to formulate sustainable patterns of knowledge to reflect the truths of the past. It is a vocation that I truly love. For some of my colleagues archaeology is just a profession, a nine-to-five job, but for me it is a way of life. I am dedicated to my work with a certain desperation and intensity, almost as if it were a virus coursing through my veins. When I die I want it to be while on an archaeological dig; I would like to think of my ashes being scattered over an ancient ruin. Ashes to ashes, and so forth.

PART ONE

1

Discovering the Cave of
John the Baptist

The Suba cave must be the most unusual archaeological site that I have ever excavated. During many years spent digging in Israel/Palestine I have been party to the recovery of a wide variety of ancient vestiges, from city walls and opulent town houses to burial caves and industrial installations, but none of this prepared me for the appearance of the strange remains in this cave. There were so many anomalies in the archaeological record that trying to puzzle it all out gave me numerous sleepless nights. Finding the cave in the first place was an incredible stroke of luck. Luck is an important feature of archaeological work: some archaeologists have a nose for important discoveries and possess the instincts of bloodhounds, others are not so lucky, however hard they might persevere in the search for the discovery of a lifetime. Some important discoveries simply fall into the lap of those who are least expecting it.

Before I say something about the circumstances of the discovery of the cave and the story of how we went about excavating it, I should first explain where the cave is located, to set the scene. The cave is in the hills immediately west of Jerusalem, about ten minutes' drive by car from the modern outskirts of the city. Forging their way between the undulating hills are narrow valleys, almost V-shaped in profile, with the flanking slopes covered with trees or agricultural terraces that were built in serried fashion (*plate 1a*). The countryside round about was originally cultivated with Mediterranean-type crops: vineyards and olive groves, orchards of fruit trees, and some grain crops in the valleys. The valleys are dry watercourses (wadis) running from east to west and one only sees water flowing in them when there is a substantial fall of rainfall during the winter months (averaging around 600 mm per year). The cave is located at the bottom of a hill slope on the northern side of one of these valleys, referred to on the local maps by its Arabic names, Wadi esh-Shemmarin and Wadi Ismail (or today in Hebrew, as Nahal Tzova). Ancient roads were once visible leading to the wadi and cave from the direction of Ain Karim and Sataf in the south-east, and from the direction of Suba in the north-east. These roads were only for local use, mostly for villagers and farmers transporting their agricultural produce. The closest main highways in ancient times, the one leading from Jaffa to Jerusalem and the one from Gaza to Jerusalem, were located a couple of kilometres away to the north and south of the cave, respectively. One thing is certain: the cave was not established at this location because of any proximity to a main road.

The cave is located about a kilometre away from the ancient settlement of Suba on top of a hill, a good fifteen-minute walk away but close enough to postulate a connection between the two. The valley (Wadi esh-Shemmarin) in which the cave is situated is quite narrow and it narrows even further – almost to a bottleneck – in the immediate vicinity of the cave. The appearance of the valley floor – now occupied by the kibbutz orchards – has changed substantially, and so it was fascinating looking at aerial photographs dating back to the early part of the twentieth century. These show ancient terraces built at regular intervals along the length of the valley, with a fenced path running parallel to it, along the southern edge. But, at the point next to the cave, a massive barrier wall once existed – crossing the valley like the wall of a dam – and it was here, just below the wall (and protected by it), that the path crossed over to the opposite side of the valley. Passing next to the entrance to the cave, the path resumed a westerly direction, eventually climbing at an oblique angle up the northern slope. Nothing of this path or of the barrier wall has survived the major changes made to the valley floor when the first orchards were planted there in the 1950s.

I saw the cave for the first time in November 1999 when doing an archaeological survey of the environs of Suba in the countryside round about Kibbutz Tzova (a collective Israeli settlement), located not too far from the village of Ain Karim. I was in the dining hall of Kibbutz Tzova one morning having breakfast when one of the members, Reuven Kalifon, a dedicated archaeological buff, approached me and enquired whether I had visited the large plastered cave whose opening was just visible under dense vegetation on one side of the narrow valley to the south of the kibbutz. I hadn't and was immediately intrigued. Later, I tentatively drove along a track leading down the side of this valley and, together with a volunteer, Arthur, who was there to help me take measurements, I made my way inside the cave by scrambling past thorny bushes into the black hole of the entrance (*plate 1b*). My eyes slowly became accustomed to the darkness within and it became possible to make out the general shape of the cave. It was much larger than I had thought it would be, and it was elongated like a long hall (*plate 2a*). Using a tape measure we found that it had a length of about 24 metres and a width of 3.5 metres. I crawled up to the side wall on the left, dragging the tape measure in one hand and holding a drawing board with the other. It was at this point that I became aware of a set of drawings incised into the wall of the cave, hidden behind piled-up boulders. There were also drawings on the opposite wall of the cave. One of the drawings was that of a figure of a man that looked like it could be John the Baptist (*plate 2b*). It reminded me of representations of John the Baptist that I had seen in early Byzantine art. There were also drawings of a hand or arm, a head, crosses and other symbols. It was all very exciting. At first glance the style of the drawings seemed to indicate that they were of Byzantine-to-Early Islamic-period date (made between the fourth to eleventh centuries), but I was still uncertain about this at that time. Perhaps, I thought, this cave might have been connected in some way with the local Byzantine traditions of John the Baptist having spent his childhood in the wilderness (cf. Luke 1:80), and the fact that this place was situated not too far away from John's traditional birthplace at Ain Karim (with the nativity stories there going back to at least the sixth century) was also quite suggestive. Clearly, the cave needed proper archaeological excavation. There were undoubtedly mysteries here that needed to be solved by digging.

I had spent many months in the countryside of Suba investigating a variety of ancient features, but the Cave of John the Baptist was not like anything I had encountered before, it seemed to be unique. All I had been expecting to find on that chilly morning in November 1999 was a simple water container and nothing more. Up to that point I had crawled about in quite a few caves scattered around Suba, among them water cisterns and burial caves (Iron Age and Roman), but none of these was special in any way. The new cave was not only unusually large, it also had very thick plastered walls, which was not common. In the late 1980s a British archaeological team led by Richard Harper and Denys Pringle conducted excavations at nearby Suba, revealing the remains of a twelfth-century Crusader castle (named Belmont in the sources) within the ruins of an Ottoman village abandoned in 1948, at the time of the establishing of the State of Israel. The massive walls of its fortifications, with a sloping revetment and the arched doorways of some of its buildings, are most impressive. Since they did not investigate the surrounding countryside, I thought that it might be an interesting project of landscape archaeology to have a look at the ancient agricultural field systems around Suba and the water-management systems connected with the ancient spring situated further down towards the foot of the hill. I was hoping that the new findings might in some way help to illuminate the important discoveries made by the original British team working at the Crusader fortress. So, together with Professor Shimon Dar, of the Bar Ilan University, we began investigating the spring of Ain Suba and its environs, a nearby reservoir (filled almost to its brim with mud), and an extensive system of agricultural terraces extending down the slopes of the hill in every direction. The lands of Suba belong to Kibbutz Tzova and so we were lucky to have their full cooperation in regard to our exploratory pursuits. One of their members, Ya´aqov Ha-Tsubai, even took us to see the prime archaeological sites that he knew of in the area round about the kibbutz. Much of the survey work entailed briskly walking around in the fields and terraces, looking at rock-cut installations, climbing walls and embankments, crawling into holes in the ground, and picking up broken bits of ancient pottery. One of the team members, Jo Clarke, kindly supplied us every Friday with lumps of Danish blue cheese and bottles of white wine, which helped keep us focused and gave us a sense of satisfaction, even when the work was proceeding slowly and nothing much was being found.

John the Baptist is one of the most intriguing of the characters in the Gospels and I had always wondered whether some evidence confirming the substance of his early childhood and early baptism procedures might some day turn up in an archaeological excavation. The discovery of the cave at Suba therefore raised all sorts of questions relating to the antiquity of the traditions connecting John the Baptist to the Ain Karim region west of Jerusalem. On the day of the discovery of the cave the first thing I did was to go through my library to find my copy of a book written by D. Baldi and B. Bagatti, entitled *Saint Jean-Baptist: Dans Les Souvenirs de sa Patrie*, to see what they had to say about these traditions. The general consensus of opinion among scholars I found was that there was a degree of uncertainty about how ancient these traditions might be.

Hence, it seemed to me to be quite fortuitous that the cave I had chanced upon seemed to be connected to the cult of John the Baptist (if, of course, my initial interpretation of the drawings was correct). The answers, I felt, lay in the depths of soil inside the cave. But should I be the one to excavate the cave, I asked myself. I had to think things over very carefully. Dedicating oneself to the task of excavating a given archaeological site is always a serious undertaking and one has always to be absolutely sure that there is a scientific justification for such work before beginning digging. I wasn't quite sure that I wanted the responsibility. Also, from past experience, I knew that one cannot predict what one will find and some excavations drag on for many years and even decades. Did I really want to get involved in a long-term project digging at the Cave of John the Baptist? I now pondered long and hard but finally, I decided that not only was the excavation worthwhile scientifically, it was also a personal opportunity not to be missed. I now needed to begin raising funds for the dig, to gather together a professional team to undertake the digging and to get the official permits sorted out.

I flew back to my home in London and began seeking financial sponsorship for the excavation at the cave. Archaeological excavations are extremely expensive and all too frequently one has to get one's begging cap out and hope that some benefactor will materialise and offer to cover the costs. Eventually, I spoke by telephone to Joseph Peeples of the Jerusalem Historical Society in Texas, who became very excited about the ancient drawings and the potential that there was in the cave for excavation. Joe was an avuncular sort of person, with a winning sense of humour and enthusiasm. We began making plans and Joe then set out to raise the funds to enable us to conduct at least one season of excavations at the cave. It was at this point that he suggested that a friend of his, Professor James Tabor, might like to join the proposed project as Associate Director, and that his university, the University of North Carolina at Charlotte, might perhaps serve as the overall academic sponsor of the project. Several telephone conversations later and everything had been sorted out and we were all set to begin the work. When I flew back to Jerusalem a month later, I had high hopes for the success of the planned excavation and in an optimistic vein I felt that within a relatively short period of digging we would surely be able to clarify the entire history of the cave and the exact date of the drawings on its walls as well. Little did I know then that it would actually take much longer – almost three years in fact – to obtain all of the answers we were seeking to the many questions that kept buzzing around inside our heads.

From the outset I kept a diary recording the progress of the excavations. It was totally distinct from the type of official record usually kept by archaeologists on excavations, such as stratigraphical field registrars (for the recording of loci and baskets) with measurements and sketch plans, and logbooks of one sort or another. The idea behind writing these progress reports was that it meant I was able to keep friends and sponsors informed by e-mail about what was happening on the dig, almost on a daily basis. Many of these reports were written upon returning from the dig and sometimes even before I had had time to shower or rest, and so they naturally possess a raw edge and a sense of immediacy. Three years on and it is still fun reading through these reports – one gets that immediate rush as if one is participating all over again in the trials and tribulations of the project and in the minutiae of the day-to-day digging. They also remind me of the many people who were associated with the dig; I am so grateful to the many hundreds of amazing volunteers who came on the dig, got excited and worked extremely hard, contributing not only their physical labour but also their hearts and minds. The great thing these reports convey is the exhilaration and passion that we all felt as the dig proceeded, with every new day shedding further light on the mystery of the Cave of John the Baptist.

We were now ready to dig. The tools had largely been bought, the archaeological staff had been organised and the official permit to dig at the site had been applied for. I couldn't wait to begin working at the cave.

2

The Cave and the Birthplace of John the Baptist

Towards the end of February 2000, my team began dealing with the many logistical and organisational details connected with setting up an excavation at the cave. Permits were obtained from Kibbutz Tzova and from the Israel Antiquities Authority, and arrangements were made for permanent office and laboratory space to be established at our dig headquarters in the British School of Archaeology in the Sheikh Jarrah neighbourhood of Jerusalem. A heavy fall of snow had brought an almond tree crashing down over the entrance to the cave and it needed to be sawn up with an electrical chainsaw borrowed from the kibbutz. In advance of the arrival of James Tabor and his students from the States, we spent a couple of days clearing away weeds, vegetation and overgrowth from in and around the entrance to the cave, as well as from around the adjacent terraces. Work began early in March and Tabor's students turned out to be an extremely enthusiastic bunch of people with a wonderful sense of adventure. I had never met Tabor before but was impressed by his archaeological knowledge and willingness to 'get his hands dirty' by digging with everyone else, as well as by the admirable way that he took care of his students (*plate 2c*). During the first ten days of excavation we worked in two different locations: in the area of the porch in front of the cave, and within the cave itself. A mixture of pottery from different periods was found in the dig, with the latest dating from Ottoman times, consisting of fragments of distinctive black water jugs originally made in Gaza, mixed with rubbish and animal bones that had been chucked into the cave by peasants working in the fields outside.

While the dig was in progress I felt I needed to know more about the ancient sites in the vicinity of the cave. The closest was that of Suba. Indeed, a path once led down the valley to the cave from the direction of its main spring of water, Ain Suba, a distance of about fifteen minutes' walk. Ancient Suba is located on a prominent hill on the outskirts of Kibbutz Tzova, and on its summit and slopes one may still see the rather dilapidated houses of an Arab village that was abandoned by its inhabitants during the fighting there in 1948. Lower still on the slopes of the hill and in the landscape all around there used to be a dense network of agricultural terraces and fields enclosed with stone fences. The site was already visited by explorers and visitors in the eighteenth century, and the main attraction was the impressive fortifications of the Crusader castle, Belmont (it flourished in 1170 and was subsequently conquered by Saladin in 1187), sections of which were visible beneath the outlying houses of the Ottoman village [note 2.1]. There was also the erroneous misidentification of the site as that of Modi'in, hometown of the Maccabees, a mistake that could be traced back to the time of the Crusaders themselves who thought that the nearby site of Abu-Ghosh was the Emmaus of the New Testament. In 1738, Richard Pococke, passing through the region, wrote:

> We went a mile to the foot of the hill of the Maccabees, as they [his guides] called it, which is to the north-west; they have some tradition, but I know not on what foundation, that the Maccabees fled to this hill in time of war, and defended themselves on it. We went up the hill, saw many openings to grottos, and in one part, a cistern and ten arched rooms; we descended to what they call the fountain of Mecca [i.e. Ain Suba], over which there is a sepulchral cave: We went around the hill of Mecca [probably named after the nearby *maqam* – holy site – of Sheikh Ibrahim] into the valley which they call the valley of Terebinth, and, they say, it is the vale of Elah . . .

Suba was also visited by a number of important explorers in the nineteenth century, notably by Victor Guérin in April 1863 and later by Claude Reignier Conder during the Survey of Western Palestine in the 1870s. They all noted that the hill had the remains of ancient defence walls, gates, vaulted rooms of good masonry, and rock-cut burial caves. In the late 1980s the site was targeted for archaeological research by the British School of Archaeology, and the excavators uncovered substantial portions of the Crusader castle, as well as some earlier remains, including a mosaic floor from the Byzantine period, and potsherds and isolated artefacts from the Iron Age, Persian and Hellenistic periods [note 2.2]. On the edges of the hill, particularly to the north and east, were burial caves identified as being of Iron Age and Early Roman type, which have also been investigated by archaeologists in recent decades.

On the slope of the hill towards the south of the village was the spring of Ain Suba and in Ottoman times the women of the village would go down to fill jars with water. It was a fair distance and they could only get there by descending the stony path winding down the southern slope of the hill, passing on the right the olive press of the village, the holy site of Sheikh Ibrahim with a magnificent ancient oak tree, and scattered tombs of the local cemetery represented by piles of small stones. Next to the spring there was a flight of ancient steps to help people reach the outlet; a few of these steps were uncovered during a dig and on them were found scattered bullet cartridges – mute evidence of the killing that took place there in 1948. In the nineteenth century and later, the irrigated terraces below the spring of Ain Suba were cultivated with numerous fruit trees, including quinces, oranges, lemons and pomegranates [note 2.3]. The spring itself and the area around it are rich in archaeological remains. Natural water ebbs out of the side of an aquifer in a rocky scarp located underground, within a structure comprising two well-constructed vaulted chambers of excellent masonry dating from the Early Roman period. The quality of the construction of these vaults suggests that it was once originally part of a larger building complex – perhaps an agricultural estate or a bath-house – but these remains are still buried beneath the ground; one day I should like to excavate them. A complex system of rock-cut channels (later replaced by an arched tunnel in the Byzantine period) led the water from the springhouse towards a large plastered reservoir (it was found choked with silt and clay) and along a rocky scarp towards the terraced fields. The reservoir was cleaned out almost single-handedly by Reuven Kalifon from the Kibbutz, and the rock scarp with its complex system of winding rock-cut channels was cleared by groups of enthusiastic American teenagers. At the far end of the scarp, to the south, a large rock-hewn cave dwelling was partially excavated – probably the 'sepulchral cave' Richard Pococke saw in 1738 – and running above the scarp the remarkable remains of a fortification wall were uncovered during a dig that I made at the site.

The segment of fortification wall investigated at Suba had a preserved height of four to five metres and was built of regular courses of very large boulders, fieldstones and roughly trimmed rectangular blocks.

Small fieldstones had been hammered into the interstices to ensure that the wall was completely stable. The construction style resembled fortification walls from the Iron Age and earlier; none of its stones bore the telltale signs of dentate tooling (resulting from the use of a hammer with teeth or a chisel with a serrated edge) that would suggest a wall of later date (i.e. Persian, Hellenistic, or later). We were only able to uncover its outer face because the inner parts are buried beneath the modern orchards of the kibbutz. The distance between the place where we discovered this wall and the 'tell' itself (i.e. the hill of Suba, or the castle of Belmont) was so great that we at first thought this fortification must be part of the defences of a solitary tower or bastion guarding the spring. However, looking at an aerial photograph of Suba (scale 1:1000) we could detect a very clear line extending from the area of our segment of fortification wall towards the south and then swinging through the fields, running all the way towards the hill of Suba.

We spent a day surveying this possible line of the wall. We divided ourselves into three teams and set off, having first eaten cheese and biscuits washed down with white wine. The group that I was with followed the line of the wall for a length of about 140 metres from the direction of the spring of Ain Suba towards the south. Not far along this line was the outlet of another, smaller, spring (Ain Haraba) and it was here that the wall could be seen turning to the west; at one point we could see the thickness of the wall which was 2.5 metres. The orchards of the kibbutz broke up the continuation of the line of the wall but the second team was able to pick up additional small segments of the wall at intervals running towards the north-west, before it finally disappeared. We had now traced the line of the fortification wall for a distance of up to 460 metres. The third team working to the south-east of the hill were not as successful since they had only encountered terraces and caves, including finding the entrance to a tomb with loculi (*kokhim*) dating from the first century AD. They did, however, come across one segment of wall with a corner built of massive stones that appeared to be remnants of a tower. Altogether, the results of the survey were quite conclusive: ancient Suba comprised not just the hill itself, which would have served as the settlement's 'acropolis', but also the large plateau-like area to the south, extending as far as the spring, and this must have been the 'lower city'. How densely built up it was, is anyone's guess; future excavations may be able to unravel this point. We all went away very excited about the discoveries – it is not every day that one finds fortifications surrounding a city! It was now quite clear that Suba in antiquity was a much larger settlement than anyone had previously thought. This helped explain why such an enormous amount of effort had been made to develop the water installations at the spring of Suba, probably from as early as the Iron Age period. Was our cave somehow linked to these water installations of Suba, I asked myself.

The excavations at the cave were proceeding quite nicely and I felt very pleased about the progress we were making. Early every morning, when there was hardly any light in the sky, we reached the cave breathing in the fresh dew filtering between the trees of the orchards, flowing like water down the valley and hugging the lower sides of the terraced hills. The first thing Rafi Lewis, our site manager, would do was to ensure that there was a big pot of black coffee bubbling on the stove. Altogether we were a group of about ten to twenty people. Fortified with coffee and biscuits, we then set about digging with enthusiasm, cutting up the ground with pickaxes, heaving stones, lifting buckets of soil out of the cave and up the steps of the entrance porch to where it was then dumped on to a spoil heap outside, pushing wheelbarrows, climbing ladders and scraping the ground surfaces with trowels and brushes until the sweat shone on our brows and the muscles in our backs began seriously objecting to this merciless toil (*plate 3a*). Breakfast was in the kibbutz canteen just up the hill and at about eight o'clock we would pile into the vehicles and head off for our meal. Well-nourished, we then resumed work, and fervent digging continued throughout the morning. Rafi would walk around the excavation, ensuring that the tools were being used safely and reminding people to drink water because it was so easy to forget and become dehydrated. Discussion took place in the different areas of the excavation as to the significance and interpretation of the features uncovered. All excavation is a process of destruction, and so it is up to the scientific integrity of the archaeologist to ensure that every small bit of evidence, however insignificant it might seem to be, is recorded for posterity. This meant that I was constantly circulating the excavation checking out the different kinds of features as they were slowly being unearthed. 'Yes, you can dig this out, it's just a layer of rubble', or, 'Hang on there, dig carefully, because I think you are just about to expose a floor.' Sometimes the digging in one area had to be stopped while photographs were taken and scaled drawings were made of the ancient features as they emerged from the ground. The ground plan constantly needed updating by our surveyor/draughtsman Fadi Amirah. Pottery was systematically collected during the digging and placed within a bucket with a label marked with the exact location it had come from; every bucket was given a number which was logged into the Field Diary. The diggers would soon reach the point in the late morning when they began feeling tired and sweaty, but they still remained buoyed up by the discoveries being made, and their spirits were lifted by shouts of encouragement across the cave, with joking and story-telling, all of which helped to spur the work along. By this time, the sun would be high in the sky and the pace of the work naturally began to slacken. Those working inside the cave began suffering from the sluggish air, while those sorting for potsherds in the soil outside the cave slowly began withdrawing towards the shade of the orchard trees. This was the point where we would begin cleaning up, straightening the earthen sections between the digging areas (known as 'baulks'), collecting the tools together for storage within the cave and making a final record of the stratigraphy as it stood at the end of that day. We then all went off for a well-deserved lunch in the kibbutz canteen.

What was surprising even at this early stage (2000) of the excavations in the cave was the appearance in the fills of soil of very large quantities of Early Roman pottery (first century AD) mixed with what appeared to be Byzantine-period pottery (fourth to seventh century AD). What was all this Roman material doing there, we asked ourselves. We then came across fragments of Roman shattered jars and jugs lying on an earthen living surface (a 'living surface' is basically a hard earthen area trampled by feet, and is to be distinguished from a 'floor' cut into rock or a pavement made of stone and cement) which was identified on the basis of burning patches and flat-lying potsherds. This surface could be seen extending up against the plastered walls within the niche in the east wall of the cave. This was very exciting and totally unexpected. But what did it all mean? Would this not suggest that the drawings were from the Roman period rather than the Byzantine?

Puzzled and tired after the strenuous digging operations during the day, I spent the evenings writing up my notes and thinking things over. Our cave was within walking distance of Suba and our survey had revealed that it had been a large town in ancient times. As a result of his researches in the country in 1838 and 1852, the pioneering scholar Robinson had identified this site with Prophet Samuel's home at Ramathaim-Zophim, but the overall reasoning behind this identification was quite weak. It seemed far more preferable in my mind to locate Ramathaim-Zophim at a different site altogether, the one appropriately named Neby Samwil (Prophet Samuel) north of Jerusalem [note 2.4]. Other scholars suggested identifying our site as Seboim mentioned in Nehemiah 11:34 and in a rabbinical text as well, but here also the case that was made was not very convincing. In fact, Seboim should not be sought in our region at all, but in the district of Lydda, in the vicinity of Ramleh and between Lod and Ono (close to the sites of Hadid and Nabalat) [note 2.5]. Since the traditional Arabic name of our village was Sobah it seems much more reasonable in my opinion to accept that it is the same as the toponym Suba mentioned in II Samuel 23: 36, as the place of origin of one of King David's heroes: 'Igal the son of Nathan of Sobah . . .'. Furthermore, in the Septuagint version of Joshua 15:59a, reference is made there to this place having been located next to Karem/Beth Haccerem (Ain Karim). A place called Suba is also mentioned in a papyrus found in Wadi Muraba'at (Papyrus No. 18), dating to the time of the reign of Nero (i.e. to AD 55 or 56) (*illustration 2.1*). This document was written in Aramaic and is a bond resulting from a transaction made between various individuals. Literally translated, it reads: 'Year 2 to Caesar Nero at Suba [?] received Avshalom son of Hanon from Suba [?], residing in Signah, the following message: I Zechariah son of Yehohanan [John] from . . ., residing in Kesalon, owes you [Avshalom son of Hanon] 20 silver zuzi . . .' There is a slight problem in the actual reading of the letters of the name 'Suba'. One

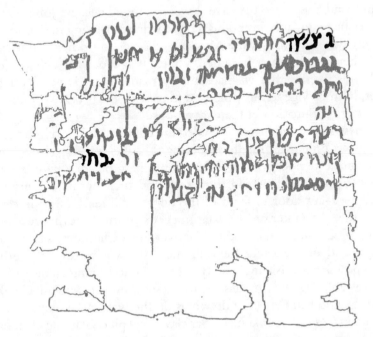

2.1

23

scholar (Milik) transcribed it as 'Suya' and then later as 'Sina'. The name appears twice in the document but only in its first instance can one actually make out the letters of the name properly. Joseph Naveh wrote that: 'the reading "Suba" is possible if we assume that the *bet* was written in a very cursive form' [note 2.6]. The reading of the name Suba does make sense here since it was mentioned together with another place name, Kesalon, which, by all accounts, is the Arab village Kasla, located south-west of Kiryat Jearim, and about six kilometres to the west of Suba [note 2.7]. It is interesting to note as an aside that the scholar David Flusser once got extremely excited about this papyrus and about the appearance of the names Zechariah and Yohanan (John) together, writing (perhaps hastily) that 'it is possible that this man was from the family of John the Baptist' [note 2.8].

Later in March 2000, we resumed work in the cave not with students (who had had to return to their studies in the States) but with local workers. Our fund-raiser, Joe Peeples, had come all the way from the States to see the results of the excavations and also to introduce me to John C. Whitehead who was visiting Jerusalem at that time. John had served as the deputy Secretary of State in President Ronald Reagan's administration in the mid-1980s. One morning John visited us and, in the company of his charming daughter, Anne Whitehead, crawled on his hands and knees into the cave. I was impressed because John was in an immaculate suit and tie and his next scheduled meeting that morning (I learnt) was with the Prime Minister of Israel and other dignitaries. Both father and daughter became quite excited about the cave project and the discoveries that we had already made there. Dusting off his clothes, John very generously pledged to provide the necessary funds for the further continuation of the excavations.

The new stage of the work included the entire clearance of the porch area (3.6 × 1.9 metres), first by exposing the fallen roofing slabs above the Byzantine-period living surface (lifting them out one by one with the help of metal chains and a tractor), and then by uncovering the stepped rock-cut floor in front of the doorway leading into the cave. Within the cave interior we continued excavating the heavy over-burden of Ottoman fills located above the earlier deposits at the southern end of the cave. Beneath these fills we began uncovering superimposed Early Islamic and Byzantine period living surfaces. We were now able to stand on the same living surfaces that were used by the Christians who had made the drawings on the walls. In the uppermost of these surfaces was a sunken circular clay-lined pit containing charcoal.

We took samples and these were later radiocarbon-dated to the Early Islamic period. There was some disappointment that we had found nothing at all on the floors except for pottery, but at the same time we retained high hopes that more interesting remains were to be found should we dig deeper.

Slowly we removed the layers of soil and debris in the cave. It was not an easy task. As we proceeded with the digging I developed a number of working theories regarding the significance of the drawings on the walls of the cave and the identity of the various people who used the cave. The drawing of John the Baptist on one of the cave walls had to signify, I reasoned, that at some point in time in the Byzantine period Christians used the cave to commemorate his memory. But what was the cave doing at this isolated location and at such a distance from nearby towns and villages? Surely one would have expected to find a cave such as this *within* Ain Karim, the traditional birthplace of John the Baptist? I realised that in order fully to understand the significance of our cave and its connection to the local tradition of John the Baptist, I needed to gain a much broader picture of the history and archaeology of Ain Karim itself.

Early Christian sources regarded Ain Karim not only as the birthplace of John the Baptist, but also as the area in which he spent his youth and early adult life. The fact that John later attracted masses of people while baptising at the Jordan River, and that they came from 'all the country of Judaea, and all they of Jerusalem' (Mark 1:5), is highly significant when trying to work out John's initial focus of influence and also where his hometown might originally have been. Another point to remark upon is the reference that was made to the great interest (and gossip) that arose 'through all the hill country°[οδρεινή]' (Luke 1:65) as a result of the peculiar events connected to John's birth, which also indicates that we are dealing with a place somewhere in the territory of Jerusalem. The often-quoted passage referring to Mary, who was pregnant with Jesus, visiting the mother of John the Baptist is also significant: 'Mary arose and went with haste into the hill country, to a city of Judah, and she entered the house of Zacharias and greeted Elizabeth.' (Luke 1:39–40). Strangely, we are not told the exact name of the place (except that it was in the Judah region) and perhaps the writer of the Gospel of Luke had no particular interest in specifying the geographical location of John's birthplace, in much the same way as there was no apparent interest among the Gospel writers in acknowledging the exact place of John's burial. However, one could point out that it would make no sense for a reference to be made to a place in the hills without actually naming it, unless it was clear to everyone which place was being alluded to, in much the same way as a mention of 'the capital city on the Thames River' would be understood by many in southern England as referring to the city of London [note 2.9]. Hence, I would think that the reference in Luke must have been given from a Jerusalemite's point of view, i.e. it naturally pointed to the hilly zone to the west of Jerusalem (to distinguish it from the arid wilderness east of Jerusalem) and indirectly it also indicated the existence there of a central village or town. It is interesting to note that in the *Protoevangelium of James* (c. AD 150), we also hear of Mary and Joseph going into the hill country, and later of Elizabeth and the infant John who 'went up into the hill-country' [note 2.10]. According to Josephus (*Jewish War* III 3, 5 [54–5]; cf. *Antiquities* XII I, I [7]), Judaea was divided up into eleven toparchies, of which the central toparchy was that of the Jerusalem district and its surroundings, which was also referred to in AD 77 by Pliny (*Natural History* v 14, 70) as 'Orine' (Latin for 'the hilly one'), and it is plausible therefore that this was the same as 'the hill country' mentioned in Luke [note 2.11]. In later rabbinical texts this same district is referred to in Hebrew as 'Har Ha-Melekh' ('the King's Hills') and in Aramaic as 'Tor Malkah' [note 2.12]. According to these sources, this region was said to have been very fertile: vegetables could be grown there, olives and grapes, fruit, as well as doves, and so forth. Indeed, such agricultural produce was not the sort of thing that would grow well in an arid zone. There is one extra reference in the Jewish Mishnah (*Shebiith* 9:2) which would suggest that part of this area (of Judah) included the hilly country extending westwards from Jerusalem as far as the foothills region (the Shephelah). In the heart of this specific area is the village of Ain Karim and therefore it may very well have been the place that was referred to indirectly in Luke as the 'city' of Judah.

In ancient times Ain Karim was a prosperous village, or small town, nestling within the hills to the east of a broad valley basin at a short distance west of the city of Jerusalem, with a good spring of water and surrounded by rich agricultural lands. Archaeological finds at the site date back to the Middle Bronze Age (early second millennium BC); and Iron Age (eighth to sixth centuries BC) and Persian period (fifth to fourth centuries BC) pottery has been found as well but remains of houses from these periods have yet to be uncovered. People were attracted to the place because of its source of water and potential for agriculture. In the nineteenth century, the village had the reputation for growing the finest grapes and olives in the land and this must also have been the case in antiquity [note 2.13]. Today, the village with its churches, quaint stone houses, winding roads and leafy terraces is on the very edge of the western outskirts of modern Jerusalem: looming above it are the ugly apartment buildings of the Kiryat Ha-Yovel suburb and in the other direction one can see emerging on the skyline a large clump of buildings representing the Hadassah Hospital. The Arabic name for the place, Ain Karim ('the spring of the vineyard'), signifies how important this permanent source of water was for the overall livelihood of the village; an alternative transliteration of the Arabic word *karim* (with an accent on the *i*) could be an adjective meaning 'noble' or 'generous', i.e. a reference to the copious amounts of water provided by the spring, but this is generally accepted to be incorrect because the word *'Ain* is feminine and the adjective should therefore be *karima* [note 2.14].

The spring is located halfway between the two main churches and is tucked away at the base of a ruined mosque (Maqam 'Umair). In the nineteenth century, the water, which was said to have been clear and sweet, flowed via a channel down to the valley below where it was used for irrigation purposes. At times of drought large quantities of water were taken from this place by donkey to be sold to the thirsty inhabitants of Jerusalem [note 2.15]. In the early 1950s the spring was found to provide 1,135 cubic metres of water per day [note 2.16]. In Christian tradition, the spring was called the 'Spring of the Virgin' in reference to the belief that Mary, mother of Jesus, drank of its waters while staying with Elizabeth after the Annunciation. Today sewage has insidiously infiltrated the water source and a big sign on the wall now warns tourists not to try and drink the water.

The village was known in antiquity as Karem and later as Beth Haccerem ('the house of the vineyard'). It was a city of Judah (written *karem*) and according to the Septuagint version of Joshua 15:59a, it was situated between Suba (Sobah) and the settlements of Gallim (Beth Jala), Baither (Battir) and Manahath (Malcha) [note 2.17]. According to Nehemiah (3:14), the rebuilding of the Dung Gate in Jerusalem was undertaken by Malchiah, the son of Rehab, who is identified as the district governor of Beth Haccerem. Judging by a passage in Jeremiah (6:1), Beth Haccerem was a place of some significance in the Iron Age, most likely the capital of the district west of Jerusalem. The prophet Jeremiah, with his divine call and commission as 'a prophet to the nations', warned of the pending destruction from the north with the approach of the Babylonians: 'O ye Children of Benjamin [in the north], gather yourselves to flee out of the midst of Jerusalem, and to blow the trumpet in Tekoa [in the south], and to set up a sign of fire [i.e. beacons, *massa'ot*] in Beth Haccerem [in the west]: for evil appeareth out of the north, and great destruction.' What is interesting is that Jeremiah's words were dedicated entirely to Jerusalem and its very immediate vicinity, with the territory of the city clearly being demarcated by the furthermost sites of Tekoa and Beth Haccerem, to the south and west, respectively, and with the northern limit set at the border between Judah and Benjamin (probably at Gibeah/Tell el-Ful).

This indicates a range of sites specifically marking out the edges of the hinterland of the city, i.e. at a radius of about five kilometres around Jerusalem. Hence, we should expect to seek Beth Haccerem at this same distance due west of Jerusalem. Not everyone has accepted the Ain Karim = Beth Haccerem equation. Some scholars have identified Beth Haccerem at Jebel Fureidis (= Herodium), between Bethlehem and Tekoa, based on Jerome who erroneously equated it with the village of Bethacharma [note 2.18]. One scholar in particular, Yohanan Aharoni, excavated an Iron Age site at Ramat Rahel, on the outskirts of Jerusalem to the south-east, and identified it as Beth Haccerem, but his suggestion has not been generally accepted [note 2.19]. The fertile valley in the proximity of Ain Karim was referred to in Jewish rabbinic sources as Biq'at Beth Haccerem [note 2.20]. It was noted as a source of a specific kind of flat stone, still seen there today, which was used for the construction of the altar and its ramp in the Jewish Temple in Jerusalem (Mishna *middoth* 3:4). The bright red colour of the valley soils was also discussed by the sages in reference to menstrual blood: 'What colour is meant by "red"? Like the blood of a wound. . . . "Like earthy water" means [a colour like that] when water is made to float over earth from the valley of Beth Haccerem." (Mishna *niddah* 2:7) [note 2.21].

From the first century AD there is an interesting reference to Beth Haccerem in the unique Copper Scroll (3Q15), which was found in a much-deteriorated condition in March 1952 in Cave 3, about two kilometres north of Qumran (*illustration 2.2*). The word 'scroll' is perhaps the wrong word to describe this artefact, since it was not intended to be something that could easily be read and then rolled up like the rest of the Dead Sea Scrolls; hence it should best be described as a 'rolled-up copper plaque'. On palaeographical grounds (i.e. the analysis of the form of the ancient Hebrew letters) Frank Moore Cross suggested dating it to AD 25 to 70. To enable the contents to be read,

2.2

the copper plaque was first sawn up into twenty-three pieces in a laboratory in Manchester. John Allegro made his first research on the contents of this copper plaque in the early 1960s, and ever since then different scholars have been presenting new ideas and conclusions that widely differ one from the other [note 2.22]. There is general agreement, however, that the plaque contains a list of hidden treasures, though whether or not they really existed or were imaginary is still much debated. These treasures were placed at locations within a fairly restricted geographical zone extending to Jerusalem and its surroundings, and eastwards down to the lower Jordan River and northern Dead Sea region. Not surprisingly, this is the same zone in which one may assume that the sect of the Essenes (who were most likely the same as the Dead Sea Sect) moved about. The purported treasures included objects and utensils made of gold and silver, some of which are said to have originated in the Jewish Temple. The reference to Beth Haccerem appears in Column Ten and reads (my translation): 'In the pool/

reservoir [a*syh* or a*swh*] which is in Beth Haccerem, as you enter, to its left ten cubits [approximately ten metres or sixteen feet]: sixty-two talents of silver [are there]' [note 2.23]. Nobody knows where this pool/reservoir was situated except that it is probably somewhere within the general area of Ain Karim. Perhaps one of these days some archaeologist will scramble into a cave and find it (and perhaps also the talents of silver . . .).

How old is the tradition linking John the Baptist to Ain Karim? Among the apocryphal writings (literary sources not found in the New Testament) there is one interesting narrative connected to the child John that stands out. It was composed as part of a *Life of John* by the Egyptian bishop Serapion of Thmouis, who was noted for his friendship as a monk and companion of the well-known Saint Anthony who was reputed to have fought demons in the guise of wild beasts before establishing one of the earliest monasteries of like-minded hermits in the Egyptian desert. Dated to between AD 385–395 Serapion's text was apparently originally written in Greek; there are two extant versions in manuscripts of the sixteenth and eighteenth centuries written in Arabic with Syrian (Garshuni) letters and the first edition was published in 1927 [note 2.24]. One passage deals with John and the death of his mother Elizabeth when he was still only seven years and six months old and living in the desert. The child Jesus is said to have been weeping for John. Mary asked him why he was crying and Jesus told her that John 'is now weeping over her [Elizabeth's] body which is lying in the mountain.' On learning of Elizabeth's fate, Jesus, his mother and his aunt Salome climbed onto a luminous cloud: 'And they mounted the cloud which flew with them *to the wilderness of Ain Karim* and to the spot where lay the body of the blessed Elizabeth, and where the holy John was sitting' (italics: S.G.). Having descended from the cloud it departed making some noise that alarmed John. Mary and Salome then washed the body of Elizabeth 'in the spring from which she used to draw water for herself and her son'. They then shrouded and buried Elizabeth, and sat with John for seven days 'and taught him [John] how to live in the desert'. Jesus says to Mary that John will remain in the wilderness until the 'day of his showing unto Israel' (i.e. another four and a half years). Jesus promises 'to render the water of this spring of water [at Ain Karim] as sweet and delicious to him [John] as the milk he sucked from his mother' [note 2.25]. While the material contained in this fourth-century source is undoubtedly legendary in content, its importance is in the fact that it is the earliest document available linking John the Baptist to Ain

Karim which is clearly stated to be a place 'in the mountain' and with a 'spring of water'.

From the sixth to eighth centuries there are a number of sources which refer briefly to Ain Karim and its connection with the tradition of the House of Zacharias and Elizabeth, but not specifically to John the Baptist [note 2.26]. Theodosius, for example, wrote (AD 530): 'From Jerusalem it is five miles [around seven to eight kilometres] to the dwelling place of Saint Elizabeth, the mother of my Lord John the Baptist.' (The distance fits Ain Karim perfectly, even though it is not mentioned by name.) Procopius of Caesarea (AD 550–58), while outlining the emperor Justinian's programme of works conducted in Palestine, mentions briefly that 'in the monastery of holy Zacharias [there is] a well.' One has to admit that it is strange that the site of the birthplace of John was not illustrated on the mosaic map of the Holy Land at Madaba, which dates from the second half of the sixth century. Possibly this was because of the way that the map was laid out, which meant that there was an inordinate concentration of sites around Jerusalem, especially in its western parts, and there was not room for all of them to be depicted by the mosaic craftsmen [note 2.27]. Epiphanius, writing in the seventh century, refers to Ain Karim as the place of the House of Zacharias and Elizabeth: 'Also to the west of it is Mount Carmel [i.e. a garbling of the name Karim], the family home of the Forerunner.' In the *Georgian Lectionary* (eighth century) we also have the reference to a church: '28 August. In the village of Encharim, in the church of the just Elizabeth, her commemoration.' The *Commemoratorium de Casis Dei* (*c.* 808) mentions the number of clergy officiating in the church at that time: 'at St John (where he was born) two.' From the tenth century, there is a brief mention of the church by Eutychius, patriarch of Alexandria, in a work that was originally attributed to St Peter, bishop of Armenia (AD 381): 'the Church of Zacharias in the territory of Aelia [Jerusalem] witnesses the visit paid by Mary to her cousin Elizabeth.'

Ain Karim is a very special place with a mystical aura, but its narrow roads are definitely not adapted to modern traffic. As I sit here writing, my back is killing me: sharp shooting pains are crawling like hoards of tingling ants down my left leg. The accident happened while driving through Ain Karim on the way back from the Suba cave excavations. During these trips by car to and from the dig I would muse on the ancient history of the Baptist's hometown and birthplace, and on the sites which attract busloads of tourists especially during the summer months. All it needed was a slight twitch of my eye towards the steeple of the

Church of St John, combined with a car abruptly braking in front of me for no apparent reason, and the front of my car began crumpling backwards and my head and neck rushed forwards. I could hear the tearing of metal and the shatter of glass. A severe slipped disc was what I ended up with; but at least my head was intact. Now, on passing through Ain Karim, my eyes sometimes feel that they would like to wander but I force them to concentrate on the road.

There are two main places of worship of John the Baptist at Ain Karim today – the Church of St John on the northern hill and the Church of the Visitation on the southern hill – and at both of them there are archaeological remains extending back to Roman, Byzantine and medieval periods (*illustration 2.3*). But why are there two sacred sites instead of one? This was apparently because of the contradictions that were perceived by early Christians while reading the Gospels, with a reference in one place to Mary going to visit Elizabeth at the home of Zacharias (*domum Zachariae*) located within a town in the hills of Judah (Luke 1:40), and in another place to Elizabeth finding herself pregnant and then seeking seclusion for herself (Luke 1:24), with her neighbours only finding out about her pregnancy at the time of the birth (Luke 1:58). In addition, Christian tradition also had to accommodate the

2.3

whereabouts of a place of refuge for Elizabeth and the baby John while hiding from Herod's soldiers at the time of the slaughter of the innocents (Matthew 2:16), as well as taking on board the notion that in the close proximity of Ain Karim there was a 'wilderness' in which John grew up (Luke 1:80). Hence, the first of these places – the Church of St John – is said traditionally to represent the town house of John's parents and the place where he was supposedly born, and the second place – the Church of the Visitation – the place where Mary came to visit Elizabeth and the place to where Elizabeth fled from Herod's soldiers [note 2.28]. It would appear, however, that in the Byzantine period there was only one *primary* place of worship associated with John the Baptist at Ain Karim and this was at the variously named Church of the House of Zacharias, which also had an attached monastery and perhaps even a hostel, and was located on the northern hill at the spot of the present-day Church of St John.

In addition to this centre of worship, there were a number of *secondary* cult places but none of these appear to have had churches or chapels attached to them and they were probably only occasionally visited by monks at times of commemoration. This was apparently the case with the site of the 'refuge of Elizabeth and John' at the spring-house on the southern hill in the area of the present-day Church of the Visitation. Indeed, judging by the representation of the place on two *eulogia,* dating from the sixth or seventh centuries, the site consisted only of a cave with a flight of steps and a cross on a pedestal. Further afield, there was another secondary cult place at the site of the 'wilderness of John' and this, I began to think, was at the cave we have been excavating near Suba. It would appear that confusion as to the significance of the various sites associated with the tradition of John the Baptist began creeping in as a result of the construction in 1169 of a major church and monastery complex at the site of the present-day Church of the Visitation, which gave the site a significance equal to that of the Church of the Nativity of St John located on the other side of the village. The fact that there were two major churches in close proximity to each other confused the many pilgrims who reached Ain Karim in the aftermath of the Crusades, and at some point in the fourteenth century it would appear that the tradition of the visit by Mary to Elizabeth and the circumcision of John was transferred lock stock and barrel to the church on the southern hill (i.e. to the church now known as the Visitation).

What would the town have looked like at the time of John the

Baptist? The direct answer is that we do not know because not enough archaeological excavations have been conducted within the village of Ain Karim and there is still not enough information even to reconstruct the general extent of the settlement in the Early Roman period. However, there are a number of considerations that may be taken into account. First, it seems likely that the village houses of that period would have been constructed close to the main source of water, the lower spring of Ain Karim. Therefore, we may envisage built-up areas of small stone houses with flat roofs on terraces extending up the hill slopes around the spring and especially to its north and east. Second, the village houses would have overlooked or flanked the main road leading from the direction of Jerusalem to the north-west. Hence, the village would have had more of a north-westerly spread, with houses existing in the area extending from the main spring and as far as the northern hill. Indeed, excavations in the area of the Church of St John on the northern hill did bring to light remains of structures from the first century and a stepped ritual bath (*miqweh*). The gully located immediately to the west of the spring would have been used for terraced irrigation agriculture just as it had always been used up to the mid-twentieth century. It does not appear that the village extended very far up the hill to the south of the spring. This area was used for extensive terraced dry farming and rock-cut wine presses were discovered there [note 2.29]. It is most likely that the water emanating from the spring-house below the present-day Church of the Visitation would also have been used for irrigation agriculture in the terraced zone located beneath it. Tombs have also been found on the northern hill. In conclusion, it would appear that the site on the northern hill (St Johns) would have fallen within the limits of the Roman village, whereas the site on the southern hill (the Visitation) would have been outside it. Because of the nature of society in the Near East in the Roman period – with women leading much more secluded and protected lives than they do today – some of the events referred to in Luke might easily have taken place at the one location, i.e. the pregnancy, Mary's visit, and the birth of John. Hence, there is no need to seek alternative sites for these events. It is unlikely therefore that there was more than one 'House of Zacharias' at Ain Karim in the first century and the Gospel of Luke does refer only to the one house (1:40: *domum Zachariae*).

Ain Karim is also a place that I associate with my own childhood. You have to imagine a bunch of excitable youngsters clambering up on to the terraced slopes above the village, breathing in the fresh smell of crushed thyme underfoot, throwing sticks at each other, shouting, laughing: we felt we were discovering the world, unravelling the mysteries of nature. We – that is my twin brother Daniel and Yoav Broshi and myself – would skip down a narrow road that ran from the outskirts of Jerusalem to Ain Karim, nestling between steep terraced hills. Climbing the terraces and wading through thickets of brambles, we eventually gained access to the upper reaches of the village, where there was a solitary Russian church dedicated to Saint John and surrounded by nineteenth-century cottages, all in a dilapidated and ruinous state, except for one or two houses that were occupied by extremely elderly and bad-tempered nuns. These scowling nuns were followed around by hoards of mangy cats, which would hiss at us. We kept out of their way. There was one house close to the top of the hill that was in a fairly good state of repair and it was far away from those occupied by the nuns. The roof was intact and we wandered around inside the rooms, fearing that at any moment the floors might suddenly cave in. We were very excited about the house: dangling our legs over the edge of the veranda, we talked about it excitedly. We came to a decision that this was the place where we were going to live together, as in a commune. There were many things to talk about: we had to choose our rooms and work out practicalities: where were we going to get our water and what about electricity? We gazed across the wilderness all around us in the baking sun and munched on our sandwiches. We wrote our names in charcoal on one of the walls and vowed that one day we would all come back to live there.

Almost three decades have passed since that childhood escapade and a friend, Yitzhak Greenfield, told me that many changes had since taken place in the area of the Russian cottages and that I should go and see them for myself. Yitzhak is an accomplished artist who lives with his Yemenite wife, Zippora, in a house in the heart of Ain Karim, only a short walk from the village spring. I was invited to tea at their house on a cold February morning during the first season excavating the cave. He wanted to introduce me to a Franciscan brother, Reynaldo Legayada (ofm), who had officiated for a while at the Church of the Visitation in Ain Karim. I mentioned the cave that I was excavating connected to John the Baptist and my interest in the history of Ain Karim and its rich traditions. We spoke about the various Renaissance-period paintings depicting scenes from the life of John the Baptist, about the pictures made by Caravaggio and about the life of that painter in the film by the director Derek Jarman. Yitzhak had done occasional restoration work on paintings from the Church of St John, and told us that it was said that the famous El Greco himself had drawn the finger of John the Baptist in one of the paintings. Having finished Yitzhak's excellent tea, we decided to walk up to the Orthodox Russian Church and have a look around. Climbing the hill I was reminded of my childhood, but the whole place has been totally transformed. We came across many extremely industrious pilgrims at work: building, cleaning windows and gardening; they all ignored us. We arrived at the Russian Church of St John and at its western end against the outer wall we saw a stone, which, according to local tradition, was where John the Baptist once stood while preaching. As we gazed at this stone, a pilgrim in a grey raincoat scurried over, bent down into a kneeling position and sank his head on to the stone. It looked like he had fallen asleep but I expect he was just meditating. The church is quite small and had been renovated recently; nearby is the octagonal belfry with its green painted spire. We climbed higher up the hill because I very much wanted to see the house that I had visited as a teenager. Eventually we found it: the house has been completely renovated and it positively gleams; the gardens and paths round about it are also spotless and tidy. It was nothing like how I remembered it.

The main church in the core of the village of Ain Karim is the Church of the Nativity of Saint John. In Karl Baedeker's late nineteenth-century handbook for travellers, *Palestine and Syria*, it was advised that anyone wishing to visit and stay within the castellated Latin Monastery adjacent to the Church of St John, should come well prepared: 'Travellers can be accommodated on bringing letters of recommendation from the secretary of the Salvator monastery in Jerusalem' [note 2.30]. Today tourists cannot stay there but they are readily admitted into the church at the appropriate visiting times. The Church of St John is located only a stone's throw away from the main road passing through Ain Karim. The centre of Ain Karim is not well adapted to large groups of tourists and waiting buses tend to clog up the main road, with their engines chugging away noisily in order to keep the air-conditioning going. Climbing up a narrow alleyway with shops on either side, one quickly arrives at the main access portal. There used to be a headless statue of John in the small niche above the gateway but it has now gone; perhaps someone filched it in the middle of the night. The head of the statue was broken off many years ago. The statue has not been replaced and the niche remains empty.

The church has had a chequered history, with periods of building, expansion and reconstruction set against periods of infighting among its occupants, decay and abandonment (even at times serving as an animal stable). The nineteenth-century scholar Titus Tobler provided a very detailed century-by-century history of the church and the minutiae of its existence, based on numerous sources including obscure pilgrims' accounts, and his work, written in Gothic German, is indispensable to any serious student of the history of this church [note 2.31]. The earliest positive description of the church was made by Abbot Daniel (1106-1108): 'Now in this place there has been built a tall church; on the left hand as you enter this church beneath a small altar is a little cave, and in this cave John the Precursor was born. And this place was encircled by a stone wall.' While this 'tall' church has somewhat changed down the centuries, with the most recent work on the church taking place under the aegis of the Franciscans during the early twentieth century, its overall plan is not far removed from its original twelfth-century basilica layout with a nave and two aisles, a dome resting on four strong piers, and with a large altar in front of the main apse [note 2.32]. The high altar is presently dedicated to Zacharias, and the south altar to the memory of Mary's visit to Elizabeth (*illustration 2.4*). In the wall of the chapel to the right of the church is a marble grating protecting a fragment of rock

2.4

which was said to have been part of a boulder on which John the Baptist originally rested. The church pavement was still adorned in 1876 with 'old mosaics', as well as with medieval *opus sectile* paving stones. There are some interesting paintings hanging on the walls, many depicting episodes from the life of John. In the far corner of the church to the left of the altar and at the end of the northern aisle there is a flight of seven steps leading down into the crypt, which is the traditional birthplace of John the Baptist. Inserted into the blackened walls are five white marble bas-reliefs depicting scenes from the life of John. Beneath the marble table is a circular opening which marks the traditional spot where Elizabeth gave birth to John. The grotto was originally a rock-cut cave but it is now lined with masonry. The church itself is entered from the west and up a flight of steps on a projecting porch (*illustration 2.5*). The basement of this porch houses archaeological remains, including the remains of a Herodian-period structure (first century) with an adjacent stepped ritual-cleansing pool (*miqweh*), and above it two fifth- or sixth-century Byzantine chapels, one of which was a memorial chapel judging by the Greek inscription in the mosaic floor which reads: 'Hail, God's Martyr's'.

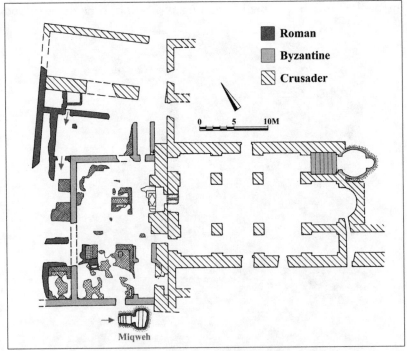

Roman

Byzantine

Crusader

Miqweh

2.5

There are no indications linking these Byzantine remains directly to the John the Baptist tradition, and the main church from this period remains unexcavated beneath the pavements of the present Church of St John. However, two marble statues of Venus and (possibly) Adonis were uncovered, suggesting that an important pagan cult centre once existed at Ain Karim in the Roman period (second to early fourth centuries) in the immediate vicinity of the present church [note 2.33]. This cult may very well have been established in an attempt to eradicate or suppress local traditions connected with John the Baptist, in much the same way as in Jerusalem (renamed 'Aelia Capitolina' by Hadrian) when the Romans erected a Temple of Venus over the spot of the Tomb of Jesus. In my opinion, the pagan shrine at Ain Karim was probably torn down and the worship of John re-established following the failed episode of paganism of Julian the Apostate (AD 361–363) who was known to have caused the desecration of the Tomb of John the Baptist at Sebaste. It was perhaps knowledge of this event in the Byzantine period that was used to elicit the appropriate sympathy (and funds) to build a major church in the name of John or Zacharias/Elizabeth at Ain Karim.

The Church of the Visitation, or Mar Zacharias, is located on the slope of the hill on the other side of the spring and a steep path leads up to its gates (*plate 4a*). According to Baedeker's calculations the distance from the spring to the church is exactly four minutes, though this does of course depend on how fast one is walking up the hill. Arriving at the site with my Franciscan friend, Reynaldo, we were ushered into the church compound as special guests and shown around by the elderly Father Ludovico Reali (ofm), who seemed particularly proud of the wonderful workmanship of the large Crusader vaults – which are visible adjacent to the present-day church – as if he himself had built them. According to tradition (at least since the fourteenth century), this was the house of Zacharias, the place where Mary visited Elizabeth, and the place where Elizabeth kept the infant John hidden from Herod's soldiers. Prior to the nineteenth century, the magnificent ruined walls and vaults of the medieval church of Mar Zacharias and its adjacent monastery were remarked upon by early travellers and pilgrims (*plate 4b*). Abbot Daniel's description (1106–1108) is the earliest that we have and describes the place as it was before the medieval buildings were erected there: 'And this place may be recognised in the rock even to the present day. And above this place there is now built a little church built on to the cave in front of it. From this cave flows very good water, and

Elizabeth and John drank this water . . .' This 'little church' probably
dates back to the Abbasid period at the earliest. Major construction
work took place at the site in 1169 with the building of the Cistercian
Abbey of St John in the Woods [note 2.34]. During a particularly
difficult winter in 1860, the vaulted twelfth-century church collapsed.
The Franciscans decided to restore it and, digging down in the following year, they found the ground was hollow and had been filled up with
stones and fills. When they cleared these fills they discovered a vaulted
chamber, rock-cut in its lower parts and with a ceiling of masonry.
Subsequent archaeological excavations exposed much of the lower parts
and it appears that the vaulted chamber was part of a subterranean water
system, with a spring-house and conduits, dating back to the Roman
period (*plate 4c*). This chamber is regarded as the traditional cave of the
'refuge' of Elizabeth and John, and on its walls are inscribed Latin
crosses.

Close to the entrance to the vaulted chamber at the Church of the
Visitation is a large stone (the so-called 'Rock of the Hiding'), which is
said to have come from the place where Elizabeth hid the infant John
(*plate 4d*). The Italian pilgrim Leonardo Frescobaldi described this stone
at the time of his visit in 1384: 'Also there is a place in the said dwelling
[Mar Zacharias], in which, when Herod sought and killed the innocents
a stone opened of itself, and in it St Elizabeth hid her son John the
Baptist, and the stone is so open to this day.' A fellow traveller, Giorgio
Gucci, said the miraculous place where John was hidden was in a wall
behind a 'large hard stone'. Relic chips of this stone may have ended up
as mementoes for pilgrims and taken abroad. Among the relics kept in
the Lateran Palace in Rome, for example, there are small bits of rock
wrapped in pieces of parchment on which one can just make out the
words in Latin: 'stone from the cave where Elizabeth . . .' and 'earth of
the grotto, Elizabeth and John . . .' [note 2.35].

There are quite a few rocks in and around Ain Karim that are
associated in one way or another with John the Baptist. We have already
mentioned the rock at the Russian Church of St John, on which he was
supposed to have stood while preaching, and then there is the fragment
of rock kept at the Church of St John which is also said to have been
part of a boulder traditionally connected to the preaching activities of
John the Baptist. This boulder was originally situated at a spot next to
the path halfway between Ain Karim and the Monastery of St John in
the Wilderness (Ain el-Habis), and in land belonging to the Armenians.
There are a number of different accounts from the sixteenth and seven-

teenth centuries relating to this boulder: Anselm of Cracow (1509) says that it was the place where Zacharias rested, while De Villamont (1600) says it was the seat of John the Baptist, and De Stochove (1630) maintains it was the stone on which St John preached. But how did a fragment of this boulder actually reach the Church of St John? The story goes that in 1721 a local man from Ain Karim, of Moghrabi (i.e. Moroccan) descent, decided to burn the rock in a kiln to make quick-lime: '. . . but hardly had he put fire to the fuel when a loud detonation took place, the oven flew into pieces, and the stones which it contained were thrown some distance. Recovered from his surprise, the Mussulman understood that the prophet Hanna [John] was angry with him on account of the sacrilege, which he had committed. In order to appease his wrath, he went and humbly took the largest fragments to the Father Superior of the Convent of St John' [note 2.36]. The rock cannot have been completely destroyed since it was still pointed out to Richard Pococke in 1738: 'We then turned to the west [from Ain Karim], and went along the side of a hill, having a valley to the right, and saw a stone, on which it is said St John preached. We then went about a mile further to the grot of St John [at Ain el-Habis].' Victor Guérin was also shown a large stone on 20 April 1863 while travelling along the path from Ain Karim (at a distance of twenty-five minutes' horse-ride from St Johns) and was told that it was there that John had preached. In his description of this trip Guérin expressed doubts about the authenticity of the stone [note 2.37].

These stories intrigued me and one day a couple of years ago I went in search of the stone, setting off with a couple of friends along the path previously taken by Pococke and Guérin, extending westwards from below the Church of the Visitation. I wanted to see the stone with my own eyes. Asking around I was surprised to find that the tradition about the stone has been forgotten by the Christian community now living in Ain Karim. Modern archaeologists surveying the landscape west of Ain Karim had also not mentioned anything out of the ordinary. So it definitely seemed worthwhile hunting for this stone. The path leading westwards in the direction of Ain el-Habis is quite clear and it steadily climbs up the slope with a regular surface, partly rock-cut, and is bordered on one side by a well-built stone fence. However, suddenly we found that the continuation of the path ended and, annoyingly, disappeared under a mass of stone and piles of soil. Clambering about it became clear to us that the continuation of this path had been destroyed by bulldozers and other mechanical equipment during the construction of the nearby Hadassah Hospital. We decided therefore to retrace our steps and to investigate the path from the other end, that is from the point of destination at Ain el-Habis, and to work our way backwards towards Ain Karim looking for prominent stones en route. We followed the path past the spring of Ain el-Khandak and around the edge of a hill with harvest towers and small caves and water cisterns along the way. Clearly pilgrims did not lack for water during their procession from Ain Karim. However, again we lost the path at exactly the point where it climbed the hill. Modern development for a new road had blurred the exact line of the path, and further up were piles of modern construction materials. Looking at the old and new maps of the area, I had to reach the sad conclusion that the site of the traditional rock of John the Baptist was utterly destroyed at the time of the construction of the Hadassah Hospital in the 1960s.

In the conclusion to his article on the birthplace of John the Baptist, Conrad Schick wrote: '. . . in Ain Karim we have the support of the name, the tradition, the history, and the locality, viz., in the mountain or hill country. Hence in these circumstances there can be little question that the required site [of the birthplace of John] can only be Ain Karim' [note 2.38]. Schick, who was of German origin, was a renowned architect and scholar, resident in Jerusalem in the latter part of the nineteenth century. He had a deep love for the antiquities of Palestine and spent much of his time examining archaeological sites, poring over Scripture and ancient sources, and writing learned articles. He examined the question of the whereabouts of the birthplace of John the Baptist very carefully in an article that was published posthumously in 1905, reaching the conclusion that the traditions associated with Ain Karim – which I have outlined above – were so strong that it would be foolish to ignore them. I would concur. My own analysis of the archaeological and textual evidence suggests that, of the two sites traditionally associated with John the Baptist in Ain Karim, the focus of the worship of John the Baptist in the Byzantine period was in the Church of the House of Zacharias which was located on the northern hill (the present Church of St John) and, interestingly enough, excavations there have brought to light remains dating back to the first century. The main church (underlying the present medieval structure) was surrounded by smaller chapels, a monastery and perhaps also a hospice. It was from this place that certain numbers of monks would set out in the Byzantine period to commemorate the cave of the 'refuge' of Elizabeth and John on the southern hill of Ain Karim. It seems reasonable that these same monks also made the journey to our cave at Suba to celebrate the memory of the child John 'in the Wilderness' (Luke 1:80). A link clearly existed between Ain Karim as the traditional birthplace of John and our cave. More digging in our cave was, I felt, necessary to clarify further the remains from the Byzantine period and the function of the remarkable drawings on the walls of the cave.

3
The Byzantine Memorial Cave

T he unique ancient drawings on the walls of the cave had to be protected somehow and I was rather worried to see people occasionally wandering about the dig who were not there by invitation. Some of these were harmless visitors who had seen the digging while walking in the countryside and simply wanted to satisfy their curiosity as to what we were getting up to. But there were others that I was more wary of, even though I hadn't seen any signs of them yet, namely illegal excavators and religious fanatics. They were the sort of people who were quite capable of committing wanton destruction just for the fun of it or, alternatively, from an unbalanced rage or zeal. Already, Kibbutz Tzova members had mentioned an Ultra-Orthodox Jewish man they had seen wandering around their grounds, searching for the location of our cave and asking specifically for 'Dr Gibson's site'. I actually knew who he was: this was the same person who had intentionally disrupted my excavations at another site, had broken into my car in broad daylight searching for human bones, and had maliciously pushed one of my assistants into the path of a bulldozer – luckily she was able to scramble to safety without a scratch. Because of the danger to my staff, that particular excavation had to be suspended before proper scientific completion. The strange thing is that this religious fanatic and others like him go around the country with identity cards supposedly giving them the authority to inspect archaeological sites on behalf of Jewish religious institutions, on the grounds that archaeologists might be desecrating ancient Jewish burial sites. Some archaeologists actually do business with these religious 'inspectors' by letting them enter their excavations and look around, fearing that by not doing so they run the risk of having their sites vandalised or that they will find their excavations swamped with hundreds of violent religious demonstrators. I have always been steadfast in my opposition to these so-called 'inspectors' and I never ever allow them on my excavations. I have seen the irreparable harm done by these vandals to some important archaeological sites in Israel and this was the last thing I wanted to happen at our site.

The cave obviously needed good protection and so we decided that the best way was to close the entrance with a permanent door. It was handcrafted and installed by Dubi, the local blacksmith of Kibbutz Tzova. It had vertical iron bars topped by archaic spearheads and strong hinges bolted into the side wall of the entrance. It turned out to be quite tasteful in appearance – fitting, I thought, to the significance of the site. Word about the discovery of the cave began getting around and this resulted in a few enquiries from journalists. We decided at that time not to inform the press of the amazing discovery of the drawings because of the fear that widespread publicity would inevitably generate a tumult of pilgrims and visitors and what we really wanted to do was to get on with the archaeological work. Later, the site could be prepared for proper visits, but meanwhile the digging had to go on undisturbed and unhindered. In any case, the last thing I wanted was some over-enthusiastic visitor falling into one of my pits and breaking his or her neck, or a mass demonstration being kindled at the dig by the Jewish Ultra Orthodox claiming that this was some kind of Jewish burial site. Over the following months, however, we did benefit from numerous visits from archaeological colleagues curious to see the cave and the drawings on its walls, voicing their ideas and offering interpretations regarding the significance of the unusual finds emerging from the cave. As we dug deeper, the mystery surrounding the significance of the finds in the cave grew.

From the outset we assumed that the drawings on the walls of the cave were to be dated to Late Antiquity (i.e. to the Byzantine or Early Islamic periods). However, when we reached the base of the wall in the eastern alcove of the cave we uncovered a floor with shattered pottery dating from the first century AD. This meant that stratigraphically the living surface was later in date than the plastered cave wall. Since we had originally assumed – at the time of the survey – that the drawings of the John the Baptist-like figure and the rest of the symbols (including the crosses) were made with incisions drawn directly into the plaster while still wet (based on the apparent smoothness within the incised grooves), the implication from the pottery on the earliest living surfaces (extending up to the plastered walls) had to be that the drawings were made in the first century or earlier. Since the cross is a Christian sign that was only used as a religious symbol from the fourth century onwards, something was obviously wrong. We were missing something. We pondered the problem very carefully and it was only when we examined once again the drawings and the surrounding walls that we finally came up with the solution. The plaster had a very hard consistency, almost like concrete, and the actual drawings had to have been created using a strong implement, perhaps something like an iron chisel. We were now able to see here and there zigzag breaks and fractures along the incised lines suggesting that the work was executed when the plaster was already dry. Second, it dawned on us that it must have been the process of the constant dripping of water from the ceiling down the walls of the cave and along the grooves of the incised lines that subsequently gave the drawings the misleading appearance of having been cut into wet plaster. I was pleased we had managed to work that problem out. The drawings could now be properly re-assigned to the Byzantine period at the earliest. The first season of excavations at the cave were drawing to a close and we were sad to see the UNCC students returning to their studies in the States.

During the next two months (April–May 2000), we continued with a series of low-key digging operations in the cave, as well as slowly clearing an area outside the cave to the east where we hoped to trace a channel that we believed brought water into the cave from the direction of the valley. We also spent many hours looking afresh at the pottery fragments which were spread out in their thousands on trestle tables. Every potsherd needed to be washed and examined, and Alexandra Drenka, our Finds Curator, supervised this work. It turned out that, apart from diagnostic examples of Byzantine pottery, there were also a few fragments that obviously dated to the Early Islamic period, some of it to as late as the Abbasid period, i.e. from the mid-eighth to eleventh centuries AD. We were still uncertain whether this material was dumped into the cave in the form of rubbish after the Christian use of the cave had ceased, or whether this rubbish belonged to monks who were still using the cave even after the country had fallen under Muslim rule. Either way, we decided to seek answers to this question during further digging operations at the cave.

I also felt that we needed to gather some basic scientific data concerning the plaster on the walls and so was happy when we were visited by chance by a local geologist, Aryeh Shimron, who had a passion for the subject. He was particularly interested in the travertine flows that could be seen overlying the plaster on the walls at the far end of the cave and was fascinated by the small stalactites also visible on the ceiling. Taking out his geologist's hammer, he collected two samples of plaster and promised to have them checked out for us in his laboratory. Meanwhile, Shimron did venture to say that, based on his visual examination of the plaster, he believed it to be of a type known to him from sites that dated *exclusively* to the Iron Age II (eighth to sixth centuries BC). This incredibly early dating astounded us. None of the pottery finds from the cave was that old – indeed the earliest pottery we had dug up at that stage was from about five hundred years *later* – and so, frankly, we all felt sceptical about Shimron's dating of the plaster. However, since we still had not got down to the rock floor of the cave, I did say to Shimron that it would only be fair for me to reserve judgment on his unusual determination until more information became available.

Following the discovery of the cave, the first things I began looking at were the written sources from the Byzantine period, to see whether there was a reference in them to our cave, but none could be found. This was not surprising, however, because there are quite a few holy Christian sites known in the Palestine region, including those with large churches and monasteries, which do not appear to have been mentioned in any of the sources. Conversely, there are also numerous names of Christian sacred sites in the sources, such as for example some of those listed in the *Commemoratorium de Casis Dei* (*c*. 808), for which we do not possess the equivalent archaeological sites on the ground. Naturally, those sites that figured in the itineraries of pilgrims came to be mentioned more frequently than sites that were located off the beaten track, however important they might be.

There are very few Christian remains in Palestine that have been identified with certainty as dating to *before* the fourth century AD and the exact significance of some of these archaeological finds is still hotly debated by scholars today [note 3.1]. Christianity became firmly established as an official religion of the Roman empire in Late Antiquity and a wealth of archaeological remains belonging to this period of time – known to local archaeologists as the Byzantine period (AD 325 to 638) – has come to light in different parts of the southern Levant. With the advent of Christianity, paganism was slowly abolished – the last pagan temple to be shut down was in Gaza in around 400 – but Jews and Samaritans were more or less tolerated by the authorities and were allowed to practise their customs and to maintain their places of prayer.

The country was now the 'Holy Land' – the place that witnessed the birth, life, crucifixion and resurrection of Jesus, as well as the other events in the Gospel narratives. Holy places of worship connected to the life of Jesus and those of his family, John the Baptist, and also many of the apostles and Old Testament figures, sprang up throughout the country. Helena, mother of Constantine, is said to have made a pilgrimage to the Holy Land (arriving in *c.* 326) to check out some of the holy sites. In Jerusalem, the site of Jesus' tomb was uncovered beneath the foundations of the Roman forum, which included a Temple of Venus, during excavation works that were supervised by Bishop Macarius on Constantine's orders [note 3.2]. The discovery of the Tomb of Jesus resulted in the construction of a magnificent basilica-*martyrium* on the spot, the remains of which are now incorporated within the present-day Church of the Holy Sepulchre. Additional churches began to be built at other sites in the country, notably at the Cave of the Nativity in Bethlehem, the Mount of Olives (Church of Eleona), and Mamre near Hebron. The strength of Christianity was consolidated between the fifth and sixth centuries, and hundreds of new churches, chapels and monasteries sprang up across the country, even in the most isolated of places. Many such buildings, particularly those with a religious function, were decorated with sumptuous mosaic floors, wall frescos and portable wooden furnishings of very high quality [note 3.3].

Institutionalised pilgrimage to the Holy Land began in the fourth century. Masses of pilgrims arrived by boat to the main ports of the country and at Dor on the northern coast, a monumental pilgrimage-church was built to accommodate some of their needs. Pilgrimage eventually became an important feature of life in Palestine and pilgrims were catered for by a number of different types of religious institutions, way-stations, hospices and even hospitals. The fact that there were so many pilgrim-tourists in the country during these centuries led to the development of a flourishing industry that produced crosses, trinkets and mementoes (*eulogia* amulets and *ampullae* flasks), portable art works (such as icons) and reliquaries. Some of the pilgrims decided to become benefactors themselves, recording their munificence in dedicatory inscriptions, and by these means wealth poured into the land. The resulting economic prosperity led to social, religious and artistic achievements that the country had rarely seen before. The movement of so many pilgrim-tourists around the country required a proper network of roads and their safety had to be taken care of by the authorities. The holy sites were scattered at different locations, with pilgrims interested in sites in and around Jerusalem as their main destination, as well as places in the Judean Hills, in the Galilean Hills, around the shores of the Sea of Galilee and in the lower Jordan Valley. Sites included not only places connected with incidents from the Old and New Testaments, but also sites that had previously been centres of pagan or Jewish worship, as well as important tombs, such as those of the Maccabees in Modi'in. One of the earliest pilgrims for whom we possess a written record of their travels is the Bordeaux Pilgrim (AD 333). Probably the best-known pilgrim's account from the Byzantine period was written by Egeria, a nun from western Spain who visited the country between AD 381 and 384 [note 3.4].

A visit to a holy site was a biblical quest to check out 'where these things were preached and done', to use the words uttered by one early pilgrim, Melito of Sardis. The motive of the pilgrim was to reach the correct and exact site mentioned in Scripture, to relive the biblical story, to experience the visual aspects of the site, to touch the stones, to take a breath of its air and to savour its characteristics. But the overall motivation was not curiosity or idle interest, but the result of deep religious conviction: there was a belief that by being physically present at a site the pilgrim would become imbued with its sanctity, almost as a receptacle filling with piety. Hence, when visiting the sites pilgrims did not act like modern tourists but spent considerable time in prayer, meditation, reading from Scripture and even taking part in processions and various rites involving relics and their adoration [note 3.5]. Although the Bible was essentially the pilgrim's guidebook, many of the visitors were simply not versed sufficiently in the topography of the land and needed written aids and maps to facilitate their journeys to the sites of the Holy Land.

An important written aid to facilitate the Christian pilgrim seeking out the imprint of the biblical narrative on the face of the Holy Land, and the whereabouts and situation of its cities, towns and villages, was the *Onomasticon* written by Eusebius (AD 260–340), a remarkable historian and writer based in Caesarea. This source is a unique lexicon of more than one thousand place names taken mainly from the Old Testament (with some names from the Gospels), accompanied by topographical explanations. While this was not in any way a comprehensive listing of *all* the places mentioned in the Bible – a feat Eusebius may very well have intended but never succeeded to do – he was able to provide geographical locations for sites whose situations would otherwise remain unknown. One may assume that when Eusebius wrote 'one can see this place to this very day', it meant that he had actually visited the place himself, or that he had managed to acquire some reliable first-hand information about it. He was particularly good when it came to places in the hill country and along the coast, but less reliable about far-flung locations. There is also some information in his work about provinces and administrative districts, about the ethnic makeup of settlements, topography and holy places, and references to roads. Written towards the end of the third century, there is very little information in the *Onomasticon* regarding his contemporary Christians and hardly any data regarding the important Christian holy sites of his time, namely the Constantinian churches in Jerusalem and Bethlehem, which seems strange. Nor is there any reference to the birthplace of John the Baptist at Ain Karim, or to the 'wilderness' of John. One explanation is that Eusebius did not actually write the *Onomasticon* as a guidebook for tourists or pilgrims and so he was not interested in making an exhaustive listing of Christian holy sites; his primary aim was that the *Onomasticon* should be used as a sourcebook to facilitate the reading of the Old Testament with the topography of the Holy Land as its backdrop. However, regardless of Eusebius' intentions, in the course of time his book did indeed become a guidebook of sorts. It may be surmised that the *Onomasticon* was originally supplied with a map, but none has survived. We know that road maps of this type did exist and the Peutinger Map of the fourth century is one example. The *Onomasticon* was also a major source of inspiration for the Madaba Map, which is dated to the second half of the sixth century. The mosaicist in some cases even copied Eusebius' mistakes [note 3.6]. Here, too, the birthplace of John the Baptist was not marked, although the places of baptism were. A Latin translation of the *Onomasticon* with quite a few additions and some corrections, was made by Jerome in AD 420.

The concept of holy places being visited by pilgrims in an institutionalised fashion for purposes of veneration hardly existed prior to the fourth century. In the first century, the Jewish Temple in Jerusalem, was, as the 'House' of God, regarded in Judaism as the only possible sacred site in the country. The veneration of other holy sites was abhorred and Jews were ostensibly not supposed to know the location of sites such as Mount Sinai, or the whereabouts of the tombs of figures such as Moses and Aaron. But in practice this was not the case, and it would appear that the notion of the veneration of tombs as holy sites had already begun from very early on. This is evident from Luke (11: 47–48) in regard to the sepulchres of ancestors, and is also clear from a passage in Matthew (23:29): 'Woe unto you, scribes and Pharisees, hypocrites! Because ye build the tombs of the prophets, and garnish the sepulchres of the righteous.' At the time of Eusebius, the proper veneration of the places associated with Jesus (and John) had still not yet been fully established and so he would not have deemed it necessary to list such sites in his *Onomasticon*. Indeed, in regard to John the Baptist, the most that Eusebius can muster is a reference to the baptism site at the Jordan, where he said some people would immerse themselves in the river. In the Byzantine period, one can trace the rapid evolution among Christian devotees from a simple dedication to the abstract notion of the sacred, harboured as it were within the general landscapes connected with scenes from the gospels, to focused acts of ritualised veneration that were conducted at very specific locations and connected with buildings designed to accommodate large numbers of worshippers and clergy. This overall process of institutionalisation was true not just for the cult of Jesus but also for the other figures associated with him, notably John the Baptist [note 3.7]. Our cave was definitely not a primary cult place for pilgrimage, but it was one of the satellite places of worship situated in the hills around Ain Karim.

On the walls within the interior of the cave are two sets of incised drawings (*illustration 3.1*). As we have seen it was these drawings that had drawn our attention to the cave in the first place and had set in motion the planning of the archaeological project. The drawings are fairly large (for example, the figure of John the Baptist is 0.7 m high) and the incised lines are cut into the plaster surface to a depth of about one centimetre. The drawings appear on the upper parts of the walls, with three on the west wall and, opposite it, three on the east wall. Apart from these drawings, the walls of the cave are completely unadorned (apart from a few drawings on the west wall of the porch *outside* the cave), which is a pity because the smooth, blank plastered walls are very suitable for the scrawling of graffiti and inscriptions. Archaeologically speaking, the drawings must be attributed to the Byzantine period. Our excavations revealed a rough earthen living surface extending across the cave at a level (two metres below the ceiling) that would have been suitable for the drawing of these images. Within the fills of this living surface we found pottery that could be dated back to the beginning of the Byzantine period, to the fourth and fifth centuries AD, and it seems likely that the drawings were executed at the same time as the establishing of this living surface. The cave was used up until the end of the Early Islamic period (i.e. to the end of the Abbasid period in the

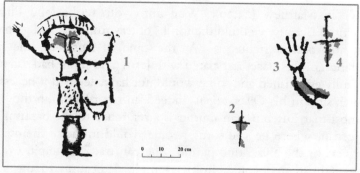

Group A

Group B

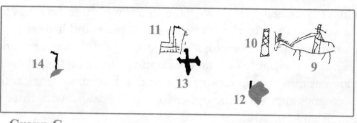

Group C

3.1

eleventh century) which saw a rapid build-up of three living surfaces and then sudden abandonment. Two radiocarbon dates were measured for charcoal from the lowest Abbasid fill and from a fire-pit cut into the latest Abbasid floor; they both provided tenth to eleventh century determinations.

The simplicity of the activities held within our cave during the Byzantine to Abbasid periods must belie the true function of this site. Many Christian sites in the Holy Land of the Byzantine period could boast a rich array of wall decorations, mosaic floors, altars, offering tables and other fittings and furnishings. Such chapels, churches and grottoes quite often had dedicatory inscriptions naming the benefactors who had given the money to build at the sites, the dates when the work was done and even sometimes the name of the site or its function. Unlike these holy sites, our cave was empty with only a very rough living surface and nothing more. It is possible, of course, that there were originally movable furnishings and vessels in the cave and that these were later packed up and taken away when the site was finally abandoned. But had this been the case, I believe we should have found something, at least a scrap, among the rubbish. Also furnishings would have required a proper paved floor in the cave and this was definitely not the case. Moreover, the way that our drawings had been organised into two distinct groups and the overall size of the images did not in any way resemble the kind of graffiti and signs – typically lightly scratched or painted – which were made by pilgrims and worshippers at other Byzantine holy sites in Palestine. The conclusion, therefore, has to be that this site was not a place for a set form of daily liturgical activities intended for large groups of people and pilgrims, but was used instead as a place of solitude, as a place of ritual seclusion, by individuals or groups of individuals, who lived a somewhat spartan existence at the cave for short periods of time. We have to imagine reed mats on the floor of the cave, perhaps a couple of rough wooden stools in one of the corners, some bedding of animal skins and woollen garments rolled up in the niche in the east wall, a few storage jars containing basic foodstuffs and water, some bowls, but nothing more. Fireplaces were lit in the area of the porch outside the cave entrance and the discovery of an iron door pivot during the excavation suggests that the entrance to the porch was closed with a wooden door.

Who were the people using the cave and where did they come from? It is uncertain how many people actually used it during the years spanning the Byzantine to Abbasid periods. It is highly unlikely, however, that it was used by a succession of isolated hermits otherwise we should have found much more of their rubbish during the excavations. Indeed, the overwhelming paucity of finds must indicate that the cave was used on only very specific and short occasions, and therefore it was not used as a permanent hermitage. Hence, I think it likely that the people who used this cave were monks seeking solitude only a couple of days every year, perhaps to mark very specific religious events in the Byzantine calendar (such as the birth of John the Baptist or his beheading, or the baptism of Jesus), and that these monks came from the Monastery of Saint John at nearby Ain Karim. Why did they choose this cave? I think that there must have been a strong oral tradition linking this cave to the story of John the Baptist in his first 'wilderness' (based on Luke 1:80: 'John was growing and becoming strong in the spirit, and he lived in the wilderness places until the day of his public shewing to Israel') and this I think is also reflected in our archaeological finds. It is possible that this was the place visited by Arculf and referred to obliquely by Adomnan in AD 685: 'This Arculf saw a clear spring in the desert, from which people say that Saint John Baptist used to drink. Its stone roof is covered with white plaster.' At the end of the Abbasid period, with the coming of the Crusaders in the twelfth century, this tradition, like many others in the hills of Jerusalem, was disrupted. The Crusaders, I believe, were aware of the tradition of John's first 'wilderness' but were hard-pressed to pinpoint it geographically, and eventually they situated it not too far away, in the next valley, as it turns out, at the site now known as Ain el-Habis.

Turning back to the evidence of the actual drawings: there are a number of matters relating to these and the person who made them, about which we can be fairly certain. First of all, the drawings were not positioned randomly within the interior of the cave, and the two sets of drawings were grouped intentionally. Second, the large size of the drawings suggests that they were not designed for the personal gratification of an individual, but were intended to be displayed to others, i.e. they were used as visual aids in a ceremony. The drawings were definitely not made for decoration in the way that we would hang pictures on the walls of our houses. Third, the overall style of the drawings and their consistent uneven workmanship must indicate that they were made by one person, evidently not a professional artist but a man who had a sense of devotion uppermost in his mind. The drawings on the walls of the cave are fairly straightforward, albeit they are 'primitive' visual images; those on the west wall consist of the figure of a man, an arm, a cross, and those on the east wall consist of a head, a staff, three crosses, and a bird. Notwithstanding the obvious simplicity of these symbols I believe the meanings behind them are actually much more complex. Therefore, we should be asking, not 'what do they represent?', but 'what are they *intended* to represent?' However, to understand these drawings and to know how they were used to 'teach' those who were looking at them, we should first define and understand briefly the nature and significance of symbolism.

The images on the walls of our cave are definitely symbols and not signs. A sign is a practical indicator of something that is known, instantly recognisable and without ambiguity of meaning. A symbol, however, while it may have recognisable features, will possess underlying and alternative meanings and associations that are not always tangible, in some cases even hidden. Jung wrote: 'Thus a word or an image is symbolic when it implies something more than its obvious and immediate meaning. It has a wider "unconscious" aspect that is never precisely defined or fully explained. Nor can we hope to define or explain it. As the mind explores the symbol, it is led to ideas that lie beyond the grasp of reason' [note 3.8]. This, of course, can sometimes be a fearful thing for the rationalist scientific mind attempting to interpret 'facts' about cultural or religious symbols. For example, how may the archaeologist analyse the degree of numinosity inherent within certain symbols? In terms of prehistoric symbols I would say that this is nigh impossible, but, for later periods, especially those relating to Paganism, Judaism and Christianity, we may be on much safer ground since these symbols were primarily used as a means of redirecting the observer towards a clarification of their faith [note 3.9]. However, one has to remain wary on such matters because even well-known artistic motifs were sometimes given mystical and spiritual meanings far beyond the simplistic connotations implicit in their appearance. In addition, one must also take into account the fact that in early art some religious figures were typically provided with an array of different attributes: Jesus, for example, was symbolically represented by a variety of images, such as the Lamb of God, the Fish, the Serpent Exalted on the Cross, and so forth.

Although the drawings are on the whole fairly crude and naïve in appearance, one can detect a certain child-like beauty shining through the images and this is probably a reflection of the sincere and pious devotion of the artist who made them. Apart from a small number of drawings on the west wall of the entrance porch (Group C), the rest of them were found as two separate sets of drawings opposite each other on the interior walls of the cave (Groups A and B). As the excavations proceeded, I had hoped that we would come across more drawings on the walls of the cave, but none was found. To make an exact copy of the ancient drawings, Fadi, our surveyor, covered the walls with plastic sheeting and used a felt pen to trace the drawings, line by line, and dot by dot. Inside the cave the large size of the drawings and the humidity worked against us: the sticky tape stopped adhering to the cave wall and shrivelled up, with the plastic sheeting slumping to the ground around us. The only solution was for Rafi and me to hold the sheeting against the wall with our bodies, while Fadi continued tracing the drawings. This worked for a while, but then the muscles in our upraised arms started throbbing with pins-and-needles jabbing into the edges of our extended fingers. After an exhausting couple of hours, we did finally manage to accomplish the task, and back in the office we reduced the enormous sheets of drawings down to a manageable scale.

In the entrance porch of the cave there are a number of drawings on the western wall (from right to left): a camel and rider; a tower/ladder; a box design; a cross; and two unclear symbols (Group C). The cross and the two unclear symbols were made in the same rough style as the Byzantine drawings within the cave, and so it is reasonable to assume that they were made by the same hand and are of the same date. However, the drawings of the camel and rider, tower/ladder and box design were done in a different style and with the use of a very delicate sharply pointed implement. I assume that these drawings are earlier than the other type, but how early is unclear. They are best seen very early in the morning when the sun casts an oblique light across the surface of the wall, enhancing the shadows of the faint lines.

The drawing of the camel with a rider on its back is the clearest of the rather faint group of drawings on the western wall of the porch (*illustration 3.2*). In the beginning we were uncertain as to what kind of animal the artist intended to draw, but the long neck and the humped back of the animal suggests a camel rather than a horse or donkey. The schematic representation of a rider seated on a baggage saddle of a type that was tied around the centre of the animal further supports the camel rather than the equine identification. The trappings used for harnessing the animal are very sketchily represented [note 3.10]. The rider is shown

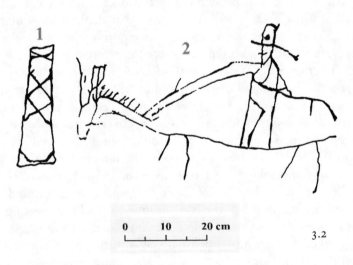

0   10   20 cm

3.2

holding a long stick to steer the animal in the right direction. Representations of camels and riders dating from the Byzantine period are known from a number of archaeological sites, for example at Nezzana and Avdat in the southern Negev Desert [note 3.11]. Camels are animals with a remarkable ability for endurance and they can survive in desert environments without water for weeks on end. By comparison a human being in a similar environment cannot survive without water for more than thirty-six hours. The camel was a sacred animal in the ancient Near East and was eaten only on very rare occasions by the Bedouin of the desert [note 3.12]. In early Christian art, the camel was perceived as a symbol of temperance. Furthermore, because of its hair (cf. Mark 1:6), the camel was also occasionally regarded as a symbol of John the Baptist [note 3.13].

In front of the camel, or to the left of it, there is a drawing of a vertical feature that may be identified either as a tower, ladder, or perhaps even as a column. The tower and ladder are both seen as symbols of man's need to reach towards the skies – as in the well-known story of the Tower of Babel – or as bridges of communication between heaven and earth, through the act of ascending and descending, as in Jacob's dream: 'And he dreamed, and behold a ladder set up on the earth, and the top of it reached to heaven; and behold the angels ascending and descending on it' (Genesis 28:12) [note 3.14]. The symbolism of the ladder was continued into later times and this is perhaps implied in the following verse: 'He who comes from above is above all; he who is of the earth belongs to the earth, and of the earth he speaks; he who comes from heaven is above all' (John 3:31). In Jewish funerary art of the first century AD, drawings of towers on stone bone boxes (ossuaries) are regarded as symbols of the *nefesh* tomb memorials. One such representation of a tower which is remarkably similar to ours, with a superimposed X-design as well, was found scratched on an ossuary, marked with the personal name 'Shimon', from a first-century tomb in the Nahal Kidron near Jerusalem [note 3.15]. The ladder as a symbol of the connection between heaven and earth also had an important significance in early Christian art [note 3.16]; and in patristic and liturgical Byzantine texts, the ladder and column, together with that of the cross, were also identified as symbols of the cosmic centre of the world. The significance of the box design (for lack of a more appropriate description) is unclear. Judging by the way the drawing was executed it was made by the same person who drew the camel and tower/ladder images. Of the later, cruder, drawings on the west wall of the porch, of which there are three, only one may be clearly identified as a 'Greek' style cross and it therefore has to be of Byzantine date.

Turning now to the drawings visible on the walls within the interior of the cave, the most striking of these in my mind has to be that of the figure of John the Baptist, which is the first drawing that one encounters on the left on the western wall (Group A) as one enters the cave. The rigid frontal pose of this figure is very typical of Byzantine-period iconography, especially for herald, soldier and prophet-like figures. At first glance one might assume that the figure is depicted in what is known as the *orans* ('one who prays') position, i.e. with both arms raised in prayer or adoration and with the palms of the hands upturned. In this case there appears to be a (very short) staff resting against the crook of the left arm [note 3.17]. This combination of upraised arms and a staff is admittedly rare but not unique in pictorial representations of holy men of that period. I would think, however, that it is much more likely that the left hand actually has a shorter arm and is holding the middle of the staff, with the right hand shown raised in benediction or in the gesture of prophecy. In fact, there are many examples of Byzantine-period depictions of prophets holding staffs, books and other objects in their left hands and with their right hands raised in this fashion [note 3.18]. Renderings of John in baptism scenes always show him using the right arm for blessing (I'll say more about this later) and with his staff clutched in his left hand or leaning against his left arm. The staff or shepherd's crook (*pedum*) in our drawing is not depicted absolutely straight and at its top there appears to be a small X-like cross.

John's head is shown oversized by comparison to the rest of his body, with a very long nose, almond-shaped eyes (now largely disfigured by the iconoclasts), small ears on either side of the face, and an oval mouth at the juncture where the neck should have been (*illustration 3.3*). The face is depicted clean-shaven, which could suggest an earlier date for the drawing because bearded representations of John the Baptist are much more typical of the later Byzantine to Early Islamic periods. The hair is set in a series of 'buns' representing curls, extending around the head from ear to ear; such hair arrangements are known from sixth-century iconography and earlier [note 3.19]. However, we must also consider the possibility that the artist may have been attempting to suggest not a hair arrangement but a cap, or, alternatively, as one visitor to the cave suggested, a clumsy rendition of a *nimbus* (or halo). The idea regarding the cap is definitely a possibility and there are one or two parallels that may be adduced for this. I am not convinced, however, that this feature

3·3

is a representation of a halo; its absence should not surprise us because many early Byzantine representations of important holy figures and saints often lack this feature. In fact, it is only in the sixth century that the *nimbus* (a Latin word meaning 'cloud', the notion being that the head of a divinity was surrounded by a luminous cloud, as a sign of sanctity, eminence and power) came to be used much more frequently in Byzantine artistic representations. Hence, I am much more inclined to see the feature around the top of the head either as a schematic depiction of a hair arrangement, or as a cap. Our depiction is very different from later artistic renderings in which John is shown as an unruly ascetic with long wavy hair and a beard, in the way that Elijah and other Old Testament prophets were frequently depicted.

Traditionally, John is described as having worn an 'outer garment of camel's-hair, and a leather girdle' (Matthew 3:4; cf. Mark 1:6) and both of these features appear to be rendered in this schematic drawing of John. The figure is shown wearing a lower garment decorated with thirty-two holes and around his waist is a belt or girdle tied towards the left. In the Byzantine period the girdle (*cincture*) was made of leather and worn over the outer garment, and was used as a purse and ornament. It was a symbol of humility and contempt extended to prophets, and the monks developed this idea and saw it as signifying vows of poverty, chastity and obedience. The hairy garment was a feature that gave early artists great difficulty when trying to depict it, after all how does one go about indicating a hairy garment without drawing the hairs? Some did it by showing ripped edges along the hem of a garment, or by using an orange-to-brown colour range in a painting, or by indicating the hairs as a convention of lines or spots. Our artist adopted the convention of spots, rendered here as a series of small holes. There are a number of Roman wall paintings from Italy showing shepherds wearing clothes with the hairs depicted as spots.

Immediately below the figure is a small oval depression which we believe was cut in order to contain a relic connected with the figure in the drawing. The size of the depression suggests that the relic itself must have been quite small, perhaps a finger-bone or a piece of cloth, or something along those lines. The relic would have been kept in place with a simple lattice of copper wires that was hammered into place in the incised lines visible along the edges of the depression. To the right of the lower body of the figure is a semi-circular feature with three lines beneath it, which is of uncertain interpretation. One possibility is that it represents a cup or bowl on a tripod, representing a chalice (used for distributing wine to the faithful), a censer (some early Byzantine examples have low feet), or an Epiphany foot-washing basin or laver (the *mandatum* tank). Alternatively, it could be a very schematic representation of a lamb, with its neck and head raised to the left, reflecting John 1:36 where the Baptist proclaims Jesus as the 'Lamb of God'. Our drawing is of a man in the guise of a shepherd holding a crooked staff (topped by a cross) and wearing a hairy garment tied with a belt, and all of this fits in well with the visual perception of John the Baptist in the Byzantine period. The fact that a depression was made below the drawing for a relic must also indicate that the figure was of some significance. The

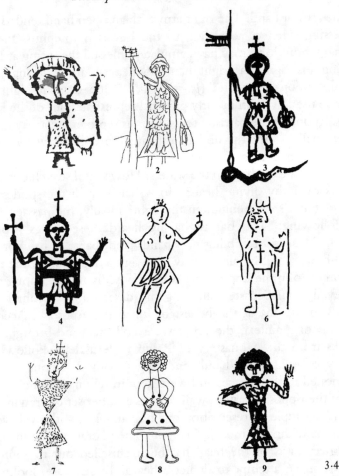

3·4

manner in which our figure was drawn resembles quite a few artistic renditions from the Byzantine period representing standing secular, military and religious figures of one sort of another, which were depicted on artefacts, mosaic floors, walls of caves, and tombstones [note 3.20] (*illustration 3.4*).

On the same wall as the figure of John the Baptist there is a life-size representation of a right arm flanked by two crosses (Group A) (*plate 5a*). This drawing probably had a number of different meanings for the onlooker. In early Christian art the hand shown issuing from a cloud was generally taken to be a symbol of the divine presence (the *Dextera Domini* or *Dextera Dei*) [note 3.21]. Indeed, there are numerous references in the Bible to the awe-inspiring majesty of God represented by the arm or hand. The right arm with an open hand tended to signify a blessing. Hence, according to the historian Josephus, the prophet Elisha (whom John may have emulated) blessed the spring at Jericho by 'raising his righteous right hand to heaven and pouring propitious libations upon the ground' (*Jewish War*, IV: 460–65). The right hand was the one used by John in early pictorial representations of the baptism of Jesus. In one of the patristic texts, John is represented as saying to Jesus: 'How shall I touch thy undefiled head? How shall I *stretch out my right hand* over thee who hast stretched out the heavens as a curtain and established the earth upon the waters? How shall I stretch out my servile fingers over thy divine head? How shall I wash the spotless and the sinless? How shall I enlighten the light? Finally, the passage ends with the following: 'The Baptist having heard these things [from Jesus], stretched out his trembling *right* hand, [and] baptised the Lord' (italics: S.G.) [note 3.22]. Finally, it may represent a depiction of the relic hand or arm of John the Baptist that was supposedly found among the bones retrieved from Sebaste following the desecration of John's tomb by pagans in AD 363 at the behest of Julian the Apostate. According to Rufinus of Aquileia, the relics were collected and brought away by monks from the Monastery of Philip in Jerusalem. Following this a variety of relic arms, hands and fingers said to belong to John are mentioned in the sources and were kept in reliquaries in churches.

On the opposite eastern wall there is another set of drawings (Group B) with a simple representation of a human head, with oval eyes, a long nose, but without a mouth (*plate 5b*). The plaster surface in the area of the lower parts of the head has been chiselled out to some degree, perhaps in an attempt to depict a beard? In any case, looking at this image the overall impression is that of the gaunt face of an ascetic. In early Christian art a representation of the head was a symbol of the whole man. This drawing most probably is a depiction of the relic head of John the Baptist and served to remind onlookers of the story of the beheading of John the Baptist by Herod Antipas at Machaerus. Since the Byzantine period numerous relic heads of John the Baptist had been in circulation and were mentioned in the sources.

The next drawing along the eastern wall is quite mysterious: it is a T-shaped sign with two semi-circular lines on either side (*plate 5c*). The entire excavation team spent a lot of time trying to interpret this symbol. One person even suggested that it was a top view of a sword, with the hilt at the top and blade pointing downwards, against a rounded platter. Having investigated all the many different types of symbols from the

Roman and Byzantine periods, it seems to me that the drawing is actually a crude rendering of a staff and serpents, i.e. the *caduceus* (Greek: 'a herald's wand'). The *caduceus* is known to many as the popular symbol of the medical profession represented by a symbolic staff surmounted by two wings and entwined with two snakes. The original symbol of the mystical staff with a snake was the attribute of the Greek and Roman god Asclepius, the healer of sickness and the patron deity of physicians. There are numerous classical statues of Asclepius depicting him as a heavy-set semi-naked man leaning with one hand on a gnarled staff around which there is a single coiled snake [note 3.23]. The symbol of a winged rod with two entwined serpents, however, was the attribute of the god Hermes/Mercury, who was the messenger of the gods, the god of the crossroads and of the merchants, and the leader of souls to the underworld. It is strange to think that the *caduceus* of the modern medical profession was not actually modelled as one would think on the attribute of Asclepius, the healer of sickness, but on the symbol for commerce and communication used as the attribute of Hermes/Mercury. The sign was apparently first used in a medical connection in 1902 when it was adopted as the insignia of the medical department of the American army. Today it is used as the emblem of the American Medical Association [note 3.24].

In the context of Christianity the symbol on the wall of the cave is most likely to be a crude combination of the *caduceus* symbol with a type of cross known as the *crux commissa* (the gallow-shaped cross). The sign was originally the last letter of the Hebrew alphabet – the *taw* (meaning 'mark') and it had the form of an X (see Ezechiel 9:4). The Church Fathers understood this to be the same as the Greek letter *taw* or the Latin T and that it was the kind of cross that Jesus might have been crucified on [note 3.25]. The central element of the symbol is perhaps a representation of the ancestral staff of John who is thus portrayed as the 'messenger' of God. There are numerous later artistic renderings of John in Byzantine and medieval art showing him holding a staff [note 3.26]. The ancestral staff has a long history in the Near East and it was regarded as a sign of distinction among townspeople, shepherds and Bedouin alike. James Neil, writing at the beginning of the twentieth century, said that 'a very short residence in Syria serves to show that the walking-stick, or staff, occupies a much more marked and important place in that land than is commonly with us' [note 3.27]. Since John was a descendant of the House of Aaron (through Elizabeth), it is possible that the artist also wished to connect him with the story of Moses who used his staff to divide the Red Sea and to liberate the Israelites from Egypt, to strike the rock in the wilderness to bring forth water (Exodus 4:2–5), and to hang on it the brazen serpent (Numbers 21:8–9). In Christianity the brazen serpent symbolised the prefiguration of the Crucifixion: 'And as Moses lifted up the serpent in the wilderness, so must the Son of Man be lifted up, that whoever in him may have eternal life' (John 3:14–15). In Exodus (4:17), we hear that God provided Moses with a commission: 'Thou shalt take this staff [*matteh*] in thy hand, whereupon thou shalt do signs.' Later, the staff was spoken of as 'Aaron's staff' that he had received as the eldest son and as a priest (Numbers 21:9). Aaron's staff may also have been the same as the 'staff of Levi' mentioned in Numbers (17:3). The church fathers also linked the idea of snakes with the sins of the flesh, and baptism was regarded as a way of redemption [note 3.28].

Further along the eastern wall is the representation of three small crosses and above them a small sign. The three crosses are undoubtedly the symbol of the crucifixion of Jesus between two thieves on the rock of Golgotha (Calvary) in Jerusalem, a scene frequently represented in early Christian art [note 3.29]. One of the earliest depictions of the three crosses on Calvary is from the wooden doors of the fifth-century church of Santa Sabina in Rome. Already in the fourth century the Christian poet Prudentius had referred to the scene of crucifixion between the two thieves as a suitable subject for church decorations [note 3.30]. The oblique sign above the crosses is unclear but it may be a rough depiction of an ascending dove, as a symbol of the spirit departing from the body (of Jesus) and as a symbol of resurrection [note 3.31]. In the Coptic Gospel of the third century, the *Pistis Sophia*, we are told: 'And after a little time my Father sent to me the Holy Spirit in the type of a dove [cf. Matthew 3.16; Luke 3.22; John 1.32] . . . the spirit draws all souls together and takes them to the place of the light' [note 3.32]. From the fourth century, the dove was the recognised symbol of the Holy Spirit and of the soul departing from the body [note 3.33].

In total there are six drawings of Christian crosses in the cave: one on the wall of the entrance porch, two on the western wall and three on the eastern wall. The cross is perhaps the most important symbol of Christian faith and salvation. There are many different forms of the cross in Byzantine art, and five of the crosses in the cave are of a type known as the Eastern 'Greek' cross, i.e. with arms and vertical components that are of equal length, as compared to the cross with a longer vertical component (which later became known as the 'Latin' cross) [note 3.34]. One of the three crosses on the eastern wall has V-shaped endings at the top and bottom, indicating that it is a version of the *nufus* cross. The cross was not used as a Christian symbol before the second quarter of the fourth century when Christianity became one of the official Roman religions; as a feature of Christian iconography it only became popular in the fifth century [note 3.35]. In the Byzantine period the cross was an important symbol of religious affiliation and cultural identity, appearing on the lintels of houses and ecclesiastical buildings, in the decorations on mosaic floors (notwithstanding Emperor Theodosius II's edict forbidding this from AD 427), and on tombstones. The cross was also used to mark the beginning and end of dedicatory inscriptions, and it appeared on numerous portable objects such as lamps, flasks and bowls, as well as on jewellery, amulets, pendants and finger-rings.

All of the Christian crosses in the cave, together with the eyes of the John the Baptist figure, had suffered from the act of iconoclasm in antiquity. Someone had come into the cave, had seen the drawings and decided to disfigure them. But it was not done at random and the vandalism appears to have been quite focused: the other symbols on the walls were left unharmed. Perhaps the reason why the eyes of the figure of John the Baptist had to be removed was to prevent them from 'capturing' the soul of the intruder in the cave. The reason for wishing to remove the crosses, however, is evident, since the cross is the supreme symbol of Christianity. The systematic vandalism, however, suggests that this was not the wanton act of a shepherd who just happened to be passing by. The fact that the crosses were systematically hacked away indicates that the person who undertook this activity had a very clear mission in mind. But who would have wanted to vandalise the drawings in this incisive way? Perhaps they were harmed as a result of the bitter iconoclastic controversy which emerged in the Christian world in the eighth century? The beginning of the iconoclastic destruction of images was in AD 726 and it ended in the east in AD 842 [note 3.36]. Alternatively, the disfiguration might have been undertaken by a deeply religious Muslim in the Ottoman period, objecting to the Christian symbols and having superstitious feelings about the eyes of the Baptist. We shall probably never know for certain who the perpetrators were.

As we have already seen, these symbols represent elements in the John the Baptist cycle of stories and these were undoubtedly interlinked in the mind of the person who made the drawings. However, what was the purpose and overall cognitive value of these drawings? Were these symbols made simply to evoke various associations of piety among those looking at them? Or were they used as primary 'visual aids' to redirect observers towards the various stages in the actual story of John the Baptist? The fact that these symbols were not scattered at different locations in the cave, but were positioned as two distinct groups, one opposite the other, had to be meaningful not just visually but also in a ritual sense. For this reason, I would suggest that the drawings were used in the Byzantine period as 'triggers' or 'cues' during the story-telling instruction of initiates on the subjects of John the Baptist and the advent of Christianity. This teaching aspect of the drawings perhaps needs further explanation. We have to imagine a senior monk (perhaps even the *hegumenos* of the Monastery of St John) standing in the middle of the cave between the two sets of drawings and facing the initiates gathered around just inside the cave entrance (see *illustration 3.5*). Pointing to the drawing of the human figure on his right he would first have related the story of the life of John the Baptist and his mission (presumably also indicating the relic that was once located in the small niche below the drawing). Then, turning to the drawing of the head on the wall to his left, he would have spoken about the beheading of John at Machaerus or Sebaste (depending on the tradition available to him). Turning back to the wall on his right he would have indicated the drawing of the arm and would have told the story of the burial of John at Sebaste, and the subsequent destruction of the tomb by pagans and the 'discovery' of the

3.5

relic of his arm there by pilgrims from Jerusalem at the time of Julian the Apostate (*c.* 363). Next, he would have indicated the symbol of the staff with serpents on the left wall and spoken about the significance of baptism in water and the descent of the holy spirit. Turning back to the right wall, he would have pointed out the drawing of the large cross and spoken about John as the Forerunner of Jesus Christ. Finally, he would have shown the three small crosses on the wall to the left, representing the Crucifixion at Golgotha and then would have spoken about the Resurrection, perhaps referring to the small symbol of the ascending dove. It is my firm belief that this has to be the significance of the drawings and the way that they were used by Christian monks in the cave during the Byzantine through to Abbasid periods. While the images on the walls of the cave cannot be defined as particularly 'artistic', it does seem likely that they were regarded by onlookers as primary coded symbols charged with a particular spiritual message of revelation concerning John the Baptist in this cave of his first 'wilderness'.

Very few artistic portrayals of John the Baptist exist in the Near East and in the southern Levant in particular, and so the discovery of his drawing *in situ* on the wall of a cave that was also dedicated to him is an important discovery. I was disappointed to learn that there are so few ancient artistic renderings of John. There was one image from Nazareth, incised on to a very small plastered stone (only 10.5 cm high), that was originally published as a Byzantine representation of John the Baptist, but recent research has shown it to be a rendering of a Christian soldier instead, dating from the mid-fifth century at the earliest [note 3.37]. Some of the earliest representations of John the Baptist are in baptism scenes, which appear as decorations on the sides of metal *ampullae* and ceramic *eulogia* tokens, probably dating from the sixth or seventh centuries [note 3.38]. In these scenes, John is depicted as a man wearing a long tunic and with two outstretched hands to the right of Jesus who is shown as a central bearded figure submerged up to his chest in the waters of the Jordan, with a descending dove above his head and with a winged angel on his left. One of the *eulogia* tokens represents John the Baptist as a bearded haloed man to the left of the central standing figure of Jesus, with a schematic descending dove over Jesus' head, and with the figure of an angel (without wings?) on the right.

The head of John the Baptist was depicted in the guise of a tragic prophet in a wall mosaic to the left of the apse of the Byzantine church at the magnificent Saint Catherine's monastery situated at the foot of Mount Sinai in Egypt. The mosaic has been dated to the sixth century to the time of Justinian, and it may very well have been executed by expert craftsmen who came there from as far away as Constantinople [note 3.39]. There is also a wonderful painted icon representing the figure of John the Baptist from the Monastery of Saint Catherine, but it is now in the Kiev Museum. It was painted locally and is dated to around the sixth century AD. It shows a standing bearded figure, with his right hand raised and with his left hand holding a scroll inscribed with the Greek text of John 1:29. He wears a long brown garment, and a girdle and a cape of sheepskin (the *melote*) which are clear attributes of desert hermits; he also wears sandals [note 3.40]. Another icon from this monastery, dating from the tenth century, is a triptych with a scene showing the baptism of Jesus in the Jordan. Jesus is shown naked in the river; John is bearded and fully clothed, and his right hand extends to the head of Jesus. Above is an ascending dove (largely destroyed) and on the opposite side of the river are two angels [note 3.41].

A blurred medieval painting of John the Baptist, shown flanking the Pantocrator, with the Virgin Mary on the other side, appears on the wall of a niche within the Chapel of St Mary (known today as the Cave of Elias) at Qarantal near Jericho. The chapel itself was mentioned by the pilgrim Theodoric (*c.* 1175). A watercolour copy of the wall painting was made by the explorer Claude R. Conder, who visited the spot on 17 December 1873. In a letter sent that day to the Palestine Exploration Fund in London, Conder grumbled to the Secetary, Walter Besant, about the conditions of his work: 'Do you know we are working in the Jordan Valley unguarded except by the wild Arabs . . .' [note 3.42]. An excellent example of a later Crusader-period painting of John the Baptist holding a scroll with a Latin text (taken from John 1:29) appears on one of the columns of the Church of the Nativity in Bethlehem [note 3.43]. Much later wall paintings representing John the Baptist are known from the caves and hermitages in the Judean Desert: for example, a nineteenth-century painting of John holding in his right hand a cross in the Cave of Arcadios close to the Monastery of Mar Saba [note 3.44].

Some early paintings of John the Baptist are known from a number of Coptic monasteries in Egypt, dating from the Byzantine to Early Islamic periods. These include a painting of John in baptism scenes at Bawit, one of which shows John with his hand resting on the head of Jesus and the other with his hand on Jesus' shoulder. In both paintings angels attend Jesus holding towels. There is also a cycle of paintings depicting the Massacre of the Innocents, followed by a painting of Elizabeth fleeing with John. Finally, there is a medallion painting of Zacharias, father of

John the Baptist, with grey hair and beard, and wearing the same garments as those worn by John the Baptist in another medallion painting. At Abiad there is a painting of John, and at the Monastery of St Macarius (Abu Makar) there is a full-frontal figure of John the Baptist standing in an arcade holding a medallion with the representation of the Agnus Dei in the form of a horned ram. John is haloed and bearded, with black hair. He wears a red tunic fastened with a belt and is also wearing a mantle. In the quaintly named Chapel of the Four Living Creatures at the Monastery of St Anthony, there is also a wall painting depicting John, represented with Mary and two apocalyptic beasts [note 3.45].

Crossing the main highway which sweeps past the northern wall of the Old City of Jerusalem one cannot help but feel an immense sadness because this road, known as Route Number One, is like an invisible chasm, deep and bottomless, dividing East from West Jerusalem and separating Palestinian from Israeli. In a way, this road is like a symbol of the ever-widening wedge lodged in the bedrock of mistrust that exists in this part of the world. Having set off from the Albright Institute of Archaeological Research on Salah ed-Din Street in East Jerusalem, Tom McCollough, a Resident Fellow at the Institute, and I crossed over Route Number One and a few minutes later entered the neighbourhood of Musrara in West Jerusalem. Eventually we reached the doorway of the house of the antiquities collector Lenny Wolfe. I had come to see whether or not he had representations of John the Baptist in among the many early Christian amulets in his collection. His house was nothing like I had expected. We drank Turkish coffee in his kitchen with breadcrumbs and the remnants of his breakfast still scattered on the table. There was a smell of solid living in the air. With bright beady eyes and a sharp Scottish twang in his voice, Lenny asked me about my research. His dog barked and continued barking which almost completely drowned out my voice as I explained my interest in John the Baptist. The dog continued barking and was getting on my nerves. 'Do you really love dogs?' I asked Lenny. 'Not really, actually I hate them.' Clearly the dog was there to guard the house rather than anything else. We proceeded down into the cavern-like basement of his house which was full of unexpected treasures arranged with a certain satisfying sense of chaos. There was dust everywhere and a large three-inch spider casually climbing the wall. It was the sort of place I like, with piles of papers all over the place, boxes, half-opened catalogues and books, dusty cabinets full of disorganised antiquities, scattered coins and amulets on the tables, a sculpture or two, heaps of lamps and juglets spread out over the floors, a computer and a library. I could see that this was the sort of person who took an immense enjoyment in his work, as I mulled over the artefacts while sipping a good double-malt whisky and munching on crystallised ginger. Among the amulets in Wolfe's collection there was one that I was immediately drawn to, depicting the baptism of Jesus in the Jordan with an angel on his left and the figure of John the Baptist on his right (*illustration 3.6*). Amulets of this sort were quite frequently produced in the Eastern Mediterranean area and particularly in the Holy Land, where they were sold to pilgrims and Christian travellers together with other trinkets, crosses and supposed relics. This one is a lead souvenir badge and probably dates to the fourteenth or fifteenth centuries, or later.

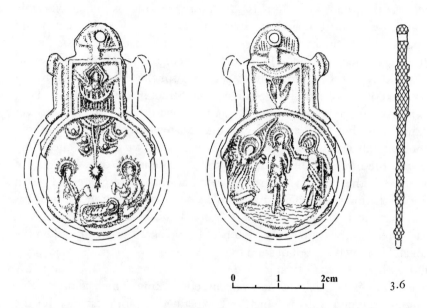

3.6

The exciting thing that I found when looking at the extant ancient artistic portrayals of John the Baptist is that the one from the cave at Suba appears to be not only one of the earliest in existence in the entire southern Levant but also the only one directly connected to a cult site dedicated solely to John the Baptist. None of the other major archaeological sites associated with John the Baptist has any significant early artistic depictions of John. However, early artistic portrayals of John do definitely exist, though in the West rather than the East, perhaps through an accident of archaeological discovery. Early representations of John the Baptist appear in wall paintings in the catacombs of Rome

3.7

(*illustration 3.7*). The first comes from the Catacomb of Callixtus (Chapel of the Sacraments A3 left-hand corner) and is dated to the second half of the third century. The scene is of a semi-naked adult figure, with a clean-shaven face, with his right hand resting on the head of a small child-like figure standing to the left. Some doubts have been expressed as to whether this scene reflects the baptism by John and it has even been suggested that the large figure might perhaps be 'marking' the forehead of the smaller figure instead. This seems unlikely because the overall posture of the large man is identical to that of the later standard renderings of John baptising Jesus in the Jordan. John is frequently shown to the right of the standing Jesus, his body is always shown slightly bent forward for the ceremony and he is always shown using the right hand in bestowing baptism. In any case, the hand is shown visibly resting on *top* of the head of the small figure. The small size of Jesus is also well paralleled. However, there are also differences: John is usually depicted in such scenes wearing more garments, and his staff is missing, the figure of Jesus is shown fully clothed; the descending dove is missing, and there are no indications of water. The second painting comes from the Catacomb of St Peter and St Marcellinus and it is dated to the late third century. It also consists of a representation of a large man (John) on the right and a small figure (Jesus) on the left. The figure of John has been badly preserved and one can only see the top of his head and his right hand resting on the head of Jesus. Jesus is depicted as a naked child and he stands in a pool of water. Above him is the dove shown in profile with much detail, and rays are emitted from the bird down and over Jesus' entire body [note 3.46].

71

3.8

John the Baptist appears in a number of mosaic depictions of the Baptism of Jesus in Ravenna (*illustration 3.8*). The first is from the mosaic in the crown of the dome of the Neoniano Baptistry, dating from around AD 440 to 450. The full-frontal and bearded Jesus is depicted naked and standing up to waist level in the water. On the right is a bearded person personifying the Jordan River. On the left John stands with his left leg raised on a rock, while he baptises the head of Jesus with a bowl held in his right hand. A dove is seen descending directly to the bowl. In John's left arm is a long bejewelled staff topped by a cross. A similar depiction of John appears in the mosaic dome of the Arian Baptistery, dated to the first half of the sixth century. The naked, beardless Jesus is depicted at the centre of the scene, standing in the waters of the Jordan River flowing from an amphora. The Jordan is personified here as a seated figure on the left, leaning against the amphora. On the right, John the Baptist is perched (uncomfortably) on a rock, clad in a hairy garment and with a shepherd's crook in his left hand. His right hand extends towards the head of Jesus. The dove as the Holy Spirit is shown above the head of Jesus [note 3.47].

Further representations of John appear on baptism scenes depicted on artefacts (*illustration 3.9*). The first is an ivory plaque of the sixth century, probably made in north Italy and now in the British Museum collections. It shows Jesus as a youth without a beard, waist-high in the Jordan River (with the personification of the Jordan at the lower right). John stands on a rock on the left with his right hand on the head of Jesus. Behind is an angel (?) holding a shawl with which to wrap Jesus. Above is the right hand of God holding the tail of the dove that descends down to the bowl with which John baptises [note 3.48]. Another baptism scene appears on a small wooden reliquary box with a painted cover; it

3.9

is now part of the treasure of the Capella Sancta Sanctorum of the Lateran in the Vatican collections. It has a number of painted scenes connected with the life of Jesus, including a scene of baptism in the lower right-hand corner. This shows a full-frontal naked figure of a bearded Jesus standing in the waters of the Jordan. Above is the descending dove with the hand of God at the top. John is seen on the bank of the river, stooping forwards and baptising Jesus' head using his right hand. There are two haloed onlookers behind John. On the opposite bank, to the right of Jesus, are two winged angels, one of whom holds a cloth to dry Jesus. The scene is dated to the late sixth or early seventh century and may have been made in Palestine and brought back to Italy by a pilgrim [note 3.49].

During a break in the excavations I travelled to the city of Florence, whose patron saint happens to be John the Baptist. In the centre of Florence is the Baptistry of San Giovanni (St John), an octagonal building next door to the Duomo, with representations of the life and death of John the Baptist on the interior and exterior of the building. The baptistery is one of the oldest buildings in Florence, with foundations dating back to the sixth or seventh century. I very much wanted to see the interior, and so I suffered the indignity of being shuffled along within a milling crowd of tourists and schoolchildren, around the building and then into the interior. The southern door has a series of twenty cast panels (out of twenty-eight) depicting in relief scenes from the life of John and it was made by Andrea Pisano da Pontedera in 1336. I liked the combination of statuary above the southern door with poor old John the Baptist seemingly as an afterthought wedged between the executioner and Salome; it was made by

Vincenzo Danti (1571). I then went to have a look at the eastern door, which (according to Vasari's *Lives*) Michelangelo called 'door of paradise' because of its beauty. Above this door is Andrea Sansovino's sculptural group called the *Baptism of Christ* (1502). Inside the building and wrapped around the cupola are four bands of colourful mosaics depicting the life of John the Baptist which was put together by craftsmen in the thirteenth century. These mosaicists began their work in 1225 – apparently the artist Cimabue who flourished during 1272 to 1302 made some of the early portions – and the work continued into the fourteenth century. What I found interesting was the sequencing of the events of John's life both on the door and in the mosaics. For instance, they show pictures of John baptising his followers in the mountainous regions *before* the pictures of John baptising Jesus in the Jordan. The font inside the building was used to baptise many Florentines, including the famous Dante Alighieri himself. Nearby, the Museo dell'Opera del Duomo has various sculptures of John and a small collection of relic artefacts as well.

The life of John the Baptist was also depicted in numerous Renaissance paintings, in a cycle of subjects, which included Zacharias in the temple; the birth and naming of John; John in the wilderness; John preaching; John's imprisonment; the feast of Herod; the dance of Salome; and the beheading of John and his burial. He was also depicted in some paintings as a saint, seated to the left of Christ and holding in his arms a lamp and scroll bearing the words 'Ecce Agnus Dei' (Behold the Lamb of God) [note 3.50]. John also appeared in pictures of the Madonna and Child, either as an infant (slightly older than Jesus) or as a youth. In some scenes the Madonna and Child are shown flanked by standing saints, including the adult John the Baptist. The portrayals of John as an infant show him wearing a hairy animal skin, with a baptising bowl and/or staff topped by a cross. There are numerous pictures depicting John as a youth or as a clean-shaven young man, with those by Caravaggio perhaps the most sensuous: smooth-faced youths in lascivious attitudes clearly reflecting his sexual predilection for young nubile boys [note 3.51]. There are also paintings depicting John as the gaunt ascetic with a beard and hollow cheeks, with the figurative elements remaining the same: clothing of hairy skin, with the purple or red cloak, the baptising bowl and the staff. There are pictures depicting the baptism of Jesus and with John as a mature individual. He is usually shown bending over the semi-nude Jesus, wading in the Jordan Valley, and holding a baptising bowl over his head. There are also pictures of the beheading, of Salome dancing or holding the charger with the head of John, and a few rare depictions of the family of John with Elizabeth and Zacharias, and of the nativity scene.

We continued digging at the Suba cave with small groups of local volunteers and workers throughout the summer of 2000, uncovering an impressive sequence of living surfaces made of tamped soil, one above the other, and separated by layers of silt and mud. Associated with these surfaces were enormous quantities of pottery dating back to the Early Roman period, to the first century AD and perhaps even a little earlier. I was baffled by the enormous quantity of pottery turning up. What was it doing here and where had it all come from? One suggestion someone made was that it represented rubbish dumps brought to the cave from elsewhere, perhaps from buildings that we postulated might have existed on the terraced ridge above the cave, with pottery being thrown down through the vertical shaft piercing the cave's ceiling. Instinctively, I felt this was unlikely because of the way that pottery was so evenly spaced out on the surfaces, without the tell-tale heaps of pottery that one would expect to find had this material been dumped there indiscriminately.

The question we now asked ourselves was: how did the water get into the cave in the first place? Initially we thought that the water might have been brought to the cave by aqueduct from as far away as the spring of Ain Suba, but because of the relatively large distance involved and the lack of any archaeological traces for an aqueduct on the ground, we had to abandon this explanation. This meant that the only other reasonable source of water for the cave had to be the winter rains. The discovery of parts of two water-settling basins outside the cave hugging the edge of the valley towards the east helped confirm this notion. It amazed me that people had apparently been living in the cave in the Early Roman period and it also amazed me that these layers upon layers of soil had not been cleaned out and dumped outside in subsequent periods, which is common practice at caves in the Near East. Was there a reason for this and perhaps this was linked to the cave having been associated with John the Baptist? I now realised that to answer properly the many new questions arising from the excavations and to elucidate further the identity of the people who were using the cave in the Early Roman period, we would have to expand the area of the excavations and gather more detailed information. I began making plans for excavations at the cave during the following year. First, we definitely needed to get down to the bottom of the cave and, second, we needed to expand the area of the excavation towards the centre of the cave.

Clearly, we also needed to know something about the area outside the cave and so excavations beneath the terraces round about the cave would have to be done as well. I realised that to get the kind of results we needed was not going to be an easy task and could take much longer than we had initially expected.

Winter was now almost upon us and preparations had to be made to protect the cave from flooding because the entrance was at a much lower level than the ground surface of the valley outside (at 631 metres above sea level). With the help of a bulldozer borrowed from the kibbutz, we cut a large drainage ditch from one side of the valley to the other, thus ensuring that any flood of winter rains gushing down the valley would be diverted to the opposite side of the valley and away from the entrance to our cave. We spent the winter months sorting through the huge quantities of pottery from the excavations. Much of the preliminary marking and counting of the potsherds had already been done by our team by the time Noël Siver, an expert conservator of pottery and other ancient artefacts, travelled from London to our headquarters at the British School of Archaeology in Jerusalem. Even before unpacking her luggage, Noël had begun the enormous task of sorting through endless numbers of bags of pottery, sorting out ceramic types by fabric, colour and shape, and then seeking to establish 'mends' between the many thousands of potsherds. This was a wondrous jigsaw puzzle, spread out on the tables in our office and even on makeshift tables set up in the gardens outside. Luckily, there was little rain or high wind and so the material could be left safely overnight on the tables. Noël was amazing and turned the British School into a hive of activity, dedicating herself entirely to the task of sorting the pottery, from early in the morning until the failing light in the evening.

4

The Cave of the Wilderness

The discoveries that we had made in the cave during the previous year were indeed remarkable. There could be no doubt that in Late Antiquity (i.e. the Byzantine and Early Islamic periods) the cave had been regarded by Christian monks from Ain Karim as a holy place dedicated to John the Baptist, but why did the monks choose this specific cave in the first place and how old was the tradition linking the cave to John the Baptist?

The digging at the cave was resumed in the spring of 2001 and we had high hopes that we might solve the remaining mysteries of the site. There were still quite a few matters for which we were seeking answers: what was the function and exact date of the living surfaces that we had been finding in the cave under the Christian levels? And what about the Early Roman pottery (mostly from the first century AD) that we had already found: had the cave been used as a dump for rubbish or were people already living in the cave at this time? Was there a flight of steps leading down into the cave or was there a sudden drop down to the floor immediately below the entrance? When had the cave first been used and how would we be able to determine this? What did the settling basins east of the cave look like and how were they fed with water? And were there any ancient buildings situated on the rocky ridge above the entrance to the cave?

The workforce this time consisted of local people together with another group of volunteers from the States, once again led by James Tabor, all of whom showed enthusiasm and excitement as the dig progressed. The sponsorship for this part of the work was provided by the Foundation for Biblical Archaeology, a non-profit organisation based in the State of North Carolina, run by 'the red-head', Sheila Bishop, who also joined us for the dig and allowed me to fuss around her pointing out possible floors (indicated by flat-lying potsherds) at almost every spot where she felt inclined to sink her trowel into the ground. Two field archaeologists who had not worked at the site before also joined our team: Nick Slope and Egon Lass. British-born Nick supervised the excavations on the ridge above the cave and managed to keep us all rolling in laughter with his unique brand of humour, even though he was professionally disappointed when nothing much was found in his area except for rocky ground ('bedrock city' Nick decided to call it). But he did eventually find a sinkhole around the postulated shaft entrance leading to the cave's ceiling, and one rough wall running inexplicably diagonally down the slope (*plate 3b*). However, this excavation did help to clarify something quite important: it was now clear that the pottery that we had been retrieving in the excavations in the cave below could not have been dumped there from the rocky ridge above it. Indeed, the soil layers which we exposed above the natural rock hardly contained pottery at all, nor was there any evidence there of buildings or houses, even of the simplest kind. This was a breakthrough and meant that the provenance of the enormous amounts of pottery had to have been from activities taking place *inside* the cave. Much better results were obtained in the area of the settling basins located to the east of the cave entrance (where James Tabor and Sheila Bishop were working): the shape of these basins was now clear and more of the massive rock-cut and plastered walls surrounding them emerged. It became evident that water had been diverted into one of these basins via a channel extending from the direction of the valley floor.

Egon's responsibility was over the digging operations within the cave itself and he immediately set about uncovering the sequence of living surfaces in the area located just inside the entrance. We discussed the necessity to find out how the surfaces in the cave might have been used in antiquity and decided that the method of flotation seemed the best procedure open to us. Hence, Egon collected samples of soil from the surfaces, bagged them and took them away for flotation. This method included washing the soil in water, sieving and drying it, and then examining the resulting dusty residue under magnifying goggles, and extracting and saving samples with the use of tweezers. Egon is an expert at this procedure and has done this sort of work at quite a few archaeological sites in Israel. The sort of micro-artefacts he tends to find when he does this kind of flotation can barely be seen with the naked eye and may include minute fragments of pottery, beads and sometimes very small coins, carbonised plant remains such as seeds and bits of wood, crushed animal bones, fish bones, snails, fibres and so forth. However diminutive in size, such bits and pieces will provide the empirical evidence needed for reconstructing the daily activities of those ancient peoples who were using the floors. Rubbish will naturally be cleared away from functioning floors, but the tell-tale signs will always remain behind for flotation experts such as Egon to find. However, Egon was astonished to be confronted with a picture that he had never encountered before. On processing the material from the living surfaces in the cave, he came across enormous quantities of crushed particles of pottery and virtually nothing else. This was most puzzling and something quite different from the plethora of micro-artefacts that he had been finding on floors and living surfaces at other sites. The picture that Egon was getting was of people who were coming to our cave in antiquity, breaking pottery vessels there and then going away again. This was very strange.

Slowly, as the dig proceeded, a sequence of living surfaces immediately within the cave entrance was excavated, recorded and then removed. Associated with one of these surfaces, in the south-west corner of the cave, was a semi-circular installation consisting of a line of stones surrounding a mass of potsherds. If there had been doubts as to whether or not these surfaces were floors that people were using to tread on, rather than just hardened layers of soil or consolidated tip lines forming beneath standing water, such thoughts could be finally banished with the discovery of this installation. We were now on the lookout for additional installations connected with the living surfaces. Close to the bottom of the cave we uncovered tamped layers of hard marl (*huwwar*, in Arabic) above layers of stones, which were deliberately placed there to support the compact plaster surfaces laid above them.

While the excavation was in progress I had already been speculating that the floors and installations uncovered in the cave might have been connected with certain Jewish ritual water-cleansing activities of the Early Roman period. This was still only a hunch, but it felt right and fitted well with the bits of evidence we had been finding. Indeed, the pottery from the fills beneath the earliest Byzantine floor in the cave could be dated to the second to fourth centuries AD. Hence, while we had no evidence of actual floors from this phase, it seemed quite likely that the cave had indeed been in continuous use from the early first century AD and through the centuries, all the way to the first appearance of Christian monks in the fifth or sixth centuries AD. Judging by the latest pottery we had been finding we could also now envisage an unbroken sequence in the cave extending through the period of Late Antiquity, with people using the cave until the time of the Crusaders in the early twelfth century. Although this was exciting, we still needed much more data to fill in our picture of the history of the cave and also further information about the nature of the activities practised there particularly during the earlier periods.

Sometimes when I think that my ideas are somewhat confused and contradictory, my mind will clear and the interpretation of salient archaeological facts will suddenly stand out in sharp relief as though a lens has suddenly brought them into proper focus. The result is that all the facts seem to fall into place and a definite historical pattern begins emerging. This is what happened one day during the digging when it suddenly dawned on me that the Byzantine monks could not just have chosen this cave at random because it suited their rituals. They must have adopted the cave precisely because of the existence of an oral tradition connected to this place, extending back in time, perhaps even to the days of John the Baptist himself. That the monks would have alighted upon a cave that just happened to have been used at the time of John the Baptist was highly unlikely, especially if my assumption was correct that this cave was originally an unusual water grotto already used for bathing purposes in the first century AD. We all felt that we might actually be on the brink of a unique and potentially sensational discovery. However, there was still much more digging to be done to understand the character of the Early Roman period remains in the cave. The first thing I felt I needed to do, however, was to clarify in my own mind the character of the existing traditions relating to the very early stages in the life of John. Could this be the actual cave to which Elizabeth fled with the baby John while she was being chased by the soldiers of Herod? Perhaps this same cave was one of the places that young John lived in during his sojourn in the 'wilderness'?

The infancy narrative of John the Baptist in the Gospel of Luke (1:5–80) is unique and does not appear in any of the other gospels [note 4.1]. Hence, it is the only source of information about John's birth and formative years. While it has been shown quite convincingly that the Lukan infancy narrative is basically a literary construct and had been provided in order to make clear to the reader the subordination of John to Jesus, we should not hastily assume therefore that the bare essentials of the information contained within this narrative were also all made up [note 4.2]. I think it a reasonable assumption that the narrative was created based on credible information derived from oral traditions or documents transmitted by Baptist groups. One scholar has recently stated that the material in the infancy narrative 'has been so heavily worked over by a Christian author that it is hard to claim any historical value for the story at all' [note 4.3]. Having given some thought to this, I am not certain that this is true. Indeed, by excluding everything that might conceivably be regarded as legendary in content (such as the angel's revelation to Zacharias, his subsequent dumbness, and so forth), or that might have been added as literary adaptations in order to lend further credence to the Jesus story (such as the ordering of events so that they might closely match those of the infancy narrative of Jesus), we are still left with a core of information that might very well have had a basis in the reality of John's early life [note 4.4].

Both of John's parents were of priestly descent (Luke 1:5). John's father Zacharias was from 'the division of Abijah', which was the eighth division of the Zadokite course (cf. I Chronicles 24:10). There were twenty-four priestly courses and priests were elected from among a small number of families and the succession was hereditary (Josephus, *Jewish War*, IV: 155 [8]). It should be remembered that all Sadducees were officiating priests at that time but not all priests were Sadducees. Zacharias himself was appointed by lot with the task of burning incense on an altar in the Holy Temple (cf. Exodus 30:1–10; 37: 25–28; I Maccabees 4:49).

Elizabeth also came from a priestly background, from the prestigious House of Aaron (Luke 1:5). Since Elizabeth (Elisheva in Hebrew) was a name that was very rarely used in the first century, (judging by the fact that there are hardly any inscriptions with that name from that century) this makes it all the more unlikely that she was a legendary figure, otherwise a much more common name would have been allocated to her. Zacharias and Elizabeth are depicted in Luke as elderly people (Luke 1:7, 18, 36), but they need not have been more than middle-aged in our own modern terms. Elizabeth's seniority, however, is clearly acknowledged by the fact that Mary is the one who sets out to visit Elizabeth and not the other way round. Elizabeth was apparently barren, though admittedly the medical problem could very well have been with Zacharias. This part of the text is most likely to be legendary and would have been added in order to emphasise the wondrous birth of John.

The next segment in the narrative deals with Zacharias and his encounter with Gabriel the Angel of God, next to the Altar of the

Incense at the Temple in Jerusalem (Luke 1:8–22). Zacharias is told that
Elizabeth will conceive a son and that he should be named John and
eventually that he would become great before God. Following the
Annunciation, Zacharias is struck dumb as a sign that God would fulfil
his promise. This part also seems to be legendary, though as a priest
Zacharias would undoubtedly have officiated in the Temple. The next
passage deals with the arrival of Mary to visit Elizabeth (Luke 1:39) in
the 'hill country' of Judah near Jerusalem. The exact filial relationship
between Mary and Elizabeth is unclear: they are assumed to be cousins,
but the Greek word in Luke 1:36 actually only means kinswoman
(συγγενίς). The presentation of Elizabeth's baby leaping in her womb
because of Mary's privilege (Luke 1:39–45) must be an addition that was
necessary in order to establish from the outset John's subordination to
Jesus. Following the birth, another legendary episode occurs regarding
the naming of John and the restoration of Zacharias' speech. On the
eighth day John was circumcised and named (Luke 1:59). Zacharias is
then filled with the spirit and speaks about the future role of his son as
a prophet. Finally, we are told that 'John was growing and becoming
strong in the spirit, and he lived in the wilderness places until the day of
his public shewing to Israel' (Luke 1: 80).

In the centuries following John's death a number of infancy narratives
were apparently in circulation; one of these may very well have been
derived from a Baptist source, though none has apparently survived.
Some scholars believe that Luke 1: 5–80 was originally an independent
birth narrative of John produced by a Baptist group, and that it was
subsequently heavily edited and elaborated so that it might fit into the
overall perspective of Luke's gospel [note 4.5]. Without going into all
the later largely apocryphal references to John's birth and youth (such
as, for example, in the early-second-century *Gospel of the Ebionites* or in
the *Pistis Sophia* of the third century), I should like to bring the reader's
attention to the more interesting and detailed *Protevangelium of James*
which purports to have been written by the half-brother of Jesus, but
actually dates from the mid-second century at the earliest [note 4.6].
The *Protevangelium* recounts how Zacharias, while acting as a priest in
the Temple, was struck dumb and therefore was substituted by the priest
Samuel instead. Mary visited her 'kinswoman' Elizabeth and then made
a prayer, with John subsequently leaping for joy in her womb (as in the
Luke account). The sixteen-year-old Mary eventually stayed there for
three months. When Joseph found that Mary was pregnant he initially
believed her to have been defiled, but, on informing the priest Annas of

these circumstances, Joseph found himself to be disbelieved and is told that one way or another he must have consummated the marriage. Joseph and Mary were then both tested with the 'water of the conviction of the Lord', which may be a reference to a dipping in a Jewish ritual cleansing pool (a *miqweh*) but by what procedure we are not told. They are then sent into the wilderness of the hill country, even though no sin had become apparent. Meanwhile, the soldiers of Herod the Great, in their search for the infant John, eventually came to Zacharias in the Temple in Jerusalem, but when he refused to provide them with information about John's whereabouts, he was summarily despatched at the altar in the forecourt of the Temple. We are then told what ultimately happened to Elizabeth and John: 'But Elizabeth, when she heard that John was sought for [by Herod's soldiers], took him and went up into the hill-country. And she looked around [to see] where she could hide him, and there was no hiding-place. And Elizabeth groaned aloud and said: "O mountain of God, receive me, a mother, with my child." For Elizabeth could not go up [further] for fear. And immediately the mountain was rent asunder and received her. And that mountain made a light to gleam for her; for an angel was with them and protected them' [note 4.7]. This appears to be a reference to a cave with an aperture through which the interior was lit up.

This is probably the earliest account referring to Elizabeth and the infant John hiding in a cave in the hill country close to Jerusalem and it is a theme which is maintained in many of the later Christian traditions relating to Ain Karim as the hometown of John. There is of course one major problem in all of this: the place of Elizabeth's residence (the one mentioned in Luke) and the cave to where Elizabeth flees (mentioned in the *Protevangelium*) could not both be at the same location or even in the same proximity. If Ain Karim is the place where Elizabeth and Zacharias lived, then the cave where John was eventually hidden must have been situated in the countryside in the hinterland of the settlement and it makes clear sense that this would have been in the opposite direction from Jerusalem where Herod's soldiers would have come from, i.e. at a place in the hills west of Ain Karim. While the narrative of the *Protevangelium* is undoubtedly apocryphal in its overall concept, the specific reference to a cave in which John was hidden from Herod's soldiers may actually have been based on an oral tradition that already existed in the second century. If so, then the cave at Suba could be a very good candidate for this cave, since it is located west of Ain Karim, on the one hand, and within it we had been finding pottery dating back to the second and first centuries. Perhaps this was the tradition connected to the cave at Suba that led to this place being venerated by Christian monks in the Byzantine period?

The image of Elizabeth fleeing to the mountain with the baby John clutched in her arms and with Herod's soldiers in hot pursuit, was a subject that later became well represented in early Byzantine art. A number of ceramic medallions (*eulogia*), for example, are known depicting the flight of Elizabeth and are dated to the sixth to seventh centuries. It is quite possible that they are based on similar pictorial representations appearing in mosaics or on wall paintings at the churches near where these tokens were being produced. Since they are quite small (up to ten centimetres in diameter), they could easily be carried away as mementoes by visiting pilgrims. One of these medallions is said to have come from Ain Karim and is now kept in Bobbio in Italy (*illustration 4.1*) [note 4.8]. Elizabeth's name appears in the surrounding Greek inscription, which reads: 'A blessing of the Lord from the refuge of St Elizabeth'. Elizabeth is shown with a halo around her head and she looks back at the Roman soldier brandishing a sword in one hand and attempting to hold on to her dangling shawl with the other. The baby John (also with a halo) is clutched tightly in Elizabeth's arms, away from the soldier. Above their heads is a winged angel with its head towards Elizabeth and feet towards the soldier. On the right is the 'hill country'

4.1

represented by a curved shape that looks almost like a French loaf of bread (hills similarly depicted appear in a sixth-century mosaic map of the Holy Land at Madaba) and at its centre, just within the reach of baby John's arms, is a blurred symbol. What this was became clear when a fragment of yet another token (not made from the same mould) was uncovered during excavations in the courtyard of the 'Monastery of the Virgins' near the Temple Mount in Jerusalem [note 4.9]. It shows a loaf-shaped hill with at its centre an image of two flights of steps (presumably leading down to a cave) and above it a large cross on a pedestal. It would be nice to think that we have here a representation of the cave that we were digging at Suba, but this is unlikely. Although Byzantine monks were clearly visiting our Suba cave and were aware of a tradition connecting it to John the Baptist, the actual place of pilgrimage connected with Elizabeth and John's 'refuge' had by the early Byzantine period shifted back to Ain Karim, closer in fact to the traditional place of the House of Zacharias. Hence, what we actually have in the Bobbio medallion is the earliest representation of the traditional cave of John the Baptist, the one at Ain Karim. The monks who came to our Suba cave in the Byzantine period were evidently aware of the two caves associated with John in Ain Karim itself, notably the grotto of the nativity of John beneath the main church of the House of Zacharias (the present-day Church of St John) and the refuge of Elizabeth and John next to a spring on the other side of the village (the so-called Church of the Visitation). There was also evidently a strong tradition regarding John in the Wilderness (based on Luke 1: 80) and I believe a specific cave was pointed out and visited on given occasions marked in the Byzantine calendar. But where was this 'wilderness' and how could the fertile region near Ain Karim, with valleys sown with wheat, and with terraced slopes laden with vineyards and olive groves, be properly described as a 'wilderness'? The key question we were now asking ourselves was: is it possible that our cave at Suba was the traditional Byzantine period 'Cave of John in the Wilderness' and how does this square with the traditional spot which is pointed out at Ain el-Habis?

In the minds of many, John spent his childhood in the barren wilderness in the Judaean Desert, where there is little vegetation and hardly any water, a region that begins in the undulating hills east of Jerusalem and extends down towards the Jordan Valley. Nobody in their right mind would ever want to wander off into this wilderness aimlessly, without food and water. Some years ago, a woman resident in Jerusalem decided to go on a long walk into this rocky wilderness east of the city.

She walked and walked and then finally died. Her broken body was found at the bottom of one of the dry gorges. There seemed to be no apparent reason for her actions, unless of course she had decided purposefully to end her own life, which is a possibility. In any case, the mystery of her death was never solved. The wilderness is a magical place with an enhanced potential for solitude, with its arid rocks and little caves, the dry rasp of shrubs, slithering lizards and smelly beetles. But it is also an inhospitable and dangerous place. Those who know its language well are the Bedouin and they survive because they have learned to be sensitive to its dangers: they do not get lost, they do not get sunstroke and they do not get swept away in the flash floods in winter. They know every one of the paths intimately and they walk around with a very clear mental image of the topographical lay of the land: every wadi (dry valley), hill and rocky crevice is known to them. More important, they know all the places where one might obtain life-sustaining water; they know the quality of the water at each cistern or water-hole and where to go should one of the sources suddenly go dry. They also dress appropriately and know where to find shelter in the midst of what may seem to be absolute desolation; they can recognise every single nook and cranny where one might take cover until the harsh rays of the sun abate. They are walking mines of information about the desert wildlife and what to do when stung by a scorpion or when receiving a snake-bite. What is unfortunate is that nowadays Bedouin youngsters are rapidly forgetting the fine traditions of the wilderness, as they are slowly becoming entranced by the glitter and temptations of the Western world.

In the Old Testament, the wilderness and desert were referred to by different terms, but the most popular ones used were *midbar* and *shmamah* (for example, Deuteronomy 32:10 and Isaiah 64:10). The term *midbar* is an all-encompassing one which could be used for very different types of landscape. At times it was a term used to denote the true desert (such as the Sinai Desert), which was largely empty and devoid of human settlement. However, it was also used in reference to the arid wilderness (such as the Judaean Desert) that could to a certain extent support basic human existence. Annual rainfall there averages at 300mm in the west parts of the region but drops to a mere 50 to 100mm on the very edges of the Jordan Valley to the east. Since the Israelites are reputed to have spent forty years in the desert, one would expect to find some sympathy about it in their writings, but, in fact, the *midbar* of the Old Testament is portrayed as a rather fearsome, bad and desolate place, where hunger and thirst were always waiting, and full of harmful animals, snakes and scorpions.

Some wildernesses, such as the Judaean Desert, served as a refuge for Jewish insurgents rebelling against the authority of the Romans at the time of the First Revolt (AD 66–70). Josephus (*Jewish Wars* VI.351), for instance, tells us that the main leaders of the revolt against the Romans, Simon ben Gioras and John of Gishala, actually requested from Titus, the Roman conqueror of Jerusalem in AD 70, that they be allowed to retreat into the desert. The wilderness was also the haven of the murderous *sicarii* (assassins) and of bandits of one sort or another. From the time of the Second Revolt (AD 132–135), letters, documents and other artefacts belonging to the fighters of Shimon Bar Kokhba and his followers, have been found in some of the cave refuges in the wilderness, indicating interestingly that many of those who fled there actually came from the upper echelons of Jewish society and were not just from the lower classes, as some historians had assumed. Throughout the first century, the Judaean Desert was a breeding ground for a number of apocalyptic and messianic movements (see the warning against false messiahs in the wilderness as expressed in Matthew 24:26) and some of their leaders even had strong revolutionary aspirations. Josephus reports on some of them: 'Moreover, imposters and deceivers called upon the mob to follow them into the desert. For they said that they would show them unmistakable marvels and signs that would be wrought in harmony with God's design. Many were, in fact, persuaded and paid the penalty of their folly . . .' (*Antiquities* 20. 167–8). We hear for instance of the Egyptian who led four thousand people into the wilderness: 'At this time there came to Jerusalem from Egypt a man who declared that he was a prophet and advised the masses of the common people to go with him to the mountain called the Mount of Olives . . .' (*Antiquities* 20.169–172; cf. *Jewish Wars* II.261). This is probably the same Egyptian who, according to Acts 21:38, 'recently stirred up a revolt and led the 4000 men of the *sicarii* out into the wilderness'. There were also others, such as Theudas in AD 44–48 who led his followers down to the Jordan Valley, where they were slaughtered by the Romans [note 4.10].

One can understand why a wilderness – such as the Judaean Desert – would have been an attraction for religious-minded people and especially for those with an ascetic bent, such as John the Baptist. Strange as it may seem, self-inflicted asceticism was regarded in the first century as a pious activity even when this was the result of alienation; apparently hunger was only deemed dishonourable at that time if it resulted from poverty. Bannus is a good case in point. According to Josephus (*Vita* 11–12), who lived with this man for three years in the wilderness, Bannus would wear 'only such clothing as trees provided, feeding on such things as grew of themselves'. He also took frequent ablutions of cold water as a medium of purification. The fact that Josephus went to live with him for such a long time must indicate that Bannus' activities were known to the public at large and that he had attracted a following. That people like Bannus and John the Baptist could acquire fame must indicate that such ascetic behaviour was on the whole unusual, otherwise Josephus would not have bothered to mention them [note 4.11]. Some scholars have suggested that John might originally have become an ascetic while living as a member of the sect of the Essenes, but this seems highly unlikely. While the Essenes did live in a very harsh environment next to the Dead Sea, they did not actually assume an ascetic lifestyle themselves [note 4.12].

According to the Gospels, John began his ministry in the wilderness next to the Jordan River, 'preaching a baptism of repentance for the forgiveness of sin' (Mark 1:4). There can be no doubt that this 'wilderness' and the area close to the Jordan River are one and the same, since the people who came there to be baptised travelled all the way from Jerusalem and Judaea (Mark 1:4–5). Matthew (3:1) names the area where John came preaching as the 'wilderness of Judaea', and since he then immediately goes on to refer to John's baptism activities at the Jordan (3:5–6), we may assume that he too regarded the wilderness of Judaea and the Jordan as being in the same general region [note 4.13]. Luke (3:2–3), however, makes a very clear separation between the wilderness and the Jordan River: 'The word of God came to John the son of Zachariah in the wilderness; and he went into all the region around the Jordan.' Hence, the wilderness from which John came and the Jordan River region to which he went to were two different places. This logically follows on from Luke 1:80 where we hear that John spent his youth in the wilderness of the hill country: 'John was growing and becoming strong in the spirit, and he lived in the wilderness places until the day of his public shewing to Israel.' The Greek word ἔρημος ('wilderness') does not necessarily imply a desert without water, but can indicate a desolate or lonely region, an area used for grazing, and without cultivation, a place of solitude, i.e. the kind of place where nomads, shepherds and ascetics thrive [note 4.14]. Hence, one should probably interpret the meaning of *erêmos* in Luke 1:80 as indicating that the youth John lived in a place of *solitude* at some location outside the immediate area of his hometown (Ain Karim). It is interesting to note that elsewhere in the Gospels the 'wilderness' does not necessarily mean a desert, as in when Jesus retreated from the crowds to seek solitude (Mark 1:35; 1:45; Luke 4:42). Only much later, as an adult man, did John descend to preach and to baptise in another 'wilderness' near the lower Jordan River, to fulfill the prophecy of Isaiah 40:3 regarding the preparation for the return of Elijah: 'The voice of him that crieth in the wilderness. Prepare ye the way of the Lord, make straight in the desert a highway for our God' [note 4.15].

What do we know about the circumstances of John's life as a youth and as a young adult prior to his descent to the Jordan River? Actually, we know very little, except that as a child who had not yet reached the age of twelve (the year of the 'shewing unto Israel') John apparently took the unusual step of not living at home. By comparison to John, Jesus led a much more balanced childhood with the full support and protection of his parents until he came of age. Origen wrote of John the Baptist in the fourth century, that 'it is easy to understand why this special child could not live with his parents but must retire from the world, leaving the tumult of the town and the business of man and the neighbourhood of cities, to live in the desert where the air is purer, the sky more open, and God closer and more familiar.' However, this is the sort of thing that might make sense to an adult, but it is unlikely to have been the behaviour of a child. And so why did John leave his parents? One could assume some sickness or tragedy resulting in the death of his parents, especially since they are already depicted in Luke as elderly people at the time of John's birth (Luke 1:7, 18, 36). According to Matthew (23:35) and Luke (11:51), John's father, Zacharias, was deliberately murdered by Herod's soldiers between the temple and the altar, while John was still a baby. However, this episode may very well have been a legendary construct imitating the popular version of the untimely end of the post-exilic prophet Zechariah whose blood bespattered the walls of the Temple [note 4.16].

In regard to the demise of Elizabeth, nothing is mentioned in the Gospels, but in one of the apocryphal works, the life of John by Serapion, written between AD 385 and 395, we do hear that the death of Elizabeth occurred when John was still only seven years and six months old and living in the desert. Judging by the general attitudes of present-day traditional Near Eastern families, it is hard to believe that John would have been neglected by his immediate family, or, in the event of the sudden death of his parents, even by his extended family of uncles, aunts and cousins. Kinship, after all, was always paramount among family members, as the story of Mary visiting Elizabeth clearly illustrates. John was also reputed to be from a family with priestly lineage and so even if he was disliked by his relatives, it is unlikely that he would have been an abandoned child and it is inconceivable therefore that John would have strayed any great distance from the place of his birth. Hence, if we are to assume an early death for John's parents, it may very well be that his relatives, upon realising that he was a sensitive child who did not necessarily mix in well with his contemporaries, purposefully allowed John to become a shepherd boy with the duty of the tending of sheep or goats in the solitude of the hills round about his hometown. Indeed, the sight of very young Bedouin and farm boys shepherding their flocks along with brisk professionalism is not at all an uncommon phenomenon in the southern Levant today. Since Ain Karim was in the midst of a rural heartland, the common areas given over to pasturage would naturally have been located at some distance from the town. Hence, John probably had to spend considerable periods of time alone in the hills at a distance of up to a couple of kilometres from his home. This interpretation fits in quite well with Luke 1:80 (with a few additions of my own in brackets): 'John was growing and becoming strong in the spirit [in his hometown], and he lived in the wilderness places [as a shepherd boy] until the day of his public shewing to Israel.'

The mystique of the places of solitude in the hills of Jerusalem, the sense of the holy achieved through hardship, asceticism and a certain amount of food deprivation, and a deep interest in ancient prophecy all probably led John, as a young man working as a shepherd, to reflect deeply about his life, about the future of his Jewish brethren and about the nature of the end of days. The prophet Elijah was probably the person he spoke to in his mind, as he clarified to himself his forthcoming mission to the Jordan, mouthing words perhaps similar in sentiment to those written almost two thousand years later in a poem by Hermann Hesse, though the image John had clearly was that of Elijah and not of death (though, strangely, abrupt death was indeed the ultimate end to his mission): 'You will come to me too some day/ You will not forget me/ And the torment ends/ And the fetter breaks' [note 4.17].

What would John have looked like? How you look is always a matter of great concern for people in every society, whether ancient or modern. Clothing is not just to cover the body for reasons of modesty or to provide it with warmth, it is also a language in itself: what you wear can indicate where you are from, your wealth and social status, and your profession. The Bible is full of expressions relating to garments of one sort or another, and they are used as symbols and metaphors for greatness and triumph, sadness and defeat. As a rural priest, John's father Zacharias would have worn garments of distinction: the main item being a coat extending down to the ankles and tied with a girdle made of fine twisted linen (cf. Exodus 28:39) and a headdress or turban. John, however, is described as having worn an 'outer garment of camel's-hair, and a leather girdle' (Matthew 3:4; cf. Mark 1:6), echoing the appearance of the prophet Elijah himself: 'a man possessing a hair garment, with a leather belt girded about his loins' (II Kings 1:8). However, not all hairy garments were made of camel skins, as one may understand from the following: 'They were stoned, they were sawn asunder, were tempted, were slain with the sword, they wandered about in sheepskins and goatskins; being destitute, afflicted, tormented' (Hebrews 11: 37). Indeed, the rough hairy garment or cloak was worn not just by prophets (Zechariah 13:4: 'neither shall they wear a hairy mantle [*aderet*] to deceive'), but by poor shepherds as well (Jeremiah 43:12: 'as a shepherd puts on his outer garment [*beged*]'). There are some in the first century who took the ascetic look much further than even John: as we have seen, Bannus, according to Josephus, wore only clothing made out of vegetal material taken from trees. The girdle itself was a strip of skin which was tied around the waist as a kind of belt (Exodus 29:9; Lev. 8:7) but it was definitely not a leather loincloth [note 4.18]. In contrast to John's rough appearance, most Jewish men at that time wore an ankle-length dress-like garment, typically made of linen (cotton was not used at that time), with a girdle or belt tied at the waist. They probably also had some form of head-covering or turban. Sandals were made of leather and were strapped to the feet.

The description of John's manner of dress has been regarded by some as legendary but it does ring true for a number of reasons. First, John would have wanted to emulate the Hebrew prophet Elijah in some way (see full discussion in Chapter Five), especially as I believe he was preparing for his return at the Jordan River. John's 'outer garment of camel's-hair' was probably a garment similar to the mantle (*aderet*) worn by Elijah and Elisha (according to Zechariah 13:4 this mantle was hairy): 'And Elijah took his mantle (*aderet*), and wrapped it together, and smote the waters [of the Jordan], and they were divided hither and thither, so that they two went over on dry ground' (II Kings 2:8). Elisha repeated the same event (II Kings 2:13–14). Second, because of the lengthy period of time that John had spent as a shepherd in the hills near his

4.2

hometown, wearing a hairy top-garment would have been quite natural to him (*illustration 4.2*). In the nineteenth century, the shepherd in the Jerusalem region wore an unbleached calico shirt gathered in round the waist by a red leather belt, and James Neil has described the appearance of this John-like figure as follows: 'over the kamise, in wet or cold weather, and during the night, the shepherd, like all peasants, wears a thick, warm, sleeveless, sack-like outer garment, made of camel's hair, invariable as to material, shape, and colour, the latter being dark brown of different shades, with whitish perpendicular stripes. This is the common overcoat of the agricultural labourer and of all the working classes of the country districts' [note 4.19].

John is presumed to have led an ascetic lifestyle. Some scholars have suggested, therefore, that at some point in his life John took a vow and became a Nazarite (Numbers 6:1–21), which would have meant that he would not have been able to cut his hair, to come into contact with a corpse, or to eat grapes or imbibe wine. However, there is no evidence that John was at any time a Nazarite, or that he had long matted hair and a beard because of any vow. Unfortunately, we have no information whatsoever regarding the appearance of his face or hair. In Luke (7:33) we are told that 'John the Baptist came neither eating bread nor drinking wine . . .'; indeed, the matter of the wine was also raised by the angel Gabriel when informing Zacharias that Elizabeth was about to give birth to John: 'But he must drink no wine and strong drink at all' (Luke 1:15). However, while there may have been times when John abstained from bread and wine as a fasting procedure because of his obsession with purity, the point behind Luke 7:33 is the contrast of the manner in which John and Jesus conducted themselves in front of their followers. While fasting was probably a feature of John's lifestyle and was also practised by his disciples (Matthew 9:14, where John's disciples compare themselves to those of Jesus who do not fast; cf. Mark 2:18), this does not mean that it was used either as a penitential measure or as a means of inclining the mind to visionary experiences (as with the later Byzantine monks).

We are also told in the Gospels that John survived on 'locusts and wild honey' (Mark 1:6; cf. Matthew 3:4) and both of these would have been deemed by him to be natural and pure, as opposed to bread and wine (of Luke 7:33) which were processed by man and so were not free from the suspicion of impurity [note 4.20]. Israelites were permitted to eat locusts according to the Levitical code (Leviticus 11:21–23) [note 4.21] and this practice was continued by Jews well into the Roman period, as is made clear from the Mishna (*hullin* 3:7): 'Among locusts [these are clean]: all that have four legs, four wings, and jointed legs, and whose wings cover the greater part of their bodies.' In addition, we hear that locusts were pickled in brine (M. *terumoth* 10:9; cf. M. *abodah zarah* 2:7). Locusts were not considered flesh and so were exempted from the prohibitions regarding cooking with milk. Locusts and honey were also acceptable foods among members of the Essene sect. The locusts were cooked by roasting or boiling, but they had to be fresh and were 'put into the fire or water while still alive . . .' The honey was acceptable so long as it did not include the larvae of bees [note 4.22]. The honey (*devash*) mentioned in Mark 1:6 must have been the honey of bees and not honey made from fruits because of John's apparent abhorrence of processed foods for reasons of purity. There are a number of references to the honey of bees in the Bible [note 4.23]. In Judges (14:8) there is the story of Samson who 'turned aside to see the carcase of the lion: and, behold, there was a swarm [*adat*] of bees and honey in the carcase of the lion.' In the first book of Samuel (14:25–27), the Children of Israel arrive in a wood and 'there was honey upon the ground', presumably in the fissures and clefts of the rocks (see also Psalm 81:16: 'with honey out of the rock should I have satisfied thee'). In the nineteenth century, Bedouin would collect the honey in skins and jars and bring them into Jerusalem for sale [note 4.24].

In the Near East the locust was regarded for many thousands of years as an acceptable article of food. Henry Layard, during his excavations at ancient Nineveh, uncovered a chamber leading to the possible banqueting hall of Sennecharib, and on one of the walls he found a relief of men bearing dried locusts fixed on to rods (or skewers), as well as pomegranates, animals and tables with cakes and fruits (*illustration 4.3*). Layard observed that in his time locusts were 'still sold in the markets of many towns in Arabia' [note 4.25]. In nineteenth-century Medina, for example, locusts were sold as articles of food in shops. They were plunged into salted boiling water, dried in the sun and eaten with butter, but only by the poorest beggars, and even the Bedouin there would

4.3

speak of eating them with disgust and loathing [note 4.26]. While visiting the Near East in 1865, the Reverend F. W. Holland, of the Palestine Exploration Fund, noted that locusts were eaten by Arabs near Mecca, as well as 'in Beyrout by some of the Arabs and black servants there, and also by the Arabs on the east of the Jordan' [note 4.27]. In Arabia, in the early twentieth century, we hear that: 'the natives dismember the insects, pulling off legs and wings, but not the head, and while still alive roast them in a pan over a hot fire; and after being thoroughly dried in the sun, they can be stored away in sacks. The taste is said by them to be akin to that of fish' [note 4.28]. There are a number of ancient sources describing peoples who consumed locusts as food, indicating that it was a common practice extending back in time not only in Arabia but also in Africa. Two of these refer to the eating habits of the Ethiopians: Pliny (*Historia Naturalis*, IX.35) tells us about some tribes who 'subsist on nothing but locusts, which are smoke-dried and salted as their provision for the year'; and Strabo (*Geography*, XVI.4:12) mentions that they blind the locusts first with smoke and then 'pound them with salt, [to] make them into cakes'. Today, in some parts of Africa, locusts are dipped in honey and eaten cold, or dropped into hot oil which provides a food somewhat resembling potato chips.

In Palestine we also hear of locusts serving as a food source. Charles Thompson (1794), wrote that 'locusts are brought to market in large quantities, and purchased by the common people; and that they are frequently seen upon the banks of the River Jordan, of the same form as ours, but much larger; and being either fried in oil, or dried in the sun, are accounted a good sort of food.' Apparently, locusts could be eaten not just as fully developed insects but even while still in an earlier stage of development, as larvae. Chichester Hart wrote: 'Locusts in some places are esteemed a great delicacy. There are various ways of dressing them. Sometimes they are boiled and devilled, sometimes ground and pounded and made into cakes with flour, sometimes they are smoked, or roasted, or fried, or stewed in butter. Amongst the Moorish Arabs they are held in high esteem as a stimulant, and in Central Arabia they are regarded as a dainty. Their taste is by no means unpleasant when roasted and dried' [note 4.29]. The naturalist H. B. Tristram also reported on them being eaten in nineteenth-century Palestine: '. . . I found that locusts are eaten by the Jehalin, a tribe in the south-east of Judaea, by most tribes in the Jordan Valley, and by the Beni Hasan in the Gilead. I found them very good when eaten after the Arab fashion, stewed with butter. They tasted somewhat like shrimps, but with less flavour. When we consider how easily and invariably locusts can be procured in the Judaean wilderness, we find no difficulty in the account of the fare of the Baptist, and we see how idle was the controversy raised on the conjecture that the "locusts" of Matthew 3:4 meant the fruit of the Carob or Locust Tree' [note 4.30].

Plagues of locusts, however, were feared, and many regarded them not as a potential source of food but as a destructive pest and as a threat to agricultural crops. They had a long history of devastation in different parts of the Near East, which is also reflected in the Bible. The scene of devastation that might result from a plague of locusts is described in a number of places: Exodus (10: 5–6, 13, 15); Amos (7:1) and Joel (1:22–2:10). Syria and Palestine suffered invasions of locusts at different points in time: in 1114, for example, there is a notice in the sources relating to a major earthquake and a plague of locusts which came in its wake and impoverished the countryside. Huge swarms of locusts would invade Palestine at intervals of every eleven to thirteen years. Originating in the low savannas of the Sudan, the Desert Locust (*Schistocerca gregaria*) would appear in the late winter or early spring and have a devastating effect on the plant-life that was encountered en route through the Near East, from Egypt and all the way to Anatolia. The adults of this species of locust can reach lengths of between six and nine centimetres. Locusts are the most destructive type of insect in the world; it has been estimated that in a single day a swarm of 50 million locusts can consume enough food to feed five hundred people for one year. There are, however, two other species of locusts which sometimes appeared in the region: the European Locust (*Locusta migratoria* L.), which was only sporadically seen in the more humid habitats of Palestine, and the Moroccan Locust (*Dociostaurus maroccanus*) which does not do as much harm as the other two species [note 4.31].

Since the ancients did not have pesticides, the only way that they could deflect the devastating approach of the locusts was to light large bonfires and try and suffocate them in the smoke. A locust attack occurred in Palestine in 1865 and the futile attempts that were made to prevent them from succeeding was described by the Reverend F. W. Holland: 'when they [the locusts] approach a village the people turn out, light fires round their fields, dig trenches and fill them with water, and endeavour to beat them back with their cloaks and the branches of trees; but the locusts appear to prefer death to a retreat. They swarm up the trees and strip them of every leaf; olives and even oaks are not spared by them, but they attack the apricots and mulberries first' [note 4.32].

Jerusalem and its vicinity suffered from a ferocious attack of swarming locusts in the summer of 1915: 'Attention was drawn to them by the sudden darkening of the bright sunshine, and then by the veritable shower of their excretions, which fell thick and fast and resembled those of mice . . .' [note 4.33]. A description of swarming locusts in the Sinai region in 1930 was provided by Major Jarvis, who served as the governor of that region for the British Government: '. . . for the next four months they drifted about the Peninsula [of Sinai] in vast swarms about five miles wide and fifteen miles long. Unless one has seen a locust swarm it is almost impossible to imagine it, and hopeless to even attempt to guess at the number of millions of insects that are passing overhead or crawling in dense masses on the ground. The expression that the sun is darkened is not an exaggeration, as though there is no question of an eclipse, it is an actual fact that when a big swarm is flying there is an appreciable shadow across the sun' [note 4.34]. The swarming locusts in the Sinai were dealt with by patrols from the Egyptian Ministry of Agriculture, using flame-guns and scattering damp bran impregnated with arsenic. Jarvis wrote that 'a darting mass of flame licking up hundreds of thousands of insects is very thrilling and spectacular to watch . . .'

In later patristic texts and apocryphal writings, John's diet was regarded as sufficiently strange to warrant further explanation. Clement thought of John's diet as carrying 'temperance to the extreme', as he put it. In the *Gospel of the Ebionites* (dating from the beginning of the second century), the text of Matthew 3:4 is modified to read like a version of Numbers 11:8, with the word 'locust' (ἀκρίς) being replaced by the similarly-sounding word 'cake' (ἐγκρίς): 'and his [John's] food, as it saith, was wild honey, the taste of which was that of manna, as a cake dipped in oil.' Epiphanius (*Haer.* 30.13.4f), commenting on this, was rather displeased: 'Thus they were resolved to pervert the word of truth into a lie and to put a cake in the place of locusts' [note 4.35]. But the revulsion generally felt by theological writers regarding the eating of locusts continued, and in a commentary by Theophylact, the locusts were explained away as either plants or wild fruits. In the thirteenth century, Jacques de Vitry was told by a Syrian monk, from a monastery near the Jordan, that the monks of his monastery ate a type of plant or vegetation called 'langustae' or 'locustae' and that this must have been the same as the 'locusts' eaten by John [note 4.36]. The pilgrim Felix Fabri (1480–1483) was one of the first to discuss all the possible alternatives for the 'locusts' of John the Baptist, during a visit he made to the Jordan Valley between 1480 and 1483: 'Others say that pods grow there on certain bushes [probably *Prosopis farcta*], wherein are grains of seed like beans, whereof St John is said to have eaten. The whole plain was covered with these when I was in this wilderness, but the beans in these pods were hard, like stones, and I could not split any of them with my teeth' [note 4.37]. Gradually, however, the explanation that came to be the more 'reasonable' was that the 'locusts' must actually refer to the fruit of the carob tree and later it became commonly known in medieval literature as 'St John's bread' from the 'locust tree'. The tree is not mentioned in the Bible [note 4.38].

I have to admit that I have never ever liked the taste of the fruit of the carob tree: the pods are dry, flat, sickle-shaped and brown, and they have a sickly-sweet taste. The carob tree (*Ceratonia siliqua*; Hebrew *haruv*; Arabic *harruba* or *harrnub*) is large and sturdy, with evergreen dark-leaved foliage and widespread branches (blossoming between August and October), and it prospers individually or in clumps within a hilly environment, but it does not like too high an elevation where temperatures might drop considerably at night. If left to grow, the trunk of the tree can be quite thick with diameters of between five and ten metres. The tree is also highly resistant and can renew itself even after being cut down or burnt in a brush fire. A young tree will produce fruit after about ten years. The Hebrew or Aramaic name for the tree, *haruv*, may originally have come from the word *herev* ('sword') because of the sickle shape of its fruit. The seeds of the carob fruit weigh 0.18 to 0.21 grams and this is basically the same weight as that of the carat, a word which comes from the Latin *ceratonia* (the standard American weight for the Karat is 0.2 grams) [note 4.39]. Pollen remains indicate the sporadic presence of the carob in the region for over 45,000 years, with the earliest carbonised remains of the tree dating back to Neolithic times. Although utilised in Roman and Byzantine periods, their present-day widespread distribution is apparently a much later phenomenon from the tenth century onwards [note 4.40]. The carob tree had various uses in the nineteenth century: its fruit was used in the making of a kind of honey or jam by the local inhabitants, and its wood was used for making agricultural implements or was burnt in kilns to produce charcoal. Many carob trees were deemed sacred and ancient examples have been preserved next to the tombs of Moslem sheikhs and other holy men [note 4.41]. In the area of Ain Karim, for example, there is a very large and ancient carob tree at Horvat Sa'adim near the tomb of Sheikh Ahmed. The carob tree and its fruit were used for a number of different purposes from the Roman period and onwards in the region of Israel/Palestine. In the Gospel of Luke (15:16) in the Parable of the Prodigal Son we hear about the use of the carob as a food for pigs: 'And he would fain have filled his belly with the *husks* that the swine did eat' (italics: S.G.). In rabbinic writings the carob was also mentioned more than sixty times, among other things as a food for livestock: sheep and goats, and beasts of burden (e.g. M. *meaaserot* 3:4; M. *shabbath* 24:2; cf. M. *peah* 2:4; M. *baba bathra* 2:7, 4:8) [note 4.42]. But it would appear that the carob pods were never actually eaten by humans except in dire straits, notwithstanding the fact that they have a considerable dietary value, since they are rich in sugar, store well and are cheap to obtain [note 4.43]. Numerous pilgrims and travellers to Palestine have mentioned the carob – in areas close to Jerusalem, in the hills of Hebron, near Nablus and on Mount Tabor – and particularly because of the apparently mistaken notion, which had become popular since medieval times, that John the Baptist must have consumed carob pods instead of locusts.

If we are correct in assuming that John the Baptist, as a child and as a young adult, lived the existence of a shepherd with his flocks in the areas of pasturage in the hills of Judah, close to his hometown (Ain Karim), then we must also assume that he was used to spending long periods of time taking shelter in secluded caves, sleeping there at nights, and using them to store his few possessions, as well as water and food. Caves have been used for dwelling purposes since prehistoric times and there are still many people today in different parts of the world who live as troglodytes ('troglodyte' is the Greek word for 'a person who gets into or lives in a hole') but they tend to be looked down upon by house dwellers. Even in Britain people were still living in caves in 1974 [note 4.44]. In the Near East, taking shelter in a cave makes sense because it is the most efficient way of taking cover from the burning rays of the sun during the summer months. In the winter months the cave can also be a warm cocoon-like retreat from the battering rain and wind. However, taking shelter in a cave and living in it are two different things. Those living in towns or villages converted their available caves into storage areas and water cisterns, or as subterranean hideaways. Taking up permanent residence in a cave was generally regarded in antiquity as a lowly mode of existence by comparison with those whose abode was in stone or mud-brick houses [note 4.45]. In Ottoman times, for example, cave-dwellers were not even taxed, as opposed to those living in houses above ground, however rude and basic their man-made structures might be. Living in damp caves cannot have been a healthy exercise and one can imagine cave-dwellers suffering from respiratory diseases developed as a result of airborne spores.

Archaeological research has shown that in the hills of Israel/Palestine large numbers of caves were used on a seasonal or temporary basis by peasants or shepherds. In agricultural areas peasants used caves at the time of the harvest seasons when their crops and fruits were ripening and needed to be diligently protected. Caves were also used for the temporary storage of jars containing wine and olive oil, before transportation to market. In areas of pasturage, shepherds made use of caves to sleep in and fenced animal pens were frequently erected in front of them for their flocks. I myself have excavated quite a few shelters and caves used by peasants and shepherds during an archaeological project conducted in the area of Modi'in, the hometown of the Maccabees. These caves were usually natural or showed signs of being roughly hewn, and as one would expect there were very few finds within them. At one end of the cave there was usually a rock-cut shelf or bed, on which one might imagine a peasant or shepherd wrapping himself up in a cloak and bedding down for the night. In the walls there were sometimes small niches and these might have been used for storing one or two possessions. The sparse finds would include: scattered charcoal from fireplaces, an animal bone or two, and (if one was lucky) a few potsherds from a broken water jug or cooking pot. This was to be expected because a person living in such a cave would have had very few possessions: bedding, clothes, a mat, perhaps a stool, a few ceramic vessels, and basic foodstuffs that were usually kept in sacks or bags hung from the ceiling to keep the insects away.

I am a bit of a speleologist myself and have always enjoyed the exploration of caves, especially those used in ancient times. I must have already visited many hundreds of caves and there are still many more waiting for me. There are, of course, dangers that the explorer must take into consideration when crawling around caves: for instance, the ceiling of a cave or tunnel might suddenly collapse inwards and trap one underground. This is particularly true of the scores of winding subterranean tunnels used by Jews fleeing from the Romans in the early second century AD, which I spent time investigating at Givat Titura in Modi'in. One can only crawl through on hands and knees, and sometimes wriggling is the only way one can get from one part of the system to another. I do love the thrill of danger but I always try to take sensible measures. There is, however, a danger lurking in the caves that can be quite deadly: it is known as relapsing fever. In 1933, for example,

Dorothy Garrod's dig at a prehistoric cave in the Carmel came to an abrupt halt and was officially closed down by the authorities. A group of archaeologists tried to visit the site, and Betty Murray wrote: 'They had been to Dorothy Garrod's dig which is in rather a mess as they've got an outbreak of fever caught from ticks which probably live on the bats in one of the caves. Everyone working in that cave has got it, so the Ministry of Health have ordered it to be closed' [note 4.46]. I know this disease very well because I nearly died of it myself more than twenty years ago. It was at the end of a lengthy excavation of a Byzantine-period monastery at Ras et-Tawil near Jerusalem. Beneath the chapel was a grotto and it was here that I became infected. Little did I know then but immediately below the ground surface were many small ticks (known as *Ornithodorus tholozani*). Under the microscope they look like something from an 'Invasion from Mars' film: each tick has a flat, oval body with depressions in the upper shell and eight spindly legs, but it is no larger than 5 mm in size. These ticks wait in the ground, sometimes for years without feeding, and awaken only when sensing the body heat of an animal or human. The ticks emerge and proceed to extract their 'donations' of fresh blood by puncturing the skin and inserting a kind of local anaesthetic in the process. Some of these ticks carry a germ (known as *Borrelia persica*) and while drinking the blood they can infect the bloodstream of their host and it is this which causes relapsing fever. I remember feeling extremely weak and put this down to exhaustion during the closing days of the dig, but I then began suffering from headaches and general nausea. I had extremely strange hallucinatory dreams. Suddenly in the background I could hear hammering and this became more and more intense. When I opened my eyes, I could see an archaeologist friend of mine standing at the door and looking down at me in amazement: I was sprawled on the floor amid broken furniture, scattered books, plates and bottles. The flat was in shambles. Apparently I had been lying there in a dazed state for about a week, and nobody seemed to know where I had disappeared to. Following a lengthy hospitalisation, I eventually returned to life, extremely thin and weak, propping myself up with the help of a walking stick. A couple of years ago, I came across an article about relapsing fever and its appearance at sites in various parts of the country by the Israeli entomologist Rafi Lidror. I was quite chuffed to find myself included in one of his charts [note 4.47].

In medieval times and as late as the nineteenth century, the first 'wilderness' of John was a very well-defined geographical zone in the minds of Christian travellers and pilgrims, an area with terraced hills, springs and woodland, positioned within the triangle extending between Beth Jala, Ain Karim and Suba, to the south-west of Jerusalem. This was the place where the site of the traditional 'Cave of John the Baptist in the Wilderness' was believed to have existed. The cave was conveniently pointed out in the centre of this area, at a place called Ain el-Habis overlooking the Soreq Valley, and with a path linking it to Ain Karim to the east and with another path extending across the top of the hill to the south and down to the traditional spring of St Philip (Ain el-Hanniyeh) and Walaje in the Rephaim Valley on the other side. Ain el-Habis is located three kilometres to the west of Ain Karim, or a ride of one hour by horseback according to the Baedeker Guide of 1876, and it is located on the southern slope of the Soreq Valley, opposite Sataf. The Arabic name of the site, Ain el-Habis, means the 'Spring of the Hermit or Hermitage', but it is also known as Ain el-Habs, the 'Spring of the Prison' or 'Religious Endowment' [note 4.48]. The site was visited by numerous scholars and explorers in the nineteenth century. The French traveller Victor Guérin reached Ain el-Habis on 20 April 1863 along a path leading from the direction of Ain Karim. Claude Conder twice visited the site at the time of the Survey of Western Palestine: on the 17 January 1874, when he measured what he described as 'the curious Hermit's cave of El Habis', and again in 1881 before he set off for his survey of Transjordan [note 4.49]. The property was purchased by the Latin Patriarchate in 1850–1855. An altar was placed in the cave, but otherwise nobody lived at the site, except for a Muslim guard. The site was in ruins until it was bought by the Franciscans in 1911: a small two-roomed building with plastered walls and a tin roof was erected over the site of the old church, another five-roomed building was constructed above the site of the convent, and a stone wall was built to surround the general property. The present appearance of the site is the result of the extensive construction works which were made there in 1923, based on the designs of the architect A. Barluzzi [note 4.50]. From 1975 to 2000, the site was rented by the Melkites, but the property has now reverted back to the custodianship of the Franciscans [note 4.51].

We reached the Monastery of St John in the Wilderness at Ain el-Habis by car along a winding and narrow road past rows of chicken coops and industrial sheds of the Israeli village (*moshav*) of Even Sapir. It was a cold day and I was wearing the wrong type of clothes: when Fadi Amirah (the surveyor) and I set off early that morning to measure the

4.4

traditional cave of St John in the wilderness, I had wrongly thought that the day would turn out to be hot, but instead the sky remained overcast and I spent the day shivering in my thin shirt. We were met at the gate by one of the two Franciscans now resident at the site, Brother Sergio, whom I had been introduced to the previous year. The cave is located on the edge of a rocky scarp beneath the modern monastery buildings, next to a clear spring of water, and is surrounded by numerous plants and flowers. The character of the place is truly wonderful and exhilarating, and it was a pleasure working there (notwithstanding the cold) (*illustration 4.4, plate 6a*).

The cave is approached by a flight of seven steep and slippery rock-cut steps [note 4.52]. The original entrance appears to have an irregular-shaped hole – visible in an engraving by Cornelius de Bruyn from 1681 – but a collapse of part of the roof led to the insertion in 1911 of a cement column construction on the right-hand side of the entrance. The cave plan is irregular in shape (7.25 × 3.3 m) and height (2.6 m) and the surface of the rocky walls shows many signs of tooling and other modifications and at one place along the southern wall one can see a small incised cross (*illustrations 4.5*). Until a couple of years ago the interior walls were plastered but the Melkites, who had been living at

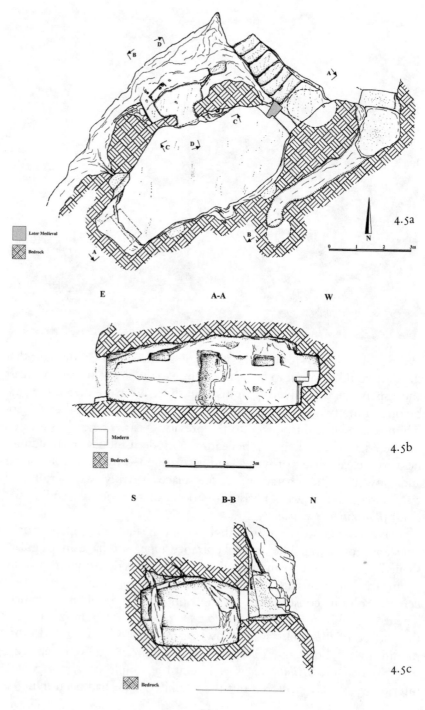

Later Medieval

Bedrock

4.5a

N

0 1 2 3m

E A-A W

Modern

Bedrock

0 1 2 3m

4.5b

S B-B N

Bedrock

4.5c

the site since the 1970s, had chipped it all off. At the far end of the cave is the traditional 'bed' of John the Baptist, which is a rock-cut shelf (1.9 m in length) with a modern altar built over it (*plate 6c*). There are a number of cupboard-like recesses cut into the walls, a hole in the wall for ventilation, a bowl-like depression in a recess above the floor (perhaps to hold a lamp), and a large window in the north wall of the cave which leads outside to a narrow rock-cut 'veranda' where one can sit, dangle one's legs and enjoy the view of the Soreq Valley below. Originally the veranda was covered by an arch of which only one small portion has survived.

The pool, located at the foot of the cave, is fed with water which flows through a rock-cut tunnel (almost five metres in length) from a natural aquifer further up the slope and in the heart of the mountain. Measuring this tunnel was quite tough since it meant getting wet. However, I can never resist tunnels and caves. Climbing up through a hole in the ceiling at the far end of the tunnel, I found myself immediately beneath the monastery, with some of the wooden rafters supporting its pavement seemingly at the point of collapse. It would appear that there are a number of outlets for the water and that the best of these carried the water to the pool next to the cave. According to Conder, the tunnel originally discharged its water into a small rock-cut basin and that this was later replaced by a much larger tank prior to his second visit to the site in 1881. The entire water system clearly deserves a special study and I think I shall have to go back next year to do this. Along the side of the mountain, beyond the pool, I could see further rock-cuttings which I also examined and recorded. These rock-cuttings are all that has survived of the back wall of a structure which appears to have collapsed completely downslope. The cupboard recesses and the plaster on the rock wall resemble that which is visible in the Cave of St John, suggesting that at some point in time there were a number of caves/structures scattered around the pool.

I had a look at the foundations of the walls in and around the monastery but most of them looked modern with one or two walls which might be medieval, but nothing at all like the ancient walls which are visible at the Chapel of St Elizabeth, some five minutes' walk upslope from the spring (see below). So where was the ancient church above the spring mentioned by some of the early travellers to the site? Perhaps the architect Barluzzi's work here in 1923 was so comprehensive that it managed to eradicate all traces of earlier buildings? Guérin visited the site in 1863 and remarked that next to the spring there was a ruin that may have been a place of piety, but otherwise he said very little, except that two or three carob trees were growing there. Conder mentions that in 1881 there were 'walls of a ruined upper storey' on the rocky ledge above the cave and that its west wall had windows with pointed arches; further east there were buildings (or a tower) 'built in the face of a rude cave'. These remains are quite clearly represented in two engravings: one made by Cornelius de Bruyn in the seventeenth century and the other by an anonymous engraver in the nineteenth century [note 4.53].

The earliest reference to the cave at Ain el-Habis was provided by the pilgrim Felix Fabri. Although he did not visit the site, he was aware of it and wrote that 'the caves in which he dwelt as a young man are shown to this day', i.e. he was referring to the cave of the 'Refuge' (at the Visitation) and the cave of the 'Wilderness' (at Ain el-Habis). Clearer information about the site was provided by Francesco Suriano (in 1485), who mentions a spring, the place where John lived, and an abandoned monastery: 'Likewise in the desert of St John is a most beautiful fountain. In this place the Christians made a monastery, which is at present uninhabited. To this place for its great amenities we used to go very often with my sons and friars for recreation and consolation of the spirit.' Elsewhere, he wrote: 'This desert is very pleasant and delightful, full of little wild pine trees high on the slope of a mountain, with a beautiful good fountain. To which place I sometimes used to go with my Friars for my spiritual recreation. There is there a church and a monastery, in which the monks used to live. Now it is empty through fear of the infidels.' Brother Pietro Pagolo Rucellai (1500) also refers to a church at the site, containing a stone that was used by John as a bed, near the spring and *above* the cave in which he lived.

There were numerous visitors to the site in the sixteenth century. Pierre Mésenge (1507), Canon of Rouen, set out for Jerusalem in April 1507, passing Ain Karim and its two churches, and mentioning that at a distance of four 'bowshots' from the Church of the Visitation was a small wood in which John the Baptist did penance. According to a Spanish Franciscan pilgrim, in a manuscript dated to between 1553 and 1555, he first visited St Philip's Fountain (Ain el-Hanniyeh) in the Rephaim Valley, and then:

Next we visited the Desert and the Cave of St John the Baptist and the spring whence he drew his water. In this desert the Baptist began to do penance while yet a child of five, so that his life should be wholly without stain. There is here a large church which we saw almost entirely in ruins and used as an enclosure for sheep and pack-horses. Desert and surrounding hills are very rugged, and the region well lends itself to meditation and prayer. Subsequently the spring disperses itself among the rocks. The place is distant from the home of the Baptist's parents three or four miles, which distance we covered when we visited the house of Zacharias and Elisabeth.

The pilgrim then continued on to Ain Karim. Leonhart Rauwolf (1573) took a similar route to the site: 'From thence [the Fountain of Philip] we came over high, rough and steep hills into the deserts, where St John the Baptist did lead his life in his young age, there is nothing to be seen but a very ancient chapel, and hard by it a delicate spring on the top of a hill, where we went to refresh ourselves a little, with eating and drinking of what we had taken along with us. About the roads grow many trees, by the inhabitants called *charnubi*, the fruit whereof is called St John's Bread in our country, and is brought to us in great plenty.'

Perhaps one of the most important visitors to the site in the sixteenth century was Giovanni Zuallardo, who has provided a very important engraving of the site of Ain el-Habis, showing in the centre of the picture a building on top of a hill which is identified as the ruined monastery (*illustration 4.6*). Next to it, on the left and below, are two openings of a spring and pool. On the slope further below is a large

4.6

opening representing the Cave of John the Baptist. On the right is the Rephaim Valley and behind it wooded areas. To the left is the Soreq Valley and one can see the path leading from Ain el-Habis towards the Church of the Visitation which is depicted surrounded by an enclosure wall with a gate. Zuallardo, who was originally of Flemish extraction (and so perhaps his name was originally Johann Schwallart), proceeded with his party in 1586 from Ain Karim to Ain Habis. His description of the site is as follows:

> Going from there [the Church of the Visitation at Ain Karim], we had a desire to continue two or three miles more, in order to visit the wilderness where St John the Baptist was guided and comforted by the Holy Spirit . . . And on arriving at the wilderness, though the path was very irritating and dangerous . . . I was very happy indeed to see a rather austere place, to us delightful, where that Holy Man [i.e. John] spent so much time. . . . at present there is not as much wood as there was in the past and it is very rough and hard, and remote from every human habitation. The cave or cavern, where he dwelt, celebrated in the hymn that is sung in church and begins 'Antra deserti . . .' is carved in the rock, in the middle, and faces the slope of a mountain full of saplings, [the slope] resembles more a precipice or cliff, meeting the deep valley that is opposite. The cave is very big inside and at the end has an elevation like an altar where the saint slept. The ascent to this [cave] is very difficult and the entrance narrow, joined to which there is a very good fountain of water that is possible to see in two places – above and below. For above there had been a church and a little monastery of which nothing remains except certain parts of walls that are almost all destroyed' [note 4.54].

On arriving back in Rome, Zuallardo had his drawings 'improved' by expert engravers there. His drawings were so well done that they were also reproduced in the publications of subsequent travellers to the area, notably Fürer, Cotovicus and Sandys.

Ain Habis was visited in the seventeenth century by George Sandys, who was one of the first English travellers to produce a reliable and lucid account of his journey through the Holy Land and it quickly made him an authority in his own time [note 4.55]. The son of the Archbishop of York, Sandys decided to make an escape from his wrecked marriage in England and from the litigation associated with it. He set out on his travels to the Near East by way of Europe in 1610. Eventually, at the age of thirty-three, he arrived at the gates of Jerusalem. During an excursion to sites around the city in the spring of 1611, Sandys arrived at the site of St John in the Wilderness, a site which impressed him enormously. Like many before him, he came from the direction of the Spring of St Philip (Ain el-Hanniyeh), remarking about the route: 'yet seemeth it strange unto me, that a chariot should hardly be able to pass those rocky and declining mountains, where almost a horse can hardly keep footing.' On the Cave of John the Baptist, he wrote:

> Having traveled about a mile and a half further, we came to the cave where John the Baptist is said to have lived from the age of seven, until such time as he went unto the Wilderness by Jordan; sequestered from the abode of men, and feeding on such wild nourishment as these uninhabited places afforded. This cave is seated on the northern side of a desert mountain (only beholding to the Locust tree) hewn out of the precipitating rock; so as difficultly to be ascended or descended to: entered at the east corner, and receiving light from a window in the side. At the upper end there is a bench of the self same rock, whereon (as they say) he accustomed to sleep; of which whoso breaks a piece off, stands forthwith excommunicate. Over this on a little flat, stands the ruins of a monastery, on the south side naturally walled up with the steep of a mountain: from whence there gusheth a living spring, which enterth the rock, and again bursteth forth beneath the mouth of the cave; a place that would make solitariness delightful, and stand in comparison with the turbulent pomp of cities. This overlooketh a profound valley, on the far side hemmed with aspiring mountains; whereof some are cut (or naturally so) in degrees like allies, which would be else unaccessably fruitless; whose levels yet bear the stumps of decayed vines; shadowed not rarely with olives and locusts. And surely I think that all or most of those mountains have bin so husbanded; else could this little country have never sustained such a multitude of people [note 4.56].

Sandys then proceeded on to Jerusalem via Ain Karim.

From the seventeenth century there are a number of additional descriptions of the site by De Thevenot (1686) and Henry Maundrell (1697). De Thevenot wrote that '. . . and from thence [Battir] by very bad way came to the Desert of St John Baptist, where after a pretty long ascent, we found a very old ruinous building, which heretofore was a monastery: under these ruins is a cave, where that Saint lived, and there you see the bed whereon he lay, which is the hard rock cut in shape of a bed. This grott is on the side of a hill, at the foot of which, there is a very stony valley or precipice, then another mountain, which intercepts the view, so that it is encompassed round with hills. There is a spring of excellent water by the side of this cave, and near to it we dined.' Henry Maundrell wrote:

> A little beyond this fountain [Ain el-Hanniyeh], we came to that which they call the village of St Philip [Walaje]; at which ascending a very steep hill, we arrived at the Wilderness of St John: a wilderness it is call'd, as being very rocky and mountainous; but is well cultivated, and produced plenty of corn and vines and olive trees. After a good hours travel in this wilderness, we came to the cave and fountain, where, as they say, the Baptist excers'd those sever austerities related of him, Matt. 3.4. Near this cell there still grow some old locust trees, the monuments of the ignorance of the middle times. These the fryars aver to be the very same that yielded substance to the Baptist; and the popish pilgrims, who dare not be wiser than such blind guides, gather the fruit of them, and carry it away with great devotion.

There are two descriptions of the site from the eighteenth century which are worthwhile mentioning. The first is by N. Crouch (Richard Burton) (1719): 'The desert of John Baptist; riding eight miles further [from Ain el-Hanniyeh] we came to John Baptist's fountain, his chamber, and a rock with a place cut out of it like a bench for a bed; if a person breaks off any part of this rock he is immediately excommunicated.' The second passage is by Richard Pococke (1738). Having described his visit to Ain Karim, including the Church of St John, the Church of the Visitation and the stone where John preached, Pococke then goes on to say:

> We then went about a mile further to the grot of St John, to which they say, Elizabeth fled with him, on the cruel decree of Herod to destroy the young children; it is said, she died when he was three years old, and that he continued in this grot, until he was thirty years of age, when he went into the desert near Jordan, to preach and baptise. We went higher up the hill, a littler further to the west, and came to a large grotto which they call the Sepulchre of Elizabeth. On

the hill, opposite to the Grotto of St John, there is a village, which, if I mistake not, they call the village of St John, or of the desert [Sataf]; and to the northwest, is a village on a high hill, called Zuba [Suba], which, some say, was Modin, where the Maccabees were born and interred; but they seem to be mistaken, as that place was in the tribe of Dan [note 4.57].

To sum up, it is clear that there are four separate features to be noted at the site: the Cave of John the Baptist; the spring with its tunnel and pool system; the buildings on the rocky ridge above the cave; and the buildings associated with the Tomb of Elizabeth further up the slope. The date of the cave and the adjoining water system is unknown [note 4.58]. In the sources mentioned above, dating back to the late fifteenth century, there is mention of a building complex on the rocky ridge above the cave and that it contained a chapel or a church. Unfortunately, no such structure has been seen by modern explorers. In fact, there are no evident ancient remains in the area of the spring dating from before the medieval period.

The Chapel or Tomb of Elizabeth is situated within a building further upslope from the spring of Ain el-Habis, to the south, which today serves as a retreat for a small number of nuns from the Swiss community of the Sisters of Grandchamp (*plate 6b*). A steeply ascending path leads straight up to this building and I arrived there one morning with the surveyor, Fadi Amirah, at the invitation of one of the nuns living there, Sister Maatje Dekker. It was a glorious day (the sun was at its most intense) and we immediately set forth to explore and to measure the building. We made a thorough examination. We were very lucky because the Sister allowed us complete access to every single part of the building, including even their private rooms and bathrooms. This meant that we could see bits of masonry and other ancient features that had completely escaped the eyes of earlier explorers. We climbed up and down the walls and across the rooftops. Although the building here appears to be much more ancient than the date of the buildings in the monastery close to the spring, the only clear reference to this building appears in a description by Richard Pococke from 1738 who calls it 'a large grotto which they call the Sepulchre of Elizabeth'. This seems quite strange and it appears to me that many of the earlier references to a church 'above' the Cave of St John might actually refer to this building and not to a building on the ridge immediately overlooking the cave. Guérin, who visited the site in 1863, refers to the building as a small chapel over the supposed tomb of Elizabeth, and says that new building works had just been completed before his arrival there. The exact whereabouts of the tomb of Elizabeth is unknown: various locations have been suggested, including Sebaste or its vicinity. In the early twentieth century, the cave of Elizabeth was regarded by the inhabitants from Walaje and refugees from Ain Karem as the birthplace of the Muslim woman Salamiya, and with her tomb situated in a grove of oaks near Sataf (i.e. at Sheikh Ubeid) opposite Ain el-Habis. Salamiya was the granddaughter of Sheikh el-Badr, a semi-legendary rainmaker among Palestinians [note 4.59].

The core structure within these buildings is clearly ancient and it contains in its ground floor a chapel (6.3 × 4 metres) dedicated to John's mother, Elizabeth (*illustration 4.7*). The chapel has a barrel-vaulted ceiling and is positioned towards the east but where one would have expected to find a regular rounded apse there is an arched rectangular niche instead, with a sunken oblong hollow in it said to be the 'tomb' of Elizabeth (*plate 6d*). I had a very careful look at this empty 'tomb' but

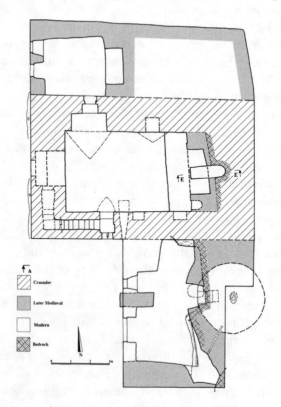

4.7a

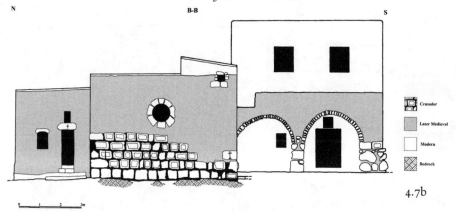

4.7b

other than observing that its length and breadth (1.9 × 0.6 m) would have been suitable for a body and that it was rock-cut, there is very little more to say about it. By the way, I could not actually see the original floor of the hollow. Presumably it was rock-cut but it is now coated with what seems to be some kind of soft yellow mortar (0.6 m below the paving of the chapel). I am sure that with the help of a trowel I could easily ascertain the depth of the original floor, but I thought that digging around at the bottom of the supposed tomb of Saint Elizabeth would be taking matters a bit too far. The barrel-vaulted interior of the chapel itself has been substantially renovated and the walls are now entirely covered with modern mortar. I am told by Sister Maatje – who showed me photographs to confirm this – that a painted decorated band originally existed on the plaster along the lower edge of the interior southern wall and was still visible before the renovations. Some scholars have expressed doubts that this chamber served as a chapel when the original building was constructed in the twelfth century. I beg to differ for several reasons. First, our survey shows that the chamber was definitely part of the original Crusader building and that it was not in any way a feature of the later building work at the site. There can be no doubt that the rock-cuttings in the face of this scarp, notably the hollowed out area of the so-called 'tomb', would have been visible to the builders. Second, the chamber was positioned towards the direction of prayer in the east and the 'tomb' very clearly served as a focus for worshippers and so it must have had some religious significance. I am not too bothered by the fact that the apse is not of the usual rounded type, especially if one takes into consideration that the east wall of the chamber, above the tomb, is a sheer rocky scarp (some 8 metres high). Finally, the main entrance in the south was so low that one had to bend

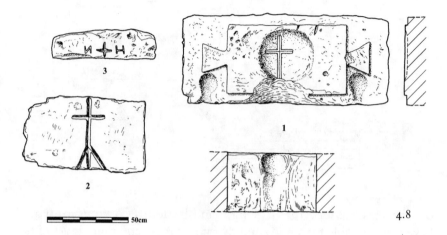

on entering and this is typical of doorways leading to chapels, the idea being that the person entering would be forced to acknowledge the sanctity of the place. The lintel of the entrance was decorated with a *tabula ansata*, with a sunken central circular motif and two small rounded side-features lower down (now defaced) (*illustration 4.8*). At a later stage a Latin cross was added in the central circle. Previous explorers had noticed the Russian letters И + H (standing for 'Jesus of Nazareth') flanking the cross but I could not see them myself even though I made a very detailed drawing of the lintel. Perhaps these markings were once in the low-cut circular features below the triangular 'ears' of the *tabula ansata* but this would mean that the letters had been obliterated only in the last couple of decades which seems unlikely. However, on another lintel above the northern doorway to the chapel, on the opposite side of the building, there is actually a small incised cross flanked by the Russian letters И + H and so perhaps previous visitors had got the two lintels mixed up in their descriptions.

The original ancient structure is quite impressive: it was oblong (11.4 × 7.2 metres, with walls 1.4 to 1.8 metres thick), built on two levels against the rocky scarp rising sharply to the east and its original height is thought to have been about 10 metres. We were able to pinpoint the south-western corner of the upper storey of the original building (which has mostly vanished) within one of the Sisters' rooms; luckily the original masonry had not been plastered over like some of the other walls. This indicated that the upper storey was set back to the east with a large open balcony above the roof of the chapel to the west. On the left, within the entrance to the chapel below, is a steep flight of twenty-three steps leading up to the balcony. This type of arrangement of steps running 'inside' the thickness of a wall is extremely typical of the architecture of the Crusader period and there are many known parallels. The original outer masonry is similar to that of rural Crusader towers known around Jerusalem (for example at Jaba') and even further afield, although there was one difference in the larger quantity of marginal-drafted stones actually used and not just for the cornerstones as one would normally expect [note 4.60].

The entire structure had evidently undergone a number of serious restorations in the history of its existence. Our examination of the masonry made this quite clear. In particular, the south-west and north-west corners of the original building showed signs of almost total collapse at one point and subsequent rebuilding. Some of the original stones were later used in this rebuild, including stones that were refaced. Thus, it would seem that a couple of hundred years after the abandonment of the Crusader building, restoration began and this also included the extension of the original building complex to the south and north. Judging by written sources, this must have taken place by the fifteenth century at the latest. The northern extension now has only one room on the west (connected by a doorway to the chapel), which is strange, because, according to our measurements, its exterior wall extends much further to the east. Also, when we had a look at the large sunken niche in the east wall of the room, it looked suspiciously like it could be a blocked-up doorway. Could there be a 'hidden' room on the east side of this northern extension? Since the walls of the chamber are plastered over there was no way that we could prove our theory, but Fadi and I enjoyed conjuring up in our minds all sorts of possible reasons why such a room would have been walled up. We also shared our excitement with the nuns who suggested that perhaps at some stage a hole could be made in the wall to see whether or not there is a room or cavity behind. This is something I would love to do in the future. The ground floor of the southern extension of the building now contains one room built up against the length of a rocky scarp to the east. It transpires that these are the private quarters of Sister Maatje, who told us that in the winter the room gets quite humid and sometimes during a downpour of rain the rocky walls stream with water next to her bed. Hidden behind a curtain at the base of the rock scarp is an iron door with steps leading down into a circular cistern. The west wall of the room originally had two large arched openings and it would seem that this was where the stables were located.

It was now half-way through the day and we were feeling quite hot from our exertions. My back was killing me and I was literally driving Fadi 'up the wall'; we had been climbing *all* over the building since quite early in the morning. Sister Maatje suddenly appeared to tell us that she had prepared a picnic under the trees with humous bread, fruit and coffee. I was overwhelmed by this unexpected hospitality. We were ravenous and fell upon the food, demolishing most of it within a very short space of time. The view was wonderful: across the way was the terraced slope of Sataf and its springs, and below us was the deep winding Surar or Soreq Valley. The tranquillity and beauty of the place made me realise why people would have thought this an ideal location for John's retreat. In the nineteenth century, various opinions existed as to whether Ain el-Habis could have been the 'wilderness' of John, with Guérin and Schick, for example, in favour of the tradition, and with Tobler and Sepp as sceptics thinking the site a bit too lush and fertile to have been a place of seclusion. Excavations which I conducted at Sataf, on the slope of the hill immediately opposite Ain el-Habis, showed evidence for settlements and agricultural remains dating back to the Roman and Byzantine periods and earlier. What emerged from the new work we did at Ain el-Habis is that there was nothing there that predated the Crusader period (twelfth century). Indeed, the earliest structural remains at the site were those of the Crusader-period tower-chapel (of Elizabeth) which was further up the slope from the spring and cave. There is still uncertainty regarding the date of when the traditional cave was first hewn and the earliest phase of the structures adjacent to it. The earliest available sources linking John the Baptist to Ain el-Habis do not predate the late fifteenth century [note 4.61]. These results lend credence to my belief that the Ain el-Habis cave site supplanted the Suba cave site at the time of the arrival of the Crusaders in the region.

Although traditions linking John the Baptist with Ain Karim are overwhelmingly strong, a few feeble attempts were made in the nineteenth century and more recently, to identify the birthplace and the first 'wilderness' of John the Baptist at alternative locations, and especially to the south of Jerusalem and close to Hebron. The scholar Reland, for example, proposed the site of Juttah as the birthplace of John, suggesting on philological grounds that the 'city of Judah' in Luke 1:39 should be read 'city of Juttah' (Ἰουτα) (Ἰετταν in Joshua 15:55). However, there are many historical weaknesses to this proposal, as Guérin and Schick were able to demonstrate.

A more serious proposal was made for the site of Ain al-Ma'mudiya

(Arabic for 'spring of the baptism') located close to the eastern aqueduct of Eleuthropolis, in a valley some 6.5 kilometres west of Hebron. Nearby are ruins dating from the sixth century, which appear to be those of a monastery (known as Khirbet ed-Deir). Both sites were investigated by the scholars Kopp and Stève between 1945 and 1946 [note 4.62]. Ain al-Ma'mudiya has a remarkable baptismal chamber built of large squared blocks of stone (6.65 × 3.15 m), with an entrance in its north wall and an apse in its east wall. Light was provided from a window with a rounded arch in the wall of the apse. In the southern wall of the structure is an opening leading to a curving flow-tunnel, with a barrel-vaulted ceiling, extending to a rock-cut spring-cave of irregular shape. Spring water ebbing from a natural aquifer would have been channelled along the floor of the flow tunnel. On reaching the chamber with the apse, the water spilled into a round, sunken basin. Five steps led down into this basin from the direction of the apse. It would appear to have been used as a font and the chamber itself would therefore have been used for baptismal purposes. Ruins around the chapel suggest that the chamber was part of a larger complex of structures, perhaps belonging to the monastery of Byzantine date from the fifth and sixth centuries AD (a lintel was found with a Greek inscription dedicated to Jesus Christ and mentioning Demetrius and his community).

Ain al-Ma'mudiya has been proposed as an alternative 'wilderness' of John because of references made about it by pilgrims passing through this southerly district in the fourteenth and fifteenth centuries. In November 1384, Frescobaldi and his companions, having stayed the night at Beit Gubrin, 'rose early and set out through desert country, and about midday we reached a valley, where there are some wild trees, and where there is a small church [*chiesicciuola*] in honour of St John the Baptist, which St Helena had built; and in this place came St John to do penance.' Later in the evening the travellers reached the outskirts of Hebron. Sigoli, one of Frescobaldi's fellow pilgrims, was much more specific as to the location: 'Five miles from Hebron is the desert where St John the Baptist preached, and in that place did penance.' Another visitor, Francesco Suriano (1485), clearly indicated the site by name: 'In this desert of Hebron where he [John] lived there is a church in which I said mass one Sunday for my devotion. Five braccia [cubits] from the church door is a most beautiful fountain of spring water, in which he baptised the people . . . This desert and place is called in Arabic Mamodie' [note 4.63]. Although these late references are interesting and illustrate the confusion among Christian pilgrims in the fourteenth and fifteenth centuries as to the exact location of the first 'wilderness' of John, there are no grounds for extending this tradition back in time, neither to the sixth century as Kopp and Stève claimed, nor to the twelfth century as Pringle has claimed [note 4.64]. Indeed, the source they cite from 1170, which was thought to contain a reference to the site at Ain al-Ma'mudiya, actually refers to the two sites at Ain Karim: 'Returning [from Hebron] you travel by the Church of Saint John the Baptist, where he preached the baptism of penitence in the desert [the present-day Church of the Visitation at Ain Karim]. There is a spring of water which does not fail, which at the time when he preached sprung forth when he prayed. From there the journey takes us to Saint Zacharias, where he lived with Saint Elizabeth and exercised his priesthood [the Church of St John at Ain Karim]. There Holy Mary saluted Elizabeth, whose infant exulted in her womb' [note 4.65].

Another site near Hebron, Khirbet Abu Rish, was recently excavated and one of its excavators has also linked it to the tradition of John in the wilderness, based on his interpretation of the source dating from 1170, referred to above in connection with Ain al-Ma'mudiya. The site contained a small rural monastic complex dating from the Byzantine period within lands belonging to the nearby village of Beit 'Anun. Installations found at the site are said to have been used for baptismal purposes. A Greek dedicatory inscription found in a mosaic floor refers to the excavated building as a holy place to which worshippers and pilgrims came, but one must point out that no mention is made of either John or his worship. One of the excavators has suggested that the site should be identified as Aenon (near Shalem), mentioned in John (3:22–25), because of the superficial similarity of this name with that of the nearby village of Beit 'Anun [note 4.66]. I find the suggested link made between the 'wilderness' tradition of John the Baptist and with the Ain al-Ma'mudiya and Khirbet Abu Rish sites not at all convincing and extremely tenuous to say the least, based as it is on a misreading of a text from 1170 and on later pilgrims' accounts. It would appear that in the Byzantine period the worship of the main events associated with the early life of John took place exclusively at Ain Karim, and the spot of the 'wilderness' (following Luke 1:80) must be sought therefore in its immediate vicinity. Since medieval times the traditional place of the Cave of John in the Wilderness has been pointed out at Ain el-Habis, but our work there was not able to detect archaeological remains predating the twelfth century. Conversely, our excavations at the Suba cave have indicated that it ceased to be used to celebrate John the Baptist in the eleventh century (or perhaps even in the early twelfth century), precisely at the same point in time which saw the appearance of the earliest structures at nearby Ain el-Habis. Hence, the Suba and Ain el-Habis sites appear to have been related, with the tradition of the 'wilderness' of John having first been celebrated at our cave in the early Byzantine period, and then, after the arrival of the Crusaders in the country, which saw disruption and major changes at many holy sites, the tradition was transferred to the site of Ain el-Habis, which is only a few kilometres to the south of Suba. Our cave was thereafter abandoned. The latest finds in the cave consisted of rubbish chucked into the cave by farmers in Ottoman times, and perhaps these were the same as the iconoclasts who vandalised the ancient drawings on the walls of the cave.

Our archaeological work had demonstrated that the Ain el-Habis site had supplanted our Suba cave site, and that together these sites illustrate a continuous tradition of the 'wilderness' of John the Baptist. This was remarkable and very exciting. The question we now asked ourselves was: how old is the tradition of John the Baptist at our Suba cave and could we trace it back to Roman times? Whether or not this was a possibility was something that we now needed to clarify during the continuation of our digging operations at the cave. The excavations were still very much in progress and a thick wedge of soil located in the front part of the cave had now been reduced to a depth of a couple of metres, exposing an impressive flight of rock-cut steps extending from wall to wall and descending into the cave. We felt certain that we were not far away from the rock floor of the cave. The hard work at the site was very demanding and to the excavators it seemed as if each day of digging was merging into the next one, with the removal of larger or smaller quantities of soil, rubble and bags and bags of potsherds. All the pottery that was being found in these early levels was pretty much from the first century AD, but, as we descended to deeper levels, even earlier pottery began appearing dating from the late first century BC, i.e. roughly from the time of the rule of Herod the Great. The installations and surfaces we were now finding struck me as particularly unusual, they were unlike anything I knew from other sites and they were hard to explain. There were still many questions about the cave for which we had no straight answers, but this made it all the more exciting and pushed us on to find out more.

5

Who Was John the Baptist?

Excavations at the cave continued throughout the summer and autumn of 2001. Now that so much soil and rubble had been removed from the cave, the interior looked grander than ever; the ceiling was now far above our heads (about four metres high) and I found descending the broad rock-cut steps into the cave an exhilarating experience. The acoustics were excellent: our subdued voices bounced off the walls, almost giving the impression of being inside a church. After a second year of digging we had managed to find some solutions to the mysteries of the cave, but, in doing so, we had also created many others.

Egon continued supervising the excavations, assisted by Rafi Lewis and Reuven Kalifon. Egon has a particularly sharp eye when dealing with the complexity of archaeological layers (stratigraphy), sorting out silts and washes from floors and occupational debris; his professionalism is tinged with modesty. Possessing a large grey beard and sharp eyebrows, he has the look and demeanour that many expect to see in the appearance of an archaeologist (*plate 7b*). Born in Germany and brought up in the United States, Egon has led an unusual life. He possesses an inner solitude, has sharp opinions about the world and a passion for classical music and poetry. For some years he lived with the Bedouin near Jericho, sensitively observing the circumstances of their daily lives, and recording his impressions in a journal. During our work, I came to know Egon quite well and I always wondered how he put up with me. I love thinking out aloud on a dig, whereas he ponders on matters silently while all the time methodically swinging his pick. I have a passion for drawing people into thinking about the different ways of explaining archaeological data, launching into heavy and enthusiastic discussions about interpretation and the overall historical significance of things. None of this, of course, is conducive to making rapid progress on a dig. Egon, on the other hand, was always making progress on the dig come what may, hammering away at the soil and filling buckets. Visitors also had a tendency of turning up at the cave whenever I was there, and this led to more discussions. And even more discussions. Egon was always courteous: he simply mumbled into his beard about time wasted and continued swinging the pick (*plate 7c*).

Our cave appeared to have been occupied in the first century AD by a strange group of people with a lifestyle unlike anything that any of us had encountered before at sites from this period in the Jerusalem hills. They apparently lived inside the cave but without possessing any normal domestic accoutrements such as one would expect to find. We were able to establish that when these mysterious people first arrived at the cave (round about the time of John the Baptist), the floor of the cave was covered by a thin layer of mud that met up with the steps at its southern end, and on it in some parts were scattered patches of plaster that had fallen away from the walls. These newcomers then began establishing a series of stone circles (approximately one metre in diameter) and other installations on top of this slight accumulation of mud. Why did the newcomers not simply clear out the soil? There were no signs that the cave was used for domestic purposes or even for storage. Moreover, the cave could not have been used as a source of irrigation water for the agricultural fields which were at a much higher level in the valley outside. Also the remoteness of the cave and the large scale of its interior made it unlikely that it had been used solely as a source of drinking water. Could it be that the people who began using the cave wanted to use it for ritual bathing, i.e. for baptism procedures? If so, did the fact that it seemed unlikely to have been used for other purposes contribute something to our knowledge about early Baptists and even about John the Baptist himself? Was it just a coincidence that Byzantine monks had chosen a cave to celebrate John the Baptist that four centuries earlier had been used as a place where it was quite possible to baptise a 'multitude' of people? These discoveries set me thinking about who John the Baptist might have been and whether he might have come to a cave such as the one at Suba.

Following the death of the much-hated Herod the Great, in the year 4 BC, the kingdom that he had spent so much time adorning with fortresses, palaces and temples was eventually broken up and divided up among his three sons. The central part of the country – represented by the regions of Judaea (including Jerusalem), Samaria and Idaumea – fell into the hands of Archelaus. However, he was unfit to rule and following complaints about him, was deposed by the Romans, with the area of his rule now becoming a new Roman province called Provincia Judaea. The northern and eastern regions – Galilee and Peraea (Transjordan) – were allotted to Herod Antipas (whom we shall be discussing later in connection with the death of John the Baptist). The third son, Philip, received the region of Auranitis in Syria. The Romans recognised the importance of maintaining a firm grip but at the same time thought of Palestine as a bit of a backwater. They were primarily concerned that their military superiority and juridical authority should be fully recognised and not flouted in any way, and that the population should be taxed efficiently. There was a poll tax and a land tax; the whole country must have groaned with the amount of taxes that had to be paid. Roman rule was represented by the prefect (later procurator) who was concerned with ensuring overall political stability, which left local government concerns largely in the hands of Jewish institutions. In Jerusalem, the Sanhedrin possessed supreme control over matters concerning the Jewish Temple and religious procedures.

First-century Palestine had a vibrant Jewish society, with people who were strong-willed and stubborn, as well as provincial and navel-gazing. Geographically, the country was broken into small units of landscape, each part with its own unique natural characteristics, and this meant marked differences in the daily-life routines of the inhabitants, in regard to their agricultural and commercial pursuits and even in terms of local customs. The one common denominator was the Holy Temple in Jerusalem where Jews thronged to mark the main festivals. The writings of the Jewish historian Josephus indicate that while Jewish society at that time had many divisions within it, the dominating groups were the Sadducees and the Pharisees. The Sadducees represented the ruling aristocracy, families who had amassed personal fortunes and who held important positions in the Temple and in the Sanhedrin. The Pharisees were probably the most popular and active among the general population, with strong notions regarding purification practices and religious conduct. There were also smaller groups with alternative views on religion and society, and these included the sect of the Essenes. In general, prior to the Great Revolt against the Romans in AD 66, the country underwent fluctuating periods of prosperity and peace, poverty and strife. This, combined with messianic expectations, led to a culture of social and religious disputes, tensions between the economic classes, and overall eschatological longings in regard to death and final destiny. The time was ripe for the appearance of charismatic religious figures, such as John the Baptist and Jesus.

Out on a walk on a bleak morning, I tried to gather together in my head all the facts known to me about the life of John the Baptist, to carefully think things out. What primary source materials are relevant to the study of the life of John the Baptist? One has to admit that in terms of the sources available – namely the Synoptic Gospels, the Fourth Gospel and the Acts of the Apostles, and the short passage within Josephus's historical work *Jewish Antiquities* – basic incontrovertible 'facts' about the life of John are few and far between. Too many commentators have shown themselves to be somewhat blinkered (perhaps guilelessly) by what are sometimes claimed to be the undeniable 'facts' regarding the overall circumstances of John's life and his prophetic ambitions. One has to remember that the Gospel writings were ultimately crafted with a very definite pro-Jesus bias, i.e. Jesus was portrayed there as the Messiah and within this scenario John could not be anything else but the 'Precursor'. There is therefore the distinct possibility that John had a mission all of his own with an agenda that was quite different from that of Jesus. This, of course, would have been anathema to pro-Jesus apologists and attempts would have been made to expunge any reference to an alternative agenda from the Gospels. Indeed, following the deaths of John and Jesus, it would appear that the Jesus movement became fairly antagonistic towards the Baptists and they would certainly have advised their members to shun any writings of the Baptist adherents that might have been circulating at that time. How then does one go about reconstructing the life of John, whom we all agree must have been an historical figure, when his own writings are not extant and when there are no surviving records by his immediate disciples and subsequent followers? I like to speculate that one day this situation will dramatically change and that somewhere in the Near East, perhaps in the deserts of Egypt, or in a cave near the Dead Sea, a treasure trove of documents will eventually come to light that will include not only the sayings of John the Baptist but also a proper account of his life. Until that time, however, commentators are obliged to view the historicity of the information about John the Baptist in the Gospels and in Acts with a healthy dose of suspicion, taking into account, as I stated before, that the information provided there was filtered by individuals who were more interested in the Jesus story than anything else.

It was sad looking at this wreckage of a human being. There was a wild, frantic look in his eyes as he gesticulated, pointing at the sky, spitting on the ground. His hair was dirty and matted and his clothes dishevelled and stained. At his feet were dried puddles of urine and an empty beer bottle. On the pavement behind him were a few possessions covered with a blanket. Crowds of people passed by, speeding towards their destination, nobody really caring or willing to listen. But there was a burning message he desired everyone to know, as he held aloft a tattered sign that read: 'Repent All Ye Sinners Before It Is Too Late.' He would shout angrily at the passers-by, calling on them to mend their ways, hurling random sentences and quotations from Scripture, as if he were throwing stones. God was speaking through him, he claimed. His voice was always hoarse from exertion and his ragged body would sway from side to side. I would often see him when alighting from the train at Euston station, on my way to the Institute of Archaeology in the University of London, where I was working on my doctorate in the 1980s. This man was there as a result of Prime Minister Margaret Thatcher's unwholesome 'care-in-the-community' policy, which resulted in the dumping of scores of damaged individuals on to the streets of London, instead of seeking to give them proper psychiatric care in hospitals. He made me feel terribly guilty, a feeling not lessened by my giving him loose change from my pocket. I had money in my wallet, food in my stomach and some intellectual pretensions in my head, and there he was, an anonymous face, roughly the same age as me, homeless, hungry and espousing a message that nobody really wanted to hear. One day in the middle of winter he was no longer there: perhaps he had been moved on or had been hospitalised, or perhaps he died of the cold. All that remained was a blackish stain on the pavement where he once used to sleep.

Seeing this man proclaiming Scripture made me speculate as to how he might have been received had he lived in Jewish Palestine two thousand years ago. Would he have been accorded the respect given to a supposed 'Man of God', with crowds gathering around to listen to his message and to abide by his proclamations? Or would he, like today, have been regarded as a misfit and an outcast from society? The answer is that he would most likely have been seen, even then, as a ranting and raving madman. After all, Jewish society of the first century was composed of groups of practical religious people with a very clear awareness of the Roman world as a whole, the region they lived in and how everyone fitted into the overall picture. Indeed, some parts of Palestine were highly cosmopolitan, with Romans, Greeks, Phoenicians, Samaritans, Idumaeans and Nabataeans mingling together and sometimes even living in close proximity to each other. Hence one should not portray Palestine in the first century as possessing a society with an anarchic fabric of bewildered and superstitious Jews who could be swayed by the threats and proclamations of any assertive 'prophet'-like individual passing their way. They were, instead, a people with an intensely mature and worldly outlook in regard to themselves, their beliefs and their religious leaders. The overall religious framework that was centred on Jerusalem and on the Holy Temple was in many ways quite rigid, especially in regard to the restrictions that were imposed on rank and file. There were also strict controls over Temple attendance and worship, the provision of tithes, and the conduct of everyday life, particularly in regard to matters of purification. Admittedly, the main religious groups at the time, notably the Sadducees, the Pharisees and the Essenes, all had differing perspectives regarding spiritual matters and apocalyptic expectations, but the basic structure and lifestyle of these communities on the ground level was well-defined and in some cases even fairly regimented.

Non-conformist voices were certainly to be heard 'in the desert' but these individuals were exceptions to the rule and those who did emerge found their credibility being forever questioned, which is why the Gospels constantly mention the barrage of questions that were repeatedly put to John the Baptist and Jesus by the Pharisees, the Scribes, soldiers, publicans and others. They were required to justify themselves not only to those listening to them, but also to their own followers. John at one point during his baptism activities expressed his contempt at the presence of the Pharisees (Matthew 3:7) and they 'were not baptised of him' (Luke 7:30). Their judgement of John that 'he hath the devil' (Matthew 11:18) was tantamount to their saying that it was not worthwhile listening to him.

The fact that a contemporary historian, Josephus Flavius, mentioned a fair number of such non-conformist individuals in his writings – including John the Baptist himself – does not mean they were a commonplace and widespread phenomenon. On the contrary, it was apparently only a very select number of such individuals who actually possessed the charismatic pull and the distinctive message, enabling them to become the prophets and leaders of segments of the population whether for shorter or longer periods of time. These individuals also had to possess special qualities such as the ability to cajole and to persuade, eloquence for storytelling, a creative ability for adapting parables and sayings, and a detailed knowledge of the books of the Old Testament. It must have been extremely difficult trying to convey a religious message that would be attractive enough to catch the imagination of a public already suffused with a great amount of institutionalised religion in their everyday lives. John's approach probably had the best staying power and, by modelling himself on the age-old image of the popular prophet, he was able to demonstrate a strong sense of continuity, extending back in time to his Israelite forebears. In the shorter term, Jesus had the easier task as the healer and as the man of 'signs and wonders', and he was the man of the hour partly because he could claim to have been chosen by John the Baptist himself. Popular prophets and healers, we may assume, were humoured by the religious authorities so long as they did not cross certain boundaries, by becoming anti-establishment or by attaching themselves to militant revolutionaries. This is exactly what John and Jesus did, resulting in the beheading of one and the crucifixion of the other. A person such as the man near Euston Station would not have merited this kind of attention two thousand years ago, since he would most likely have been regarded by his contemporaries as delusional and possessed, as someone whose body had been taken over by evil spirits. Since mental illness was feared at that time, much more so than today, he would probably have been shunned.

The discovery of the Suba cave led me on a quest to find out more about John and what his baptism rituals were all about. The more I was able to ascertain about him, the more exciting my quest became. But writing about someone about whom we possess very little information is an incredibly difficult task, and so when it transpires that the sparse information available about John in the Gospels might be extremely selective in regard to the facts, then the task of actually getting to the truth of things would seem insurmountable. There are some who might think contemplating such a task foolhardy, or to say the least a source of barren fruit. Scholars such as E. P. Sanders, have already pointed out how difficult it is to gather solid factual data 'about a first-century Jew who lived in a rather unimportant part of the Roman Empire' [note 5.1]. The reference is actually to Jesus but it could equally apply to John, about whom we possess even less information. But historians have been labouring for more than a century with the study of the few source materials and they have been coming up with some very good results, especially now that they can be tested against the realities of archae-ological finds on the ground and with the contents of the Dead Sea

Scrolls. There has been an enormous amount of scholarly commentary in relation to the events connected with John's birth, his prophetic mission, his sayings, his baptismal rites and the circumstances that led to his death. But there is still much that is not known. We know next to nothing about John's years as an adolescent, the development of his ideas as a young adult, the circles in society that he moved in during those early years, and the exact point in time when he moved out into the 'desert'. What would John's childhood have been like and would it have been affected in any way by the fact that he hailed from a priestly family and that his father Zacharias officiated as a priest in the Jewish Temple? When did he start to become vocal about his ideas about sin and repentance, in which he called on his fellow Jews to undergo baptism? The assumption is that John was totally dedicated to his prophetic mission almost from the outset, but is this true? His personal circumstances are also obscure. Was he at some point married or was he always a bachelor? What was he like as a person, was he an easy-going man or was he always a firebrand? What was his approach to everyday life and to what extent did his religious beliefs distance him from his interlocutors? What was his perspective on the Romans and on the strictures of the local religious establishment, and how would he have regarded acts of violence committed by his fellow Jews?

Another factor that must be considered pertains to the strengths and weaknesses of the different types of textual source material used. When looking at any given source one should keep in mind the following questions: when was it written? Who wrote it and for what purpose? What was the cultural context that saw the writing of the source in the first place, and what sort of literary model would the writer have had in mind? What language would it have been written in? Which snippets of information contained in the source may be presumed to be authentic, and which bits biased or fabricated? Also, which parts were modifications or 'corrections' made to the source as it was transmitted through time? Trying to unravel the real historical 'truth' within a textual source can be a dangerous and hazardous business. In any case 'truth' as we all know is a multi-faceted concept and one can very easily be led up the garden path. Indeed, it is sometimes the case that a primary and contemporary source will contain biased information and false data that give the impression of being historically credible. On the other hand, historically reliable data may end up being transferred first as an oral tradition and then much later within the framework of a 'secondary' written source, giving the reader the impression that the data must be of derivative or quasi-legendary character, when it is not. For this reason, one must always keep an open mind in regard to the credibility of later textual sources, which purport to relate traditions, however distant in time they may seem from the events they describe [note 5.2]. Having gone through the process of asking these questions, one hopes that the rest will then fall into place like the denouement of a detective story, by actively piecing together all the bits of information and by testing the results against the published research of fellow scholars. All of this should be undertaken by anyone wishing to set out to dispel the swirling mists of the unknown that surround the life of John the Baptist.

The primary sources of information about John the Baptist appear in the Gospel of Mark, the so-called Q source, the Gospel of Matthew, the Gospel of Luke and the Book of Acts, and the Gospel of John, with the earliest of these written and in circulation within thirty years of the events they describe [note 5.3]. The first three gospels, Mark, Matthew and Luke, resemble each other in both content and style of presentation and were written based on similar source materials. Hence, they are referred to as the Synoptic Gospels because together they (syn-) view (optic) Jesus and his story. Mark is the earliest and shortest of the canonical gospels and was a source for both Matthew and Luke, which may be regarded as literary expansions. However, Matthew and Luke share another source of material – Q (from the German word '*Quelle*' meaning source) – that is not to be found in Mark. In terms of historical reliability the best information about John the Baptist may be extracted from Mark and Matthew. However, if the same material appears in both Matthew and Luke, then there are some commentators who believe it is best to use Matthew as the source. Moreover, if the same information appears in all three of the sources, then one should rely on Mark instead. The Gospel of Matthew also includes material which is not found elsewhere, and it should perhaps be interpreted either as inherited or non-factual material. The Gospel of Luke and the Book of Acts go hand-in-hand as a two-volume work designed to describe the development of early Christianity. Within Luke there is material not found elsewhere, for example the Infancy Narrative of John the Baptist (Luke 1:5–25), and suggestions have been made that this specific portion derives from a separate Baptist source. The Fourth Gospel (John) was based on alternative sources to those of the Synoptic Gospels and, while presenting quite a lot of accurate data, the writer does display a clear anti-Jewish stance. The figure of John the Baptist was pivotal for the early followers of Jesus and this was emphasised by the fact that his story appears at the very beginning of the Gospels (except in Matthew) at the spot where logically the nativity of Jesus should have taken pride of place. Incorporated into the Gospel accounts one finds a woven mixture of history, legend and religious interpretation about John, who is presented as the Precursor of Jesus, with numerous strands of information of varying significance interspersed within the narratives, requiring serious disentangling. This information includes anecdotal segments, bits of narrative and various sayings. The Gospel writers presumably excluded anything that did not support the Jesus story. Some passages were severely tinkered with and this can be detected in the heavy-handed editing sometimes made when adapting the materials about John into the Gospels. There are also examples of sentences or bits of information that were intentionally inserted to help clarify customs or notions that would have been common in the milieu of first-century Palestine but would have been perceived to be alien to some readers of the Gospels. The Gospel narratives were written in Greek but John himself would have preached in the standard vernacular of that time, which was Aramaic. Hence one must also accept that the sense of some of his sayings (those that are deemed by scholars to be authentic) may have been lost in translation. The Gospels also include examples of interaction between John and his interlocutors. Looking at the narratives, one needs to address the matter of 'who is speaking?' and 'who is being addressed?' before going on to ask, 'what was being discussed?' There is a multiplicity of voices (internal and external) in the Gospels, with well-defined roles and relationships arranged between the speakers and the addressees.

As we have seen, the material about John the Baptist from the Gospels is supplemented by a short anecdotal passage appearing in the writings of the Jewish historian Josephus Flavius written during the years following the fall of Jerusalem in AD 70 (*Jewish Antiquities*, XVIII 116–119; for two translations of this important passage refer to the Appendix at the end of this book). Josephus' knowledge about John was definitely second-hand since he was born at least ten years after the beheading in AD 37 or 38 (*Vita* 5). The passage in Josephus is very important because it probably represents the general view that existed in first-century Palestine about the uniqueness of John's baptism procedure as opposed to the normal Jewish ritual cleansing practices of the time. The main problem with this passage is that Josephus did not feel obliged to provide any relevant information about John's life. Since we do not know whether he had first-hand access to writings about John and his beliefs, one might reach the conclusion (wrongly I think) that the description of John's baptism practices could represent Josephus' very own personal point of view but nothing more tangible than that [note 5.4].

One of the first things that anybody wants to know about the historicity of the New Testament is how to fix the events described there in time. When did these things happen and how can we be sure of the dates? Scholars have been debating this chronological issue for a very long time and, as recently as 1993, E. P. Sanders wrote: 'we are better off if we accept the accuracy of the sources in a more general way. This allows not only one of them, but even all of them to be fuzzy or wrong on some details' [note 5.5]. Historical research continues, however, fuzzy or otherwise, and some of the contributions provided by recent scholars on the subject have been quite polemical. The sad fact is that at the present time archaeology has not been able to help resolve any of the existing problems when it comes to dating specific events, though this might one day change depending on future discoveries. Hence, in order to discuss the one or two dates that we do have pertaining to John the Baptist himself, we must also attempt in tangent to establish something about the overall chronology of the life of Jesus; after all both lives intersected at important points in time.

If one accepts the premise that the 'Herod' mentioned in Luke 1:5 and Matthew 2:1 is none other than Herod the Great (whose reign lasted from 37 BC until his death in 4 BC), then, accordingly, both John and Jesus would have had to have been born by the year 4 BC, if not before. According to the Luke version of the nativity of Jesus, Mary, upon finding out that she was pregnant, spent the next three months living with Elizabeth in Judah until the birth of John (Luke 1:56–57). John was six months older than Jesus (Luke 1:26). Since Herod the Great was still alive at the time of the birth of both John and Jesus, we may assume some credibility for the story of the slaughter of the infants (those up to the age of two years old) ordered by Herod the Great (Matthew 2:16), though there is no confirmation for this story from any other external source. We do not know when this took place (if at all) but, assuming that it did, then this would have occurred when Herod was already quite ill and demented in the final years of his life leading up to his death. Herod died of cardio-renal failure, or failure of the heart and kidneys, but he had already begun suffering from major illnesses from around 7 BC, accompanied by his normal bouts of uncontrollable anger and cruelty [note 5.6]. The implication must be that John and Jesus were born at some point during the two years before the event of

Herod's death, i.e. between 6 and 4 BC. It is interesting to note that in a late-fourth-century life of John, written by the Egyptian bishop Serapion, we are told that Herod died on the same day as John's mother Elizabeth and that John was only seven years and six months old at the time. Although this information is arguably legendary, it would indicate a date in 11 BC for the birth of John, i.e. five years earlier than the upper limit given here [note 5.7].

The next bit of chronological data that must be considered is the statement made in Luke 2:1–6 that Joseph and Mary moved to Bethlehem for the birth of Jesus in view of the proclaimed census that was to be undertaken by the Roman Governor in Syria, P. Sulpicius Quirinius, by decree of Caesar Augustus. Clearly there is a problem here because historical sources indicate that Quirinius only arrived in Syria in AD 6 and that the census itself was only undertaken that year or in AD 7 [note 5.8]. Moreover, there is no historical record of an edict indicating that Augustus actually ordered the census in the first place. Since it is impossible that the census was carried out during the reign of Herod the Great (since C. Sentius Saturninus and then later P. Quintilius Varus were governing Syria at that time), Luke's information must be seriously flawed. If Jesus were born between 6 and 4 BC, this would indicate that at the time of the census Jesus was actually twelve to fourteen years of age. Many suggestions have been made to explain away this problem – the ingenuity of some of the arguments is truly amazing – but in my opinion none is convincing [note 5.9]. I think we must conclude that Luke simply got his facts in a muddle and that this piece of chronological evidence is not very useful and should be disqualified.

According to Matthew 2: 19–23, Mary and Joseph returned from Egypt, with the 'young child' Jesus, at the time when Herod's son Archelaus was still ruling a kingdom which included the regions of Judaea, Samaria and Idumaea. There are two conclusions that we may be able to derive from this information that are relevant for our discussion. First, we know that Archelaus was deposed in AD 6 and so the return from Egypt must have taken place by that date. Second, Jesus was still considered a 'young child', indicating that he must have been younger than the twelve years of age or may just have reached that age. This fits in with the earliest suggested date for the birth of Jesus in 6 BC. Hence, we may assume that John reached 'the day of his shewing unto Israel' in AD 6 (Luke 1:80).

The next chronological indicator of interest is the date of the beginning of John's mission and the fixing of this event in time according to

Luke 3:1–2: 'Now in the fifteenth year of the reign of Tiberias Caesar, Pontius Pilate being governor of Judaea, and Herod being tetrarch of Galilee, and his brother Philip tetrarch of Ituraea and of the region of Trachonitis, and Lysanias the tetrarch of Abilene, Annas and Caiaphas being the high priests, the word of God came unto John the son of Zacharias in the wilderness.' Taking into account the muddle previously created by Luke regarding the census of Quirinius, should we also accept this information as unreliable? Let us have a look at some of the dates that emerge from other sources regarding a few of the rulers and religious leaders mentioned in this passage. Tiberius is known to have succeeded Augustus in AD 14 and so his fifteenth year would work out at AD 28, unless, of course, one also counts the co-regency that began two years earlier which would indicate a date of AD 26 instead, but I think this second date unlikely. Based on information provided by Josephus (*Antiquities* XVIII, 35), we know that Pontius Pilate was appointed Prefect in AD 26, so both dates are possible. Caiaphas was High Priest in Jerusalem between AD 18–36 and this also fits in quite well. Based on this information I do think that we may regard Luke's statement as reliable testimony. If we accept the earliest date of birth for John at 6 BC then this would suggest that he took up his prophetic mission at the age of thirty-four (or alternatively thirty-two if he was born in 4 BC). This was a fairly mature age when one considers that at that time the average lifespan of an adult male was forty years. Jesus was of the same age as John but since he is said to have been six months younger, it is quite possible that he was still only thirty-three at that time (or thirty-one if born in 4 BC). Both of these ages fit the description given in Luke 3:23 of Jesus that he was 'about thirty years of age' when he came to be baptised by John.

If AD 28 is the year when John began his baptising activities in the Jordan Valley, one has to admit that there is absolute uncertainty in regard to the total length of his mission before he was arrested and imprisoned by Herod Antipas at Machaerus. I would contend, however, that John's entire mission was actually short-lived and that he was beheaded later on that same year. As we shall see, the unbearable temperatures during the late spring and summer months in the Jordan Valley suggest that John's activities there would have begun at the end of the winter months in AD 28, when the river itself was swollen with water and the climate was fairly suitable for large crowds of people to congregate there. His baptising ceremonies were so successful that within a very short period of time word began spreading and many came to be baptised, including Jesus. The fact that John had sufficient time to move from one baptismal location to another, from Bethabara to Aenon (John 3:23), a distance of some 65 km, suggests that a chunk of time (perhaps six months) did elapse from the start of his ministry. The fact that the baptising phenomenon did draw large crowds of people around John – they are described in Matthew (3:5) as 'streaming forth' (εξεπορεύετο) – and that they kept on coming to him from all walks of life, was undoubtedly perceived by Herod Antipas as a major destabilising factor in the region, one that could very easily lead to a rebellion against his rule. In any case, chronologically speaking, John could only have been executed by Antipas *before* the actual outbreak of hostilities with the Nabataeans in AD 36 because it was the disastrous outcome of this very conflict that was believed by many to have been inflicted on Antipas from the heavens because of what he had done to John (*Antiquities* XVIII, 116).

It is an absolute certainty that Jesus was crucified during the course of Pontius Pilate's administration, at some point between AD 27–36 (Mark 15:1–15), and that this could only have taken place *after* the execution of John in AD 28 and *before* the High Priest Caiaphas had been removed from his position by Vitellius in AD 36. Hence, the latest possible date for the final Passover attended by Jesus in Jerusalem must have been in the spring of AD 36. The accepted view is that the death of Jesus took place late in the 20s or early in the 30s of the first century. I personally would place the crucifixion in the year AD 30 when Jesus was thirty-six years of age, and only two years after the beheading of John.

Recently there was a tremendous ripple of excitement across the world when an article was published in the pages of an archaeological magazine, *Biblical Archaeology Review*, announcing that a 2000–year-old stone box had been found mentioning James (Ya'aqov) the brother of Jesus [note 5.10]. It sounded too good to be true. The stone box was an ossuary that was used to collect together human bones after a dead person's body had decomposed, and on one of its long sides there was an Aramaic inscription reading: 'James son of Joseph, brother of Jesus.' The artefact apparently originally came from Jerusalem from a burial cave somewhere in the lower Kidron Valley. The ossuary is now in the hands of a private collector but, judging by the rather vague statements that he has issued on the matter of provenance and on the length of time that it has been around in his possession, some scholars have rightly expressed serious doubts about the authenticity of the inscription. The ossuary itself was carved out of soft chalk and must be authentic, but the same cannot be said of the inscription. All of it, or at least part of it (perhaps the 'James son of Joseph' bit), certain scholars say may well have been added in modern times by an accomplished forger who knew his Aramaic well and knowingly wanted to increase the value of the object considerably. Recent laboratory investigations carried out by Yuval Baruch, of the Tel Aviv University, and others, do suggest that the ossuary inscription is indeed a forgery. However, even if it were somehow decided that the inscription was authentic, the fact remains that names such as James (Ya'aqov), Joseph and Jesus were very common among the Jewish population at that time which means that this inscription need not necessarily refer to *the* James, Joseph and Jesus of the Gospels.

The name 'John' was another very popular name in the first century, as was the name of John the Baptist's father Zacharias (Zakharya). Various forms of the name John have been found inscribed on ossuaries found in burial caves round about Jerusalem, in Hebrew or Aramaic scripts (Yehohanan), in Greek (Ἰωάνης) and with one rare appearance in Latin (IOHANA). One inscribed ossuary apparently came from a robbed tomb in Akeldama, at the foot of Mount Zion, with an interesting set of names indicating that it had once belonged to 'Yehohana, daughter of Yehohanan son of Theophilis the high priest' [note 5.11]. It transpires that the name John (Yehohanan), together with that of Eleazar, were the most common names used for Jewish priests at that point in time, which fits in well with the notion of John the Baptist having come from a priestly family. Among the first-century *ostraka* (inscribed potsherds) from the site of Masada, is one bearing the private name 'Yehohanan' [note 5.12]; another Yehohanan who is mentioned, 'going up to Masada' appears on an *ostrakon* found at Wadi Muraba'at [note 5.13]. The name John continued to be popular among Jews in the Byzantine period as well, and a rabbi and scribe named 'Yohanan' is mentioned in a dedicatory inscription from a mosaic floor at Susiya [note 5.14].

One would think that in common with Jewish practice, which is manifested in Hellenistic to Roman period textual sources, notably inscriptions and papyri, that John would naturally have been named after his father, Zacharias (Zakharya), had it not been for the event described in Luke 1:59 [note 5.15]. Zakharya was a fairly common name in the first century, with a number of examples found inscribed on ossuaries from that period. The name Zakharya also appears on an abecedary *ostrakon* dated to the first century [note 5.16]. Interestingly, both Zakharya and the name Yehohanan appear together in an Aramaic papyrus from Wadi Muraba'at, dated to AD 55 or 56, which also happens to mention the site of Suba. The popularity of the name Zacharias continued into the Byzantine and Umayyad periods (as late as the eighth century), but the name usually signified a remembrance of the minor Israelite prophet Zacharias (late sixth century BC) and not the father of John the Baptist, except for the rare instance of a Greek inscription from above the entrance to the 'Tomb of Absalom' in Jerusalem. There are quite a few archaeological sites in Israel/Palestine, especially in the Shephelah foothills region, bearing the Arabic name Khirbet or Beit Zikarya; but none of these, as far as one can tell, has had anything whatsoever to do with the father of John the Baptist. John's father Zacharias, son of Barachias (cf. the post-exilic prophet, the author of the biblical book Zechariah 1:1), was of Zadokite descent and Luke (1:5) says he was from 'the division of Abijah', which was the eighth division of the Zadokite course (see 1 Chronicles 24:10). According to Matthew (23:35) Zacharias was killed between the temple and the altar (cf. Luke 11:51), but the place of his burial was not recorded. A recent discovery of a Byzantine inscription in Jerusalem records a memorial to Zacharias, 'father of John' on a large sepulchre at the foot of the Mount of Olives, opposite the Temple Mount. Later, from the Crusader period, the traditional tomb of Zacharias was placed at Sebaste, adjacent to the tomb of John the Baptist. According to an account by 'Imad al-Din of the capture of the site in July 1187 by Salah ed-Din's forces, the large Crusader cathedral was described as the 'tomb' or 'sanctuary' of Zacharias. Yaqût, around 1225, also mentioned that the mosque contained the tombs of John the Baptist, his father Zacharias and other prophets. Another location for the supposed tomb of Zacharias is in Syria. It is pointed out in the Great Mosque, the Jami el-Kebir (first built in 715) in Aleppo. The tomb is located just left of the *mihrab* in the prayer hall. The tomb has been described as 'behind gilder railings and covered with a heavily embroidered cloth' [note 5.17].

The name of John's mother was Elizabeth (Elisheva in Hebrew) but, strangely, it was not a very popular name during the first century judging by the fact that there are only two examples of the name among the numerous ossuary inscriptions in existence. The first comes from an ossuary inscribed in both Greek and Aramaic and was found in a burial cave in Wadi es-Shami (near Silwan) in Jerusalem. The Aramaic inscription reads: 'Elisheva wife of Tarphon' (Elisheva att Tarphon) [note 5.18]. The inscription was published at the beginning of the twentieth century and was initially kept with the collection of antiquities belonging to the Benedictine monks on Mount Zion. The exact whereabouts of the ossuary was always thought to be unknown but a university researcher, Haggai Misgav, eventually managed to track it down in the archaeological collections of the Institute of Archaeology at the Hebrew University [note 5.19]. The only other ossuary inscription from the first century mentioning the name Elizabeth comes from a private collection. It reads: 'Yohanan son of Yosef son of Elisheva' (Yohanan bar Yosef bar Elisheva), which is a rare metronymic. The provenance of the ossuary is not known, but the strong probability is that it was found somewhere around Jerusalem. The name Elisheva continued to be a rarity among Jews even during the later Byzantine period, and perhaps this was the direct result of the popularity of the name Elizabeth among Christians at that time [note 5.20]. Outside the Holy Land, there are only two instances of the name appearing in Jewish contexts: the first in an Egyptian papyrus of AD 596 and the other on an incantation bowl from Nippur dated to just before the Arab conquest in the seventh century.

It has generally been assumed that Elizabeth and Mary, mother of Jesus, were cousins but according to Luke 1:36 all that we may assume is that Elizabeth was a kinswoman (συγγενίς) of Mary not a cousin (άνεψιά) [note 5.21]. There have been some who would go further by denying any blood relationship between the two women [note 5.22]. Elizabeth, we are told in Luke (1:5), was a descendant of the highly respected House of Aaron: 'and his [Zachariahs'] wife was of the daughters of Aaron, and her name was Elizabeth.' The House of Aaron was a priestly family whose members were always regarded as upright and holy people. Indeed, Elizabeth's progenitor, Aaron, 'took him Elisheva [Elizabeth], daughter of Amminadav, sister of Naashon, to wife . . .' (Exodus 6:23) [note 5.23]. In later periods, high expectations existed in regard to the descendants of this priestly family and this was made crystal clear in the rabbinical literature. In one of the tractates of the Mishna, we are told that Hillel (*c.* 30 BC to AD 10), having received the Law, said: 'Be of the disciples of Aaron, loving peace and pursuing peace, loving mankind and bringing them nigh to the Law.' (M. *aboth* 1:12; Danby ed., p.598). The important role that members of the House of Aaron held in the rituals that were conducted at the Jewish Temple in Jerusalem was also made clear: 'And thus they used to say: "Blessed be God, blessed be he! For that no blemish has been found in the seed of Aaron. And blessed be he that chose Aaron and his sons to serve before the Lord in the House of the Holy of Holies"' (M. *middoth* 5:4; cf. M. *taanith* 2:5). While there is no specific link between the House of Aaron and Sebaste, it is perhaps not coincidental that Byzantine-period chapels dedicated to Aaron (linked to Elizabeth) and Elijah (linked to John the Baptist) were constructed not too far away from each other to the south-east of the city of Sebaste, close to the aqueduct that brought water from Ain Haroun ('the spring of Aaron') to the city. The exact place of the tomb of Elizabeth is unknown, but as we saw in Chapter 4 some have placed it at Sebaste. In the 1170s a Moslem writer, al-Harawi, says he saw the tomb of Elizabeth at Sebaste, alongside those of John the Baptist and Elisha. The traveller John Phocas (AD 1185) also says he saw the tombs of Elizabeth and Zacharias in an underground chapel at Sebaste: 'On the right of the altar is a coffin in which is preserved the body of Saint Zacharias, the father of the Forerunner. And on the left side is a second coffin in which lies the body of Saint Elisabeth his mother.' The Tomb of Elizabeth is also said to be located at Ain el-Habis, near Ain Karim.

The epigraphist Dr Leah Di Segni lives in one of the western neighbourhoods of Jerusalem and occasionally she would very kindly give up her precious time to invite me around to discuss ancient Greek inscriptions of the Holy Land and particularly those referring to John the Baptist. Sipping from a glass of excellent quality Italian almond liquor, Leah would talk about the ancient inscriptions and their interpretation with an enthusiasm which was a joy to behold. I was surprised to learn that there are only a handful of Byzantine-period inscriptions that actually refer (sometimes indirectly) to John the Baptist. A list of six was originally published by Yiannis Meimaris in 1986, based on his doctorate submitted a decade earlier, and of these we can delete one, which, it transpires, had nothing to do with John the Baptist, but we can now also add five more [note 5.24]. In Byzantine-period inscriptions John' (Ιωάννης) was sometimes mentioned directly by name, but more usually he was referred to indirectly by using one of two titles, 'forerunner' (Πρόδρομος, 'going', literally 'running', 'before') and 'Baptist' (Βαπτιστής). Interestingly, in the New Testament the former word was only used once and not in reference to John but to Jesus having gone on ahead of his followers to the heavenly places (Hebrews 6:20). Finally, the appellation 'prophet' (προφήτης) was never given to John in Byzantine inscriptions in the way that various prophetic figures of the Old Testament were sometimes acknowledged (compare this to Matthew 11: 9–11, where John is said to be a 'prophet').

There was one inscription that puzzled me greatly, but Leah and I finally managed to work it out. In his catalogue of mosaic pavements from 1932, the doyen of Israeli classicists, Michael Avi-Yonah, listed two inscriptions from floors (nos. 26 and 67), one mentioning a benefactor named John and the other of John the Baptist himself [note 5.25]. By carefully sifting through the evidence, however, it became clear that these two inscriptions were actually one and the same and that Avi-Yonah had mistakenly published them twice with differing interpretations! The story of how this happened is worthwhile telling since it illustrates the occasional pitfalls of scholarship. It all began with an excavation by Father Vincent in 1902 of a small church or chapel paved with mosaics at a site called Beth Shi'ar or Beit Cha'ar, in the vicinity of Bir Ayyub, not far away from Bethlehem [note 5.26]. The Greek inscription in the mosaic pavement in front of the main apse was incomplete and it read: 'For the help of the benefactors . . . Cassion, John, Zacharias and John Abesombos and John . . . and the work was completed in the year . . .' Although the date had not been preserved, the style of the inscription was sufficient to suggest to scholars that it should be dated to the first half of the sixth century. Clearly the persons mentioned in the inscription, including John and Zacharias, were individual donors who had given the money to build the church/chapel in the first place and they had nothing whatsoever to do with John the Baptist or his father. So why the confusion in the first place, one might ask? In the article about his discoveries, Vincent did mention that one of the landowners nearby had stumbled upon a channel and a water installation, and that within a niche in the installation traces of a wall painting depicting two human figures was seen. The landowner was certain (so Vincent says) that this painting was a representation of the baptism scene (i.e. John and Jesus at the Jordan River). Unfortunately, the wall painting, which is said to be 'Roman', has not been published and the whole matter sounds extremely circumstantial. Indeed, the painting could easily be just a representation of monks, saints or perhaps even angels. In any case, there is no apparent connection between this installation and wall painting with the church/chapel excavated by Vincent. This was apparently the source of Avi-Yonah's confusion; hence, we may conclude that no inscription mentioning John the Baptist, or dedicated to him, has yet been found at Bir Ayyub or its vicinity.

In the southern Negev Desert at the site of Auja Hafir (ancient Nessana), a cache of wonderful papyri was uncovered by the Colt expedition [note 5.27]. One of them is Document No. 89, which was found in thirteen fragments and is dated to the late sixth to early seventh centuries. At first glance it would seem to be a fairly boring business account of a trading company and Kraemer, who translated it, called it nothing more than just a 'dry little record'. However, a closer look reveals it to contain a multitude of details about daily life, such as purchases that were made while on the journey to a 'holy mountain' (presumably Mount Sinai) and also transactions that were made dealing largely with animals and commodities (and even with child slaves), all of which is the sort of information that inevitably delights the heart of any historian. At the end of the document (lines 44 to 46), the pious Christian writer inserted a short prayer asking for the intercession of 'our Lady Mary Mother of God and Ever Virgin and of John the Forerunner and Baptist, and of all the holy saints'. The titles 'forerunner' (Πρόδρομος) and 'Baptist' (Βαπτιστής) were given in the Nessana papyrus in an abbreviated fashion.

The Greek epithet 'Prodromos' ('forerunner') was particularly popular in the Byzantine inscriptions mentioning John the Baptist. There was even a Byzantine Church of that name on the bank of the lower Jordan River honouring John the Baptist. One inscription mentioning John by the title 'Prodromos' was found on the lintel of a chapel dedicated to Elijah the Prophet at Boberiyeh, dating from the fifth or first half of the sixth century. The site is located fairly close to Sebaste where the traditional tomb of John the Baptist was situated [note 5.28]. Three more inscriptions referring to John by his title 'Prodromos' are known: two from Jerash and another from Jebel Haroun in Transjordan. The inscriptions from Jerash are both of a dedicatory nature: the first is a Greek inscription within a *tabula ansata* in a mosaic floor dated to AD 531 in the Church of St John the Baptist, which mentions its founders Bishop Paul and the donor Theodore, and refers to John by his epithet. The second Greek inscription from Jerash is also within a *tabula ansata* in a mosaic floor dated to AD 533 in the Church of the martyrs Cosmas and Damianus [note 5.29]. More recently, the epithet of John the Baptist 'Prodromos' was found inscribed with red paint on the wall plaster of a chapel at Jebel Haroun near Petra [note 5.30].

Two Byzantine period inscriptions referring to the martyrdom of John the Baptist are known from Er-Ramthaniyyeh in the Gaulanitis region (Golan) of southern Syria, and a third is known from the Hauran region further east. The ones from Er-Ramthaniyyeh relate to a large church which was dedicated to the memory of John the Baptist. It is likely that a relic of John was kept at the site as well. The third inscription comes from over the door of a church in Harran and appears in Reverend Ewing's list of inscriptions collated during his trip to the Hauran region in the late nineteenth century, and dates to between 22 March and 31 April of the year 568 [note 5.31]. It reads: 'Asarelos, the son of Talemos, the head of the tribe [of the Ghassanids?], founded this memorial of the martyrdom of St John in the first indiction of the 463rd year of the province. May he that inscribed it be remembered.' The magnificent Madaba map of the Holy Land dating from the mid-sixth century has John's name appearing next to the drawing showing the place of the baptism (Bethabara). John's name appears together with the words 'holy' and 'baptism' (βάπτισμα) [note 5.32]. Finally, Joe Zias has recently investigated a Greek inscription from the Byzantine period above the entrance to the so-called 'Tomb of Absalom' at the foot of the Mount of Olives in Jerusalem (*plate 7a*). According to Emile Puech, of the École Biblique in Jerusalem, the inscription reads as follows: 'This is the tomb of Zachariah, martyr, very pious priest, father of John' [note 5.33].

Like many of his contemporaries, John was accorded respect as an honoured teacher and preacher and so was called a rabbi (Hebrew, 'my master') (John 3:26). However, the common appellation given to John was the Baptist (or Baptiser). In Matthew 3:1 the title given in Greek is βαπτιστής, which is translated as the 'Baptist'. Josephus, confirms that John was known by the title βαπτιστοῦ ('Baptist'/'Baptiser' or alternatively the 'Immerser'): 'But to some of the Jews the destruction of Herod's army [by the Nabataean ruler Aretas] seemed to be divine vengeance, and certainly a just vengeance, for his treatment of John, surnamed the Baptist (βαπτιστοῦ)' (*Antiquities* XVIII, 116–19). What should be the correct translation of the term for John is still unclear. In the nineteenth century certain scholars suggested that the word should more properly be translated as the 'dipper' or 'submerger', though one scholar, Dale, writing in 1898 preferred the term 'purifier' instead. In any case, to refer to the prophetic figure of John as the 'dipper' or 'submerger' now sounds absolutely ludicrous. Who were the people who would actually have called John the Baptist or Baptiser? It seems unlikely that he would have been given this title by his relatives or by his followers, and so we must assume that it was applied to him by the general public and reflects the significance of the major feature associated with his preaching, i.e. baptism with water. Although ritual water purification was commonly practised among the Jewish groups of that period, it is important to note that John was the only one we know of to whom such a title was applied. Hence, to deserve this appellation John must have been able to offer Jews the ultimate in ritual and ceremonial purification through the act of immersing in water.

When I was thirteen, I fell ill with rheumatic fever and was confined to bed for a period of more than two months. I had a slight murmur on my heart as a result of my illness. Schoolmates visited to try and alleviate the boredom. This was the occasion when I wrote my first book, an ambitious pile of scribbled paper entitled *A History of Jewish Sects, Prophets and Desert Dwellers*. It was intolerably bad and ended up in the rubbish bin. The general theme of that book was the religious character of Jewish Palestine in the first century of the Common Era. Two thousand years ago saw the appearance of a variety of Jewish charismatic prophets, righteous leaders and healers in the country – among them John the Baptist and Jesus – and their authority attracted to them groups of people who felt, for all sorts of reasons, that God had perhaps deserted them and that their temple in Jerusalem was becoming polluted. The miracle-working and intense piety practised by some of these charismatic figures suggested to their followers that they might possess a link to the divine. The picture of an upsurge of Jewish religious sects and groups in the first century was fostered in the writings of the historian Josephus Flavius, who took a clear pro-Roman stance in his analysis of events. Josephus went out of his way to highlight and exaggerate the significance of these religious sects and their leaders, so that he might enhance the view that a build-up of religious confusion and gradual isolationism in the country was one of the contributing factors that eventually led to the breakdown of society which inevitably culminated in the disastrous Jewish rebellion against the Romans from AD 66 onwards. However, this manifestation of Jewish sects and religious movements in first-century Palestine was probably quite a modest phenomenon and not as commonplace as it was made out to be by Josephus. The great majority of people at that time were pro-establishment and possessed a cohesive outlook on religious life and its institutions. It was only a minority of people who were not adapted to the framework of mainstream society and felt the need to withdraw into the desert (*Antiquities* XX, 188). The fact that their leaders led a simple and ascetic life ensured that they were revered even more. Hence, the appearance of a John or a Jesus in the first century was notable precisely because it was an unusual event. This in itself did not signify turmoil in the general population or a threat against it, unless, of course, the charismatic leader and his followers decided to adopt revolutionary objectives and to take up arms [note 5.34].

In his own lifetime John the Baptist would undoubtedly have impressed those around him as someone who was following the age-old tradition of the Israelite prophets. Indeed, John was referred to as a 'prophet' and even as 'more than a prophet' in Matthew (11: 9–11), though this was not necessarily an appellation that he would have used to describe himself (John 1:21). It is quite likely however that he did see himself as a 'mouthpiece of God' and as such would have regarded himself as falling into the general mould of prophets such as Hosea: 'I have also spoken by the prophets, and I have multiplied visions, and used similitudes, by the ministry of prophets' (12:10). The ascetic lifestyle of the Israelite prophet would also have fitted John quite well: 'They wandered in the wilderness in a solitary way; they found no city to dwell in. Hungry and thirsty, their soul fainted in them' (Psalms 107: 4–5). These Israelite prophets were certainly a strange group of individuals, some behaving in ecstatic fashion and others with a certain abandon. They did odd things, such as walking around barefoot (Isaiah), wearing wooden yokes around their necks (Jeremiah), and dressing in strange garments [note 5.35]. But not everyone saw John the Baptist as a prophet: the historian Josephus depicted him as a kind of Hellenistic-type 'ethical teacher', whereas in the Christianised portrayal in the Gospels he is depicted as a subordinate of Jesus (for example Mark 9:12; Matthew 3:13) but this is largely, as I shall be arguing, the result of the controversy between the followers of John and Jesus. There were some who regarded him as Elijah incarnate, as if he were the prophet himself who had returned to life (cf. Luke 1:17; 7: 27).

One may assume that John did thrive on the element of ambiguity and uncertainty in the role that he took upon himself. The idea of John in the role of Elijah *redivivus* was something I believe was largely contrived by the early followers of Jesus and by the Gospel writers, in keeping with their view that John was the forerunner of Jesus as it was seen to be foretold in Malachi 3:1: 'Behold, I will send my messenger, and he shall prepare the way before me . . .' Hence, Matthew (11:14) reports Jesus as saying about John: 'and if ye will receive it, this is Elias, which has for to come.' In another passage, Jesus reiterates the connection between the two: 'And Jesus answered and said unto them, Elias truly shall first come, and restore all things . . . . Then the disciples understood that he spake unto them of John the Baptist.' (Matthew

17:11–13; cf. Mark 9:11–13). The Gospel of Mark is much more explicit in the introduction provided for John the Baptist: 'As it is written in the prophets, Behold, I send my messenger before thy face, which shall prepare thy way before thee' (Mark 1:2).

I would contend that John actually saw himself as the forerunner not of Jesus but of Elijah [note 5.36]. This comes across in the passage in the Fourth Gospel where John is questioned by the Pharisees and emphatically denies being a prophet, a messiah or Elijah (John 1: 21–25). More importantly, in this passage John does admit to being a baptiser and then goes on to say that he is awaiting the coming of one whose sandals he felt unworthy of even unlacing. In my opinion, the 'one' John is referring to, must be the prophet Elijah, for whom he had a great regard and who was the reason why he descended to the lower Jordan River region in the first place and why he made baptism such a strong feature of his activities. After all, the Jordan River was the place where Elijah had been taken up to heaven (II Kings 2:8) and this was the place to which he would return. Hence, John's role model may actually have been Elisha, who was an Israelite prophet and the disciple and successor of Elijah. John probably believed that Elijah's spirit rested upon him in much the same way as 'the spirit of Elijah doth rest on Elisha' (II Kings 2:15), and that he was there to prepare for the return of his master, 'the voice of him that crieth in the wilderness' (Isaiah 40:3) and in doing so the end of days would inevitably come closer: 'Behold, I will send you Elijah the prophet before the coming of the great and dreadful day of the Lord' (Malachi 4:5). However, John's perception of himself as the figure of Elisha awaiting the coming of Elijah may not have been totally accepted even by his own followers, who were perhaps hoping that eventually John would announce himself as Elijah *redivivus*. In any case, such an announcement was never made and his beheading would have been a severe blow to the expectations of his followers, apart from the personal loss of their leader, and especially since there was no sign of Elijah returning. The resulting confusion among John's followers may have created a greater ambiguity about John's role which was then fully exploited by the followers of Jesus and eventually by the Gospel writers, as I shall argue.

The prophet Elijah was originally from the Gilead region of the Transjordan, from a place called Tishbe (I Kings 17:1) and we know more about his deeds than about him as a man. He was in direct line of a group of inspired preachers and reformers. He appeared as a prophet quite abruptly and then withdrew back towards the Jordan River: 'Turn thee eastward and hide thyself by the brook Kerith which is on face of Jordan' (I Kings 17:3). With his mantle, Elijah 'smote' the waters of the Jordan. Eventually, he acknowledged Elisha as his heir and successor [note 5.37]. Elisha was the first (or at least the first mentioned) to have used the Jordan for healing purposes. He sent Na'aman the leper there: 'Go and wash in Jordan seven times, and thy flesh shall come again to thee, and thou shalt be clean' (II Kings 5:10). However, since Elisha was Elijah's successor it makes sense that he followed the purification practices at the Jordan River previously established there by his teacher. Interestingly, Elisha was also called upon to deal with the purification of the contaminated spring at Jericho by casting a vessel with salt into the waters (II Kings 2: 19–22). According to the historian Josephus, Elisha 'went out to this spring and cast into the stream an earthen ware full of salt, and then *raising his righteous right hand* to heaven and pouring propitious libations upon the ground, he besought the earth to mollify the stream and to open sweeter channels . . .' (italics: S.G.) (*Jewish War*, IV: 460–465). The spring of Jericho (Ain es-Sultan) is still there today and its waters remain sweet: it is interesting to note that the late Peter Dorrell recalled speaking to elderly refugees in present-day Jordan who had been unable to visit Jericho for twenty years or more, 'but still remember with pleasure the taste of the water from Ain es-Sultan' [note 5.38].

If my proposal that John the Baptist had taken on the role of Elisha in preparation for the return of Elijah is correct, then what was ringing in John's ears as he descended to the lower reaches of the Jordan River were the words from II Kings 2:6: 'The Lord hath sent me unto the Jordan.' John came from the region of Jerusalem with the burning desire to be present at the spot near the Jordan River where he believed Elijah had originally ascended into the heavens. It was here that John called upon his followers to purify themselves and to repent of their sins. Everything had to be ready. John must have sent out messengers to report on the imminent return of Elijah, otherwise news of his presence at the Jordan would have taken a while to circulate throughout the land. It was this news about Elijah that attracted so many people to John and not the fact that he was a baptiser. With the help of his followers, John baptised many people simultaneously. He also preached and felt confident enough even to go as far as denouncing Herodias, perhaps hinting that she was a bit like Ahab's wife Jezebel. Herod Antipas must have heard about these events with a sense of foreboding, fearing the military implications of these masses of people 'streaming forth' (Matthew 3:5).

There was a great excitement in the air and many people came to the Jordan with very high expectations. After all, one can imagine people saying to each other, if the prophet Elijah was about to return then the eventual outcome of all of this would have to be the arrival of that 'great and dreadful day of the Lord' (Malachi 4:5).

About half a day's walk from John the Baptist's stamping grounds in the lower Jordan Valley was the settlement of the Qumran sect, situated immediately north-west of the Dead Sea, one of the deepest places in the world. In 1947 a hapless teenager from the Ta'amirah Bedouin tribe – Mohammed Adh Dhib 'Issa – crawled into the darkness of a cave above the ruined settlement and came across very well preserved two-thousand-year-old scrolls which were subsequently to set the whole world of New Testament scholarship alight. The general consensus of opinion nowadays is that Qumran was a settlement belonging to the sect of the Essenes and that the scrolls came from their library. Since then, quite a few scholars suffused with the thrill of the discovery and interpretation of the Dead Sea Scrolls have been led to ask: was John the Baptist an Essene? Might it be possible that John spent part of his childhood or perhaps even part of his adult life in an Essene community such as Qumran? [note 5.39].

We were on our way back from visiting the excavation of a Roman and Byzantine Jewish village at the green oasis of Ein Gedi on the western edge of the Dead Sea shore. We – that is Rafi Lewis, Katy Galor and myself – drove northwards along the winding road, stopping off at Qumran where Katy said some Israeli excavations were in progress and we thought it might be a good chance to see what was being uncovered. I have always liked Qumran because it is such an unusual site in terms of its function, but, at the same time, there is nothing there which is really out of the ordinary: simple stone walls, small structures, channels and plastered water installations. I know of many travellers who, on arriving at Qumran for the first time, expect to see an awesome site with monumental buildings, and eventually go away terribly disappointed with what they have seen. I remember my own cousin Mark, having read an appallingly bad book (which I shall not even attempt to identify) that proposed Qumran as the place of Jesus' crucifixion, arriving back in Jerusalem after a visit to the site with a piqued look on his face: how could it be that this insignificant-looking place was the actual birthplace of the literature of the Dead Sea Scrolls? However, archaeologists never find Qumran boring and they will always be returning to investigate the mysteries of the site and the caves in its surrounding landscape.

Knowing that there might still be a scroll or two, or a heap of torn fragments, buried somewhere within a crevice at the back of one of the caves, is the sort of thing that gives the scholar a kind of buzz that ordinarily can only be obtained through smoking illegal substances. Qumran, it has to be said, is a bit like the proverbial honey pot, and it has managed to bring out the worst and the best in international scholarship.

The Dead Sea Scrolls include a variety of religious and sectarian documents and all of these apparently originated in the library of a community of people who referred to themselves as *yahad* (literally 'togetherness') and these by all accounts must be the same as the sect of the Essenes, who are mentioned briefly by Pliny the Elder and in some detail by Josephus. They are depicted in some documents as the 'sons of light' or the true Israelites preparing themselves for an apocalyptic battle against the 'sons of darkness', cutting themselves off from mainstream society and rejecting the authority of the Jewish Temple in Jerusalem and its priesthood. They were separatists with an enormous dose of piety and their lives were structured accordingly. The religious scrolls include quite a few biblical and apocryphal texts. On the basis of the content of the scrolls, palaeography (i.e. the study of the style of letters) and radiocarbon dating methods, it would appear that the earliest of the scrolls were written between 250 and 150 BC, with the bulk of the scrolls written between 100 BC and AD 70. None of the scrolls dates from later than that date. I am frequently asked, when giving public lectures, whether it is not possible that there are scrolls 'hidden away' that have been suppressed because of their controversial or inflammatory contents. People always like a conspiracy but the answer to this question is quite simple: pictures of every single one of the scrolls and of the major fragments are now in the public domain (except for the minor scraps bearing only a letter or two) and all of these may be accessed by anyone interested in doing so. Research by scholars, however, still continues apace and detailed publications are finally emerging. New advances are now also being made in the study of the scrolls by utilising the imaging procedures of digital technology, especially in regard to the clarification of unclear and blurred words in the scrolls, and with the jigsaw fitting together of seemingly disassociated torn fragments.

The rugged area of Qumran was the place chosen by the Essenes for their new order presumably because of its apparent seclusion and inhospitable surroundings. It can be hellishly hot in this area during the summer months, with temperatures sometimes reaching above forty degrees Celsius. Those living there clearly did not do so for the fun of it. Surrounding the settlement there must have been palm groves and perhaps even small gardens in the immediate vicinity, but the environment would not have sustained the herding and management of cattle. The examination of aerial reconnaissance work has delineated the existence of a complexity of features in the landscape around Qumran, with clear trails linking the site with Jericho, Ain Feshka and Ain el-Ghuweir. Hence, members of the Qumran community may very well have participated in trading ventures relating to the processing and transportation of balsam oils and commodities such as salt and bitumen, both of which are available in the Dead Sea. Jerusalem was only a day's walking distance and Jericho could be reached in a matter of hours. It is unlikely that there were more than 150 people living within the buildings at Qumran at any given time, judging by the size of the refectory and the size of the buildings [note 5.40]. The initiates lived in more temporary accommodations and in caves around the settlement for a period of two years [note 5.41]. The 'Community Rule' details the structure of their daily routine. Those living at the settlement had a fairly regimented way of existence with study, worship and daily chores from morning to night. One of the focal points in the settlement must have been the Scriptorium in which the scrolls are believed to have been written or at least read, and they were kept in locally made ceramic pots ('scroll jars'). Each person followed a strict code of conduct that was adhered to at all costs; transgressors were expelled from the community. After work community members would purify themselves, dress in clean clothes (they perceived such garments as 'holy') and then continue to the refectory for the communal meal. Although their way of life seems rigid and unbending, they sincerely believed that discipline, piety and purity would eventually lead them to a higher plane of existence.

Members of the Qumran sect had always been waiting for an apocalyptic holy war and indeed one of their scrolls deals with the battle between the sons of light and darkness and reads almost like a military manual. The scrolls were subsequently hidden away by the sectarians in caves in the cliffs behind the settlement, with the object of protecting them from the Romans at the time of their suppression of the Jewish rebellion. The members of the Qumran sect – the Essenes – appear to have entered the fray without any concern for their own survival. There are no signs, for instance, of attempts being made to fortify their settlement in advance of the arrival of the Romans. The fact that so many scrolls (close to 900), complete or in fragments, have been found in the caves at Qumran must indicate that the Romans eventually slaughtered the entire community. The end was so complete that there was nobody left to reclaim the scrolls.

The possibility that John the Baptist might at some point have lived with the Essenes in their 'monastery' at Qumran has been an idea that scholars have been flirting with ever since the momentous discovery of the Dead Sea Scrolls and the subsequent excavations by Roland de Vaux at the site. However, there is no evidence to support this theory, though even some recent books on Qumran and the Dead Sea Scrolls have put forward this view. None of the scrolls contains writings that could be said to relate to John's activities in any way. Some have suggested that John only spent the early years of his life with the Essenes and that some catalyst resulted in him being banished from the community or that he left of his own accord. Others have suggested that while John did not live with the Essenes at Qumran he was heavily influenced by their beliefs. According to Luke 1:80 John the Baptist is said to have spent part of his youth in the wilderness, but nowhere does it say that this was at the Jordan River or near the Dead Sea, indeed there is no reason even to believe that John grew up in the Judaean Desert region. The fact that the Essenes were in the habit of adopting children into their community, as reported by Josephus (*Jewish War* II: 120), does not signify necessarily that John would have been among them. Indeed, John's father had officiated in the Temple in Jerusalem, whose administration was hated by the Essenes. While it would not have served the purposes of a Gospel writer to mention any Essene connection to John, this does not explain why the historian Josephus, who knew the Essenes well and described them at some length, did not bother to mention such a connection in his description of John the Baptist; unless, of course, there was no such connection. While certain similarities may be posited between the beliefs of John and the Essenes, the dissimilarities are even greater. While the sect regarded the 'the voice of him that crieth in the wilderness' (Isaiah 40:3) as a reference to themselves, John, in my view, regarded it as a reference to the need to prepare for the return of Elijah. The Essenes were basically separatists and firm believers in pre-destination, which is the belief that God is omniscient and omnipotent and that humans have no free will of their own. However, John gave every pious Jew the right to choose to be baptised and to repent of their sins, implying a belief that God delegated a certain degree of free will to man. The geographical proximity between the area of John's activities at the Jordan and the Essene settlement at Qumran also does not indicate any specific relationship between the two, and the suggestion that John's followers may have belonged to some 'peripheral' group of ascetic Essenes is also extremely hypothetical [note 5.42]. When John took up his mission and descended to the lower Jordan River region, it is most likely that he would have been fully aware of the existence of the sect of the Essenes, their teachings and the situation of their settlement. He may even have had hope that some of the Essene community members might feel inclined to leave Qumran and join up with his movement instead. But there is absolutely no evidence that John himself was an Essene or that he had lived with them either early on in his life or as an adult.

One day a friend rang me to say that he had just heard a report on the news saying that the skeleton of John the Baptist had been unearthed at Qumran by an American professor, Richard Freund. Since I knew that Magen Broshi had been digging there with Hanan Eshel, the first thing I did was to send Broshi an e-mail asking him if there was any validity to this report and if he could send me a copy of the press release. He replied that some part of a skeleton had indeed been found, and that he would send me a press release issued by Freund [note 5.43]. The press release eventually came through my fax machine: it had been issued by the Office of Communications of Freund's university and was entitled *University of Hartford Archaeologist Finds Remains of Man Who May Be the Missing Link Between Judaism and Christianity*. It spoke about the discovery at Qumran of a complete skeleton of a man with a ceramic vessel next to it dating from the first century, which Freund thought must be the tomb of the 'Teacher of Righteousness' of the Qumran community, a religious leader mentioned in some of the Dead Sea Scrolls, whom he identified as John the Baptist because of the 'orientation of the body in the ground and other evidence' [note 5.44]. The press release also mentioned that bone material from the skeleton had been sent for radiocarbon dating and for DNA testing. It took a while for the mists surrounding the discovery and subsequent controversy to clear, but Broshi and Eshel eventually produced a proper report on the discovery [note 5.45]. The cemetery at Qumran is quite large – there are approximately 1200 graves – and the bodies are all oriented north to south. A small number of graves were found with the bodies positioned towards the east, but these are apparently late Bedouin burials as the anthropologist Joe Zias was able to show. The purported skeleton of John the Baptist was found in Tomb 1,000, which was investigated at the eastern extremity of the cemetery located east of the settlement itself. According to Broshi and Eshel, 'there is not a scintilla of evidence for asserting that the bones are of John the Baptist'. They argue that the skeleton was found with its head intact, protected by two stones, which would not fit the Gospel description of John the Baptist being beheaded. However, a beheading does not necessarily imply that the body would have been buried separately from the head and we are not told whether their anthropological examination of the cervical vertebrae of the skeleton indicated that there was no evidence of decapitation. The size of the tomb chamber suggested that the bones must have belonged to a person of some importance in the Qumran community, and Broshi and Eshel proposed that it was of a *mevaqqer* (overseer) mentioned in the scrolls. While I agree with the excavators that the suggestion that the Qumran grave might contain the bones of John the Baptist 'is the purest speculation, devoid of the slightest evidence', to be fair the same has to be said about the *mevaqqer* theory and so the mystery remains.

The hard digging operations at the cave at Suba were intensified in the mad rush to get as much done as possible before the onset of winter. The danger that the cave could be broken into became a reality at the end of 2001 when we found the iron door at the entrance twisted and broken. The intruders had used such force that the metal bolts holding the door to the wall had fallen out. Thankfully, no harm was done to the ancient drawings on the walls of the cave – one wonders whether the intruders had even noticed them – but they did carry away with them items of digging equipment. We had the door put back and reinforced (with additional wall bolts), hoping that this would prevent the intruders from returning.

The winter rains that year were quite strong and a large body of water rapidly accumulated within the excavated area of the cave. Hence, Rafi, with the help of Reuven from the kibbutz, spent valuable time slopping water out of the cave in buckets. We realised that since this was evidently going to occur every year, it was worthwhile investing in a mechanised water pump, which we did. We spent the winter months sorting through the enormous amounts of pottery derived from the excavation, counting more than 50,000 potsherds from the Roman levels alone, and putting together a series of charts illustrating the seriation and frequency of every single vessel type – mostly jugs, with a smaller quantity of jars and cooking pots – from each level and living surface excavated. The importance of this work was that we could now pinpoint the changes that occurred within each class of ceramic vessel represented in the cave, spanning the 150-year period from *c.* 50 BC to AD 150. We also spent a lot of time discussing among ourselves the significance of the finds that we had been unearthing. The full flight of rock-cut steps extending into the cave had now been uncovered and they were very impressive. Clearly the intent behind cutting these steps was for people to enter the cave itself and to descend the steps in order to reach the water, suggesting that the water also served for bathing purposes and not just for collecting water, otherwise people would have simply dipped their storage jars vertically into the water from a shaft in the ceiling. Indeed, the act of collecting water at the bottom of a flight of steps is far more difficult than any other kind of water-gathering procedures. Discussions took place regarding the installations – the stone circles and meandering walls – found on the earthen floors in the front of the cave, and the general consensus was that they had to reflect certain ritual procedures performed in the cave during the course of the first century AD. This conclusion was strengthened as the excavations proceeded.

The discoveries we were now making at the cave evidently indicated that something very unusual happened there in the Early Roman period, during the hundred years or so from the end of the first century BC to the early second century AD. Further investigations were necessary.

6

The Baptism of John

We were back at the Suba cave in the spring of 2002 and continued digging through the summer, with the help of a number of individuals and small groups of volunteers, under the constant, watchful eye of Egon. The goal of the new work in the cave was quite ambitious: to extend the area of the excavation substantially to the south, towards the centre of the cave (to just below the shaft in the ceiling). Our plan was to uncover the same sequence of archaeological layers previously encountered in earlier seasons of excavations – from the Ottoman, Early Islamic, Byzantine and Early Roman periods – and to completely dig this area down to the rock floor of the cave. This would give us a second chance to examine all the archaeological remains and to seek confirmation of their dating and interpretation. There were numerous unanswered questions that we were determined to solve during this new phase of the operations. The task of excavating such a large area by the end of the summer before the onset of the autumn rains was going to be tough, but Egon expressed confidence in taking on this challenge, even if it meant excavating there single-handedly, should we run out of money and workers. Because of the dodgy political situation, there were fewer and fewer volunteers working with us in 2002, but Egon was lucky to have had the stalwart support of Rafi Lewis and Reuven Kalifon throughout. Hard work ensued and large quantities of soil were shifted.

Digging down in the new area through the Ottoman fills, we uncovered a rough circle of boulders, rubble and piles of burnt material. The latter contained much charcoal and because of its location we interpreted it as collapse or dumped material that had got into the cave through the rock shaft in the ceiling. As the excavation proceeded, we reached a series of surfaces, dating from the Byzantine and Early Islamic periods, and these were without doubt a continuation of the floors seen in previous seasons to the north. We were slightly disappointed that no further information could be gleaned on the activities that took place in the cave during this time period and nothing unexpected was found, except for a shallow hearth associated with the uppermost living surface. Once we reached the Early Roman levels, however, we did make some exciting discoveries that helped to shed light on the character of the activities that took place at that time in the cave. Associated with the living surfaces from this period were numerous small circular installations with walls built of stones. As we got deeper, many more of these stone installations were encountered, so many of them in fact that it felt like we were excavating a prehistoric site. These circular installations were all empty except for one that had some shattered pottery on top of a floor paved with flat slabs of stone. Finally, we got down to the plastered rock floor of the cave, beneath a layer of mud containing parts of a crushed storage jar. The floor was flat and there were no additional steps. We also found a mass of fallen plaster, with the fragments mostly face down that had collapsed from the western wall of the cave. The mud layer contained basalt grinding stones and examples of pottery dating from the late second century BC to the late first century BC. Hence, the collapse of the plaster must have occurred at this time. Surprisingly, no attempts were ever made to replaster the western wall.

How does one interpret an archaeological discovery when it appears to be unparalleled and unique, and inconsistent with prevailing patterns of knowledge? Archaeologists usually solve such problems by extending and deepening their digs over larger areas, always hoping that more information will provide more knowledge, and that is exactly what we decided to do in 2002. We hoped that by enlarging the dig it would eventually provide us with a better overview of what went on in the cave, especially in the Early Roman period, and that clearer explanations regarding the various functions of the cave would emerge as a result of this increase of new knowledge. But, as we dug deeper and over a wider area, the mystery of the cave actually grew instead of decreasing: things did not always add up, more and more anomalies in the archaeological record emerged. None of the archaeological features from the Early Roman period – from the time of John the Baptist – was of a sort that had been found before and this made the challenge even greater. We all felt – me, James Tabor, Egon Lass and the rest of the crew – that the results needed rigorously testing by obtaining further data; and so we continued digging, gathering evidence and running a variety of scientific tests to check the strength of our conclusions and the veracity of our theories. Finally, we put together all the basic facts that had been revealed to us about the cave and examined all the nuances of the data. The results were quite astounding.

One afternoon, when the digging had ceased for the day and every-body had gone home, I drove back to the cave. I felt I needed to look at it, to think things out quietly and without distraction. Our recent excavations had shown that the cave had been used and abandoned well before the Early Roman period, but we were still not sure how old the cave was. It seemed to me that, for anybody wanting to re-use the cave for water-gathering purposes in the first century AD, the most logical thing would have been to clean it out, restore the plaster on its walls, clear the settling basins outside the cave and get the water-diversion channels working again. This was commonly done at cisterns, reservoirs and pools elsewhere: after all, the whole point of water conservation is to gather the largest amount of rainwater possible within a given installation and to prevent the water from evaporating [note 6.1]. From experience I knew that water installations were frequently re-used from century to century, since it was easier to renovate old cisterns than to hew out new ones. Cleaning and repairing a water installation ensured that water did not seep out through cracks in the walls or percolate through holes in the floor, and that contaminants were excluded so that the water could be rendered hygienic for drinking and washing purposes. Strangely, not only did our mysterious people in the first century not do cleaning or repairs at the cave, but they seem to have gone out of their way to prevent it from properly functioning again as a reservoir. They completely abandoned the settling basins, purposefully packing the upper parts with stones, and going so far as building a retaining wall right across the area. They even blocked up the vertical shaft in the cave's ceiling with stones and mortar, covering over the rocky area above the cave with a layer of soil. Within the cave they established living surfaces, but without making any attempt to remove the silts and mud that were accumulating there during each winter. Tamping down the ground created some of the surfaces, others were provided with a consolidation base of stone or marl, apparently to deal with the problem of mud. To deal with the rainwater gushing into the cave, channels were dug along the edges of the cave walls and this ensured the rapid passage of the water from the entrance to the inner end of the cave. They also built bizarre stone installations – almost prehistoric in appearance – on top of the living surfaces, consisting of various types of rough stone circles or semi-circles, one of which had a floor of stone paving; another was found packed with broken pottery (*plate 8a*). Associated with the lowest living surfaces, which probably date to the early first century AD, was a pathway with parallel lines of stones and a narrow space in between, leading from the steps along the length of the chamber towards the pool of water at the back of the cave. This path extended past a circular installation on the left and with stones pushed to both sides, and then past a pile of fallen plaster which was surrounded by a line of stones (perhaps to prevent people from stubbing their toes on the jagged pieces of plaster sticking out of the mud). It was evident that the people who were using the cave in the first century came in through the entrance, placed items or personal belongings in the alcove to the right, undertook certain activities connected with the installations on the living surface in front of them, and then made their way fairly unimpeded across the muddy surface to the source of water at the back of the cave.

The excavations in the cave revealed a series of superimposed living surfaces (two metres thick) from the Early Roman period and each floor was interfaced with layers of silt and mud of varying thickness (*plate 8b*). The geomorphologist, Neil Munro, studied this deposit with great enthusiasm and helped us gain a clearer picture of how the silt and mud layers got there. During the wet rainy months of the year (November to February), water flushed into the cave from the side of the valley and, as is the case today, smaller amounts also entered it from the slope of the hill above the cave. The settling basins whose function it was to prevent soil, silt and detritus (leaves and other organic matter) from entering the cave were no longer functioning in the Early Roman period and this meant that water was channelled fairly indiscriminately into the cave. On flushing through the cave entrance, gradually or rapidly, the water would spread across the living surface like a sheet, depositing mud and silt residues in the process, and then would flow along the channels cut along the edges of the walls to the back of the cave. The amount of water that collected in the cave depended on the quantity of rainfall that descended in any given year (averaging 600 mm annually in this region). At times of heavy rainfall it is possible that even the front part of the cave remained partially under water for at least some months of the year, especially in early spring. During the dry season (March to October) when the water in the cave began to evaporate, the waterline would slowly have sunk and the deeper part of the water would have receded inwards towards the back of the cave. Hence, the people using the cave evidently had a clear dependence on the water that was collected in the cave during the flooding interludes of the winter months. But what did they actually use the water for?

It did seem wholly inexplicable that a large plastered cave such as this would not have been regularly cleaned out and used more efficiently for water-storage purposes in the Early Roman period. In antiquity water was deemed a very valuable commodity, especially for those forced to endure seven dry months every year. For this reason it does seem extremely odd that people were establishing their living surfaces and installations over such a large area of the cave, instead of simply cleaning out the muddy deposits. This is something I had never encountered before when excavating ancient water-storage installations and this made it all the more puzzling. There is also the fact that there are so many of these living surfaces, extending in time over more than a hundred-year period, indicating that this was not just a one-off or fluke situation. The people using the cave came back every year and did the same things in the cave that they had done the previous year. Each time the occupants had the opportunity to clean the cave but they decided not to. Why? While the dig was in progress, it seemed to me that the best way to gain a proper insight into the character of the people using the cave in the Early Roman period was to excavate their living surfaces and installations as carefully as we could to extract every scrap of information possible. This did slow down the pace of the excavation quite considerably and made it more costly, but it was well worth the effort.

We began by studying the ceramics. Every single potsherd, however small, was collected during the excavation. We also sieved every bucket of soil before dumping it outside. This procedure of total collection meant that we were not only able to count every single fragment of pottery recovered, but we were also able to classify every piece according to its fabric and vessel type on a computerised database. More than 100,000 fragments of pottery had been recovered from the living surfaces and associated fills from the Early Roman period. Rafi Lewis bravely undertook the work of counting the sherds. Altogether, this was a staggering quantity of pottery in proportion to the size of the area excavated. Where had all this pottery come from? we wondered. At first, we thought that it might possibly have been dumped from somewhere outside the cave, particularly from the area of the rocky ridge above. However, subsequent excavations on the ridge did not reveal any buildings at all and the associated fills uncovered there, dating from the Early Roman period, were almost sterile, with only a few associated potsherds. Another possibility raised was that these were dumps derived from a pottery kiln. However, no kiln was found and the examination of the pottery itself did not reveal distorted pottery (known as 'wasters'), slag or any other by-products normally found in kiln dumps. Indeed, the excavation of the living surfaces revealed an evenly spaced distribution of flat-lined potsherds rather than the higgledy-piggledy piles which one would expect to find had the pottery been dumped there indiscriminately. The distribution pattern of the potsherds also indicated that they came from vessels that had been broken on the spot and there was absolutely no evidence that the potsherds had been washed into the cave. Noël Siver's careful conservation work showed that while there were vessels with ancient breaks, not one vessel was found intact, which is quite strange considering the massive quantity of pottery recovered. This suggests, I would contend, that the breakage of the pottery vessels was deliberate and it was part of the strange practices that were undertaken in the cave.

We were able to obtain a good typological range of pottery vessels for the entire sequence of living surfaces. Chronologically, the pottery fragments from the earliest surfaces could be dated to the end of the first century BC whereas those from the top end of the sequence could be

6.1

dated to the early second century AD (*illustration 6.1*). By counting the vessel rims and by estimating the percentages of their preserved parts, we were able to establish the minimum number of vessels that would have been broken on each one of the living surfaces (or at least in the areas we excavated), and which vessel types actually dominated the pottery repertoire. We were also able to monitor even minor typological fluctuations in the rim shapes of the dominant vessels as they appeared in the sequence, allowing us to prepare very detailed charts with drawings of the vessel types and sub-types. This was quite an unusual pottery assemblage and it differed considerably from the normal mixture of pottery from that period at contemporary sites. It was extremely odd that the assemblage did not represent a complete array of ceramic types, such as storage and transport vessels, cooking vessels, plates, kraters, bottles, perfume juglets, lamps, imported wares (such as the red gloss *terra sigillata*) and so forth. Such vessels are normally found in domestic contexts of towns and villages, and to a lesser degree in small rural farms. In addition, there were almost no lamps (only two fragments found out of some 100,000 potsherds) and this was also quite strange considering that we were inside a cave. The pottery assemblage from the cave was dominated by very large quantities of one-handled jugs (with a superficial resemblance in shape to modern wine decanters), with considerably smaller quantities of storage jars and cooking pots. This was unusual. Ordinarily, the large storage jar would have been the better vessel for facilitating simple water retrieval and transportation over the distance between the source of water (in this case, our cave) and a household within a settlement (Suba). A jug, however, was a medium-to-small vessel of limited function and in towns it was usually only used as tableware, which is the reason why only very small quantities of such vessels are usually found. Because of this vessel's limited capacity it would hardly have been used for conveying water from a source of water to a settlement, especially in our case where Suba is located more than a kilometre away from the cave. In any case, Suba has a number of good springs of water and it would not have made sense for it to be conveyed over such a great distance. It is suggested that the reason for the overwhelming dominance of the one-handled jug in the pottery repertoire of the cave was because the people using them were involved in some specialised activity connected with water. Indeed, the jug was an ideal vessel for filling with water and for pouring, and so could perhaps be used to facilitate ritual cleansing (baptismal) rites. It was not, however, at all useful for storage purposes or for the transportation of water.

Apart from pottery, very little else was found on the living surfaces. This was disappointing because we very much wanted to come across finds that could help to explain how the surfaces were actually used and by whom. (Ordinarily, when excavating domestic floors at other sites, one would come across quite a lot of rubbish, such as animal bones and food remains, ashy and lime pockets of fill, metal fragments and bits of discarded building materials.) There were also no glass vessels, coins, nor objects made out of metal or stone. The lack of such finds on the living surfaces was completely out of balance with the great quantities of pottery that was uncovered, indicating that the surfaces could not have been used for domestic purposes. There were also no fireplaces.

The next step was to undertake flotation procedures on the soil samples taken from the living surfaces: perhaps here one would find some clues. Egon Lass collected more than 500 kilos of soil samples from the surfaces, weighing each sample separately, washing them on a metal screen within a barrel of water, and then drying them in the sun. The results were quite revealing. As we had expected, there were very large quantities of small crushed potsherds present in the samples (15.2 per cent per kilo), larger in fact than at any other site seen by Egon (where it usually amounts to no more than 1–2 per cent per kilo). The very sparse finds consisted of a few botanical remains, a small number of eggshell particles and five fish bones. Although one could suggest that these infinitesimal finds attest to occasional vegetarian meals, it seems more likely that they reached the cave unintentionally while adhering to the insides of cooking vessels. In any case, the results from the excavations and from the flotation procedures have made it clear that these living surfaces could not have been used for domestic activities, otherwise we would have found much more evidence of botanical remains, such as olive stones, wheat grain and animal bones. Indeed, the marked lack of animal bones from the Early Roman levels (in contrast to those from the later Byzantine/Early Islamic and Ottoman levels) was also confirmed by the archaeozoologist Ed Maher.

During the excavations a number of unusual carved stones were found embedded in the living surfaces. These were also helpful in the reconstruction of the activities in the cave in the first century. One of these was discovered the previous year, on the right hand side, as one entered the cave. It was rectangular (0.6 × 0.37 m) with a circular saucer-like depression in its top, with a vague resemblance to Roman-type altars (*illustration 6.2*). We were not sure what it was used for and some

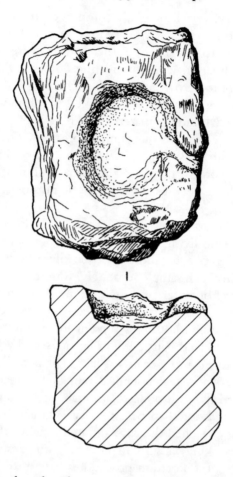

6.2

of us thought that the altar resemblance was perhaps not coincidental after all. It was definitely not used for domestic purposes, such as for the pounding or grinding of foodstuffs, otherwise signs of smoothness and polishing would have been visible within the circular depression. Also the stone itself was soft, so soft in fact that I could easily scratch the surface of the stone with just a fingernail. As we dug deeper, Egon drew my attention to a much larger oval-shaped stone that was emerging from underneath the so-called 'Altar' stone (*plate 9a*). This lower stone (1.25 × 0.63 m) had a singular depression on its upper surface, hollowed out remarkably like the imprint of a human right-foot, with the outline of the toes pointing outwards and with the rounded heel at the other end (*illustration 6.3*). Leading to it was a channel extending from a small saucer-like depression (we archaeologists call them 'cup-marks').

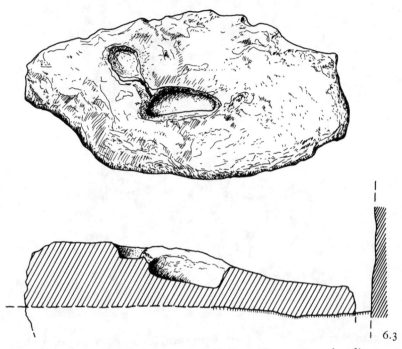

6.3

At the time of this discovery, we had great fun getting the diggers to model their right feet within the depression, while we clicked away with our cameras. Of all the people there, Rafi Lewis's right foot (size 42 cm) was the only one with the perfect fit! I also tried and found that I could just get my (slightly larger) right foot into the depression. An important point to mention is that it was not at all possible to insert the left foot because the depression had been shaped specifically only for the form of a right foot. I tried inserting my right foot backwards, i.e. in the opposite direction, with my toes towards the heel of the depression, but again without success. We concluded therefore that the stone must have been used in the Early Roman period for foot anointing: the initiatory would have stood facing west with his back against the wall, with his right foot inserted into the foot-like depression and with his left foot resting on the living surface (*illustration 6.4*). The saucer-like depression probably served as the base for a one-handled jug, similar to those found in the hundreds in the cave. It could have contained either water or oil, but the fact that there is a small groove extending from the cup-mark to the foot depression, suggests that it was the latter. After all, water could be splashed around but every attempt would have been made to conserve precious oil dripping down the jug.

6.4

The existence of only one foot depression and specifically only the one to accommodate the right foot has to indicate that the stone was connected with cultic practices and not with daily ablutions. In our reconstruction of this event, we believe that it was another person rather than the initiatory himself who would have administered the washing and anointing of the foot with oil from a jug. This discovery was very special and nothing like it, as far as I knew, had ever been found before at an Early Roman site in Israel/Palestine. In fact, there was a clear prohibition against graven images, which was largely adhered to by the local Jewish population. Indeed, this prohibition was also made clear in rabbinical writings: 'If a man found fragments of images, they are permitted. If he found [a fragment] in the shape of a hand or the shape of a foot, these are forbidden, since an object the like of these is worshipped' [note 6.2].

Background research showed me that the anointing and washing of feet was an ancient practice in the ancient Near East and I found the general subject fascinating. There are numerous references to foot-washing in the Old Testament. For example, we hear of Abraham washing the feet of the three angels as an act of hospitality (Genesis 18:4; see also Genesis 19:2), and of Abigail washing the feet of the servants of David at Carmel (I Samuel 25:41). It was usually regarded as a functional duty to rinse away dirt and was performed when greeting travellers or guests, but rarely was it an activity associated with specific water-cleansing rituals. In Exodus (30:19), however, there is a passage dealing with Aaron and his sons who were ritually required to wash their feet and hands in a basin of copper located between the Tent of Meeting and the Altar of God. Elsewhere, there is also an interesting reference to a covenant being struck by the dipping of a foot in oil (Deuteronomy 33:24). Shoes or sandals are also referred to as having been removed (hence also having to be washed) before entering a holy place: 'Put off your shoes from your feet, for the place on which you are standing is holy ground' (Exodus 3:5; also Joshua 5:15). In antiquity, the foot was regarded as a symbol of humility and of willing servitude because the foot was the part of the human body closest to the dust of the ground. Unlatching the thongs of a sandal or unloosing the shoe of a person was regarded as a servile function in Roman times as well. Hence, in one rabbinical text, it is said, 'all works which a slave performs for his master, a disciple should do for his teacher, except undoing shoe straps' (Ketubot 96a). When John the Baptist, speaking perhaps of the Messiah or of Elijah, proclaims him to be the one 'whose sandals I am not fit to take off', this is usually interpreted as a reflection of John's humility (Matthew 3:11; see also Mark 1:7; John 1:27; Luke 3:16; Acts 13:25), but a further exegesis is one which implies a context whereby, had John managed to unlatch the sandals, the next step would have been by necessity the washing of the feet. Indeed, John, in this clear ritual-cleansing vein immediately goes on to say: '*That* one [i.e. the Messiah or Elijah] will baptise you with holy spirit and with fire.'

When was this foot-washing performed? We lack specific information regarding the different circumstances during which foot-washing was undertaken among Jews in Early Roman Palestine. One may surmise, for instance, that the cleansing of feet was essential in agricultural pursuits, such as the treading of grapes and the pressing of olives. What we do have, however, is information regarding the two stages of ritual cleansing that were engaged in prior to a Jewish meal: namely immersion in a ritual bath (baptism) and the washing of hands. The washing of the feet appears to have been undertaken by Jews as part of the overall process of ritual cleansing, whereas the washing of feet *after* a meal seems only to have been practised by Jesus and those associated with him (John 13:4–7). Excavations in the Jewish Quarter in the Old City of Jerusalem brought to light well preserved remains of households dating from the first century AD and in the basements were numerous stepped bathing installations for ritual cleansing (*miqwa'ot*) with small footbaths next to the entrances [note 6.3]. In the Mishna (*miqwa'ot* 9:2) it is stated explicitly: 'None may immerse themselves [in the *miqweh*] with the dust on his feet. [Just as] a kettle may not be immersed with the soot that is thereon unless it has been scraped.' The ritualistic washing of hands prior to the partaking of food in first-century Jewish households was common practice and interlinked with the use of stone vessels. Stone vessels were very fashionable within Jewish society because they were deemed ritually unsusceptible to defilement as opposed to receptacles made out of processed materials, such as fired pottery, metal or glass. In the later Jewish Rabbinical writings of the Mishna, stone vessels are mentioned for the purpose of ritually cleansing hands: 'they may not . . . pour [water] over the hands, save only in a vessel; and only vessels that have a tightly stopped-up cover [i.e. a lid] afford protection.' (Yadaim 1:2; ed. Danby). The quantity of water is specified as a quarter of a *log* or more but one must assume that in the first century the quantity was more likely to have been assessed rather than measured. Of the three main types of vessels that generally characterise the stone vessel assemblage of that time – cylindrical mugs, small open vessels and large jars – it seems reasonable to assume that the large jars were actually used to contain the ritual water and the reference in John 2:6 to six stone jars used 'for the Jewish rites of purification' at Cana may be adduced as proof of this. However, the stone vessels that were used for the act of 'pouring' the water are more likely to have been the cylindrical mugs. These mugs are probably the same as the 'cups' mentioned in Mishna *Parah* 3:2: '[In Jerusalem] . . . they brought oxen with doors laid upon their backs, and on these the children sat bearing in their hands cups of stone. When they reached [the spring or pool of] Siloam they alighted and filled the cups with water and got up again and sat upon the boards' [note 6.4].

On the basis of the evidence that I have just discussed, I should like to propose a reconstruction of the procedure of ritual cleansing before a meal in a typical Jerusalem household of the first century AD, and the place that the washing of feet had in this process. If, let us say, the head of the household had just come back from the marketplace, where conceivably he could have been exposed to certain impurities from items sold there, or might have come into contact with a leper begging for alms while on his way back, it was incumbent on that person to totally immerse himself in a ritual pool (*miqweh*) located in the basement of his house. Having disrobed, the person would first wash his legs and feet in a stone basin next to the entrance to the ritual pool: this was to ensure that extraneous matter (such as leaves or insects, or clods of mud) would not be introduced into the pool itself. Having immersed in the ritual pool, the person would then put on a robe and climb the steps to the *triclinium* (dining area) of the house to partake of a meal. At the entrance to the room there would have been two large stone pots (about three feet high) next to a stone table on which there were a number of vessels including stone cups. Taking a cup, the person would dip it into the water in the stone pot and would then wash his hands over the second empty pot.

Against this background one may re-examine a number of passages in the New Testament relating to procedures of cleansing prior to meals. In Mark (7:2–3), for instance, we read: 'And when they [Pharisees and scribes in Jerusalem] saw some of his [Jesus'] disciples eat bread with defiled, that is to say, with unwashed hands, they found fault. For the Pharisees and all the Jews, except they wash their hands oft, eat not, holding the tradition of the elders.' Later in Mark (7:5) the following appears: 'Then the Pharisees and Scribes asked him [Jesus], Why walk thy disciples [who had just come from the market place] according to the tradition of the elders, but eat bread with unwashed hands?' Clearly the Jewish practice at that time was for the hands to be washed before eating and especially if one had just come in from a place with possible impurity and pollution, such as a marketplace. The hands were purified by pouring water over them or by dipping them into water. In Luke (11:38) we read: 'And when the Pharisee saw it, he marvelled that he [Jesus] had not first washed before dinner.' Either the reference here is to total immersion in a ritual pool (*miqweh*) or the reference here is to hand-washing with the use of a 'water pot' (John 2:6). It is unlikely that hand-washing was a substitute for total body immersion in a pool as Dale once suggested [note 6.5], otherwise we would have an absurd situation whereby a person sitting down to a meal with ritually cleansed hands would be placing food into a body that was still in a state of uncleanness.

The story of Jesus' washing of the feet of his disciples is recounted in an interesting but complicated passage in John chapter 13. The scene is the last Passover meal which Jesus and his disciples attend. The disciples had already undergone general immersion in water prior to the meal (John 13:10) and we may assume that the participants had also ritually washed their hands. The supper having ended, Jesus got up and disrobed except for a towel, which he wrapped around his middle. 'After that he poureth water into a basin, and began to wash the disciples' feet, and to wipe them with the towel wherewith he was girded' (John 13:5). As the dialogue between Jesus and Peter makes clear, the disciples are not at all sure of the implications of Jesus' act, since the washing of feet by another person was deemed a servile activity at that time. Later, Jesus did explain his actions: 'If I then, your Lord and Master, have washed your feet; ye also ought to wash one another's feet. For I have given you an example, that ye should do as I have done to you' (John 13: 14–15). Interestingly, for completeness, Simon Peter asks of Jesus to wash 'not my feet only, but also my hands and my head'. Jesus replied that this was unnecessary because 'He that is washed [already by total immersion and with the washing of hands before the meal] needeth not save to wash his feet' (John 13:10).

Another instance of feet-washing is the story of the washing of the feet of Jesus in the House of the Pharisee: the woman who did so (with her tears) undertaking this action as a token of humility and penitence and thus her sins were forgiven (Luke 7:37–38, 46). This woman is said very specifically to have used perfumed oil on Jesus' feet after they had been washed. In another story (John 12:3) relating to Jesus tarrying at Bethany (el-'Azariyeh), a village close to Jerusalem, Mary anoints the feet of Jesus with perfumed oil, said to be quite costly, before drying them with her hair. Interestingly, as I discussed earlier, the footprint stone from the cave was probably used for anointing with oil, but, unlike the references in the Gospels to the anointing of *both* feet, our stone was used only for one foot. This fact must indicate that the ritual of anointing that was undertaken in the cave was purely symbolic, since there would have been no practical use for an installation for the anointing of just one foot and not the other. There is also no evidence that the anointing of the feet in the cave was associated in some way with the partaking of a meal. In later Christian thinking, Jesus' act in washing the feet of his disciples (John 13:5) was regarded as part of the process of purification in preparation for the future, a symbolic washing away of the First Man (i.e. Adam, 'man of dust'). The ceremony of the washing of the feet (*pedilavium*) was part of the church liturgy of Maundy Thursday and was traditionally performed by the bishops. Twelve men would be led into the church and the celebrant would then proceed to wash and dry the feet of each in turn. Sometimes epiphany tanks were built for this ceremony: in Egyptian monasteries, for example, the *lakan* (or *mandatum* tank) was situated on the west side of the nave of the church [note 6.6].

Cultic stones with images of a foot or feet chiselled into them as outlines or hollowed-out imprints were, I found, of great antiquity in the Near East and many of them had a sacred or religious significance. They are usually taken to allude to human or divine presence. Sometimes the image of the foot was taken as a metaphor for the setting out on a journey, or as a notion of passage, or as a manifestation of an epiphany. Probably the earliest footprint incised into a cave wall was found at Gezer, in the western foothills of Israel, and it was attributed to the Neolithic period [note 6.7]. Footprints of human and divine significance are also known from Graeco-Roman monuments in Mediterranean countries, in Egypt and the Near East [note 6.8]. However, some of the footprints seem to be of fairly modern origin or are downright forgeries, such as the footprint of the child Jesus on a rock that was supposedly 'found' fifteen years ago in the Coptic town of Pekha-Issous and is now kept in the Church of the Virgin Mary at Sakha Kafr el-Sheikh. J. S. Buckingham, a traveller in the Near East in the early nineteenth century, had the following remarks to make on the phenomenon:

The quality which rocks formerly possessed, of receiving impressions from the weight of men and animals, seems to have been almost too general to render it a rarity. The mark of Adam's foot on the peak of Ceylon is visited by pilgrims of all classes; and considering his reputed size, it is scarcely to be wondered at. The impression of the entire figure of Moses is shown in the granite mountains of Horeb and Sinai, when the rock became soft at the presumption of Moses, in wishing to see the face of God as he passed. The print of the foot of Mohammed's camel, when he was taken up, beast and all, by the angel Gabriel into heaven, is also shown on the same holy mountain; and considering that, according to Mohammedan belief, the animal was large enough to have one foot at Mecca, another on Damascus, a third on Cairo, and a fourth on Mount Sinai, the enormity of his weight might be almost sufficient to account for this also. At Jerusalem, and in the other parts of the Holy Land, one can scarcely move a hundred yards without seeing marks of fingers, elbows, knees, and toes, as if imprinted in wax [note 6.9].

Another doubter was Mark Twain when confronted with the supposed footprints of Saint Peter in Rome. He says that when shown the ashes of St Peter, he stood there with reverence, but when they showed us the print of Peter's face in the hard stone of the prison wall and said he made it by falling up against it, we doubted. And when, also, the monk at St Sebastian showed us a paving stone with two great footprints in it and said Peter's feet made those, we lacked confidence again. Such things do not impress one. The monks said that angels came and liberated Peter from prison by night, and he started away from Rome by the Appian Way. The Saviour met him and told him to go back, which he did. Peter left those footprints in the stone upon which he stood at the time. It was not stated how it was ever discovered whose footprints they were, seeing the interview occurred secretly and at night. The print of the face in prison was that of a man of common size; the footprints were those of a man ten or twelve feet high. The discrepancy confirmed our belief [note 6.10].

Strangely, John the Baptist is the only major Christian figure without any cultic footprint attached to him. There are, however, many thousands of examples of footprints on stones locked away in churches and mosques and museums, attributed to Jesus, Mohammed and a variety of other holy figures. Perhaps the best known footprint stone in Jerusalem is the one said to be that of Jesus in the octagonal Chapel of the Ascension located on the Mount of Olives (et-Tur), which has been pointed out there since the time of the Crusades but could date back to the earlier circular church there in the Byzantine period [note 6.11]. Entering the building, there is an oblong marble enclosure on the floor in which one is shown the impression of a right foot positioned towards the south in the rock. Baedeker's Guide states that: 'since the time of the Frankish domination this footprint has been so variously described, that it must have been frequently renewed since then' [note 6.12]. According to tradition, this church marks the spot where Jesus is said to have ascended to heaven (Luke 24:50–52). The Franciscan Bernardino Amico in the late sixteenth century made a plan of the chapel and indicated on it the exact position of the footprint. Amico wrote: '. . . on the pavement of the hard marble floor is impressed, as in wax, the print of our Saviour Jesus Christ, and these are the last vestiges he left on ascending into heaven . . . The other foot-print, according to hearsay, has been removed by the Moslems; and they keep it in their temple with much veneration, as also this one in the said Mount [i.e. the Chapel of the Ascension] which is also a mosque of theirs . . .' [note 6.13]. The second footprint was apparently removed *c.* 1200 to the Aqsa Mosque, where it was placed in the lower part of the southern wall, to the west of the *mihrab* (prayer niche) [note 6.14]. There were apparently a number of other sites on the Mount of Olives where footprints of Jesus were pointed out. In the mid-sixteenth century, for example, an anonymous Spanish Franciscan pilgrim described passing through the Kidron Valley at the foot of the mountain and seeing 'the marks of his feet imprinted on the rock' at a place where Jesus, captive and bound, was said to have fallen down 'being pushed by many'.

Wandering around the Topkapi Palace during my trip to Istanbul, I stumbled upon the aptly named Hall of Relics. I was actually hunting for the arm of John the Baptist (housed elsewhere), but was fascinated by two stone objects on display bearing the reputed footprints of Mohammed the Prophet [note 6.15]. The first is a slab of orange-brown stone with a highly polished exterior and on it the outline of a right foot, with the toes especially well delineated. The stone was cracked near the heel and a wire threaded through two mending holes holds the artefact together. The second stone has a print of the left foot and it seems to have been chiselled out of a dark black rock and covered with a reddish-yellow paint (with traces of an Arabic inscription). Glancing also very briefly at the hairs said to be from the beard of Mohammed and then at a casket said to contain dust from his tomb (I held my breath and tried not to sneeze), I eventually departed from the Hall of Relics and continued with my search for the arm of John the Baptist.

Numerous footprints of Mohammed are known throughout the Near East, and Tewfik Canaan, who was one of the most important ethnographers working in Palestine in the early twentieth century, refers to quite a few examples from Palestine; researchers are still using his scholarly works today. One section of his book entitled *Mohammedan Saints and Sanctuaries in Palestine* deals with the interesting subject of the imprints in solid rock of the feet and hands of Muslim saints (*weli*-singular, *awlia*-plural). Fifty per cent of these consisted of the imprints of feet, with smaller numbers of the hands, and even fewer numbers of the head, knees, or the whole body. Canaan mentions the following imprints said to be of Mohammed from Jerusalem: the twelve footprints (as well as an imprint of his head) on the rock (*sakhra*) beneath the Dome of the Rock on the Haram al-Sharif; a single footprint of Mohammed on a separate stone at the Dome of the Rock; a single footprint (thought to be of Mohammed) between the villages of Deir Ghassaneh and Ain ed-Deir; and another single footprint in the Haram al-Khalil in Hebron. Canaan also studied the local Palestinian traditions regarding the footprints of Abraham, Lot, Mary and Jesus. At Beit Jala (southwest of Jerusalem), locals told Canaan the following story about the imprint of the knees and hands of Mary seen at Bir Ono: Mary and the infant Jesus were passing along a road and, when wishing to quench their thirst at a water cistern, found that it was dry. Mary decided to pray: 'Become full, O well, so that the young child may drink!' When the cistern miraculously filled up to its brim from a subterranean source, Mary and Jesus bent down to drink and, in so doing, left impressions of their knees in the rock [note 6.16].

Based on my interpretation of the evidence being uncovered at the Suba cave dating from the first century AD, I reached the conclusion that the cave can only have been used for ritual bathing (*illustration 6.5*). The question that now needed to be asked was whether we could describe

6.5

it as a Jewish *miqweh*? At the time of John the Baptist and throughout the first century, the Jewish population in Palestine had a very distinctive practice of purification in water within ritual baths known as *miqwa'ot* (singular, *miqweh*; 'a gathering of waters'). This practice developed as a result of Jewish concerns about the possibility of contracting a state of ritual impurity (through contact with a corpse, semen, menstrual blood, and so forth). Such a contamination was deemed abhorrent, especially for those living within Jerusalem and in such a close proximity to the house of God at the Jewish Temple. Hence, there was an urgent desire to acquire the opposite state by immersing in water within a purposely built (or hewn) installation (a bath or a pool), so that the pollutions of the flesh might be removed on a regular basis.

The basis for our information about what was or was not permitted at that time appears in rabbinic sources: the tractates *Miqwa'ot* in the Mishna and Tosefta. There were stringent religious regulations (*halakhot*) in existence in regard to certain constructional details and how the installations were to be used. A *miqweh* had to be supplied with 'pure' water derived from natural sources throughout the year and even during the long dry season, and it had to contain a minimum of forty *seah* of water (the equivalent of less than one cubic metre) so that a person might be properly immersed (if not standing, then lying down). There was a possibility of adding drawn water, according to the sources, so long as the original amount of water did not decrease to below the minimum requirement of water. Hence, an additional body of water, known as the *osar* (the 'treasury') could be connected to the *miqweh*, and linked by pipe or channel. There was, of course, the problem of the water becoming dirty or stagnant (though not impure), but the *miqweh* was not used for daily ablutions for the purpose of keeping clean. Indeed, people appear to have washed themselves (or parts of their bodies, notably the feet and hands) before entering the ritual bath (M. *miqwa'ot* 9:2). The *miqweh* was required, according to the sources, to be sunken into the ground, either through construction or by the process of hewing into the rock, and into it natural water would flow derived from a spring or from surface rainwater in the winter seasons. There was, of course, the problem of silting (M. *miqwa'ot* 2:6). On the basis of archaeological finds we know that many of these installations had flights of steps leading down into them and extending across the entire breadth of the chamber. These ubiquitous steps, however, were not referred to in the sources (*illustration 6.6*) [note 6.17]. The walls of these chambers were plastered; ceilings were either natural rock or barrel-vaulted with

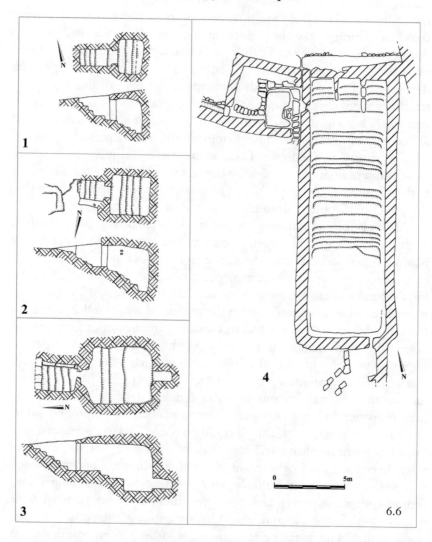

1

2

3

4

6.6

0   5m

masonry. I myself have recorded a number of *miqweh* installations during surveys around Jerusalem and have excavated others at Sataf (Sheikh Ubeid) to the south-west of Jerusalem and at Tell el-Ful (Gibeah of Saul) to the north-west of Jerusalem. Some *miqwa'ot* were small, especially in towns and cities, but larger installations are known, particularly close to highways, and they probably serviced pilgrims en route to the Jewish Temple in Jerusalem during the festival periods [note 6.18]. To accommodate the masses of pilgrims flocking up to Jerusalem, bath-houses and swimming pools were also used for ritual cleansing [note 6.19]. Large stepped *miqwa'ot* are known from the Qumran settlement of the sect of the Essenes [note 6.20].

The *miqweh* was also used for the purifying of contaminated vessels (e.g. M. *miqwa'ot* 2:9–10, 5:6, 6:1, 10:1; cf. Mark 7:4). It is not surprising, therefore, that in the excavation of *miqwa'ot* at Jericho and Jerusalem, some were found to contain quantities of ceramic vessels, perhaps abandoned during the process of cleansing. At Jericho, in one *miqweh*, located in the northern sector of the main Hasmonean palace, hundreds of intact ceramic vessels (mainly bowls) of the first century BC were found in a silt layer on the floor of one installation. This is what Netzer, the exacavator, had to say about it: 'In our view, this phenomenon has a simple and unambiguous explanation. During a prolonged period, perhaps even a decade, the pools were not cleaned . . . Over the years the silt carried by the influx was deposited on the bottom of the pools, and together with this accumulation of silt, the pools became a repository for ceramic vessels which fell into them from time to time' [note 6.21]. A large concentration of pottery was also found trapped beneath a collapse of ashlars in the lower part of a *miqweh*, dating to the first century BC, which was uncovered in the Jewish Quarter excavations in the Old City of Jerusalem. The concentration of pottery found there mainly consisted of an unspecified number of small bowls, mostly intact [note 6.22].

The fact that the cave at Suba was definitely being used for water ablutions of a ritual nature during the Early Roman period, as we had been able to ascertain during the excavation, indicates that it must also have been perceived of as a place which fitted the Jewish religious prescriptions of the time regarding *miqwa'ot*, or those approximating them. However, we had also reached the conclusion that the cave had been hewn and plastered many centuries before the Early Roman period, perhaps in the early Hellenistic period or earlier. For this reason, I believe that our Suba cave may actually have been a prototype and model (or one of them) for the appearance of *miqwa'ot* in Jerusalem and the Judean Hills during the first century BC. Indeed, hitherto, little was known about the origins of the *miqweh*, and it was suggested that in the earlier stages of this practice, Jews might have achieved a state of ritual purity by simply immersing themselves in various natural bodies of water, such as a spring, a river or a lake. Hence, some scholars have suggested that this kind of installation was an innovation of the Late Hellenistic period at the earliest and that it was the manifestation of the need for proper purification procedures which ultimately gave birth to the type of installation and not the other way round. Our discoveries at Suba may very well change this perception about the origins of the *miqweh*. It cannot be coincidental, in my opinion, that our cave bears all the hallmarks of the ritual purification pool, which later became so characteristic of the first century AD.

What do we know about how a *miqweh* was used in the first century AD? Ritual bathing was practised individually (i.e. no more than one person would enter the installation at a time), and it was done regularly and whenever deemed necessary. The purpose of the immersion was to ritually cleanse the flesh of the contaminated person in pure water. It was neither used for the cleansing of the soul nor for the redemption of sins, or for any other rituals (except for the conversion of proselytes following their acceptance of the Torah and circumcision: M. *pesahim* 8:8). One assumes that disrobing took place before the immersion and that new garments were put on immediately afterwards. Ritual bathing could be conducted in the comfort of one's own home, or indeed even in your palace if you had one (*plate 9b*), but there were also public *miqwa'ot* positioned close to the Temple in Jerusalem. Peasants and other workers (quarrymen or lime burners) could cleanse themselves in installations within farms or even at fairly isolated locations in the fields. The *miqweh* was not used for general cleaning and ablution purposes: this was done in alternative installations located within the house, or in a public bath-house instead. The fact that so many *miqwa'ot* are known in the landscapes of greater Jerusalem is a very clear reflection of the preoccupation that Jerusalemites had in the first century with the concept of separating and fixing the boundary between the pure and the impure. It is not surprising therefore that it should have been from this exact area that John the Baptist emerged with his firm ideas about purification and baptism.

It was like a breath of fresh air having Ronny Reich visit us one morning at the dig at the Suba cave. Ronny is one of the leading experts on the subject of Jewish ritual pools (*miqwa'ot*), having dug quite a few of them during his excavations in Jerusalem, and having written his doctoral thesis on the subject in 1990. So it was great to get the benefit of his opinion about the results of our work. The first comment he made on entering was that there could be no doubt that the features in the front part of the cave, namely the porch, the large entrance and the broad steps, resembled features known to him in *miqwa'ot* dating from the Early Roman period.

According to Ronny the use of the broad steps strongly suggested to him that the cave was used primarily for bathing purposes, otherwise, as he pointed out, the steps would only have hindered people trying to get to the water and the whole exercise would inevitably have become a labour-intensive activity. Also, the presence of stratified silts and living surfaces in the cave from the first century did not at all make sense in the context of a water reservoir. The fact that nobody had bothered to clear away the mud was also quite meaningful. Functioning reservoirs and cisterns were ordinarily cleaned out at least once a year (usually in late autumn and before the first rains) and the plaster on the walls was also renewed or repaired at that time. However, the phenomenon of silts gathering within a *miqweh* was referred to quite clearly in rabbinic texts. For instance, in reference to the minimum quantity of water required in a *miqweh* for it to be ritually permissible, we hear that: 'if the mud was scraped up [from the pool and heaped] by the sides, and three *logs* of water drained down therein, it remains valid [for cleansing purposes]; but if the mud was removed away [from the pool] and three *logs* rained down therefrom [into the pool] it becomes invalid' (M. *miqwa'ot* 2:6). Elsewhere, we are told of certain damming operations that were made inside the *miqweh*: 'if the water of an immersion pool was too shallow it may be dammed [to one side] even with bundles of sticks or reeds, that the level of water may be raised, and so he may go down and immerse himself' (M. *miqwa'ot* 7:7). It is quite possible that the water source at the back of our cave was also edged in this fashion, to ensure access to the water during the immersion procedures.

In the Early Roman period, between the late first century BC and the early second century AD, a religious sect took over the cave at Suba and practised baptism rites and foot-anointing there. This was quite clear from the archaeological finds. Because of the very specific character of these activities (combined with the later Byzantine tradition about the cave), it is likely that it was John the Baptist himself who initiated the baptism procedures at the cave in the early first century AD. On the floors of the cave we found a variety of installations testifying to the fact that certain rituals accompanied the water-immersion activities there. To understand this further, I felt it imperative that I make a study of the rituals of baptism as performed by John the Baptist during his sojourn in the lower Jordan Valley. So much has been written about John's baptism of Jesus, but, at the same time, very little is actually known about the specifics of that event [note 6.23]. The key matter which I shall be addressing here is whether or not there is sufficient evidence to reconstruct the *tangible* aspects of the ceremony of baptism as performed by

John at the Jordan. If so, then we might have something to compare with the archaeological finds from the cave at Suba.

In the gospels we hear that John came to the 'wilderness' region of the lower Jordan River and 'preached the baptism of repentance unto remission of sins' (Mark 1:4; cf. Luke 3:3). One may ask why John went to the Jordan River in the first place. After all, this region was inhospitable and also at some distance from the population to whom John ultimately wanted to preach. The answer to this is, as I suggested in the previous chapter, that John deliberately went to the Jordan River to prepare for the return of Elijah. John was not seeking ascetic seclusion for himself at the Jordan River but clearly wanted to attract to him as many people as possible. The events at the Jordan River would have taken place not at the beginning of his mission but at its end, i.e. John had already previously established a strong reputation for himself as the 'Baptiser' in the region of Jerusalem and in the hills of Judah. His activities in the Jerusalem hills may actually have been spread out over many years, whereas the time he spent at the Jordan may have been fairly limited. Hence, John's purpose at the Jordan was to preach, to call on the people of Israel to repent their sins, to be baptised by him and then to prepare the way for the coming of Elijah and to hasten the arrival of the Kingdom of God. The belief that John was the forerunner of Elijah is what ultimately attracted people to make the long journey to the isolated region of the Jordan River in the first place, rather than his baptising activity, even though this was the main aspect of the ceremony he performed there. The fact that John was known as the 'Baptist' (or 'Baptiser') rather than as 'prophet' means that he was better known for the lustrations he performed than for his preaching/teaching and exhortation/instruction.

In keeping with his role as Elisha awaiting the return of Elijah, John would have adhered to the general concept of ritual cleansing with water going back to the time of the Israelite prophets (e.g. Ezekiel 36:25: 'Then will I sprinkle clean water upon you, and ye shall be clean: from all your filthiness, and from all your idols, will I cleanse you.') and especially would have identified with the symbolism of the waters of the deluge having rid the world of sin, and with the concept of the 'crossing' of the Israelites from Egyptian bondage across the Red Sea and then later across the Jordan River into the Promised Land. Indeed, it is quite possible that John would have modelled himself on the cleansing procedure advocated by the prophet Elisha at the Jordan River for Na'aman the Leper (2 Kings 5: 10–14). This procedure included three

1a. General view of the terraced hills west of Jerusalem.

1b. The entrance to the cave after excavation.

2a. The interior of the cave at the beginning of the excavations.

(*Left*) 2b. The incised drawing of John the Baptist on the wall of the cave.

(*Below*) 2c. Excavations in progress in the cave at an early stage of the work. The man wielding the pick is Professor James Tabor.

(*Above*) 3a. Climbing a ladder in the stepped porch area of the cave.

(*Below*) 3b. Digging in 'bedrock city' on the ridge above the cave.

4a. The Church of the Visitation (Mar Zacharias) from the gateway to the compound, Ain Karim.
4b. Photograph taken between 1885 and 1897 at Mar Zacharias (with the 'upper' medieval chapel on the right) towards the Russian Church of St John. (PEF/Schick/126/2.)

(*Left*) 4c. Vaulted chamber in the 'lower' chapel of the Church of the Visitation.

(*Below*) 4d. The 'Rock of the Hiding' at the Church of the Visitation.

5a. Suba cave: arm and cross on western wall of cave.

(*Above*) 5b. Suba cave: head on eastern wall of cave.

(*Right*) 5c. Suba cave: staff and serpents.

(*Left*) 6a. Ain el-Habis: View of the monastery (above) and the entrance to the Cave of John the Baptist.

(*Above*) 6b. Ain el-Habis: The Chapel or Tomb of Elizabeth: south-west corner of Crusader tower, with the entrance to the chapel on the right.

6c. Ain el-Habis: altar above 'bed' of John the Baptist.

6d. Ain el-Habis: the Chapel or Tomb of Elizabeth: the tomb is visible in the sunken area at the east end of the chapel.

7a. The so-called 'Tomb of Absalom' in the Kidron Valley in Jerusalem. Above the entrance is an inscription in Greek indicating that this was the tomb of Zachariah, father of John the Baptist.

(*Below*) 7b. Egon Lass taking samples inside the cave.

7c. Egon Lass and Reuven Kalifon dismantling the mass of collapsed plaster.

8a. Circle of stones from one of the Early Roman living surfaces.

8b. Section across the fills excavated in the cave, showing the accumulation of layers from the different periods.

9a. The 'Footstep' stone beneath the 'Altar' stone.

9b. View of entrance to ritual bath (miqweh) at Machaerus.

9c. The Greek Orthodox Patriarch Irineos (centre), between two bishops, during a visit to the cave.

10a. Eastern basin with floor and fireplace from the Iron Age II period.

10b. The stepped porch in front of the entrance to the cave.

10c. Shattered Hellenistic pottery on the floor of the cave.

11a. Qasr el–Yehud from the north–east.

11b. The Epiphany ceremonies at the Jordan River in progress.

(*Above*) 12a. Tell el–Kharrar: the 'Cave of John the Baptist'.
The skull was found in a pit in the foreground of the picture.
(*Below*) 12b. Tell el–Kharrar: Roman pool.

3a. Machaerus: general view of portico surrounding courtyard (the columns have been reconstructed).

13b. Machaerus: caldarium of bathhouse.

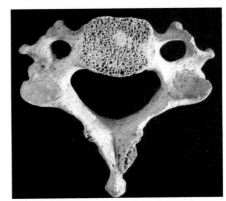

13c. Horvat Ethri: a cervical vertebra with clear evidence of decapitation.

14a. Steps leading down to the Tomb of John the Baptist.

14b. The underground Tomb of John the Baptist. Note the 'pigeon-holes' leading to the *loculi*-graves and the barrel-vaulted ceiling.

14c. Arched alcove which was probably the place of the tomb of John the Baptist with the basalt door in the foreground.

15a. The interior of the Cathedral, looking south-west. Note the door (left) connecting the cathedral with the cloisters (?) further south (see No. 66 in illustration 9.18). On the right is the chapel (right).

15b. A crown of relics from the Church of John the Baptist (Muristan) in Jerusalem. (Photograph by John Garstang from the 1920s courtesy of the Palestine Exploration Fund, London).

15d. The façade of the Church of John the Baptist (Muristan) in Jerusalem.

15c. Façade of Crusader Cathedral of St John at Sebaste.

16a. Two reliquaries (centre and right) containing relic fingers of John the Baptist in the Museo dell' Opera del Duomo, Florence.

(*Below and bottom right*)16b & d. Reliquaries containing a relic finger of John the Baptist in the Museo dell' Opera del Duomo, Florence

16c. Stand with a painting of the head of St John on a platter and with skull relics within the circular depression on the right. Church of John the Baptist (Muristan) in Jerusalem.

activities: first, standing on the bank of the Jordan and calling on the Divine name; second, the prophet striking his (right) hand over the place of the immersion; third, helping with the bathing process, with the person being dipped seven times into the Jordan River.

As a Jew from a priestly background, John's baptism procedures must have had their origins in the common practice of Jewish ritual immersion in *miqwa'ot,* which, as we have seen, was undertaken for the purpose of the purification of the flesh of the body from ritual uncleanness. However, there was much more to John's baptism procedures than just immersion to remove pollution, otherwise he would not have acquired the reputation that he definitely had. As opposed to normal Jewish immersion procedures, which were carried out whenever a person was deemed to have been contaminated with pollution or needing purification (i.e. before prayers), John's procedure would appear to have been a one-off event, which means that people went to the Jordan to be immersed and then after this event of purification returned home to await the coming of Elijah (or of the Messiah).

What is not stated in the sources, however, is that John would most likely have exhorted those who came to him to maintain their purity thereafter by frequent immersions in their *miqwa'ot* back home. John's baptism also appears to have been a group activity, unlike the individual immersions common at that time. Hence, there can be no doubt that John's baptism was distinctive and that it was intrinsically linked to the preparation for future events, as is clear from John 3:25: 'then there arose a question between some of John's disciples and the Jews about purifying . . .' Judging by the sources available to us, namely Josephus and the gospels, it would appear that John's baptism procedure was a kind of initiation by purification, but one which only occurred after a person had undergone repentance (with a confession of sins) and regeneration.

In a way, this procedure resembles the order of events during the Jewish conversion process at that time: the proselyte was immersed in a *miqweh,* but only after he had first accepted the Torah holy writings and had undergone circumcision [note 6.24]. John's arrangements at the Jordan site were not exclusive to a select band of chosen followers. On the contrary, judging by Josephus (*Antiquities* XVIII, 116–119), John was there for *all* of the people of Israel.

By comparison, the sect of the Essenes at nearby Qumran – with which some scholars believe (incorrectly) that John was connected to at an earlier stage of his life – practised exclusivity and the goal of their immersion process was simply to maintain the ritual purity and sanctity of their community [note 6.25]. Those who were immersed were members of the community or initiates who were taking part in the induction process into the fold. Immersion among the Essenes was an individual activity and only differed from normal Jewish practices in the sense that the person wishing to be purified had first to adopt a pious and repentant attitude (resembling John's call for repentance): 'It is by the holy spirit uniting him to his truth that he can be cleansed from all his iniquities . . . It is by humbling his soul to all God's statutes that his flesh can be cleansed by sprinkling with waters of purification and by sanctifying himself with waters of purity' (1QS 3, 7–9). Clearly, one may understand this as reflecting a belief that external purification with water was only effective if it were connected with the concept of the inner being having been made ready for the divine holy spirit [note 6.26].

An important source of information about John's baptism procedure appears in the writings of Josephus (*Antiquities* XVIII, 116–19; see the Appendix in this book). The passage is very important because it represents the general view that must have existed in first-century Palestine in regard to the uniqueness of John's baptism (βάπτισμα) as opposed to the normal Jewish ritual cleansing practices of that time. What emerges from Josephus' description is that there were two main activities relating to the procedure of John's baptism. People first gathered to listen to him and subsequently he asked them to lead righteous lives, both towards each other and towards God. This part of the ceremony included the cleansing of souls and the purging of sins. Only those who had completed this part of the procedure were then allowed to proceed to the next step, which was to immerse in water in order to purify their flesh from pollutants in the normal fashion of that time.

The principal source of information that we have regarding John's baptism of Jesus is in Mark (1:9–11): 'And it came to pass in those days, that Jesus came from Nazareth in Galilee, and was baptised of John in the Jordan. And straightaway coming up out of the water, he saw the heavens rent asunder, and the Spirit as a dove descending upon him: and a voice came out of the heavens, Thou art my beloved son . . .' We may assume the authenticity of this passage simply because it was such a terrible embarrassment to the early followers of Jesus. The assumption underlying this passage is that Jesus, in having accepted baptism from John, must have beforehand also repented of his sins (Mark 1:4). This concept was so irksome to the other Gospel writers that a conversation between John and Jesus was inserted into Matthew (3:13–17) and the material was heavily edited in Luke (3:21–22) to make it quite clear to the reader that Jesus was without sin and could not in any way have been a subordinate of John. The second point of interest in the passage from Mark is that the descent of the dove (representing the *shekhina* – the divine presence) and the sound of the voice from the heavens (*bath kol*), both occur only *after* Jesus came out of the water. I think we may assume that the voice from the heavens was something quite specific to the Jesus story, but, at the same time, there may very well have been some expectation among those who gathered to be baptised by John that they too would experience the descent of the holy spirit on them.

By combining bits of information taken from 2 Kings (5: 10–14), Josephus (*Antiquities* XVIII, 116–19) and Mark (1:9–11), and by using some common sense, we may reconstruct a tentative picture of the process of baptism as practised by John at the Jordan River. Crowds of people gathered there to listen to his teachings or exhortations. Since they are said to have come from Jerusalem and the central hilly country (Mark 1:4), we must assume some temporary shelters were set up at the site as accommodation. Fasting may very well have occurred before the ceremony (cf. Mark 2:3). The whole procedure would have been monitored and organised by John's followers. John then spoke to those gathered there, asking them to lead righteous and pious lives. He may have devised a set of prayers that were read by his disciples (cf. Luke 11:1). Subsequently, the souls of the people gathered there were cleansed and there was a remission of sins. How this was practically done is not made clear, but it may have been performed with the sprinkling of some water or by calling on the divine name. In any case, this stage of the ceremony took place immediately before the immersion. Only those who had completed this part of the procedure were then allowed to proceed on to the next step. Standing on the bank of the Jordan River, John would have called on the divine name and would have raised his right hand in blessing over the place of the immersion, perhaps also pouring libations (cf. Josephus, *Jewish War*, IV: 460–5). The people who gathered there then immersed themselves in the river, dipping themselves seven times in the water, in order to purify the flesh of their bodies from contamination. On emerging from the water, John would have called again on the divine name and asking for the holy spirit (the *shekhina*) to descend upon the crowd. The ceremony may have ended with doves (symbols of the special relationship between God and the Chosen People) being let loose from cages [note 6.27].

There is no evidence that Jesus himself did any baptising following the death of John, but a short time before this occurred we do hear that Jesus was baptising with his disciples in the hill country near Jerusalem (John 3:22; contradicted slightly in 4:2) [note 6.28]. Jesus could have baptised in a cave such as the one at Suba and he may very well have been sent there as a protégé of John to gain experience in the procedures of baptism and to continue spreading the word about his teachings. The Suba cave was in the hinterland of John's birthplace at Ain Karim and, as I have already pointed out, it is conceivable that John originally used it for baptism purposes before he descended to the Jordan River.

On the basis of the suggested baptism procedure at the Jordan River, how might this procedure have been undertaken at the Suba cave itself? Since the cave was located at some distance from a town or village, there would have been ample space for people to gather near the entrance to the cave and to listen to his teachings. Entering the cave, John would have asked those gathered there to lead righteous and pious lives and this may have been accompanied with the reading of prayers. The cleansing of the souls and the remission of their sins then followed this. This part of the procedure would have taken place on the living surface with the stone installations in the front part of the cave. Continuing to the back of the cave and standing at the edge of the water, John would have called on the divine name and would have raised his right hand in blessing. Finally, people would have begun immersing themselves in the water, dipping seven times, and then as they came out John would have called for the holy spirit to descend upon the purified. Later, a foot-anointing ritual, involving the use of oil, was undertaken in the front of the cave. Perhaps it signified that initiates, after having been baptised, were ready to set out on the journey towards the 'great and dreadful day of the Lord' (Malachi 4:5).

Following the death of Jesus, his followers settled in Jerusalem and its vicinity. These followers included his disciples and the community leaders, consisting of Simon-Peter and James the Just, the brother (or half-brother) of Jesus. They encountered persecution at the hands of the Jewish population in Jerusalem (who called them the *minim*, i.e. apostates), with Stephen, one of the members of the community, being stoned to death and becoming the first of the Christian martyrs. Basically, these Judaeo-Christians regarded themselves as Jews in their general way of life and observance of Jewish customs. They decided to abandon Jerusalem (*c.* AD 66) on the eve of the revolt against the Romans and subsequently made their way to Pella in Transjordan. This event may have allowed the followers of John to consolidate their position in the surroundings of Jerusalem. Indeed, in the Suba cave there is evidence of a continued presence there until the early second century. According to Eusebius, the followers of Jesus returned to the environs of Jerusalem following the destruction of the city in AD 70 (we know the names of the officiating bishops at that time) and remained until AD 135. Under Hadrian, direct access to the city was no longer possible to Jews, even those professing a belief in Jesus, but gentile Christians were allowed into the Roman city (newly named as Aelia Capitolina) and they even had serving bishops there. Hitherto, very little has been found in the archaeological record in the region of Palestine, which could be associated with Judaeo-Christians or the gentile followers of Jesus. Excavations beneath a fifth-century church at Capernaum brought to light the remains of a structure which, it was suggested, might have been an early house of prayer (*domus ecclesiae*) from the early centuries identified as the 'House of Peter', though this interpretation has been strongly criticised [note 6.29]. As one scholar, Yoram Tsafrir, has stated: 'The lack of Christian finds from Palestine before the fourth century does not point to the absence of Christians in the country, but, rather, to the inability of archaeology to identify their remains' [note 6.30].

In the Acts of the Apostles we hear about three different kinds of baptism practices which were undertaken by the followers of Jesus after his death. The first was undertaken in the normal Jewish fashion with immersion in water and it differed only in that it was accompanied by 'miracles and signs' and was without the descent of the holy spirit (Acts 8:13, 16): 'for as yet he [the holy spirit] was fallen upon none of them: only they were baptised [by Philip] in the name of the Lord Jesus.' The second kind of baptism included both the immersion in the water and the descent of the holy spirit. The story of Philip and the Ethiopian eunuch, from about AD 33, is quite revealing in this respect (Acts 8:36–39). On reaching 'a certain water' (which may have been a *miqweh*) the eunuch asks Philip: 'See, here is water; what doth hinder me to be baptised?' Upon proclaiming his belief in Jesus, the eunuch, who is accompanied by Philip, 'went down both into the water'. The next stage after 'they were come up out of the water' was the descent of the 'spirit of the Lord'. The third kind of baptism was performed by the Apostles themselves on individuals who had already previously been immersed and it involved (not necessarily in any given order) the laying-on of hands, the 'giving' of the holy spirit and also the overseeing of the act of repentance (Acts 8:17) [note 6.31].

An interesting passage exists in Acts relating to an Alexandrian Jew who was active in Ephesus at the same time as Paul (Acts 18:24–25). It confirms that John's baptism was still regarded as distinctive: 'And a certain Jew named Apollos, born at Alexandria, an eloquent man and mighty in the scriptures, came to Ephesus. This man was instructed in the way of the Lord; and being fervent in the spirit, he spake and taught diligently the things of the Lord, knowing only the baptism of John.' The next chapter in Acts (19:1–6) is enlightening in regard to the differing baptism procedures that Paul discovered when he arrived at Ephesus: 'He said unto them [the disciples of Apollos?], Have ye received the Holy Ghost since ye believed? And they said unto him, We have not so much as heard whether there be any Holy Ghost. And he said unto them, Unto what then were ye baptised? And they said, Unto John's baptism. Then said Paul, John verily baptised with the baptism of repentance, saying unto the people, that they should believe on him which should come after him, that is, on Christ Jesus. When they heard this, they were baptised in the name of the Lord Jesus. And when Paul had laid his hands upon them, the Holy Ghost came on them; and they spake with tongues, and prophesied.' This passage makes it clear that there were elements in John's baptism that differed from those practised by the followers of Jesus (i.e. the Apostles' baptism). John did not use the laying-on-of-hands in his ceremony, and nor was there any speaking in tongues. In the baptism of the Apostles the holy spirit was said to descend in the name of Jesus Christ. Indeed, in Mark (1:8), John says: 'I indeed have baptised you with water, but he [Jesus] shall baptise you with the Holy Ghost.'

The exact nature of the relationship between Jesus and John has intrigued many readers of the gospels [note 6.32]. The only point of contact mentioned was at the baptism at the Jordan River and even there Jesus was only part of a multitude of people. Strange as it may seem, the impression is that they hardly knew each other, even though Jesus probably stayed on as a follower of John after the baptism. The Gospel writers laboured hard to reflect John's support and recognition of Jesus. John was regarded as one of the leading prophetic figures of his generation and Jesus needed his stamp of approval so that later on he could press forward with his own mission. Apart from the clear respect that Jesus extends to John, there are also other strands of information in the Gospels suggesting tension between the two men, and there was undoubtedly vocal conflict between the followers of the two individuals as well. The fact that the only source of information about the relationship between the two men is in the Gospels (Josephus does not go into the subject at all) is complicated by the fact that the Gospel writers were clearly at pains to try to emphasise John's subordination to Jesus and this definitely must have led to biases in their accounts.

I think there cannot be any doubt that Jesus did actually go down to the Jordan River and that he did undergo the process of baptism. But why would Jesus have wanted to be baptised? Indeed, in the later second-century Gospel of the Nazoraeans, Jesus is stated to question the necessity of being baptised since he had not sinned [note 6.33]. On the matter of the kinship between the two we do have the testimony given in Luke (1:36) and one scholar has suggested that Jesus might even have met with John while on a pilgrimage to the Jewish festivities in Jerusalem, which is an interesting proposal but there is no evidence for this [note 6.34]. What is clear is that news of John's prophetic activities did eventually reach the ears of Jesus in the Galilee and that acting on this information he made the four-day trip to the Jordan Valley to participate in the baptism ceremonies being performed there. He must have been intrigued by what he heard and saw. Notwithstanding matters of kinship, Luke (3:21) makes it clear that Jesus was only one of many people being baptised there and that he was given no preferential treatment. In the account of the baptism in Mark (1:11; cf. Matthew 3:17), Jesus, on coming out of the water after the immersion procedure, hears a voice from Heaven (*bath kol*) which proclaims him to be the 'beloved son'. This may have been a crucial personal experience for Jesus, but neither John nor those baptised with him seem to have been aware of it. Indeed, had the knowledge of the importance of Jesus been publicly revealed at that time (as is implied in Matthew 3: 14–15), then surely John would have proclaimed the fact and thereafter all of his followers would have followed Jesus. But this is not the case and the mission of Jesus really only began *after* the death of John.

The next point one needs to give some thought to is the length of time that Jesus stayed at the Jordan with John's followers. Most of the multitude who came to be baptised at the Jordan immediately returned home or went somewhere else. However, on the basis of John 3:26, it would appear that Jesus spent some time at the Jordan. Hence, we may conclude that John took him on as an apprentice baptiser and that being kin may actually have helped him in this regard. The fact that Jesus was later baptising (near Jerusalem) in parallel to John (at Aenon) suggests that John intentionally sent his followers to different parts of the country to help spread word of his teachings and to baptise in his name. The followers may have been divided up into roving bands with their own leaders (John 3:22; 4:2).

How long did Jesus stay at the Jordan River? We cannot know for certain, but, in any case, his sojourn there was sufficiently long to impress his character upon some of John's followers, resulting in two of them deciding to follow him (but perhaps while he was still only the leader of one of John's bands). One of these was Andrew, brother of Simon (later called Peter) (John 1:35, 40). His other disciples were Simon, Philip, Nathanael and a further unnamed individual (John 1:41, 44–45). It is quite probable that at some point Jesus began asserting his own views and ideas about matters of religious practice and purification (John 3:25; cf. Mark 2:18). John, on hearing that Jesus was not keeping to the exact form of his teachings, may have disapproved. It was perhaps at this stage that Jesus revealed to his followers and others the profound experience that had changed his life while at the Jordan. This is perhaps reflected in the polemic held between Jesus, priests, lawyers and elders, in regard to the substance of John's baptism and whether it was of divine or human origin (Mark 11:30–32; Matt. 21:25–26; Luke 20:4–6).

Of great concern to the gospel writers was that John should recognise the authority of Jesus. Hence, Matthew (3:14) has John remonstrating with Jesus at the site of the baptism: 'and John would have hindered him, saying, I have need to be baptised of thee, and comest thou to me?' While Herod Antipas at Machaerus imprisoned John, he was extended certain privileges, including access to his followers, and they told him about Jesus' new activities (Matthew 11:2–4; Luke 7:18–20). Two of these he sent to Jesus to enquire whether he was 'the one who is come' or there might still be another (ἕτερον which would strictly mean 'a second' or 'one quite different'; cf. ἄλλον, 'another', in Luke 7:19). On face value, this question would seem strange if one were to accept that the recognition of Jesus had already taken place at the time of the baptism. For this reason, quite a few scholars have advocated its historicity. My own interpretation is that it reflects John's impatience or anger towards Jesus, which had been growing since Jesus had turned away from John's teachings and ushered in his own religious practices and teachings. One of the most serious causes for this disillusionment was the fact that Jesus showed little interest in baptising, to such an extent that he frequently came into contact with menstrual emissions, corpses, lepers and unclean spirits, and was not particularly concerned with adherence to the basic Jewish laws regarding washing before food. The point that John tried to make was: here I am cooped up in Herod's prison and facing possible death, and meanwhile all I hear is that you are not following my teachings, you are not preparing for the coming of Elijah, and you are dabbling in 'signs and wonders' (healing and exorcising) instead. Jesus seems to have been a disappointment to John, but the Gospel writers managed to gloss over this by suggesting that John did eventually realise that Jesus was the intended one after all.

So who were the people who were using the Suba cave in the Early Roman period? Clearly, nobody lives inside a water reservoir unless there is good reason for doing so. I can think of at least three groups of people who might have wanted to use the cave as a shelter during the Early Roman period: (1) farmers, (2) rebels/refugees or bandits, and (3) members of a religious sect. Since the cave is located in a fertile valley with good cultivable soil, it would have been an ideal temporary shelter for local farmers during the harvest seasons, and a storage space for their agricultural produce. However, the strange stone installations that were found on the living surfaces and the unusual stone with the hollowed footprint are not the sort of features that would be consistent had the occupants of the cave been farmers. The absence of botanical remains of agricultural produce is also an important consideration. Another factor that goes against the cave having been used by farmers are the enormous quantities of pottery that were found in the cave, which were certainly far beyond their limited needs; also the fact that jugs dominated the pottery assemblage rather than storage jars (as one would have expected) is significant and does not support the cave having been used as a storage area. If the intention of the farmer had been to use the cave solely as a source of water, then one would expect that some attempt would have been made to clean it out and to re-plaster the walls. Having excavated numerous agricultural sites from this period in different regions of Israel and knowing the sort of sparse remains that are usually left behind, I find it highly unlikely that peasants were the actual occupants of this cave in the first century.

The second possibility is that the cave was used by rebels and refugees or by bandits as a hiding place from the Romans. Once again, there are no archaeological remains of purely domestic activities in the cave, as one should expect, such as fireplaces, ovens and stone beds. Indeed, the excavation of quite a few hiding tunnel complexes in the hills of Judah and in the lowlands of the Shephelah dating from the early second century have shown how adaptable and motivated the Jews usually were in such difficult surroundings: hewing chambers, building walls and making arrangement for all the domestic amenities necessary [note

6.35]. Hence, it is highly unlikely that refugees made the strange installations on the surfaces or the footprint stone. The presence of very large quantities of pottery in the cave is also not at all consistent with the lifestyle of fleeing refugees or rebels, who would normally take along with them their most valuable of objects, such as money, documents and deeds, jewellery, metal and glass vessels, and so forth; this is the picture that has emerged from the excavation of refuge caves in the Judaean Desert [note 6.36]. Moreover, the living surfaces unearthed in our cave testify to their use over an extended period of time (late first century BC to early second century AD), which does not fit in with what we know about the short time periods that the Jewish people were in a state of rebellion against the Roman authorities and army, i.e. during the years of the First Revolt (AD 66–70) and the Second Revolt (AD 132–135).

The most convincing explanation for such Early Roman-period remains is that they reflect the activities of a religious sect who used the space to conduct rituals that were associated with water-purification rites. The lack of domestic amenities in the cave makes it unlikely that people lived there. They would probably only have gathered at the cave for ritual purposes, or whenever it was deemed necessary. Pure water would have collected within the cave by natural means during the winter months, flowing across the living surfaces in the front and centre of the cave and eventually pooling at the back of the interior. Those who came to the cave brought with them large quantities of pottery and left most of it (if not all of it) behind. Since not one vessel was found intact, this suggests that vessels were broken intentionally. Jugs, along with smaller quantities of jars and cooking pots, dominated the pottery retrieved from every single living surface. This extraordinary quantity of one-handled jugs, which is out of all proportion to the percentage of such vessels that are known from other excavated sites, strongly indicates that they had a very important role in the water rituals carried out in the cave.

The size of the cave, the very large quantity of pottery found there, the presence of numerous installations on the living surfaces, suggests that many people were using the cave at the same time. Access to the cave was via a stepped porch and through a large entrance, with further steps extending into the cave; with the build-up of the living surfaces, the lower steps immediately within the cave slowly disappeared. The fact that lamps were not represented in the pottery assemblage means that the only light in the cave was the natural light that poured through the large entrance; the resulting semi-darkness, we can imagine, would certainly have heightened the expectations of those entering the cave. In the late winter and early spring, the entire area in the cave was probably still quite muddy, which would explain why some of the living surfaces were consolidated with layers of small stones and marl, to make sure that nobody fell and broke their necks while crossing the surfaces towards the water at the back of the cave. The niche in the east wall of the cave, just within the entrance, would have made an ideal space for the placing of clothes after disrobing. In the summer months there is a constant temperature of 26 degrees centigrade in the cave, which is quite pleasant when there are soaring temperatures outside. The circular installations must have been connected with the people crossing this area towards the source of water. The fact that crushed potsherds were found in two of them suggests that they were used for holding ceramic vessels. On the earliest of the living surfaces, a pathway bordered by rows of stones was found leading across the area to the back of the cave. In the summer and early autumn months, owing to the heat and evaporation, the level of the water at the back of the cave would slowly have dropped, making it increasingly difficult for any person wanting to immerse themselves in it. This may explain the prevalence of jugs in the cave: these would have been very handy for the pouring of water from the depleted waters at the back of the cave. Close to the front of the cave was the stone with the hollowed-out shape of a foot in its upper surface, which clearly as we have seen had some ritual function. The size and weight of the stone also implies that it had been deliberately brought into the cave. In the later living surfaces, alternative stones with hollowed-out circular areas came to be used instead.

It seems likely that the water baptism rituals performed in the cave were the common denominator of the rituals undertaken by the people who came to the cave. This was not a solitary exercise and the archaeological features suggest that groups of people who gathered at the cave came together to experience ritual immersion in water and to undergo other rites together, including the anointing of feet with oil. This differed considerably from the Jewish practice of that time of daily immersion on an individual basis in a small stepped pool (*miqweh*) located within the basements of private homes or alongside farmsteads. The Suba cave was positioned at the right distance from nearby settlements: close enough for access but distant enough for it to have served as a place where people in the company of others could undergo the experience of ritual self-discovery associated with baptism in water far away from the hullabaloo of daily life.

There is no evidence that anybody actually lived at the cave. It stands to reason that the ritual activities performed in the Suba cave must have been undertaken by a person with a great amount of charisma and the respect of many, and why not John the Baptist? After all, the cave is located not far west of his reputed hometown at Ain Karim, and there must have been places where he went to try out his ideas about baptism. Where better than in a cave that was linked to ritual water-cleansing practices extending back in time and linking John to his Israelite fore-bears? The water-ritual activities in the cave went on for more than one hundred years, and judging by the archaeological finds, hardly any changes were made to the manner in which these activities were undertaken in the cave. It seems to me that it was no coincidence that monks in the Byzantine period chose to celebrate and worship John the Baptist in exactly the same spot that was used for ritual baptism by an unusual Jewish sect from the time of John the Baptist himself. One may speculate that the monks came to this cave precisely because it was known locally as the 'Cave of John the Baptist'. I am a firm believer in the concept of the longevity of collective memory and in the power of oral tradition, and the fact that Byzantine textual sources do not appear to mention the cave does not mean that these traditions did not exist, but that they were simply left unrecorded [note 6.37]. For this reason, I think we may assume an association between this cave and John the Baptist from the first century AD and through the centuries until Byzantine times. In archaeological terms, sporadic pottery finds were indeed found in the cave bridging the Early Roman and Byzantine periods. Hence, the tradition connecting John the Baptist to this cave was probably passed on from century to century until the Byzantine period and then was maintained there to the early Islamic period, and as late as the eleventh century or thereabouts. I have already mentioned that a cave of John the Baptist existed somewhere in the mountains of Palestine, and is mentioned in an account by Adomnan from AD 685 about the travels of Bishop Arculf: 'This Arculf saw a clear spring in the desert. Its stone roof is covered with lime plaster. The Evangelists write that John Baptist's "food was locusts and wild honey" [Matthew 3:4], and in the desert where John used to live, our friend Arculf saw locusts of an extremely small type.' This might very well be a description of our cave but the lack of any specific topographical indicator in Adomnan renders his description suggestive but nothing more [note 6.38].

Assuming that this was a cave used by John the Baptist himself, are there any references to this place in the Gospels? Unfortunately, there are none, or at least none referring specifically to John the Baptist, but this is not surprising since the Gospel accounts were more interested in highlighting the role John played in the baptism of Jesus and were not particularly interested in delving into the details of his early life and the various places where he would have preached and baptised as a young adult. However, there is one possible reference to our cave in a brief passage about Jesus during a sojourn in the countryside around Jerusalem. We are told that this occurred after Jesus had been baptised by John at Bethabara (John 1:28), where he had been joined by two of John's disciples (John 1:37). Later that same year, Jesus was in Jerusalem to attend Passover (John 2:23). Immediately following this, he and his two new disciples went to baptise in the hills nearby: 'After these things [in Jerusalem] came Jesus and his disciples into the land of Judaea; and there he tarried with them, and baptised' (John 3:22). Where exactly were these baptism activities undertaken? Had the reference been to the Jordan River then this would have been clearly specified, but this was not the case. Indeed, we are also told in tangent that: 'John also was baptising at Aenon near Salim . . .' (John 3:23) and the point that was being made was that John (and Jesus) were not at the usual spot along the lower Jordan River but were both at two entirely different spots altogether. It seems unlikely that Jesus would have dared to take over baptism activities at sites along the Jordan River so soon after having been baptised by John, since this was definitely regarded as John's territory and it would easily have been interpreted as an act of defiance against his authority.

If, however, as I believe, John regarded Jesus as one of his protégés, he might very well have sent Jesus intentionally to visit the scene of his early baptism activities and especially in Jerusalem and close to his hometown (Ain Karim), and our Suba cave was just that place. In another passage we hear that 'when therefore the Lord knew how the Pharisees had heard that Jesus made and baptised more disciples than John (though Jesus himself baptised not, but his disciples), He left Judea, and departed into Galilee' (John 4:1–3). On his way to the Galilee we are told that Jesus passed through Samaria, which would make sense if he was travelling from Jerusalem northwards along the watershed route. Many scholars have found the interpretation of the meaning behind these apparent baptism activities by Jesus in the hills of Jerusalem a complicated matter. Clearly, the words 'though Jesus himself baptised not, but his disciples' must be a later gloss, inserted because it was probably seen to be odd that Jesus was acting as a baptiser himself when his mission had already been revealed to him when he was baptised by John. Farrar wrote about this difficult baptism episode: 'Theologians have sought for all kinds of subtle and profound explanations of this baptism by the disciples. Nothing, however, that has been suggested throws any further light upon the subject, and we can only believe that Jesus permitted for a time this simple and beautiful rite as a sign of discipleship . . .' [note 6.39].

7

The Original Shape and Function of the Cave

S ometimes the most interesting archaeological finds are made at the end of a dig. In our case interesting finds were made at the Suba cave at almost every stage of the project, with the discovery of Byzantine-period wall drawings at the beginning of the work; the evidence of Early Roman baptism rituals appearing halfway through the work, and the exciting discovery of Iron Age pottery right at the end of the dig. I was running around Jerusalem sorting out the latter-stage administrative logistics when I received a cellphone call from Rafi. In a breathless voice, he told me: 'Egon and I have just found Iron Age pottery inside the settling basin next to the entrance to the cave. This means our cave is far more ancient than we thought it was, doesn't it?'

Perched on the steps of the cave I spent a lot of time thinking about the original shape of the Suba cave (*illustration 7.1*). This was not a natural cave – it was completely hewn out of the rock by human hands. It was elongated like a hall, extending from south to north for a distance of twenty-four metres, with a breadth of four metres from wall to wall, and with a total depth approaching five metres from ceiling to floor. A small shaft cut into the ceiling – almost like a chimney – linked the cave to the area above and outside. Twelve broad steps led down from the entrance into the cave. Immediately to the right, as one entered the cave, there was an alcove of irregular appearance. The entrance itself was large and allowed a person to enter in an upright position. In front of the entrance was a porch with seven steps leading into it (*plate 10b*). The steps and walls and ceiling of the porch were plastered, and the ceiling was built of large slabs of stone projecting one above the other in corbelled fashion. Next to the porch – to its east – were two rock-

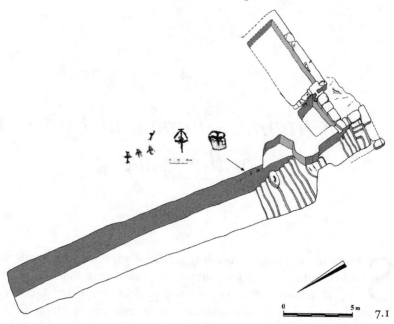

7.1

cut rectangular basins with plastered walls, one deeper than the other. A channel was found that diverted water from the valley into one of the basins; it was covered with small flat slabs of stone. An overflow channel also linked the smaller of the two basins with the porch in front of the cave. There can be no doubt that this artificial cave was pre-planned and not created in stages: in other words, the shape of the cave today is the same as those hewing it originally conceived it, with settling basins, a porch, an entrance, an alcove off to one side and a flight of steps leading into the large interior, and so forth. There is absolutely no evidence that the cave was ever enlarged or expanded.

The cave was cut out of living rock – block by block – following natural seams appearing between the fairly thin geological layers. The top layer of rock was left to serve as the roof of the cave. Usually quarrymen would get out their chisels, mattocks and metal rods, and through sheer hard work, sweat, and the exertion of muscles, would cut out lumps of rock by chiselling around them, working in different directions until the overall shape of the cave (rectangular or circular) was obtained. A lot of hard work, it would seem. However, the work in our cave must have been far less complicated because the layers of rock were naturally thin and the seams separating them facilitated the removal of regular-shaped blocks with only a limited expenditure of labour. All that was needed was to break up the blocks with a few tools and then for the blocks to be shifted out of the cave and hauled away on donkeys to be sold locally or in Jerusalem. Even small blocks of stones when slightly tapped would fall into bits in the form of perfect tiles or bricks. These pristine-looking stones were frequently encountered by the volunteers digging with us in the cave and I kept on being asked whether these stones were natural or man-made.

The peculiarities of the limestone in this district ensured that it was in great demand in antiquity, a fact that was even remarked upon in early rabbinical writings. Apparently, the altar of the Jewish Temple itself was built of stones brought from hereabouts: 'The stones of the ramp and the stones of the altar [of the Jewish Temple in Jerusalem] were alike taken from the valley of Beth Haccerem [Ain Karim], where they were quarried from below virgin stone and brought from thence as whole stones upon which no [tool made of] iron had been lifted up. For iron renders [the stones] invalid . . .' [note 7.1]. In the early twentieth century, stones used for pavements were brought to Jerusalem from the district of Ain Karim and the quality of the stone was much praised. These stones were flat and smooth, and there were two types: hard and soft. The first of these types was called in Arabic *maqadem* and was used for the construction of domes, arches and pavements of streets, and the other was called *lat* and was used to cover conduits and for the lining of burial cists [note 7.2].

Once the overall shape of the cave had been achieved by the quarrymen, work began on preparing the plaster that was needed to coat the walls of the cave. This was necessary because water channelled into an unplastered cave would rapidly percolate through natural cracks or seep out between the geological seams in the rock walls. The whole point was to contain water within the cave. Lime plaster was made using limestone, primarily composed of calcium carbonate, which was burnt at a heat of at least 900 degrees Celsius causing the release of carbon dioxide. The resulting quicklime (calcium oxide) would have been brought from nearby limekilns, where it was then mixed with large quantities of crushed chalk aggregate and water, thus beginning the transformation of the quicklime back into calcium carbonate [note 7.3]. The resulting mixture was then rapidly added to the walls of the cave in two basic layers: the first to smooth out irregularities in the side walls which were fairly rough owing to the quarrying process, and the second to create a smooth upper surface that would be completely impervious to standing water lapping up against it. Jabbing marks were cut into the surface of the lower plaster layer while still soft so that the upper plaster would adhere to it properly. The surface of the outer layer was extremely well smoothed – with a yellow to orange hue – and one can still make out the trowel marks of the plasterers. The walls, alcove, steps and floor of the cave were eventually plastered and only its ceiling was left unplastered. Similarly, the stepped entrance-porch, settling basins and channel outside the cave entrance, were also plastered.

How did water accumulate in the cave? The results of our excavations show that an impressive amount of human effort went into creating a system that ensured that the cave was always filled to its capacity with water. It was an amazing feat of engineering (*illustration 7.2*). There were two principal sources of rainwater: the first was from the hill slope above the cave. Our excavations showed that a large and deep oblong space had been hewn quite aggressively into the rock surface above the cave, and that it was extended as far back as possible into the side of the hill. The aim of this artificial 'trough' was to collect by degrees the run-off surface rainwater draining from the slope of the hill, and to divert it down and into the cave through the rectangular shaft located in its ceiling. Bits of walls that we exposed in the excavation led us to believe that steps led down around the edges of the 'trough' to the shaft opening.

The second source of water was from the valley itself. A massive

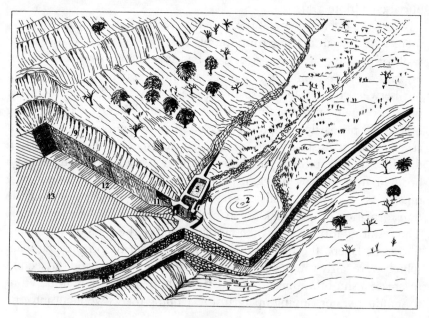

7.2

barrier wall built from one side of the valley to the other eventually halted rainwater rushing along the bed of the valley during the winter months: a large pond of water was thus created behind it. The wall was not found in the excavations but it is quite prominent in aerial photographs from the early twentieth century. Kibbutz members remember seeing the wall and recall it having been destroyed during bulldozing activities relating to the placing of new pipes by the Israeli authorities to carry water and oil along the valley floor. Until recently the piled-up blocks of stone that obviously came from this ruined barrier wall were still visible close to the cave entrance.

The water was then channelled artificially from the pond towards the cave and one such channel, covered with flat slabs of stone to prevent it from silting up, was found in the excavations. Water diverted towards the cave was first siphoned through a settling basin to ensure that it was properly filtered of silt, leaves and other detritus. The clean water was then allowed to flow into the stepped porch and subsequently down into the interior of the cave. The fact that the porch itself was plastered indicates that at times of maximum capacity water was also contained within the porch area as well.

There can be no doubt that the cave was originally intended to hold water. But why was the cave established at this location in the first place? The cave could be said to be dangerously close to the bed of the valley and at times of substantial flooding it would have been under constant threat of silting and a risk for those who had the difficult task of maintaining it. One possibility is that it was chosen because a natural flow or trickle of water from an aquifer was originally spotted at this location, perhaps at the far end of the so-called 'trough', where there appears to be a concave depression (perhaps natural) in the side of the hill, and that consequently the cave was hewn out by those who had hopes of enlarging such a trickle into a proper source of water. However, as far as I can see, there is no evidence for such speculation. Indeed, the build-up of the travertine flows visible on the inner walls of the cave, and of stalactites on the ceiling at the back of the cave, could easily have been created by the gradual percolation of rainwater through natural rock. Moreover, the shape of the cave does not at all resemble spring-caves and none of them have plastered walls. Several spring-caves have been studied in recent years in the Judaean Hills and they are nothing like our cave [note 7.4]. I believe that the location of the cave was deliberate and that it demonstrates sheer engineering brilliance. For this elaborate water system to entrap rainwater from two different sources – the hill-slope and the valley – there was only one possible location for the cave: it had to be at the sensitive juncture between these two topographical zones.

Water in ancient Palestine was a very precious commodity and for many of its inhabitants water was much more valuable than gold and could mean the difference between life and death. The country has few natural water resources, such as lakes, perennial rivers and springs, and in the highland regions, in particular, there were only a very small number of springs. For this reason, great efforts were made to devise methods of conserving rainwater for drinking and irrigation purposes from very early times. Much thought was put into the shape and appearance of cisterns and reservoirs, and those who made them followed certain basic rules. The entrance, for example, was usually via a small shaft opening in the ceiling of the cave and this facilitated the lowering of jars into the interior to fill them with water. The openings were kept small to prevent evaporation, especially during the hot summer months, and to prevent the infiltration of dirt and detritus. Keeping the entrance small also helped to exclude light from the cave since it could stimulate the growth of green mosses and fungi. The entrance was usually capped with a stone or metal lid. It was essential that the greatest amount of water be stored in the cave and so very rarely were steps built inside them. If a cave did have steps, they were narrow and placed to one side. In smaller cisterns, wooden ladders were used, or handgrips and footholds were cut into the wall beneath the shaft opening. Cisterns tended to be round or rectangular in plan and bell-shaped in section. Those reservoirs used for irrigation purposes were intentionally positioned on the slopes above the fields so that water could be siphoned off when necessary. The cisterns were usually cleaned out in the autumn and their walls were frequently repaired and re-plastered before the first rains.

As we know, our cave does not fit the normal definition of a cistern: the elongated shape of the cave is unusual; it has broad steps in both the porch area and within the cave itself to ensure that many people could gain easy access to its interior; the large size of the entrance would also have facilitated the traffic of people in and out of the cave and would have provided the interior with light (it would also have stimulated the growth of fungi and mosses) (*illustration 7.3*). The size of the interior of the cave is also unique – large reservoirs for drinking purposes, as we shall see, are known but only in the midst of cities and not at isolated locations in the middle of the countryside. Peasants would have made

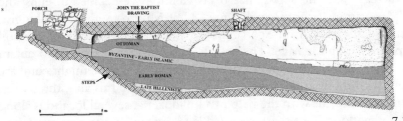

7.3

do with water collected in much smaller and more regular-shaped cisterns. The fact that our cave was hewn at a level that was substantially lower than the surface of the valley floor outside clearly indicates that it cannot have served as a source of water for irrigating fields. There can be no doubt that a concerted effort went into hewing this cave, with its external basins and channels, its barrier wall across the valley, and the scooping-out of the 'trough' depression on the hill-slope above. This has to suggest that the project was originally a community-based affair and not the result of the enterprising will of an individual or even a family.

Since this water system was purposefully built for water-gathering but not specifically for either drinking or irrigation purposes, I would suggest that its main function was as a place connected with bathing practices. The broad steps in the cave extending from wall to wall physically took up valuable space, and would not have been useful had the sole intention been to facilitate people collecting water. Indeed, it would have been physically difficult for people to scoop water into containers from the steps, or to dip their jars, unless, of course, the water level was very high, but then this would have obviated the need for steps in the first place. It would have made much more sense to cut away the entire area immediately within the entrance: this way much more water would have been accessible close to the entrance and the dipping of jars would have been relatively easy. The presence of steps inside the cave was definitely intentional and since we were not situated within a city, the only conclusion that one may come up with is that the steps facilitated efficient bathing procedures. The effort and cost that went into the construction of this cave, combined with the odd location in a valley, located at some distance from the nearest town (Suba) or village (Sataf) and main highways, suggests in my mind that the type of bathing which took place here was not for hygienic cleansing purposes but must have been connected with certain religious practices.

To investigate alternative perspectives on the construction and date of the cave and the appearance of its vicinity, we decided to enlist the help of various scientific colleagues. Neil Munro, a geomorphologist, came all the way from Scotland to make a detailed study of the soil deposits within the cave. The first thing he needed to do was to obtain information about the soils of the valley itself, so that he might compare them with those in the cave's interior. To achieve this aim, three deep trenches were cut with the help of a bulldozer at several locations along the valley floor. This work revealed layers of soil and stones, extending down to the rocky bed of the valley, which is, at its deepest point, 3.5 metres below the present surface of the kibbutz orchard. A thin and sterile layer of soil was found at the bottom of this sequence above rock and the top of this layer probably represents the ground surface from the Iron Age or earlier. Downstream, about fifty metres or so to the west, outside the entrance to the cave, a diversion channel was uncovered which originally brought water from the surface of the valley to the settling basins. It was found only half a metre below the present surface of the kibbutz orchard.

The evidence from these excavations suggests that there was hardly any soil accumulation in the valley bed before the Late Hellenistic period, which means that the large barrier wall, crossing the valley outside the cave, had to have served as a dam rather than as a terrace. The pottery found in the second and much thicker layer in the pits dug by Neil could be dated to the Late Hellenistic period, i.e. from the late second century to late first century BC. This soil would have accumulated within the valley as a result of substantial erosion, probably brought on by deforestation practices. Widespread cutting down of trees on the slopes of hills would inevitably have led to unprotected soil being washed down into the valley by the winter rains. The only way to retain the soil on the slopes of the hills, following such tree removal on a massive scale, was to initiate the construction of agricultural terraces. For this reason, we may assume that the hundreds of agricultural terraces that are visible lining the slopes of the hills, on either side of the valley, cannot be older than the Late Hellenistic period [note 7.5]. The valley bed in the Late Hellenistic period had sloping ground extending from east to west, tilting precariously towards the cave entrance. Perhaps it indicates that at that time the barrier wall was in a state of collapse or had been breached partially. In the winter, following heavy rainfalls, water would rush down the valley and, because of the angle of the slope, some of it would flow straight into the cave, dragging with it quantities of silt and soil. It is possible, therefore, that attempts were made to put the older water system back into use in the Hellenistic period, but that this had to be abandoned precisely because of the dramatic rise in the level of the ground surface of the valley outside. This may also explain why there was such an enormous build-up of soil in the cave during the subsequent Early Roman period.

Early on in the excavation, Dr Aryeh Shimron, from the Geological Survey in Jerusalem, had visited the site and examined the plaster on the walls of the cave; he also took samples away with him and had a look at them under a microscope in his laboratory. Having compared the consistency of our plaster to samples which he had collected from installations at a variety of other archaeological sites of different dates, Shimron came to the conclusion that the plaster adhering to the walls of our cave must date to the Iron Age II period at the latest (i.e. to some point in time between the eighth and sixth centuries BC).

This was quite astonishing, and during the early stage of the excavation it did seem to be inconsistent with our archaeological findings, which had only brought to light Late Hellenistic material on the rock floor of the cave. In stratigraphical terms, however, we had to concede that we had not uncovered direct evidence for the date of the *construction* of the cave, but only a date for the earliest possible time that a layer of mud had accumulated on the floor of the cave. All we could say, therefore, was that the hewing and plastering of the cave must have occurred at some point in time *before* the Late Hellenistic period, and theoretically this could have been a couple of years or a couple of hundred years. But archaeologists always need something a bit more tangible than just a probability. At one point, we had found a little pottery that seemed to be of Iron Age date in a trench excavated by Sheila Bishop behind the southern wall of the entrance porch, but we were not quite sure of its significance at the time. However, clear and incontrovertible evidence from the Iron Age did emerge during the final few days of the excavation (sod's law) in the eastern of the two settling basins located next to the stepped porch of the cave (*Plate 10a*). It was here that an earthen living surface was uncovered with scattered pottery and a circular fireplace, indicating quite clearly that this plastered basin was no longer used for the purpose of filtering rainwater and that people had decided to live inside the basin, perhaps only temporarily. Beneath this, further layers of fill were found descending to yet another hard earthen living surface located immediately above the plastered floor of the pool. On it was a considerable quantity of shattered ceramic jugs, storage jars, holemouth jars, cooking pots and bowls – the ancient breaks indicating that some of this material could indeed be restored. This material dated to the Iron Age II, i.e. to the eighth to sixth centuries BC. Since these surfaces evidently postdated the construction of the basin, and indeed the porch of the cave, and since we had already established that the whole water system was built at one time and not in stages, there was now no doubt in our minds that the cave had to have been in use at some point before or during the Iron Age II. But when exactly was this cave first hewn and plastered?

The most common scientific chronometric technique in use today in archaeology is the radiocarbon dating method (14C), and Dr Elisabetta Boaretto of the Radiocarbon Dating Laboratory at the Weizmann Institute visited us on a number of occasions, taking away various samples of charcoal from different locations in the cave. She had been able to obtain some good determinations for charcoal from the Abbasid-period floors and an additional number from the lower Hellenistic and Roman levels. Unfortunately, we had not been able to find any charcoal that conceivably could be associated with the time of the actual hewing of the cave. Elisabetta, therefore, suggested that we break open fragments of the wall plaster to see if we could detect there trapped charcoal particles from the time it was made, which could then be dated using the finer radiocarbon accelerated-dating method available, but although we cracked open quite a few fragments nothing turned up from the plaster at the back of the cave. We did, however, obtain a calibrated radiocarbon determination for a plaster patching of a hole in the east wall of the cave: 770–400 BC.

The next thing we attempted to do was to see whether we could get a dating for the travertine build-up (flowstone) – resulting from the seepage of water – over the surface of the plastered wall at the back of the cave, using the sophisticated uranium–thorium dating method. In the spring of 2001, Dr Mira Matthews and Dr Avner Ayalon of the Geological Survey in Jerusalem came to the cave and took away a sample of the travertine for this test. Hitherto, the uranium–thorium dating method has rarely been used on archaeological materials derived from sites in Israel/Palestine. The method works as follows: the technique uses the properties of the radioactive half-life of uranium-238 and thorium-230. The half-life of uranium-238 is 4.5 billion years, that is to say, in that period of time half of the original amount is still uranium while the other half has lost protons to form a different element, which is more stable. The half-life of thorium-230 is only 75,380 years. For this technique to be successful, the sample tested must take up uranium-238 and no thorium, then immediately be closed off so it would not be able to take in more. Such environmental conditions are usually only possible in caves and in areas of deep water and land falls [note 7.6]. By comparing the amounts of uranium and thorium obtained, Mira was thus able to make an accurate estimation of the age of the flowstone from our cave. Taking into consideration all the possible error factors, Mira successfully obtained two separate ages from this sample: 2600 +/- 100 and 2260=/-100 years BP (i.e. before present, and in this case, 2002. 'We geologists', Mira explained to me, 'do not really like all these BC and AD dates, it is just too confusing'). The first of these, from the earliest build up of flowstone on the plaster surface, would indicate a date of 598 BC, and the second from a later build up, giving a date of 258 BC. Using the first of these determinations, which is the earliest of the two, we must assume that the hewing and plastering of the cave was undertaken at some point in the Late Iron Age (*c.* sixth century BC). This result fitted in quite well with the radiocarbon dates obtained inside and outside the cave (eighth to fifth centuries BC) and with the pottery finds (eighth to sixth centuries BC) as well.

The Late Iron Age date for the water system at Suba provided by the uranium–thorium technique, if accepted, and there is no reason to suspect that any error has occurred since a number of tests were made, means that our cave was hewn and plastered at the time of the divided monarchy when the Israelite people had already become firmly established in the territory of Judah in the central highlands of Palestine. In recent years, scholars have expressed great scepticism in regard to the historicity of the biblical account relating to the origins of the Israelites, and hot debates and controversies have ensued between those holding extreme views. One group of scholars – the Copenhagen School, as they are known – believe that there is hardly anything historical at all that might be elicited from the biblical account regarding the history of the Israelites before the Persian period. The traditional view was that the Israelites arrived either by means of conquest (as in the biblical account) or by peaceful infiltration.

Others have examined in some detail the archaeological remains from the Early Iron Age in the highland regions, and they suggest that this was a period that saw the fluctuation and gelling together of disparate peoples arriving from many different directions, some of them dis-enfranchised farmers from the lowlands, others tribal pastoralists from inland regions, perhaps even from beyond the Jordan, and sedentarising nomads from the deserts as well. These people (sometimes called the 'proto-Israelites') led a fairly simple family-based way of life in the twelfth century BC in small, scattered villages, located at intervals of about five kilometres from each other, with subsistence agriculture being undertaken in the valleys, logging of the woodland on the slopes of hills and some terracing and the herding of animals. It is believed that their engineering skills were not very advanced; that they did not even have plastered cisterns, and that some water was brought from natural springs and that rainwater was collected in large jars (*pithoi*). It was only about four hundred years later, however, in the eighth century BC, according to current thinking, that large water systems first came to be established in the royal Israelite cities and towns. These were quite impressive and indicate that a high level of engineering expertise became available to the population at that time. They were designed as part of the overall urban setup and were constructed to cater for the daily needs of the inhabitants (drinking and washing), as well as to provide sufficient water at times of war when the towns were under prolonged siege [note 7.7]. The discovery at Suba fits in quite well with prevailing scholarly opinion regarding the engineering abilities of the Israelites in the Late Iron Age period. However, it also indicates that large water systems were also being created in the countryside of the highland regions and not just within cities and towns.. The corollary of all this is that the water system at Suba must have been created by a community-based group of people and that some of them must have had extremely good engineering skills.

Now that we knew that our cave was from the Late Iron Age, we felt it worthwhile consulting one of the leading experts on ancient water systems in Israel, Dr Tsvika Tsuk. His interest is primarily in water systems that predate the Hellenistic period and his doctoral thesis was on this very subject. He visited the Suba cave with us in October 2002. He was fascinated with the cave and thought that it should be compared to examples of large plastered reservoirs known from the Amman Citadel, Beth Shemesh and Beer Sheba, but with an added reservation that all of these had been found *within* cities and that, as far as he could tell, barrier walls and settling basins had never been found at these sites either [note 7.8]. The Beth Shemesh reservoir is perhaps the closest of the examples mentioned by Tsuk and I visited it myself recently. The Geologist Shimron was quite right about the plaster on its walls: it did look remarkably like the plaster from our cave. The Beth Shemesh cave also had a number of characteristics that were fairly similar to ours: it was rock-hewn and had steps leading down to the entrance (in this case the steps were partly built and quite narrow); there was a small niche on the right just inside the entrance (resembling our alcove); there was a water channel which collected rainwater extending to the steps and entrance, and a vertical shaft facilitating the drawing of water through the ceiling of the cave to the surface of the city above [note 7.9].

However, while inspecting our cave, Tsuk remarked that he thought it strange that our cave was located at such a distance from the nearest Iron Age settlement (Suba). He was also puzzled as to why there should have been a need for such a large reservoir at this location, when it evidently was not being used for irrigation purposes for the fields in the valley outside the cave; nor was there any evidence for a water wheel (similar to the Egyptian *shaduf*) having been employed to lift water to the level of the ground surface outside. Nor could the cave have been used for the watering of herded animals since no arrangements to facilitate this were found. While he remained convinced that the cave must have been used primarily as a source of drinking water, he could not answer the question as to why a vertical pit for filling jars was not cut immediately inside the entrance to facilitate water-collection procedures. He did agree with me that the steps would have made the whole process of water gathering quite labour-intensive. There was also no apparent reason why the entrance to a reservoir should be so large. After all, a small entrance or access shaft would exclude light from the cave and would prevent the growth of algae and other contaminants inside. Also it would have kept to a minimum levels of evaporation during the hot summer months.

It seemed to me that the mystery of the original function of the cave had intensified following Tsuk's visit. Why would such an enormous reservoir have been hewn at a spot so far away from human habitations? we asked ourselves. Why were no attempts made to utilise the water for irrigation purposes or for watering animals? And why would it have been used solely for drinking purposes in the middle of nowhere and far away from main roads?

The Old Testament is a major source of information about the different kinds of water-storage installations that were available in the Iron Age and through to Persian times – with frequent references to springs, cisterns, wells, and the underground water systems in the towns [note 7.10]. Our cave was probably referred to by the Hebrew word *bor*, which generally means a hole or cavity in the ground for the storage of water (Exodus 21:33; 1 Chronicles 11:18; elsewhere it was used in reference to a pit, a grave and a dungeon: Genesis 37:24; Ezekiel 32:23;

Exodus 12:29); but what about all the features in the area outside our cave, notably the barrier wall, the channels and settling basins. How would they have been collectively referred to? Looking through the Old Testament, one comes across references to mysterious *gbym* (singular, *gbi*), and these have been translated in the past, with some uncertainty, as 'ditches' or 'pools', but in my opinion these could very well have been artificial 'ponds' for collecting rainwater behind barrier walls built in the valleys. In II Kings 3:16–17, for example, we read: 'And he [Elisha] said, Thus saith the Lord, Make this valley full of *gbym*. For thus saith the Lord, Ye shall not see the wind, neither shall ye see rain; yet that valley shall be filled with water, that ye may drink, both ye and your cattle, and your beasts.' This passage makes it clear that the *gbym* were features in the landscape of a valley and that water was gathered there even at times when water was scarce [note 7.11]. Further support for this interpretation may be found in a passage in Jeremiah 14: 3–4, describing the outcome of a ferocious drought: 'And their nobles [of Jerusalem] have sent their little ones to the waters: they came to the *gbym*, and found no water; they returned with their vessels empty; they were ashamed and confounded, and covered their heads. Because the ground is chapped, for there was no rain in the earth . . .' Hence, the *gbym* were large artificial 'ponds' in the ground (outside the cities) that were filled with rainwater during the winter months and would have remained in use at least until the beginning of the summer when they would eventually have dried up. These 'ponds' were established behind stone-built barrier walls or dams, extending from one side of the valley to the other. They would have been used for drinking purposes (using ceramic sherds as scoops: Isaiah 30:14), as well as for the watering of animals. Channels would have been cut across the levelled ground surface to facilitate the siphoning of water from the ponds, at the peak of the winter rains, and towards the reservoirs that were cut into the edges of the valleys. Our cave, I believe, was one such reservoir (*bor*) that was fed by an artificial pond (*gbi*).

So what was the function of the cave? The first thing to consider is the fact that a great amount of labour and engineering skill was put into creating this water system in the first place. It was a massive undertaking. Not only was it necessary for enormous quantities of rock to be taken out of the cave and from the ridge above it, but great quantities of quicklime also had to be brought to the cave for the plastering of the walls and its adjacent installations. Woodland in the immediate area of the cave also had to be cleared and a large barrier wall erected across the valley. All of this would have required a lot of labour. Because of the proximity to Suba, one may suggest that these people came from that settlement. But why did they not create this water system closer by, instead of at this isolated and unprotected location over a kilometre away? It simply does not make sense when one considers that water rights in antiquity were a serious business. The cave was definitely not used as a source of irrigation water and this is because it is situated well below the level of the actual valley floor outside. Indeed, the geomorphological work has also shown that there was hardly any soil in this section of the valley at that time. The cave was also an unlikely source of drinking water: it was too distant from the settlement of Suba (which had its own springs) nor was it close to any major highway. Hence, the only people who might have been able to drink from the waters of this cave would have been small numbers of local farmers, herdsmen and the occasional passer-by. I cannot believe that such an amazing water system was created for the benefit of such a limited number of people. We are left, therefore, with only one other possibility: that the cave was used for ritual purposes and that this probably involved bathing.

How would the cave have been used? The whole concept of sacred space and the identification of cult sites in landscapes is a fascinating one, but unfortunately not enough research has been done on the subject. Indeed, much of what we know about religious practices in Old Testament times in Palestine is derived from the archaeological study of temples, altars, ritual furnishings and offerings found within town and village sites [note 7.12]. Sacred space is usually perceived of as being harboured within the confines of religious buildings – a temple or shrine – but the reality is that in ancient times the dwelling places of the gods, spirits and cultic beings could be anywhere in the landscape, even at locations with no apparent ritualistic features, such as in a tree, a cave, a water cistern or spring, a pile of stones, or even within an entire valley or mountain. This, of course, causes practical problems for archaeologists when attempting to identify isolated cult sites at natural locations outside of settlements [note 7.13]. How does one identify cultic sites, which are devoid of material artefacts connected with religious activities? Does this lack of cultic accoutrements – sculptures, figurines, altars – lessen in some way the importance of these places as mediators between the worshippers and the gods/spirits? [note 7.14]. In our case we have a cave with water in the side of a mountain in a valley. In the mists of time, the idea of the mountain was perceived in the Near East as a symbol of the entire earth, as the general abode of the divine.

Passing through the door of the cave beneath the mountain was to enter a 'deep pit' full of water 'and darkness was upon the face of the deep'. 'And the Spirit of God moved upon the face of the waters' (Genesis 1:2). The holy mountain in Jerusalem was the hill of Zion on which the Jewish Temple was eventually built, and 'streams' or 'rivers' were said to issue from beneath the mountain (Psalms 45:4). Entering it was a process of both initiation and consecration, since the doorway to a sacred space may have imitated that of the supreme door leading into the Jewish Temple. One may imagine those being ushered into the cave with the summons: 'This is the Gate of the Lord. The righteous shall enter into it' (Psalm 117:19–20).

But what does the Old Testament actually tell us about ritual activities connected with water? Of the sanctity of water in ancient Israelite ritual there can be no doubt. Indeed, as we have seen, in the book of Genesis (1:2), the spirit of God was said to hover over the face of the waters. In the book of Numbers (22) there is mention of a purification ritual involving first the washing of a person's clothes and then the bathing (*rehaz*) of the flesh in the water (verses 7–8). There is also a reference to a 'clean place' (*makom tahor*), which could very well have been a place such as our cave. Coming into contact with a corpse presented problems: the contaminated person would remain unclean for seven days and so, on the third day, he would be required to purify himself (12). We are told that the first part of the process required that the 'water of separation had to be sprinkled upon him', otherwise he ran the risk of having his soul cut off from Israel (13). The process is clarified further: the ashes of the heifer of purification were mixed with running water in a vessel (18): 'and a clean person [*ish tahor*] shall take hyssop and dip it [*taval*] in the water, and sprinkle it upon the tent, and upon all the vessels, and upon the persons that were there, and upon him that touched a bone, or one slain, or a grave.' And in verse 20: 'And the clean person shall sprinkle upon the unclean on the third day, and on the seventh day he shall purify himself, and wash his clothes, and bath [*rehaz*] himself in water, and shall be clean at *erev* [i.e. night-time].' Isaiah (1:16) spoke of an apocalyptic repentance that included water: 'wash [*rehaz*] you, make you clean; put away the evil of your doings from before mine eyes; cease to do evil.' In the days of the prophets, people came to them rather than to physicians to deal with their ailments. In 2 Kings 5: 10–14, one hears about Na'aman the Leper who cleansed himself in the Jordan. He was probably not a leper but suffered from a skin disease (psoriasis) [note 7.15]. In the sense of Leviticus 13:13,

Na'aman's body had become 'invaded' by the unclean; it did not necessarily require curing and the condition could be dealt with ceremonially. Hence, he was sent by the prophet Elisha: 'Go and wash [*rehaz*] in Jordan seven times and thy flesh shall come again to thee, and thou shalt be clean' (2 Kings V: 10, 11, 14). Na'aman seemed to be annoyed that Elisha did not undertake the ceremony himself, suggesting that this might have been normal practice at the time. Na'aman had expected Elisha to do the following: to stand on the bank of the Jordan and to call on the name of God, to strike his hand over the place, and to help with the bathing process. Finally, 'he [Na'aman] went down, and dipped [*taval*] himself seven times in the Jordan, according to the saying of the man of God [i.e. Elisha], and his flesh came again like unto the flesh of a little child, and he was clean.'

The new evidence showed that the cave at Suba was already more than seven hundred years old at the time of the birth of John the Baptist. It was a place, I believe, that must have possessed a hoary Israelite tradition of ritualistic bathing going back into the mists of time, perhaps it was one of those 'clean places' where you could go and bath like Na'aman the Leper and come out again with your skin feeling as soft as a child's. The cave was evidently used throughout the Iron Age and until the time of the destruction of Jerusalem by the Babylonians in 586/587 BC, which also saw the razing of the Jewish Temple. The discovery of habitation levels inside the second silting basin located outside the cave, with numerous fragments of pottery vessels dating to the eighth to sixth centuries BC, proved that the cave had indeed been used in the Late Iron Age period. The fact that Iron Age pottery was not found on the floor of the cave itself suggested that the cave was regularly cleaned out, at least until the end of that period. What happened during the Persian and early Hellenistic periods, is unclear, but one thing is certain: very little soil accumulated inside.

There was some accumulation of silt and mud washed into the cave in the late Hellenistic period. When we excavated the floor of the cave, we did come across a thin layer of mud (about 30 centimetres thick) and in it were basalt grinding stones and a jumble of Late Hellenistic pottery, of which the latest could be dated to between the late second and first centuries BC (*plate 10c*). We also found a mass of fragmented plaster, with the fragments face down, which had collapsed from the western wall, evidently prior to the earliest Early Roman living surface being established. The fact that this plaster had collapsed not on to a layer of mud dating from the Iron Age or Persian periods but from the Late

Hellenistic period clearly indicates that the cave floor had already been thoroughly cleaned out in the Hellenistic period. Surprisingly, no attempts were ever made to re-plaster the western wall. But why was the cave cleaned out in the first place and for what purpose?

It has generally been assumed that the intense concern with ritual washing and purification was a characteristic feature that was very specific to Jewish life in the Early Roman period, and that, in the preceding periods, particularly at the time of the Israelite kingdom of Judah during the Iron Age, it played only a very marginal role in daily and religious life. However, the discovery of the Suba cave may change this thinking. The general appearance of this cave and its features – with a porch, a large entrance, a flight of steps leading into the cave and extending the entire breadth of the installation, and a niche in the side wall – bears an extraordinary resemblance to the appearance of the later *miqwa'ot*. It was also plastered and was fed with 'pure' water. The only major difference is the exaggerated length of the interior of the cave, since the back wall of the *miqweh* was usually located close to the bottom of the flight of steps. The similarities were so striking that quite a few archaeologists visiting our site, at an earlier stage of the excavation (when we only had Roman pottery and no inkling of the Iron Age date of construction), seemed to be absolutely convinced that this cave must have been originally constructed as a *miqweh* or as a hybrid *miqweh/ reservoir*. John the Baptist or his followers would have chosen the cave precisely because of the ancient traditions of ritual bathing associated with it. There would have been no point in John practising his procedures of baptism within the confines of his hometown. A cave such as this would have been ideal for his purposes.

I like to think that the Suba cave was frequented not only by John the Baptist during the early stages of his life, but also by Jesus himself, arriving at the cave following his baptism by John at the Jordan River, to see for himself where it had all begun for his teacher, John the Baptist. An account regarding the infancy of John appears in the *Protevangelium of James* (of mid-second century date) and we hear of Elizabeth hiding within a cave in the 'hill country' while fleeing from the soldiers of Herod the Great. While there can be no doubt that the *Protevangelium* is a legendary narrative, one does wonder whether the mention of a cave is based on an oral tradition that may have been factual. Indeed, we have found living surfaces in our cave corresponding in date to the early second century. However, since the geographical situation of the cave was left vague in the *Protevangelium*, the possibility that it refers to our cave will have to remain in the realm of speculation. During the excavations, we were visited by numerous Christians who felt a special affinity to the cave and to the religious electricity inherent in that place. Whether you are a believer or not, one feels it every time one enters the place. On one occasion we were visited by three Greek Orthodox bishops and they all expressed great interest in the finds and especially in the drawing of John the Baptist on the wall of the cave (*plate 9c*). Indeed, one of the bishops, named Irineous, who is now the Patriarch of Jerusalem, declared there and then that our cave was a 'holy place'.

Conclusion

Most of the work of digging at the Suba cave was completed by 2003. All that remained to do was a little bit more work in the area outside the cave, in the area of the settling basins, and in the area of the shaft entrance on the rocky ridge above the cave so that we could obtain information about how the surface runoff was originally diverted into the cave. As far as the interior of the cave was concerned, I felt that we had now extracted as much information as we could about its origins, history and functions. Purposefully, we had not excavated the cave in its entirety but only about two thirds of it. This was intentional so that future archaeologists, perhaps with better scientific skills than our own, might be able to check on the veracity of our conclusions. A good scientific excavation is not just one where the digging procedures and methods are exacting, but also one in which a balanced and unprejudiced view is kept in regard to the interpretation of the evidence as it emerges from the ground. The whole process of archaeological excavation is by its nature a destructive one: what you dig is almost immediately gone and if you do not record the features you have been excavating properly, then that evidence will be lost for ever. Hence, it is incumbent upon the archaeologist to address the publication of the discoveries in as swift a fashion as possible, so that fellow-scholars and everyone else in the world might keep abreast of the discoveries and their interpretation. The years of digging at the cave were now at an end. We were exhausted but also overjoyed with the results that had been obtained. The time had now come to gather together all the clues, to set in motion the process of study and analysis, and to begin putting together a comprehensive picture of the history and significance of the cave.

Conclusion

Recently, I visited the Minoan palace at Knossos in Crete for the first time and I was looking forward to exploring this archaeological site in my own way. I was there with a friend. As we passed through the gates to the site, a grey-haired woman approached us. 'May I take you around?' she asked. We declined her offer but she was persistent. 'But it will be difficult for you to see the site all by yourselves,' she insisted, and then explained: 'After all, the stones all look more or less the same.' 'Don't worry,' I told her, 'I *am* an archaeologist.' She was not at all flummoxed by this reply. 'Well, then,' she said, 'I shall take you around as a guide instead.' The need for some form of explanation is essential for every visitor reaching an archaeological site, and my little knowledge of Knossos was based on some reading and a look at the site plan. I can imagine that one day the very same thing will occur at the Cave of John the Baptist at Suba. Guides will hover around its entrance and will offer to take visitors and pilgrims into the cave, to explain the significance of the archaeological discoveries there and the meaning of the ancient drawings. This book will probably be on sale in a shop in the vicinity of the cave, perhaps hidden behind stacks of postcards, and shirts and mugs with the printed image of the drawing of John the Baptist on them. However, all of this is still very much in the future. Hitherto, we have managed to keep knowledge of the discovery of this cave under wraps so as to allow us some breathing space while we pursued three years of archaeological investigations. The last thing I would have wanted was for us to be swamped with visitors while we were still in the midst of puzzling things out at the cave. This excavation turned out to be one of the most challenging and exciting projects of my career. But the time has now come to inform the world of these discoveries and to begin seeking appropriate funding so that we might protect the site for posterity.

The first part of this book has dealt with the exciting story of the discovery of the cave and the significance of its finds. There can be no doubt that in the minds of the Christian monks who came to this place in the Byzantine period, this was the cave that had been used by John the Baptist when he was in his 'first' wilderness (reflecting Luke 1:80). The monks probably visited the cave once a year to reflect on the sanctity of the place and to commemorate calendar dates marking either John's birth or death. Drawings were subsequently incised into the walls of the cave to tell the story of John's life and his place in Christianity, perhaps for the edification of novice monks. The oral tradition connecting John to this cave was sufficiently strong that the monks felt no obligation to scrawl on to the wall of the cave the words 'wilderness of John the Baptist', which, of course, is very annoying to archaeologists who love to have everything clearly spelt out. The Byzantine tradition at the cave was maintained continuously until close to the twelfth century, at which point it was disrupted, presumably because of the heavy-handed behaviour of the Crusaders which forced many local Christians to flee for their lives. This resulted in the tradition of the 'wilderness of John the Baptist' being transferred to the site of Ain el-Habis located not too far away in the Soreq valley, to the south of the Suba cave.

The excavations in the lower parts of our Suba cave revealed some startling evidence dating from the time of John the Baptist and the first century AD. Apparently, the inner end of the cave was used for baptism purposes, whereas the surfaces in the front of the cave were used for strange rituals involving the construction of stone circles, the breaking of large quantities of jugs and the use of a large stone for foot-anointing. There can be no doubt that these activities reflect the beliefs of a particular group of Jews with a unique approach towards purification in water. Hence, the cave was most probably used by John the Baptist during his sojourn in the hill country, because of the proximity to his hometown at Ain Karim, and it was also certainly used during the course of the first century by his followers or by a group of Jews who were baptists. It cannot be coincidental that the cave that was chosen in the first century AD had an antiquity connected with ritual bathing reaching back all the way to the Iron Age, to the early first millennium BC. Since John the Baptist appears to have regarded himself as a successor to the Israelite prophets, what better than to choose a place to conduct his rituals of baptism where there was already an established tradition of ritual cleansing extending back to their time?

This book is also the result of my personal quest to find out more about the life of John the Baptist, and to study the archaeological sites which have traditionally been associated with him, notably Ain Karim (his birthplace), the many baptism sites in the lower Jordan Valley (the place of his mission), Machaerus (where he was beheaded) and the city of Sebaste (where he was buried). John came from a rural priestly background and apparently as a shepherd boy spent a lot of time by himself in the hills around his hometown. While tending his flocks of sheep or goats, John matured into a young man with a very particular set of views about purity and baptism and about the imminent return of the prophet Elijah. People from the vicinity of Jerusalem began responding to John's teaching and eventually came to be baptised by him. The growth of interest in his message led to John shifting his location to the lower Jordan River, to the traditional spot where Elijah had ascended into the sky and where John believed he was about to reappear. His reputation grew and many people came to be baptised by John, including Jesus, who appears then to have stayed on as one of his followers. John began spreading word of his teachings in other parts of the country, and he did this by despatching roving bands of his followers who were led by chosen individuals. One of these groups was led by Jesus in the hills close to Jerusalem, and he may even have come to the Suba cave. John, meanwhile, moved northwards and set up a temporary centre at Aenon, perhaps with the intention of attracting people from the Galilee. Herod Antipas regarded the rapid growth of John's power and influence as dangerous to the stability of territory under his rule, and he brought this situation to an immediate end by arresting John and executing him. The event of John's death was extremely traumatic for his followers. Subsequently, it triggered a rift between the followers of John and the followers of Jesus and each group apparently immediately began consolidating their own independent teachings. The Gospel writers later downplayed the significance of John as a prophet of the people, in order to boost the story of Jesus and his ministry, and to spread the word that John the Baptist had been the 'forerunner' of Jesus the Messiah.

Digging at the Suba cave was an adventure and momentous discoveries were made there. I am very grateful to everyone who helped with this project of excavation, it was truly a collaborative effort and part of the success of the dig was because of the enthusiasm and excitement of the team members who stuck with the project all the way to the end. The dig at the cave opened the door to an archaeological investigation into the life of John the Baptist. He was a real historical person and there may now be archaeological support for this as well. Clear and unequivocal archaeological evidence was uncovered indicating that complex baptism rituals were being undertaken in the cave of Suba during the first century AD, at the time of John the Baptist and later. These rituals were quite distinct from those practised by the Jews of that time. This cave was later used by Byzantine monks to commemorate the memory of John the Baptist in the wilderness. Could this just be a coincidence? I think not. I sincerely hope that the readers of this book enjoyed following our progress and deliberations as we excavated in the fascinating Cave of John the Baptist and that one day they will visit the cave for themselves.

PART TWO

8

Beyond the Jordan and a Beheading

Our cave had provided important and unique evidence regarding John the Baptist, his early life, the whereabouts of his first 'wilderness', the rituals of baptism which he practised, and the subsequent cult of John the Baptist in the Byzantine period. But there were a number of subjects relating to the life of John the Baptist about which the cave was able to contribute very little. I was fascinated, especially, by the whereabouts of the baptism site in the lower Jordan River, I also wanted to find out more about the place of the decapitation of John which was said to be at Machaerus; to investigate John's tomb at Sebaste, and to find out more about the cult of the Baptist and the dispersal of his relics from the Byzantine period onward. Hence, I began an investigation which led me to many of the principal sites, including the lower Jordan River.

In 1867, the famous American author, Mark Twain, meandered along the bank of the Jordan River, complaining incessantly: 'It was such a dreary, repulsive, horrible solitude!' he wrote. 'It was the "wilderness" where John preached, with camel's hair about his loins – raiment indeed – but he could never have got his locusts and wild honey here. We were moping along down through this dreadful place, every man in the rear. Our guards – two gorgeous young Arab sheikhs, with cargoes of swords, guns, pistols, and daggers on board – were loafing ahead' [note 8.1]. Twain was uninterested in the dusty landscape and all he wanted to do was to get back to a bit of civilisation as fast as his donkey could take him. John the Baptist could wait. The lower Jordan River has always held a great fascination for travellers and pilgrims alike. Some have loved it and others have loathed it. More than two decades earlier, in 1845, the adventurer Alexander William Kinglake described a hot and frustrating ride down the Jordan Valley in his book *Eothen*, which has remained a gem of literary workmanship ever since it was published. 'About mid-day,' he wrote, 'I began to examine my map, and to question my guide, who at last fell on his knees, and confessed that he knew nothing of the country in which we were. I was thus thrown upon my own resources, and calculating that on the preceding day, we had nearly performed a two-day journey, I concluded that the Dead Sea must be near.' Later, while struggling to find a bridge across the Jordan River with some difficulty, one of Kinglake's servants suggested to him that perhaps the guide should be put to death for causing all the confusion in the first place. With considerable enjoyment and an acerbic wit, Kinglake mused about committing such an act:

> . . . whilst the question of his [the guide's] life, and death was debated, he was riding in front of our party, and there was something in the anxious writhing of his supple limbs that seemed to express a sense of his false position, and struck me as highly comic; I had no crochet at that time against the punishment of death, but I was unused to blood, and the proposed victim looked so thoroughly capable of enjoying life (if he could only get to the other side of the river) that I thought it would be hard for him to die, merely to give me a character for energy. Acting on the result of these considerations, and reserving to myself a free, and unfettered discretion to have the poor villain shot at any future moment, I magnanimously decided that for the present he should live, and not die [note 8.2].

Unlike many other travellers and pilgrims who passed through the region and expressed a profound interest in its significance as the place of John's baptism of Jesus, Kinglake expressed no interest whatsoever in instructing his readers regarding the history of the place, and the continuation of his narrative provides further adventures and witty stories but all about himself.

The Jordan River flows along the remarkable geological feature known as the Syro-African rift valley. Formed by the confluence of streams at the foot of Mount Hermon, the river first enters the Sea of Galilee and then meanders to the south for quite a distance (166 kilometres) until it reaches the Plains of Jericho and the Dead Sea. Its steep and muddy banks contiguous to the river are overgrown with dense vegetation and are rich in wildlife. There are various fords along its length. The lower Jordan Valley was a place of transition and crossing, resounding with biblical memories. The fords at this location were referred to as Bethabara ('house of crossing': Joshua 2:7; Judges 7:24). This is the place where Joshua Ben Nun crossed into the Promised Land with the Israelites (Joshua 3–4) after having received the leadership from Moses at Mount Nebo. These were also the stamping grounds of the prophet Elijah, and his disciple Elisha, and it was here that they both miraculously divided the waters of the Jordan by smiting it with a hairy mantle (2 Kings 2: 7–14). Eventually, Elijah went up from this spot to heaven in a blazing chariot. In the Roman period, there was a great amount of activity in the region: Jericho was a prosperous town, with palm groves and balsam plantations, and Herod the Great had constructed his winter palaces nearby. The sect of the Essenes had their headquarters near the north-western shore of the Dead Sea. Many travellers passed along the highway linking Transjordan with western Palestine. There were also roads running to the north towards the Sea of Galilee, and a road leading westwards towards Jerusalem. Many people used these roads to transfer goods such as dates, balsam oil, and 'loaves' of asphalt and sacks of salt from the Dead Sea.

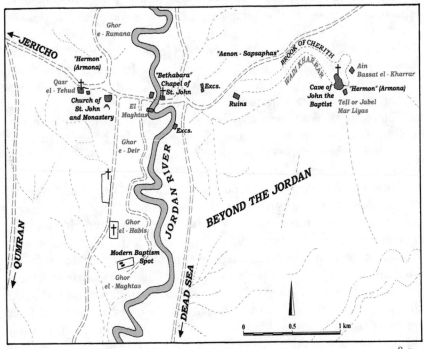

8.1

In the Synoptic Gospels we are told that John the Baptist preached a baptism of repentance in the general 'wilderness' region of the Jordan (Mark 1:5; Matthew 3:5–6, 13; Luke 3:3). However, the location given in John (1:28; 3:26) is much more specific: it was at a place called 'Bethabara beyond Jordan' (*illustration 8.1*) [note 8.3]. We are also told that this place was 'where John at *first* baptised' (italics: S.G.) (John 10:40). It does make sense that John would have chosen to go back to the spot where he believed Elijah must have ascended into the sky, on the right (east) bank of the river (2 Kings 2: 7–14) and close to the fords (Judges 7:24). Jesus lived there for a while following the death of John (John 10:40). Bethabara was also referred to by Josephus (*Jewish War* IV: 419–421) as a walled village called Bethennabris (Βηθεννάβρίν) It was to this place that some fugitives fled after their town Gadara had been captured by Vespasian in AD 68. The fugitives were subsequently hunted down by Placidus and he chased and eliminated them next to the banks of the River Jordan. In later periods, the location of Bethabara was extended to include part of the west bank as well. Origen (c. AD 185–254) suggests that the baptism was effected by John at Bethabara '*alongside* the Jordan' (italics: S.G.) (IV, 280), and Eusebius (AD 260–340) mentions that the place was located east of Jericho, and that in his time 'many believing brothers who, wishing to be reborn, are baptised in the living current' (*Onom.* 58:18–20). It was also depicted on the mosaic map of Madaba, dating to the second half of the sixth century (*illustration 8.2*), with the Greek inscription: 'Bethabara (Βεθαβαρά) [the sanctuary of] of John the Baptist' [note 8.4]. There is also a reference in John (1:28) to 'Bethany beyond Jordan where John was baptising.' Either this name refers to another location east of the Jordan (which seems unlikely) or it may have been another name for Bethabara itself (cf. Bethennabris in Josephus). In any case, it should not be confused with the Bethany to the south-east of Jerusalem, where Jesus stayed and where Lazarus lived (Mark 11:1; John 11) [note 8.5].

With the intention of attending the Greek Orthodox Epiphany celebrations at the baptism site on the west bank of the Jordan River, I set off early one morning in January, speeding down the winding highway leading from Jerusalem towards the Jordan Valley. Soon we reached a signpost that directed us off the highway towards the Monastery of St John, or Qasr el-Yehud. Turning the vehicle to the east we drove along a narrow road pitted with holes until we reached a gate in a fence that marks the Israeli side of the border between Israel and Jordan. Qasr el-Yehud is located within the military zone further along the continuation of this road behind the fence. The gate was closed. Rafi

8.2

Lewis had been in touch with the military authorities the previous day and they had assured him that the gate would be open for the Epiphany celebrations. We waited. We got out of the vehicle and stretched our legs. The air was crisp and tangy with a saline edge to it. Using his mobile phone, Rafi rang the military representative he had previously been in contact with, but there was no answer. We waited. We then supposed that we were at the wrong location, and that there might actually be another entry to the baptism site further south, and so we drove along the road parallel with the border fence. There was a magnificent view of the lower Jordan Valley and in the distance we could make out the northern tip of the Dead Sea. We then met with an Israeli border-patrol vehicle: the soldiers gazed at us warily, perhaps not used to seeing civilians along this stretch of road. Apparently there was no additional entry to the baptism site and we were told to go back to the place we had come from, to the closed gate. We waited and then had a picnic breakfast under the trees. Eventually, a military jeep came whizzing by and we hailed it. The soldier in the front turned out to be the officer in charge of this stretch of the border. It transpired that we had got there a day too early. The Epiphany celebrations at the baptism site were to take place on the following day, with the Greek Orthodox celebrations in the morning followed by those of the Ethiopian church from noon.

On the following day we arrived early – Rafi and I were joined by a friend of mine from Jerusalem, Maayan – and there in front of the gate that had been closed the previous day, we were confronted by a congregation of military vehicles clogging the area. Since the gate was only to be opened at 8.30 am, as one of the soldiers informed Rafi, we decided first to drive over to the Monastery of St Gerasmius (Deir Hajla), which was only about five minutes distant by car, to see how preparations were proceeding there for the Epiphany celebrations. At the Monastery, we found Greek flags fluttering in the wind along the main approach to the building and there was a great amount of frenetic activity going on next to the entrance. The Greek Orthodox abbot ran about trying to ensure that all of the furnishings for the ceremony at the Jordan River were being loaded appropriately on to the truck. This included a high chair for the Patriarch, incense censers, palm fronds, gilded staffs and all manner of ecclesiastical items. Finally, the truck set off, with the abbot in the car in front, and with our vehicle shadowing the entourage from behind. On arriving at the border-fence, we found that the gate had just been opened and we proceeded directly onwards along the bumpy road leading to the Monastery of St John.

I was astonished by the severity of the appearance of this monastery – it looked distinctly like a prison (*plate 11a*). The building is roughly rectangular in layout and, since its reconstruction by Greek monks in 1881, it has acquired two tower-like appendages flanking the main entrance to the building from the west, as well as a belfry and crenellations along the upper edges of its walls. The external walls were clad in 1955 with an ugly grid of modern buttresses, coated in heavy-handed fashion with cement and mortar, apparently to prevent structural collapse resulting from the 1927 earthquake. The first thing we did was to wander around the perimeter of the building to see whether we could identify signs of ancient masonry peeping out from beneath the lower parts of the walls where the modern mortar had peeled away. Entering into a partly collapsed vault on the south side of the building, we could see that the walls had not been heavily plastered and that it was possible to make out the characteristics of the ancient masonry there, with walls built of regular courses (0.25 m high) of flat rectangular stones, and with barrel-vaulted ceilings made of rubble and mortar. On one stone in the lower part of the external north wall we could make out an ancient incised cross (cut off at the top) with double V-shaped ends, as well as various other graffiti in Greek, much of it evidently modern.

Entry to the building is from the west and a number of Greek Orthodox monks from St Gerasmius were just giving the area in front of it a quick brush with a broom before the arrival of the pilgrims. Lean-on palm fronds were slung over the doorway in a picturesque fashion. Within there is a paved courtyard and various rooms, some in a state of collapse, on either side. Two flights of steps lead up to the roof and a belfry is visible in the corner. In front of us was a long barrel-vaulted chamber (4.7 m wide) extending eastwards and culminating in an apse. This is the chapel mentioned in the explorations conducted at the site in 1873 by Claude Regnier Conder for the Palestine Exploration Fund. Maayan and I wandered around the building, holding in one hand a copy of Conder's plan. Apart from the fact that the ground floor of the building still consists of four long barrel-vaulted chambers, which have been subdivided into separate chambers, the dimensions of the rooms we examined seemed to differ from those depicted on the plan, perhaps because of the restorations made as late as 1955 (with the inauguration of the chapel surmounted by a dome in 1956). Hence, I decided that there was no point in us trying to update Conder's plan: the whole complex will need to be re-measured at some later time. There was an intense smell of urine and neglect in some of the rooms and a film of powdery dust lay everywhere. In one room we came across an enormous cache of empty glass bottles. Climbing to the first floor, everything appeared to be modern and so must postdate the nineteenth-century reconstruction of the building. A cupola with four windows provided light to the chapel below. There are innumerable bullet holes in all of the upper walls. The bell still hangs in the belfry and it too has been pierced by a number of bullet holes. From the roof there is a magnificent view of the Jordan River, the baptism site and the mountains of Transjordan in the background.

Busloads of Greek and Russian worshippers had been arriving at the site for the celebrations. I estimated that there were at least one thousand people milling about outside the monastery, and some of them kept trying to squeeze themselves into the narrow chapel to light a candle and to make a prayer. A nun kept on blowing out candles and reselling them, presumably because there were not enough candles to go around. Rafi elected to follow the procession that was almost ready to make its way from the monastery down to the banks of the River Jordan. Everyone was now awaiting the imminent arrival of the Greek Orthodox Patriarch, Irineous. Maayan and I, however, went over to investigate the hillocks located immediately east of the building. Scattered on the ground surface there were many stone mosaic cubes (*tesserae*) and pottery that seemed to be Byzantine and medieval in date, together with a few modern beer bottles and shrapnel from exploded shells. Apparently, according to the ancient sources, there was some kind of chapel or altar to the east, approximately halfway between the monastery and the Jordan River, but today nothing is visible there except for a heavily fortified Israeli army outpost surrounded by lines of barbed wire and extensive mine fields. Maayan and I advanced as close as we could to the minefields, but then turned back.

Joining the throng of worshippers moving down the road leading to the Jordan River, we passed what appeared to be rectangular camps for worshippers on either side of the road, but these are no longer accessible and, judging by the signs on the fences, they are now all minefields, lethal to enter. A road extends to the south on a fairly straight line to the modern baptism site and its adjacent chapels. We proceeded, however, all the way to the east bank of the Jordan River (*plate 11b*). On reaching that place we witnessed an amazing sight: two groups of Greek Orthodox worshippers, opposite each other on both sides of the river. Those on the right bank stood on the soil of the Hashemite Kingdom of Jordan and those on the left bank stood on the soil of the State of Israel, with only a narrow ribbon of churning river serving as the border between the two countries. The baptism ceremonies proceeded on either side under the watchful eyes of the armed Jordanian and Israeli soldiers – apparently in the past some people had made attempts to jump from country to country without the use of passports.

Walking down to the river edge, I was pleasantly surprised to bump into Sister Maatje from the Convent next to the Monastery of Saint John in the Wilderness near Ain Karim. 'Hallo, Shimon,' she said, 'it is good to see you here.' Down at the waterfront, an industrious Russian monk was doing his best to dole out water to the pilgrims, which he was collecting by bucket direct from the Jordan, filling their water bottles to the brim. Some of the pilgrims, with a fierce dour look in their eyes, were even dunking their bodies in the freezing water, hoping to experience something of the sanctity of the same water that had been used to baptise Jesus. I could not help but recall that recent scientific studies had shown the Jordan River to be heavily polluted.

The procession with the Greek Orthodox Patriarch at its head had finally reached its destination and the ceremony unfolded, with prayers and the burning of incense. I felt sorry for the Patriarch, he was hemmed in on all sides by officials and cameramen, and it looked like he was not going to get the chance to see the Jordan River himself.

Climbing back up the hill towards the monastery, I reflected on the significance of the ceremony and on the beauty of the environment, albeit marred by the military earthworks and minefields, and thought about those days, many thousands of years ago, when John the Baptist himself might have wandered around in this landscape.

In the Byzantine and medieval periods it would appear that there were a great many sites associated with the memory of John's baptism of Jesus in the landscapes of the lower Jordan Valley region (eight kilometres north of the Dead Sea). Some of these were scattered next to the approach to the river from the west, others along the banks of the river, and there were additional sites inland extending up the length of Wadi Kharrar (*illustration 8.1*). Scattered between these sites were numerous hermitages and isolated cells [note 8.6] The sites are mentioned in a profusion of ancient texts and it has been a great puzzle for scholars trying to work out which source should be linked with which site. The main site along the approach to the river from the west is Qasr el-Yehud (Deir Mar Yuhanna), or the Monastery of the Prodromos (St John). Then there is the site of el-Maghtas or Bethabara, which is located at the crossing of the river itself, mainly on the east bank; and, finally, there is the site of Ain Bassat el-Kharrar and Tell Mar Liyas which are situated at the head of Wadi Kharrar [note 8.7].

The earliest positive reference to a visit made to the Jordan is that of the Bordeaux Pilgrim (AD 333). Approaching from the west bank, this pilgrim wrote: 'Five miles from there [the Dead Sea] in the Jordan is the place where the Lord was baptised by John, and above the far [eastern] bank at the same place is the hillock from which Elijah was taken up to heaven' [note 8.8] The nun Egeria (AD 384) passed through the region on her travels in the company of various monks, deacons and a presbyter, but, strangely, completely ignored the traditions relating to John the Baptist (perhaps she wrote about it elsewhere in writings about her travels which have not been preserved). Instead, she described

Bethabara as follows: 'reached the place on the Jordan where holy Joshua the son of Nun sent the children across and they passed over, as we are told' [Joshua 3, 4]. There was no mention in her narrative of any church or installation whatsoever, but there must have been some people there because she says 'we were shown a slightly raised place on the Jericho stretch of the river [presumably just east of the Qasr el-Yehud location], where the Children of Reuben and Gad and the half tribe of Manasseh made an altar [Joshua 22:10].'

The description provided by Theodosius (*c*. AD 530) refers to the church erected by order of Anastasius (AD 491–518) on the east bank of the river at Bethabara: 'At the place where my Lord was baptised is a marble column, and on top of it has been set an iron cross. There also is the Church of Saint John Baptist, which was constructed by the Emperor Anastasius. It stands on great vaults which are high enough for the times when the Jordan is in flood. The monks who reside at this church each receive six *solidi* a year from the treasury for their livelihood.' Theodosius then goes on to talk about another site (presumably inland) and it may refer to the Ain Basset el-Kharrar site: 'Where my Lord was baptised there is on the far side of the Jordan the "little hill" called Hermon . . . where Saint Elijah was taken up. The tomb of Elisha is there at the place where he blessed the spring, and a church has been constructed over the tomb.' Finally, Theodosius provides a location from the Bethabara site: 'It is five miles [8 km] from the place where my Lord was baptised to the point where the Jordan enters the Dead Sea' [note 8.9].

The next description of note is that provided by the Piacenza Pilgrim (*c*. AD 570), who begins by describing the Bethabara site: 'from there we arrived at the place where the Lord was baptised. This is the place where the Children of Israel made their crossing, and also where the sons of the prophets lost their axe-head, and where Elijah was taken up.' The pilgrim then continues and describes the Ain Basset el-Kharrar site:

In that place is the "little hill of Hermon" mentioned in the psalm [Psalm 133:3: 'as the dew of Hermon . . .']. At the foot of the mountain at seven o'clock in the morning, a cloud forms over the river, and it arrives over Jerusalem at sunrise . . . . In that part of the Jordan is the spring where Saint John used to baptise, and which is two miles from the Jordan, and Elijah was in that valley [Wadi Kharrar] when the raven brought him bread and meat. The whole valley is full of hermits . . .

The pilgrim then resumed the description of the Bethabara site: 'I kept Epiphany at the Jordan, and on that night special miracles take place at the spot where the Lord was baptised. There is an obelisk there surrounded by a screen, and in the water, where the river turned back in its bed, stands a wooden cross. On both banks there are marble steps leading down to the water.' The Piacenza Pilgrim relates how at the Jordan during Epiphany there is a large congregation and the ceremony is conducted by a priest in the presence of ministers and deacons.

The moment he starts blessing the water the Jordan turns back on itself with a roar and the water stays still till the baptism is finished. All the shipowners of Alexandria have men there with great jars of spices and balsam, and as soon as the river has been blessed, before the baptism starts, they pour them out into the water, and draw out holy water. The water they use for sprinkling their ships when they are about to set sail. After the baptism everyone goes down into the river to gain a blessing [suggesting that the location of baptism and river were somewhat distinct?]. Some wear linen, and some other materials which will serve as shrouds for burial. And after the baptism the water returns to its place . . . [The description suggests that water from the Jordan was siphoned off towards the church, or under it, for the purpose of baptism].

The pilgrim then speaks about another nearby location: 'On the bank of the Jordan there is a cave in which are cells for seven virgins. They are placed there as small girls, and when one of them dies, she is buried in her cell, and another cell is hewn from the rock, so that another girl can be placed there to make up the number. They have people outside to look after them. We went in with great reverence to pray there, but we did not see the face of a single one of them. It is said that the cloth is there which the Lord wore on his face.'

Finally, the pilgrim speaks once again about the site of Bethabara (though alternatively he could have been referring to the Qasr el-Yehud site): 'By the Jordan, not far from where the Lord was baptised is the very large Monastery of Saint John, which has two guest-houses. On both banks of the Jordan below the mountains there are serpents from which people make antidotes against poisoning' [note 8.10].

The next source of interest is the description of the penitent St Mary of Egypt who on leaving Jerusalem made her way to the Jordan where she intended to cross over to the other side:

When the sun was nearing its setting . . . I saw the Church of John the Baptist which was in the vicinity of the Jordan; and entering the sanctuary to pray I went down immediately to the river and with that holy water I washed my hands and face. I took then the life-saving and most pure sacraments of Christ the Lord in the same basilica of John the Baptist, the Forerunner. Then I ate half a loaf, drank from the water of the Jordan and lay down on the ground for the night. As soon as the light of dawn arrived, the following morning, I passed to the other side . . . [presumably back again westwards] [note 8.11].

Another interesting source of data is the work called *Pratum Spirituale* (The Spiritual Meadow), consisting of anecdotes about monastic life which was written by John Moschus (*c*. AD 575). In one story he refers to the baptism of a young monk at the Jordan River at the 'Monastery of the Eunuchs' which may very well be the church at Bethabara. Elsewhere, he relates that a certain elderly monk set out on a journey with a disciple and reached the site of Ain Basset el-Kharrar:

They crossed the river Jordan but before they reached even the first mile-post the elder began to shiver with fever. As he was unable to walk, they found a small cave and went in it so that the elder could rest. He stayed in the cave for three days, scarcely able to move and burning with fever. Then, whilst he was sleeping, he saw a figure who said to him: 'Tell me, elder, where do you want to go?' He replied: 'To Mount Sinai.' The vision then said to him: 'Please, I beg of you, do not go there,' but as he could not prevail upon the elder, he withdrew from him. Now the elder's fever attacked him more violently. Again the following night the same figure with the same appearance came to him and said: 'Why do you insist on suffering like this, good elder? Listen to me and do not go there.' The elder asked him: 'Who then are you?' The vision replied: 'I am John the Baptist and that is why I say to you: do not go there. For this little cave is greater than Mount Sinai. Many times did our Lord Jesus Christ come in here to visit me. Give me your word that you will stay here and I will give you back your health.' The elder accepted this with joy and gave his solemn word that he would remain in the cave. He was instantly restored to health and stayed there for the rest of his life. He made the cave into a church and gathered a brotherhood together there; the place is called Sapsas. Close by it and to the left is the Wadi Chorath [i.e. Kerith] to which Elijah the Tishbite was sent during a drought; it faces the Jordan [note 8.12].

The following account from AD 685 was written by Adomnan and relates to a trip taken by Bishop Arculf to the Jordan. Bishop Arculf arrived in the region from the direction of Jericho, passing Gilgal (at Tell Jiljul), and then proceeding on towards the Jordan along the ancient Roman road. The first site mentioned was the one at Bethabara and he also refers to a church on arches:

> The holy, venerable spot at which the Lord was baptised by John is permanently covered by the water of the River Jordan, and Arculf, who reached the place, and has swum across the river both ways, says that a tall wooden cross has been set up on that holy place. The water level reaches the neck of a very tall man if he were to stand there, but there are times of extreme drought when the water goes down, and would only reach his chest, and times of serious flooding when the extra water would submerge the whole cross. The position of the cross where, as we have said, the Lord was baptised, is on the *near side* of the river bed. A strong man using a sling can throw a stone from there to the far bank on the Arabian side. From this cross a stone causeway supported on arches stretches to the bank, and people approaching the cross go down a ramp and return up it to reach the bank. Right at the river's edge stands a small rectangular church which was built, so it is said, at the place where the Lord's clothes were placed when he was baptised. The fact that it is supported on four stone vaults, makes it usuable, since the water, which comes in from all four sides, is underneath it. It has a tiled roof. This remarkable church is supported, as we have said, by arches and vaults, and stands in the lower part of the valley through which the Jordan flows. [Italics: S.G.]

Adomnan then goes on to mention the Qasr el-Yehud church on the western bank: 'But in the upper part there is a great monastery for monks, which has been built on the brow of a small hill nearby, overlooking the church. There is also a church built there in honour of Saint John the Baptist which, together with the monastery, is enclosed in a single masonry wall' [note 8.13].

Epiphanius the Monk (dated to between AD 715 and 717), who approached the site from the direction of Jerusalem, mentions the Ain Basset el-Kharrar site: 'The spring of Meras is there, and, about three miles [4.8 km] beyond the Jordan a cave in which lived the Forerunner. There too is the bed on which he slept, a natural shelf in the rock of the cave, and a small chamber. Inside the cave is a sound of water, and in the room is a spring in which holy John the Forerunner used to baptise . . .'. He then goes on to refer in rapid succession to the monastery (fort) of Qasr el-Yehud and to the Bethabara church with a relic stone: 'And to the east of Jericho, about eight miles away is the Jordan, and a small fort is there containing a large church, the Holy Trinity. On the river bank is a church of the Forerunner, and in the apse of the church stands a stone on which the Forerunner was when he baptised Christ. And across the Jordan, about a mile away, is the cave of the Foreunner' [note 8.14].

In AD 724, Williband reached the monastery at Qasr el-Yehud where he stayed the night, but on the following morning he visited the Bethabara church site. One may construe from his description that the course of the river had now moved to the west which explains why the vaults beneath the church were dry:

> They rested there for a time, and then went on to the Monastery of St John the Baptist, which had about twenty monks. They stayed one night there, and then went on a mile or so to the Jordan, where the Lord was baptised. There is now a church there which is raised on stone columns, and beneath the church the very place where the Lord was baptised, which is now dry soil. At the place where they now baptise there is a wooden cross in the middle, and a small channel for water. On the feast of the Epiphany cripples and sick people come and, using the rope to steady themselves, go down to dip themselves in the water: women who are barren also come there. Our bishop Willibald bathed there in the Jordan, and they were there for one day [note 8.15].

The existence of two churches at the Jordan River: the Bethabara Church and the Qasr el-Yehud church, is also clear from the *Commemoratorium de Casis Dei* (c. 808) which mentions 'At the Jordan, the Monastery of St John and another church where pilgrims go down to the river [there are] 35 monks' [note 8.16]. The Bethabara church continued to be visited in the ninth century judging by a short reference by Bernard the Wise (AD 870).

Finally, the Russian abbot Daniel (1106–1108) has provided us with a fairly full description of his journey to the baptism sites. Arriving from the direction of Jericho and travelling for six *versts* [approximately 6.4 km, i.e. 1 *verst* = 1.067 km], he reached 'the monastery of St John the Baptist, built high on a hill [Qasr el-Yehud]. Here about 20 fathoms [213 metres] from the monastery is Mount Hermon, on the left [to the north or at Ghor er-Rumana?] near the road. It is a sandy hill, small rather than large. It is two good bowshots [213 metres] from Hermon to the old monastery of St John [Qasr el-Yehud], where there was a great church built in honour of St John the Precursor.' Abbot Daniel proceeds with a description of a site located immediately east of the Qasr el-Yehud church which is now an Israeli army outpost:

And beyond the altar of this church on a rise close by to the east there is a little altar and a small arch and in this place John the Precursor baptised Our Lord Jesus Christ; the Jordan came to this spot and turned back and overflowed its bed, frightened when it saw its creator coming to be baptised. And near this pool there used to be the Sea of Sodom [the Dead Sea] but now it is some 4 *versts* further from the place of baptism [i.e. 4.2 km to the south], for the seas seeing God, naked, standing in the waters of the Jordan, took fright and fled [i.e. the sea receded southwards – it is interesting to note that the sea has now receded 7.5 km to the south of Qasr el-Yehud] . . . From the place where Christ was baptised to the Jordan itself [i.e. from the altar and small arch location] is as far as a man can throw a small stone.

Abbot Daniel then went on to talk about the Bethabara site: 'There is a pool in the Jordan and here all the Christians come to bathe; and there is a ford here [at the Maghtas Ford] across the Jordan into Arabia; here of old the Jordan parted for the sons of Israel and the people passed through on dry land. There too Elisha struck the water with the mantle of Elijah and they crossed the Jordan on dry land; and at the same pool Mary the Egyptian crossed the waters to Father Zosimus to receive the body of Christ and, crossing the waters again, went back into the desert.' Crossing over, Daniel says that the river 'is 4 fathoms deep [approximately 42.7 m] at the middle of the bathing place, as I have measured and tested myself, for I have crossed to the far side of the Jordan and have travelled much along its bank . . . There is on this side of the Jordan at the bathing-place a sort of wood of small trees like the willow . . .'

Finally, Abbot Daniel refers to the Ain Basset el-Kharrar site: 'And there is a place here to the east some two bowshots distant from the river, where the prophet Elijah was carried up to heaven in a fiery chariot. And here also is the cave of St John the Baptist. And there is a beautiful torrent here full of water, which flows over the rocks into the Jordan; and was the water which John the Precursor of Christ drank when he was living in this holy cave. There is another remarkable cave here where the holy prophet Elijah lived with his disciple Elisha. And by the grace of God all this I have seen with my own sinful and unworthy eyes' [note 8.17].

On the basis of the available textual sources, it would appear that the Qasr el-Yehud ('Fort of the Jews') site, which is also known as the Monastery of the Prodromos (Deir Mar Yuhanna), was not built before the seventh century. The earliest reference to the site is from Adomnan's account of Arculf's travels from AD 685, and this is followed by descriptions by Williband (AD 724), Epiphanius the Monk (dated to between 715/17) and Abbot Daniel (1106–8). Further sources supply us with additional information about the site [note 8.18]. In 1114 there were twenty monks in the monastery. In 1139 the monastery was rebuilt and inhabited by six monks, all of whom were subsequently beheaded by 'Imad ad-Din Zangi (Sanginus). In 1154 we hear of Greek monks inhabiting the place. Apparently, between 1169–1172 the monastery was fortified by the Templars to protect pilgrims [note 8.19]. In 1175 Theodoric bathed in the river with other pilgrims and was able to observe the stone on which Jesus stood while being baptised. According to John Phocas (1185): 'The Monastery of the Prodromus, was completely demolished by an earthquake [probably in 1160]. But it has now been newly rebuilt by the munificent hand of our Emperor Manuel, crowned by God, Manuel Porphyogenitus Comnenus [1143–1180], because the Head of the Community [i.e. the prior] spoke freely to him about it being rebuilt.' In 1217 and 1229–1231, we hear of Greek monks at the site. Relics of John (left hand or arm) were being shown at the Qasr el-Yehud monastery in the fourteenth century and are mentioned in a few accounts. Nicolas of Poggibonsi (1336–50), for example, wrote: 'As you go straight down [to the east] you enter the said monastery [Qasr el-Yehud], and to the left you find a staircase, to the right there is the church, and in front of the door there is a portico. And the Greek monks who live in the said monastery show at the gate a box of cypress, in which they display the hand of St John the Baptist; and the hand is withered, with the fist open.' In the fifteenth century, the monastery was in ruins and the pilgrim Felix Fabri (1480–83) wrote that the site 'has now been desecrated by the dwelling therein of Arabs, who live the life of robbers therein and inhabit it as a fortress. Its altars are destroyed, and it has in some sort lost the form of a church.'

The realisation that the Bethabara site might actually be on the east bank of the Jordan River first became apparent in 1899 during a trip made there by Father Féderlin of the White Fathers in Jerusalem, who reported seeing the remains of a buried chapel on arches at the estuary of Wadi Kharrar in an area covered with tamarisk trees and bordered to the east by *lissan* marl cliffs [note 8.20]. Two other visitors to the site, Dalman in 1913 and Buzy in 1930, confirmed the existence of these ruins. Finally, a proper archaeological survey of the area was conducted by Father F.-M. Abel in 1932 and he suggested that perhaps this was the location of the main Byzantine church of St John [note 8.21]. These finds fit in with the information from the textual sources. A church dedicated to St John (which was built on arches) was erected at the site of the traditional site of the baptism at the instigation of the emperor Anastasius, in the late fifth or early sixth centuries. A monastery and two guest-houses which were connected to the church, are also mentioned in a pilgrim's account from the late sixth century. This monastery may very well have been the same as the 'Monastery of the Eunuchs' referred to by John Moschus. The church was mentioned once in the seventh century (as a church on four vaults), twice in the eighth century (as a church on vaults and with a relic stone), and finally twice in the ninth century. Thereafter, we do not hear of the church and we must assume that by the end of the ninth century it had been abandoned and afterwards remained in ruins, with most of the needs of the pilgrims now being facilitated by the Monastery of St John at Qasr el-Yehud on the west bank.

In 1997, Mohammed Waheeb, of the Jordanian Department of Antiquities, began excavating at the Bethabara site at the spot previously pointed out by Abel, about two hundred metres to the east of the Jordan River. Digging down he came across the impressive remains of a large church built above collapsed vaults, which underwent numerous stages of construction during the three hundred years of its existence. The church was of basilical plan, with nave and two aisles, marble and mosaic floors, and an apse in the east. A staircase led up to the façade of the church from the west. On the basis of the finds the church has been dated to the Byzantine and Early Islamic periods. On the east side of the main church complex, the excavators found a staircase (1.5 metres wide), built of blocks of black bituminous stone, which descended eastwards to below the actual level of the water of the Jordan River. It is surmised that the staircase was used by pilgrims during baptism ceremonies. Not far from the main church and adjacent to the staircase,

Waheeb uncovered a small chapel (6.3 × 4.3 metres) with an apse, plastered walls and a pavement of black marble. Nearby were cist graves (of two adults and a child). About 250 metres to the east of the main church is a rectangular pool (24 × 5 metres; 2 metres deep) which drained water from Wadi Kharrar and it has been dated to the Byzantine period. Steps led into the pool from the south-west corner and a channel that brought water into the pool (and a western outlet) has also been identified. It is conceivable that this pool (or another seen in the vicinity) was the result of imperial patronage at the site by Justinian (AD 527–560) with Procopius reporting that a cistern or well was built at the Monastery of St John. Nearby, archaeologists have identified additional building remains which may represent the remains of a hostel; perhaps it was one of the two mentioned in the late sixth century by the Piacenza Pilgrim [note 8.22].

It was in all the newspapers worldwide in late December 2000 with the blazing headline: 'Skull of John the Baptist Found Near Jordan.' I was intrigued, but the newspaper account did not provide many details, other than saying that John's head had been found in a cave under a church on the east bank of the Jordan River, but otherwise the details were rather sketchy. So I contacted an acquaintance of mine in Jordan, Rami Khouri, who is at present the Executive Editor of the *Daily Star* in Beirut, asking him if he could provide me with some information about the discovery. He wrote back to me as follows: 'Shimon – The skull story is not very credible; I saw the skull about two years ago and it's one of many in the area from ancient and modern burials. It's not something they found last week. I don't know why they just publicised it now. Best wishes – Rami.' It quickly transpired that the whole skull story had been a spin created by journalists. In order to clear things up the Jordanian Department of Antiquities issued a statement in January 2001 denying that the skull was that of John the Baptist [note 8.23].

I decided that I needed to see for myself the site – Ain Basset el-Kharrar – where the skull had been found, and therefore in May 2001 I set off for Jordan. But setting up a meeting with the dig director was not turning out to be an easy task. Meanwhile, I went to have a look at another archaeological site connected with John the Baptist, namely the site of the beheading at Machaerus. From there I continued on to Safi.

It poured with rain all night long, a phenomenon quite unusual at Safi at that time of year (May). A thick blanket of thousands of frogs was spread out across the land and it was impossible to drive along the roads without crushing a few of them. After a quick breakfast provided by the archaeologist Dino Politis at his dig headquarters – humous, eggs and yoghurt – we set off to see some ancient sites. Apparently a downpour of rain such as this had not been seen there since 1992. There was a fresh smell of damp soil in the air. We drove south and were amazed when we came across an enormous body of water cascading under the bridge beneath the road. One could hear the clang – almost metallic in sound – as the boulders hit each other, as well as the supports of the bridge. We proceeded southwards. Again we could see water gushing westwards, cutting past Tell Numeirah with an intense force and speed. It was an awe-inspiring demonstration of the power of nature. Even the locals were impressed: cars were stopping and drivers were hanging over the railings, gawping with astonishment at the enormous body of water crashing down from the mountain gullies, bubbling and frothing and churning up the mud. We subsequently visited the Zoar-Safi sites, including the Ayyubid or Mamluke structure in the plain, passing a sugar factory on the low ridge, and reaching the hillocks honeycombed with pits made by tomb robbers; the entire area looks like Swiss cheese. Sadly, the ancient tombs are being robbed out and nothing can be done to stop the damage. I had to drive carefully because some of the clandestine diggers were even undermining the roads in their search for antiquities. I definitely did not want my rented car collapsing into a Bronze Age tomb!

We returned northwards passing Wadi el-Hasa, which was now a raging torrent of water and crashing boulders. Eventually, we reached the Byzantine monastery of Deir Ain Abata (the Monastery of St Lot) and, after visiting the site, we proceeded to the office of the local Antiquities inspector, Halil Hamdan, a charming man with whom we sipped coffee, while he attempted to contact Mohammed Waheeb, the excavator of Ain Basset el-Kharrar, by telephone. I said goodbye to Dino and Halil and then drove northwards along the eastern edge of the Dead Sea. My meeting with Mohammed Waheeb at the baptism site had been set for noon and I wanted to get there on time. On the way, I witnessed yet another impressive display of the power of water pumping without restraint out of Wadi al-Mujib and into the Dead Sea and creating a large brown stain in the light blue waters. There were even boulders flying down the wadi, and the foundations of the bridge I was standing on shook and trembled. The police came over and indicated that they thought I should leave because there was a chance that the bridge might collapse. I proceeded northwards and eventually reached the baptism site, twenty minutes late, having driven down a number of incorrect side roads and around in circles because of misleading road signs.

Mohammed Waheeb was in his office: a man in his late thirties, with a mild manner and very courteous. After tea, during which he provided me with a pile of assorted publications relating to his work, we proceeded on foot to the site of Ain Basset el-Kharrar. Waheeb pointed out that there are fifteen sites that he has been investigating in the Wadi el-Kharrar region, extending for about two kilometres from the head of the valley and down to the eastern bank of the Jordan River. All of these had produced Byzantine remains, he told me, except for Tell Mar Liyas ('Elijah's Hill'), to which he was taking us, which had earlier material. The earliest remains that he had uncovered there were from the first century AD, including typical Early Roman pottery and the rim and handle of a stone 'measuring cup'. However, Iron Age pottery had not yet come to light there [note 8.24].

The Ain Basset el-Kharrar site that Waheeb was showing me is mentioned in a number of ancient sources dating from the sixth century to the twelfth century. Three sources from the second half of the sixth century indicate that the site used to have a number of separate locations associated with the worship of the tradition of Elijah and John the Baptist, notably a cave of Elijah in the Kerith Brook (i.e. Wadi Kharrar); a place where Elijah ascended to heaven (the 'little hill of Hermon'); a church situated over the tomb of Elisha; a spring which Elisha blessed and where John baptised, and cells that were used by the monks living there. The monastery (*laura*) was known as Sapsas, which is a garbled version of the name Sapsaphas. A source from the early eighth century describes three locations: the spring of Meras; a cave of John the Baptist, and the spring where John baptised. Finally, an early twelfth-century source described four locations: the place where Elijah ascended to heaven; a cave used by Elijah and Elisha; a cave of John the Baptist, and a spring where John drank. The name of the site – Sapsaphas – is perhaps derived from the name (Arabic *safsaf*, Hebrew *tsaftsafa*) of the fast-growing shrubby willow of the *Salicaceae* family, i.e. the *Populus euphratica Oliv.* and it can reach a height of fifteen metres when there is an abundance of water (cf. Ezekiel 17:5). The bark was used for making baskets and mats, and it also had some use in local medicine [note 8.25]. The site was also depicted on the Madaba mosaic map of the Holy Land on the right (eastern) bank of the Jordan, and the Greek text reads: 'Aenon where now is Sapsaphas [Σαπσαφᾶς].' The symbol on this sixth-century map shows an enclosed spring [note 8.26].

Waheeb explained to me that some of the water installations that he had uncovered at the site were of Roman date. The site is very fertile and the spring water (of el-Kharrar, and further east those from Ain Salim, Ain Fawara and Ain Hammam, and others) created dense vegetation in the adjacent wadi, which brings to mind the attraction that the site would certainly have had in antiquity. The area of Elijah's Hill is the property of the Greek Orthodox patriarchate.

Waheeb showed me around the dig, pointing out its salient features. First, he showed me a simple mosaic floor with red and black rosebud decorations, which apparently were part of a church. He then took me along to see a Byzantine-period 'prayer chapel', which also had its own mosaic floor. The water system was quite interesting with an open pool (*birke*) resembling many which can be seen at other monastic establishments. We then proceeded along a wall surrounding part of the site: cut into the marl below it there were three small caves and Waheeb told me that he has identified the largest of these as the traditional cave of John the Baptist (*plate 12a*). The evidence seemed quite slim. Apart from the size of the cave, there were no other finds with which to identity the cave. Since the sources also mention the traditional cave of Elijah and Elisha at the site, as well as dwelling caves (cells) used by Byzantine monks, one has to express certain reservations about this identification. It was in front of this cave that a pit (0.6 × 0.6 m) was uncovered containing the famous skull which attracted worldwide attention. It was of a 25-year-old individual and his lower jaw is missing. Waheeb chose his words very carefully, when I asked him if he thought it might be the skull of John the Baptist. Because of the size of the cave and the manner in which the skull had been deposited, Waheeb seemed to believe that the skull might have been connected in some way with the cult of John the Baptist.

Proceeding around to the central part of the hillock, Waheeb showed me a chapel with a mosaic floor and a dedicatory inscription in Greek which read: 'With the collaboration of the grace of Christ our god, under Rhetorius, the most god-loving presbyter and abbot, all the work of the monastery was done. May god the saviour grant him mercy' (*illustration 8.3*) [note 8.27]. The late fifth- or sixth-century date for this inscription fits in well with the consecration of a cave-church at the site under Patriarch Elias (AD 494–516) and with the account provided by John Moschus (*c.* AD 575). The fact that this inscription did not mention John the Baptist or the name of the actual establishment was a major disappointment for Waheeb; it showed in his face. The building remains

THCXΑ̅ΡΙΤJ(ΥΝΡΓΙCΑCJX̅Y̅
ΤΟΥΘVΗΜJ·ΕΠΙΡΗΤωΡΙΟ̆
ΤΟ̆ΘΕΟΦΙΛJΠΡΕCΒJΚΗΓJ
ΓΕΓΟΝJΤΟΠΑΝΕΡΓJΤΗCΜ̇Ν̲J̲
ΔΟΗΑΥΤωΕΛΕΟCΟΘCΟCΗ̅Ρ̅

8.3

at the top of the clump represented the eighteenth-century Greek Orthodox monastic settlement. My gut feeling is that the deep well with a round entrance that descends down to the water-table must also have been in use at this date and that many of the associated water installations coated in grey plaster are also of late date. Further along is a large stepped pool with steps leading down which has been identified as a 'baptising pool' of Roman date (*plate 12b*).

In John (3:23) we hear that John the Baptist had moved his scene of operations from Bethabara in the southern part of the Jordan Valley, to another location altogether, though whether this was to be a temporary or permanent arrangement was left unclear: 'And John too was baptising at Aenon (Αἰνών), near Salem, because there was much water there, and [people] came and were baptised.' Why did John baptise at Aenon instead of just staying at Bethabara? A puzzling question, but there are no clear-cut answers and the Gospels remain silent on this matter. One possibility, however, is that this was because of the time of year. Since the occasion appears to have been not long after the Passover observance in springtime, the river might very well have become swollen and over-flowed its banks, rendering the area of Bethabara in the lower Jordan River unsuitable for baptism purposes. The Jordan ordinarily has two banks: an inner one which marks the level of the river water, which remains more or less constant throughout the year, and an outer one which marks the top elevation of the river during the rainy season and especially in March when the river is boosted substantially by the melt-ing of the snow from the Hermon Mountain in the north. The swollen banks of the river in the Bethabara area might explain why John would have departed from the lower Jordan river, but not why he had also left behind the inland sites 'beyond Jordan' (i.e. the springs of Ain Basset el-Kharrar), unless of course John was already fearing for his life from Herod Antipas's soldiers. After all, Machaerus is not too great a distance from Bethabara.

One other possibility is that John was in the process of expanding his mission of baptism further northwards and was turning his eye towards the Galilee. Interestingly, Jesus at that time had been sent with a group of his followers to John's home ground in Jerusalem. In any case, it is unlikely, in my opinion, that John would have moved away from the immediate vicinity of the Jordan River, since, as we have shown, this region served as his main seat of operations precisely because of the expectation that he had regarding the imminent return of Elijah. Hence, I cannot envisage John having gone to any location that was more than one or two days' travel from Bethabara.

Scholars have been searching for the exact location of Aenon (a Greek word which means 'many waters', which is the plural of the word Ain, 'spring') in many different parts of Palestine: some have identified it in the locale of Jerusalem, others in Samaria, and others in the northern parts of the Jordan River. The rationale behind situating this place close to Jerusalem is that the first part of the passage in John (3:23) refers to 'Jesus [who was] baptising in Judaea with his disciples' and so the argument goes it would only make sense to compare the two if Jesus and John were both physically active in the same region. In the nineteenth century, Joseph Barclay identified Aenon at Wadi Farah to the north-east of Jerusalem. Barclay wrote that 'we passed some half dozen expansions of the stream, the water varying in depth from a few inches to a fathom or more. These pools are supplied by some half dozen springs bursting forth rocky crevices at various intervals. Verily, I thought, we have stumbled on Aenon!' Although Barclay concedes that his identification was a 'random conjecture of the moment', he does reach the 'assured conviction' that this was the place. Barclay was quite pleased to find that one of the wadis in the area to the south was known as Wadi Salim because he believed that it corresponded in some way with the place name Salem [note 8.28]. Barclay's views were later supported by the Reverend Lyman Coleman: 'About four or five miles northeast of Jerusalem, beyond the Mount of Olives, two or three below Anata, the ancient Anathoth, birthplace of Jeremiah, he [Barclay] found in the desert a succession of fountains for a mile or two gushing out from under high cliffs, πολλὰ ὕδατα, many 'pools deep enough for wading, swimming and all the immersions of the Baptists. Both [John and Jesus, with their disciples] would be nigh to each other, and have ample space. Indeed, all the conditions of the narrative are fully met here' [note 8.29].

Since the nineteenth-century attempts have been made to place Aenon and Salem in Samaria, but none of these suggestions has been very convincing. Khirbet Ainoun, located close to Tubas, to the north-east of Nablus, has usually been pointed out as the site of Aenon. However, as Guérin already pointed out in the nineteenth century, there are no springs at the site. The same argument against this identification was recently made by Jerry Murphy O'Connor [note 8.30]. There is also nothing to recommend the Salim or Salem sites, either east of Nablus or close to Ta'anik, since it is more likely that the name derives from the name of a local Palestinian clan, the Bani Salem [note 8.31].

A few textual sources indicate a location for Aenon in the Jordan Valley to the south of Beth Shean and I think that this tradition is quite a strong one. As I have already pointed out, it is unlikely that John would have moved any distance from the Jordan River since he was awaiting the return of Elijah. According to Eusebius (*Onomasticon* 40:1): 'the place is still shown today, eight miles south of Scythopolis [Beth Shean], near Salem and the Jordan.' The nun Egeria (AD 384), during her travels in the Holy Land, came to a fertile valley descending to the Jordan, with water, vineyards and trees.

> In it was a big village called Sedima; it is in the middle of a plain, and in the centre it has a fairly small hillock [a tell] shaped like a big tomb. On top is a church, and below, all round the hillock, are huge ancient foundations [fortification walls?], though only a few communities live there now.

Egeria enquired about the hill and was told that it was originally the city of Melchizedek and its name was originally Salem. After being greeted by the clergy of the church, Egeria was shown around by the presybter, who was an 'oldish man with an excellent knowledge of the Bible', who pointed out the ruins of a 'palace' and said that it was being used as a quarry for building stone.

> Then I remembered that according to the Bible it was near Salem that holy John baptised at Aenon [John 3:23]. So I asked if it was far

away. "There it is", said the holy presbyter, "two hundred yards away. If you like we can walk over there. It is from this spring that the village [of Sedima] has this excellent supply of clean water you see." Thanking him I asked him to take us, and we set off. He led us along a well-kept valley to a very neat apple orchard, and there in the middle of it he showed us a good clean spring of water which flowed in a single stream. There was a kind of pool in front of the spring at which it appears holy John Baptist administered baptism.

Egeria also relates that the place was known as 'St John's Garden' and that there were monks occupying cells in the area. The place was visited by many monks and pilgrims who would immerse themselves there. Egeria received apples as 'blessings' from the presbyter. Apparently, those 'candidates' for baptism from the village of Sedima were either baptised in the village church, Opu Melchisedech, or in the spring itself. From the spring 'they go off by torchlight singing psalms and antiphons, and accompanied by the clergy and monks' back to the village church [note 8.32]. The site was also shown on the Madaba Map of the Holy Land, dating from the second half of the sixth century, in the upper reaches of the Jordan Valley and written next to it in Greek: 'Ainon (Αἰνών) near Salem (Σαλήμ).' On ''this map the site is indicated close to Salumias [note 8.33].

About twelve kilometres (or eight miles according to Eusebius) to the south of Beth Shean (Scythopolis), there is a region which would fit Aenon perfectly. This location has numerous springs: I have counted thirteen of them in a small area of four by four kilometres and, interestingly, Ambrose in his writings (II, 1432) claimed that there were twelve springs at 'Ennon'. On the north side of this area is Tell Shalem, which undoubtedly must be Salim/Salumias (map ref. 2097–1998), and so the place where John baptised at Aenon may have been at any one of the springs in the vicinity of Tell Shalem. Abel suggested identifying Aenon at Khisas ed-Deir located about 1.5 km to the south-east of Tell Shalem [note 8.34]. Alternatively, Aenon could have been much closer, for example at Khirbet Hamed el-Fakhur, only half a kilometre to the south-west of Tell Shalem. Egeria in AD 384 visited the village of Salim (Shedima) and was told that the spring of Aenon was located very close to the village, only 200 yards away (approximately 183 metres), which she then visited. If indeed Tell Shalem was a village, then Aenon would have to be identified with Ain Ibrahim which is next to a sheikh's tomb immediately to the north-west of the ancient mound of Tell Shalem (Salim).

John's sway among those who came to him to be baptised, and the overall effects of his preaching, were so strong that Herod Antipas, son of Herod the Great, and ruler of Galilee and Peraea, looked upon him as the sort of person who was capable of leading a rebellion against him, and so as a threat to stability John had to be dealt with severely. According to Josephus (*Antiquities* XVIII, 116–119), 'Herod became alarmed. Eloquence that had so great an effect on mankind might lead to some form of sedition [or revolt]. For it looked as if they would be guided by John in everything that he did. Herod decided therefore that it would be much better to strike first and be rid of him before his work led to an uprising, than to wait for an upheaval, get involved in a difficult situation and see his mistake.' Herod's thinking rings true, especially since he had the reputation for being wily and cunning, which earned him the nickname 'the fox' (Luke 13:32).

There are two matters which arise from this: first John's message may have been much more political than we are led to believe based on the information in the Gospels, and, second, it does not appear that Herod's soldiers encountered any resistance from John's followers. Hence, it was only John's words that were political and not his actions. John was eventually brought in chains to Machaerus, a fortress-town on the southern borders of Peraea, and there executed. Later, in AD 36, when a dispute broke out between Herod Antipas and the Nabataean ruler, Aretas, over the annexation of the territory of the Tetrarch Philip, 'the whole army of Herod was destroyed' (*Aniquities* XVIII, 114) by the Nabataeans [note 8.35].

The story given in the Gospels regarding the reason for the imprisonment of John is different from the one given by Josephus, but it is in no way contradictory. According to Mark (6:17–18): 'For Herod himself had sent forth and laid hold upon John, and bound him in prison for the sake of Herodias, his brother Philip's wife: for he had married her. For John said unto Herod, It is not lawful for thee to have thy brother's wife' (cf. Matthew 14:3–4; Luke 3: 18–20). There is some confusion in Josephus as to when exactly the marriage between Herodias and Herod Antipas occurred and whether it was before or after John's death. Josephus provides us with the relevant details: '. . . Herodias, taking it into her head to flout the way of our fathers, married Herod [Antipas], her husband's brother by the same father, who was Tetrarch of Galilee [Peraea]; to do this she parted from a living husband [Philip]' (*Antiquities* XVIII, 136). The problem was in Herodias having married her two uncles, one after the other, while both were still alive, a union forbidden by Jewish law. Salome was the child of the first marriage to Herod (not to Philip as in Mark 6:17). The point John would have made in his preaching is that such a union was not in keeping with Leviticus (18:6): 'No man is to betake himself to a woman who is near of kin to him, and mate with her.' Indeed, the following unions were forbidden by Jewish law: son with mother; a man with one of his father's wives; a man with his sister or half-sister; a nephew with his aunt, and so forth. The guilty were usually put to death. In view of John's emulation of Elijah and the message that he was giving out regarding his imminent return, it is quite possible that he might have referred to Herodias as the incarnation of Jezebel, wife of Ahab, a matter which would not have been appreciated in Herod's royal household. The Gospels seem to suggest that Antipas had no plans to kill John, but that a set of circumstances led to his execution at the behest of Herodias who suggested that Salome ask for his head. This occurred on the occasion of a banquet to celebrate Herod's birthday in which he promised Salome anything that she desired because of her exquisite dancing.

People have always loved to hate her: throughout the centuries Salome has been portrayed in works of art as the evil Mona Lisa, her head tilted slightly to one side, a coy smile on her lips, a sense of drama and licentiousness in the gestures of her body and hands [note 8.36]. Scenes such as the 'Dance of Salome' and 'Salome and the head of John the Baptist on a charger' were favourite subjects for artists, and they portrayed her with underlying suggestions of hidden sexuality locked into the curves of her body, and flames of secret seduction flickering in her eyes. For many, Salome was the epitome of unruly and playful evil and delightful wickedness. She was a reminder of the dark side that can sometimes lurk within the apparent innocence of childhood. The Reverend Farrar, writing in the nineteenth century, pointed out that while some may regard Salome as having been merely an instrument in her mother's hand, the fact that she wanted John's head 'immediately with haste' (Mark 6:25) implies, as he put it, an 'ignorant girlish glee' [note 8.37].

So who was Salome? It was a popular name: there are fifty-two recorded instances of the name Salome (Hebrew: Shlomit, Shalom) in inscriptions from the Early Roman period. In the Gospels Salome was not mentioned directly by name and she is simply referred to there as 'daughter of Herodias' (Mark 6: 22). It is Josephus, in one of his writings, who actually provides us with her exact name, Salome (*Antiquities* XVIII, 136). The Greek word χοράσιον associated with her in Mark indicates that she was a 'very young girl', probably only twelve, when she danced in front of Antipas at a banquet to celebrate his birthday. Hence, she was probably born at the earliest in AD 16. Later, she is believed to have married Aristobulus, King of Lesser Armenia, but there have been some doubts about this [note 8.38]. There are two Gospel passages that deal with the story of Salome and the execution of John (Matthew 14:1–12; Mark 6: 14–29). A comparison of the two narratives is quite instructive. While the passage in Matthew is very factual in presentation, Mark's account is much more colourful. While in Matthew Salome was 'instructed' by her mother beforehand (i.e. Herodias planned the beheading in a premeditated fashion), the story in Mark is that it was the result of a whim, with Salome having to leave the banquet hall to consult with her mother: 'What shall I ask?'

There are some other minor points of difference: Antipas is referred to correctly as 'Tetrarch' in Matthew and simply as 'King' in Mark. The head of John is brought back on a charger in Matthew, but in Mark it was the executioner who brought back the head. Jacobus de Voragine (c.1230–1298) has preserved an apocryphal story of Salome's death, which represents the wishful thinking of Christian writers who could not accept the possibility that Salome might have got away with it, i.e. there had to be some final retribution for her act: 'As for her daughter [Salome], she was walking over an icy pond when the ice gave way under her and she was drowned, though one chronicle says that the earth swallowed her alive' [note 8.39].

No contemporary sculpted representation of Salome is known. However, in the 1920s an amateur archaeologist by the name of Paul Ilton, a resident of Jerusalem, bought a marble portrait of a young woman (about 4 inches high) from a man called Mussa who claimed that he had found it in a wine jar that he dug up in a cave located 'about 80 feet from the northern fortress' at Machaerus. Ilton subsequently made a visit to the site to have a look at the cave. In his book, Ilton quotes the opinions of a number of people to whom he showed this marble portrait, including R. Ben-Dor, G. Olaf Madson and G. Richter. While Ilton himself was convinced that he had bought the head of Salome, he summed up the opinions of the experts as follows: 'On strict scientific grounds it is obvious that no irrefutable identification of the statue as a likeness of Salome can be made' [note 8.40]. This sculpted head (labelled 'statuette of an Eastern Princess') still resides in a private collection and a replica of it was at one point made for Jerry Vardaman, who expressed the belief that it was indeed a likeness of Salome [note 8.41].

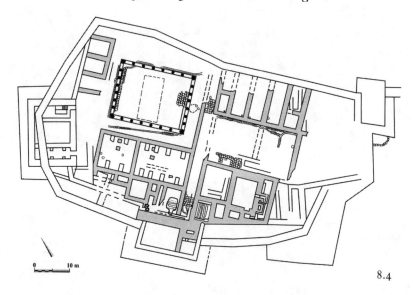

8.4

We set off from Madaba, passing the village of Libb, driving down a narrow winding road to the west, listening to James Bond theme music on a cassette. The first appearance of Machaerus (Mukawir) is quite impressive. It is a prominent mountain in a commanding position, with deep gullies all around, hollowed out reservoirs along the lower slopes, and with Roman military camps and siege-works round about. Climbing the hill, one comes across the crumbling walls of the palace which must have been the pride and joy of Herod Antipas (*illustration 8.4*). Apparently, on a clear day, one can look westwards and see the palace-fortress of Herodium near Bethlehem. It was to this place that John was brought to be imprisoned and where he finally met his death by beheading, if we are to accept the testimony of Josephus. The architectural fragments that have survived tell us that the palace was sumptuously decorated. I wandered around the palace site and wondered where John might have been brought to. Clearly he would not have been taken into the private apartments, the bath-house or to the service areas of the building complex (*plate 13a*). This leaves us with the large paved courtyard area, which had a surrounding portico of five-metre-high columns with Ionic-style capitals (*illustration 8.5, plate 13a*). This would have been a suitable location for a public engagement. The area of the courtyard has been heavily reconstructed since the excavations there, but one area of the original paving is still intact. An enormous water cistern beneath the courtyard is now the haven of nesting birds: the

245

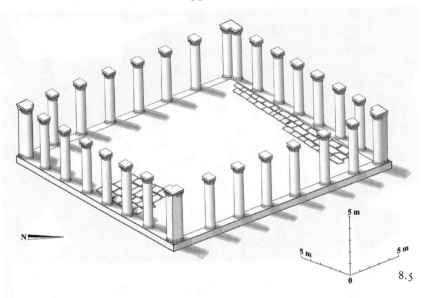

5 m

5 m   5 m

0   8.5

sound of the chirping is constant and the acoustics are amazing. Any bird lover worth their salt should come and record the singing of these birds.

Notwithstanding its importance, Machaerus was hardly visited in the nineteenth century, except by a few hardy explorers, notably Burckhardt, Tristram and Conder. Claude Regnier Conder reached the site during his survey of central Transjordan in 1881–1882 for the Palestine Exploration Fund, and described it briefly as 'stone heaps' and as the place of the 'gloomy prison' of John the Baptist [note 8.42]. Abel explored the site in January 1909 and provided photographs of the ruins and drawings of the architectural fragments he found [note 8.43]. Excavations were first conducted at the site by Jerry Vardaman in 1968, but the results were never published. However, I did manage to come across an interesting unpublished manuscript on his excavations in the library of the Hebrew University in Jerusalem [note 8.44]. The historian Nikkos Kokkinos, who knew Vardaman well, wrote to me that 'the Vardaman affair is as unusual as this man often was'. Apparently, his final report on the excavations was submitted with all the original plans and photographs for publication to the Jordanian Department of Antiquities, but all of this material was eventually lost in a fire which broke out in their warehouse. In any case, Kokkinos writes that Vardaman 'was left only with his notebooks and early versions of plans and photos, and was unable, as he told me, to reconstruct his excavation' [note 8.45]. In the early 1970s, August Strobel made a very detailed study of all the Roman siege-works in the landscape around Machaerus [note 8.46]. At the end of the 1970s, the Franciscan biblical school undertook major excavations at the site, under the general direction of Father Virgilio Corbo. Some work is still being undertaken at the site and M. Piccirillo recently excavated a few first-century tombs near the site [note 8.47].

Machaerus (Greek Μαχαιροῦς; Arabic Mekawar) was originally built by Alexander Jannaeus as a frontier fortress. Josephus (*Jewish War* VII: 163–70) describes its appearance: 'For the site that is fortified is itself a rocky eminence, rising to so great a height that on that account alone its reduction would be difficult; while nature had further contrived to render it inaccessible. For it is entrenched on all sides within ravines of a depth baffling to the eye, not easy to traverse and utterly impossible to bank up.' Later it passed into the hands of the Romans, was destroyed at one point by Gabinius, and was eventually rebuilt by Herod the Great:

> But Herod, on becoming king, regarded the place as supremely deserving of attention and of the strongest fortification, more especially from its proximity to Arabia, conveniently situated, as it was, with regard to that country, which it faces. He accordingly enclosed an extensive area with ramparts and towers and founded a city there, from which an ascent led up to the city itself. Furthermore, on the top, surrounding the actual crest, he built a wall, erecting towers at the corners, each sixty cubits high. In the centre of the enclosure he built a palace with magnificently spacious and beautiful apartments; he further provided numerous cisterns at the most convenient spots to receive the rainwater and furnish an abundant supply, as if he were vying with nature and endeavouring with these artificial defences to surpass the well-nigh impregnable strength which she had bestowed upon the site [Josephus, *Jewish War* VII: 171–77].

The site was on the southern border of the territory of Peraea. The Tetrarch Herod Antipas, one of the sons of Herod the Great, later entered into a marriage of convenience with the daughter of the Nabataean ruler Aretas, who was also a vassal of Rome. Following the liaison between Herod and Herodias, Herod decided to divorce the daughter of Aretas. She begged to be sent back to Machaerus and from there made her escape back to Nabataea. Because of the threat of war with the Nabataeans, Herod moved to Machaerus together with

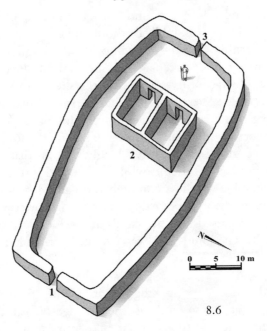

8.6

Herodias and her daughter Salome. It was at this point that the imprisonment and beheading of John took place. The site later became a refuge for Jews fleeing from Jerusalem which had been besieged by the Romans. Machaerus was also subsequently put under siege by the Roman legate Lucilius Bassus (*illustrations 8.6*). Josephus (*Jewish War* VII: 163–70) wrote that: 'This fortress it was absolutely necessary to eradicate, lest its strength should induce many to revolt; since the nature of the place was specially adapted to inspire its occupants with high hopes of security and to deter and alarm its assailants.' Eventually, its inhabitants surrendered; some were slaughtered and then the site was razed.

I had always wondered what a beheading would be like. Even as a child I was fascinated by the apparent duality within human beings, of physicality (the body) and essence (the soul), and this led me to ponder what would happen if one part of the physicality of a person, say the head, was detached from the rest of the body. Would the essence remain with the head or stay with the torso, or could it be in both places at the same time? For many thousands of years people have been puzzling over the nature and exact whereabouts of the soul of a human being: was it located in the heart, in the brain or was it something that was suffused throughout the body? Legally speaking, this is the great imponderable: when might a medical doctor, realistically and reasonably, declare a person as absolutely dead. Is this when the heart has completely stopped, or the brain has ceased to function; when the vital organs have become substantially impaired; or when the person has lost general cognition and has a permanent inability to make decisions regarding their own welfare? Death is definitely not an on-and-off switch. Establishing clinical death is made all the more difficult because there is evidence suggesting that brain cells continue to function for hours after 'death' has occurred.

In first-century Jewish Palestine, at the time of Jesus and John the Baptist, this situation was so unclear that a 'dead' person was initially regarded by the relatives as someone who had fallen into a 'state of slumber'. Hence, the body was placed in a sleeping position, wrapped in a shroud on a bed-like shelf in a burial cave, with members of the family returning from time to time to check on the situation of the body. Owing to the state of medicine at that time it is conceivable that some people were buried while still in a comatose state, with some later waking up in the tomb. This may have given rise to stories of people being raised from the dead (e.g. Lazarus). The final acceptance of death by the family, with the real act of burial taking place, was only after a period of about a year or so, when the body had completely decomposed and the bones could be gathered together for final internment in a stone box (ossuary). Many people, at the time of John the Baptist and later, believed that the essential being of a person and all rational thought was lodged in the head. Hence, in one mid-second-century source, there is a saying by Jesus about John the Baptist: 'The Lord answered and said: "Do you not know that the head of prophecy was cut off with John?" But I said: "O Lord, can it be possible to remove the head of prophecy?" The Lord said to me: "If you know what 'head' means, and that prophecy issues from the head, [then] understand what it means that "Its head was removed"'' [note 8.48].

My first thoughts about beheading occurred when I was only nine years of age, having just arrived in Israel with my mother. I remember the moment as if it was only yesterday: an English schoolboy standing with his twin brother in the midst of a Jewish Yemenite village, Tirat Shalom, watching the beheading of a chicken. I was horrified and at the same time fascinated by the spectacle: the chicken continued running around in circles in the courtyard of the house, with fluttering wings and blood spurting out of its neck, even though its head had been firmly removed with a knife from its body. For a small child a chicken had always been something that came well-packaged from the butcher's shop; it was food and was definitely not something that had once been alive. Later, in our host's house, I was presented with a bowl of chicken soup with one slice of carrot floating around on top. I was not quite sure what I should do and felt sick at the prospect of the pending main course of roasted chicken. I remember that I could not but help thinking about the beheading of human beings. My fertile young mind was able to conjure up a vivid scene: the roughness as the person was shoved to his knees, the feel of the quick thrust of cold metal against the neck, and then a few frightening seconds of shock before final closure. It is apparently a most difficult procedure to detach a head from a torso, and if decapitation with a sword or axe was not done by a professional hand, then things could go terribly wrong. An explorer from the Palestine Exploration Fund, Charles Warren, described a botched public execution that took place in 1867 of a Ta'amirah Bedouin accused of murdering a Jerusalemite:

> He was brought out for that purpose to the Jaffa Gate; but his family still seemed to think there was hope for him, and when the time was up made a last minute appeal to the widow of his victim. During the short conversation which took place with her, the convict opened his mouth, eyes and nostrils in his endeavours to hear her replies, and when he was put out of his dreadful suspense by finding her inflexible, he appeared already to be suffering the pangs of death. The execution was truly barbarous; the unfortunate man first got a cut across his shoulders, and turned around to say, 'You are hurting me'; then the amateur executioner, finding that sixteen blows did not sever the head from the body, turned the man upon his back, and sawed away at his throat as if he were killing a sheep. Eventually he managed to get the head and part of the shoulder off the trunk, and together they were left during the day for the diversion of the multitude [note 8.49].

Compared to the appalling deeds of this amateur executioner, the story of Judith's beheading of Holofernes, who was chief captain of the Assyrian army, sounds like it was a much more 'professional' affair. In this apocryphal story, we are told that Judith, the warrior woman and femme fatale combined, 'approached to his bed, and took hold of the hair of his head and said, Strengthen me, O Lord God of Israel, this day. And she smote twice upon his head with all her might, and she took away his head from him. And tumbled his body down from the bed . . .' (Judith 13: 7–9). Although Judith was a religious person practising prayer and self-denial, her act did not suit her piety, because she murdered a defenceless man, and then subsequently treated his mutilated head with disrespect by carrying it off as a trophy. Some scholars have suggested that this is the reason why the book of Judith was not included in the canon and was relegated to the apocryphal writings instead [note 8.50]. In the ancient Near East beheadings were frequently undertaken in the aftermath of hostilities so that the victorious army could have an accurate tally of the dead of the vanquished people. One Assyrian relief depicts exactly that: piles of severed heads of dead soldiers on one side and facing them scribes counting the number of the dead. There was also a custom at that time of cutting off the right hands of the casualties for tallying purposes, and some evidence of this practice has even come to light in a tomb at Jericho [note 8.51].

There are, of course, methods of execution that are worse than beheading in the sense that they involve a greater amount of suffering and indignity. Beheading, it would appear, was on the whole an easier way to die than to be hanged, drawn and quartered, garrotted, impaled, flayed or burnt alive, or torn limb from limb, crucified or stoned to death. By all accounts these were extremely painful procedures that gave victims extreme and prolonged physical suffering and mental anguish. The pain involved in some of these procedures is just too difficult for the modern mind to comprehend (though in some countries, one still hears of atrocities involving these methods). Of these methods of execution, stoning was the preferred method practised by Jews in the first century and earlier (Leviticus 20:2, 27; 24:16; Numbers 15: 35; Deuteronomy 21:21). The Romans, however, preferred crucifixion, especially for criminals and enemies of the state, and beheading as normal practice [note 8.52]. There is very little evidence for beheading during the Roman period in Palestine, but recently a cervical vertebra with clear evidence of decapitation was uncovered in 1999 from an early second-century context at Horvat Ethri, in the Judaean Shephelah, west of Jerusalem (*plate 13c*) [note 8.53]. Beheading, one has to admit, was the most dignified procedure of execution available that could have been chosen for John the Baptist. The suffering that the crucified Jesus had to endure was something very different from the swift death experience by John. Perhaps this indicates that Herod Antipas had a substantial regard for the dignity of John. Indeed, the Gospels depict Antipas as a person racked with grief and guilt over John's demise (Matthew 14:9; Mark 6:26).

9

John's Tomb at Sebaste

It is a bit of a puzzle why the Gospel writers did not indicate the exact place where John the Baptist was buried. All they say, in very sparse language, is that 'his disciples came [to Machaerus] and took up his body, and buried it, and went and told Jesus' (Matthew 14:12). Mark, who used a similar source as Matthew, added that it was only when the disciples 'heard' about John's death that they went to collect it, and that he was ultimately buried in a 'tomb' (Mark 6:29). But geographical information about the location of this tomb was not provided. Unlike the Gospel writers, early Byzantine tradition, however, is very clear as to where the tomb was located – it is placed at Sebaste (biblical Samaria), a town located in the northern hilly range of central Palestine. How correct is this tradition and why, of all places, was he buried in a Pagan town, far away from his hometown (Ain Karim) and not even, following normal practice, at the spot where he met his death? One has to remember that even Jesus, who was born in Bethlehem but grew up in Nazareth, was ultimately buried in Jerusalem close to the place of his crucifixion.

We knocked on a door. We waited for quite a while before an extremely elderly woman finally answered. She was doubled over with age. It seemed to me that her chin was almost touching her knees. But she was, as it turned out, regardless of her bent posture, the perfect hostess and slowly, painfully shuffling towards the sitting room, she beckoned us to follow her. The first thing she told us was that lunch had been laid on for our visit. It was March 1992 and this 83-year-old lady we had come to visit at her cottage in Heyshott down in West Sussex was the granddaughter of the remarkable lexicographer Sir James

Murray, compiler of the Oxford English Dictionary. But we – I was accompanied by Pamela Magrill from the British Museum – had not come to talk to her about her illustrious grandfather; we were much more interested in finding out about her trip to Palestine in 1933 to participate in the Samaria excavations. Dr Katherine Maud Elisabeth Murray – or 'Betty' to her friends – had an amazing house with shelves stacked high with books and small tables with neat piles of papers and magazines. Sitting down she trained her bright, shrewd eyes on us and in an incisive manner began asking questions. She knew exactly what was what and was quite relentless in wanting to know 'the facts': what our journey had been like, where we had come from, why we were doing research and why we should want to visit her of all people. Once she felt that we had answered all her questions properly and correctly (later I found out she had been a principal of a college) and had supped with her without breaking etiquette and embarrassing ourselves, I could see that she allowed herself to relax and an inner warmth began emanating from her. We were now able to call her Betty. She ushered us to a table and on it were photo albums and a large thick sheaf of letters she had written to her mother from the excavation camp at Samaria in 1933. 'You can take them away if you like,' she said [note 9.1]

The letters were amazing: a day-by-day account, reading almost like the screenplay of a soap opera, detailing the trials and tribulations of a bunch of archaeologists immersed in the process of excavating the site of Samaria. Betty, who was twenty-four at the time, was absolutely frank with her mother (they must have had a very close relationship) and regaled her with all the inside stories, even the embarrassing ones. In the mornings, they were all out on the dig, sweating and getting dusty, trying to puzzle out the bits of walls, practising their Arabic with the workmen. Food was not the best in the world: 'I believe everyone suffers from digestive troubles out here.' In the evenings they played bridge and listened to jazz on the gramophone ('It's more like a barrel organ than a gramophone: only you can't give it a penny to go into the next street'). Betty hated the blare of the music (since there was only a limited range of records) and hated the constant banter and complaints about anybody who was not present in the room ('What I dislike about this expedition – tho' I suppose it's common to all small communities – is the atmosphere. The moment any member of it is absent the others immediately discuss his or her faults and criticise his actions'). Instead she got on with her letters to her mother. Little did the archaeologists know that every one of their remarks and actions was being carefully monitored and recorded by the precocious Betty. One of the team members, Kathleen Kenyon (who later became a dame), had constant tantrums, stamped her foot and played a game of being aloof and superior. So Betty wrote: 'Apart from her gramophone I quite like Nancy [the daughter of the dig director], better than Kathleen, who is too superior – she has a way of talking about everything as if she has experienced everything already and found it all stale. This is coupled with the St Alban's type of home play – a tendency to throw food about, etc.' Finally, there was the dig director himself, John Crowfoot, who frequently flew into rages or went through periods of almost total indecision. All of these characters sound like they have stepped out of the pages of one of Agatha Christie's mysteries, with the one essential difference that nobody actually got murdered in Samaria.

The excavations at Samaria were conducted between 1931 and 1935, largely on behalf of the British School of Archaeology in Jerusalem. The Director, John Winter Crowfoot (1873–1959), had a varied career. Originally a graduate of Brasenose College in Oxford, his academic training was in the field of classical archaeology and early Christianity, but then he shifted direction to successful postings in education in Cairo and Sudan, ending up as the Principal of Gordon College at Khartoum [note 9.2]. This experience in administration eventually served him well when he was appointed Director of the British School in 1927. Kathleen Kenyon described him in 1960: 'his firm hand, unlimited tact and equable temperament provided ideal leadership . . .' Strange as it may seem, Crowfoot, who excavated many important sites at Jerash, Bosra and on the Ophel in Jerusalem, actually hated dirt archaeology. It was simply not his scene. This comes across quite well in Betty's letters. Betty refers to the progress on her dig, the squabbles and the problems with the locals whose lands were being excavated. There was constant friction between Betty and the archaeologists about what was needed to be done on the dig. On one occasion Crowfoot turned up just as Betty was having a difficult time with two mixed levels: 'He proceeded to change all the plans about what was to be photographed next day, to mess what had been prepared before by pulling down a lot more and further irritating me by proclaiming as discoveries things I had pointed out to him two days ago. By which time as you may gather I was in a thoroughly bad temper.' On another occasion:

However during breakfast Mr Crowfoot began to fuss and soon after breakfast down he came criticising everything and objecting to everything. I don't think he really knows much about it himself, but he is governed by two principles: a) He is terrified of destroying anything. This is the natural position of anyone looking on and not doing the thing himself. The worst of excavation is that only the actual workmen really sees and knows what is happening and as the responsibility rests on someone else, that someone else always feels uneasy and wonders if things are really as they look. But one has to take the plunge somehow and destroy if one is ever to know. b) He has learnt a lot from Kathleen's good slow methods, and wants to apply them on every occasion. Today he suddenly got cold feet and thought I was mismanaging things and wanted the dig done by trenching and not by layers. It isn't a suitable dig for that method as it really isn't much more than a trial trench itself, a very small area in which there isn't room for trial trenches. Anyway having upset everything – complained of every bit of work and that there were too many workmen and the place wasn't clean – he went off after leaving instructions with me, with the Raise [foreman], and with the workmen.

Various officials and scholars turned up to visit the dig: 'I also had visits before breakfast and lunch from . . . Peré Vincent, a charming old Dominican Father, who is a great archaeologist. He was very excited speculating what my building could be – and finally decided on a small building with two good chambers below and probably a statue of the emperors on top. I was amused when the *mukhtar* [village headman] came round. Peré V. turned to me [and] asked if the *mukhtar* could understand English and when I said No, he said he believed him to be the greatest robber in the country.' In one letter Betty reports about the interest in the Church of the Invention of the Head of John the Baptist, which had been excavated by Crowfoot the previous year: 'Today there was a constant stream of visitors, my dig is on the main line of the traffic to the Byzantine church [of St John] led by the official guide: today I had a French fashionable lady and priest – lady talking English – a German, Dutch or Austrian with an awful little English speaking man attached – a dear old Franciscan with an aged pilgrim – female with a gampy umbrella and a grey flannel dress. As the guide doesn't speak much English, all and sundry fall upon me to explain both what they have seen and what they are seeing. I get all tangled up and speak a mixture of French, English and Arabic.'

The prophecy of Micah notwithstanding, 'I will make Samaria as a heap of the field' (1:6), there is still a modern village called Sabastiyeh to the east of the ancient city, but like so many other places in the West

Bank today its inhabitants suffer considerably under the heavy yoke of Israeli occupation (*illustration 9.1*). Tourists no longer come looking for the Cathedral and Tomb of John the Baptist in the village or to look at the Church of the Head of John excavated by Crowfoot, which is sad because the ruins of the ancient site are very impressive, with remains from many different periods including those extending back to the time of King Ahab and the hated Jezebel. Originally an Iron Age city (named Shomron) of great importance, the capital of the Northern Kingdom (I Kings 16:24), founded in 876 BC, it was taken by force following Alexander the Great's invasion of the Near East, and from that time onwards the city came to acquire a fairly cosmopolitan flavour, with Hellenism at the forefront of cultural endeavour and enterprise there. It therefore became attractive to the Hasmonean rulers and was eventually destroyed in *c.* 109 or 108 BC [note 9.3].

Matters changed when Pompey arrived in the region (63 BC) and the city thus became part of the Roman province of Syria and restoration of its buildings began by Gabinius (between the years BC 57–55). Yet another drastic change occurred when Samaria was granted to Herod the

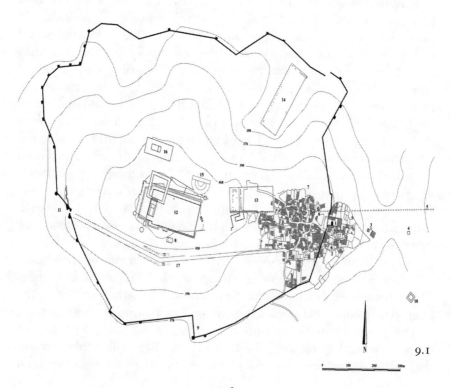

9.1

Great by Augustus. Since this was where he married Mariamne in 37 BC, he poured funds into the embellishment of the city, renamed it Sebaste in honour of his benefactor (Greek *sebastos* = Augustus) with the construction there of as many beautiful buildings as possible, including a temple and a palace. The Arab name for the present-day village, Sabastiyeh, preserves the ancient name of the site. Two of Herod's sons were executed in this city. Following the death of Herod the Great, Sebaste was under the brief rule of his son Archelaus and then under a Roman procurator (from AD 6). At the time of John the Baptist and Jesus, Sebaste was a pagan city, though this did not exclude the presence there of Samaritans and Jews as well. In the countryside thereabouts, the Samaritan presence continued to be strong and gained strength during the first century. Jews passing through Samaria found themselves constantly harassed, as the historian Josephus tells us in *Jewish War* (II: 232) [note 9.4].

Jesus visited the Samaria region himself, according to Luke (9:52; 17:11) and John (4:4–5), but according to Matthew (10:5) he did not allow his disciples to go there. The appearance of Jews at Samaria was exceptional at that time and probably also dangerous. At one of the watering-holes (Jacob's Well) in Samaria, Jesus encountered a woman who had come to draw water and asks for water. 'How is it that thou,' she asks Jesus, 'being a Jew, asketh drink of me, which am a woman of Samaria? For the Jews have no dealings with Samaritans' (John 4: 9). Much later, we hear that Philip goes to Samaria (c. 33 AD) and finally manages to baptise some of the inhabitants (Acts 8:5): 'Then Philip went down to the city of Samaria, and preached Christ unto them.' Also in Acts 8:14: 'Now when the Apostles which were at Jerusalem heard that Samaria had received the word of God, they sent unto them Peter and John.' While there was some Christian presence in Samaria during the following centuries, it would not appear to have been very substantial until the early Byzantine period.

There are two sites at Sebaste connected with the John the Baptist tradition and we shall look at them separately. The first is the small Church of the Invention of the Head of John, situated within the area of the ruins of the ancient town, marking the supposed spot of the palace where John was imprisoned and later beheaded. The second site, located some 600 metres further to the east, is the very large Cathedral of St John located in the midst of the present-day village of Sabastiyeh, marking the spot of the tomb of John [note 9.5].

The ruined Church of the Invention of the Head of John the Baptist is located on the southern brow of the acropolis and on a terrace just above the main columned street of the ancient town. This building was first seen by officers of the British Royal Engineers, C. R. Conder and H. H. Kitchener, during their survey of the site in the 1870s, even marking it on the topographical map that they prepared of the site and of its antiquities [note 9.6]. I am not sure that Crowfoot who excavated the building realised that the building was already visible to explorers in the nineteenth century, otherwise he would not have written that he had 'stumbled more or less by chance in 1931' on an 'undiscovered' church. (It is true, however, that explorers in the nineteenth century, Edward Robinson among them, had tried to identify signs of a Christian edifice among the ruins outside the village because of the references given in the writings by Phocas and Burchard, but without success) [note 9.7].

Crowfoot originally tackled the excavation of this area of fields – known to the locals as 'Aqtan el Deir' (Lands of the Monastery) – hoping to find a continuation of a much earlier Israelite wall that he was tracing. Almost immediately, Crowfoot came upon a jumble of walls, patches of decorated mosaic floors and water cisterns, which he identified as the remains of a Greek monastery of the sixth or seventh centuries, though medieval pottery and a coin of King Amaury (1162–73) were also found in one of the cisterns. Further traces of monastic buildings could be identified (but were not excavated) to the north and west, and the working theory that Crowfoot developed was

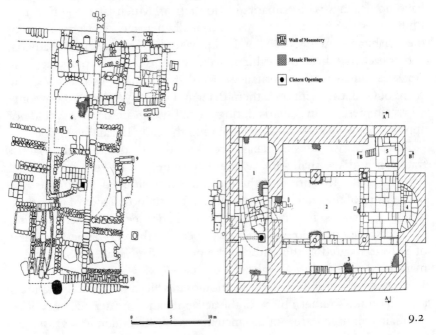

Wall of Monastery

Mosaic Floors

Cistern Openings

0   5   10 m

9.2

9.3

that the lands of this Byzantine monastery stretched for a distance of some 220 metres along the terrace. The church was apparently located at the heart of this monastic complex (*illustration 9.2*).

Access to the church was from the west, via a paved narthex-like porch and an entrance that could be barricaded from the inside with a slot-bar. The interior of the church is almost square (14.6 × 13 m) and a single apse, square on the outside, protruded towards the east. The ceiling of the building was originally domed and was supported on four columns which were later encased in masonry in the form of piers. In appearance this church largely dates from the final stage of its construction in the twelfth century. Nothing much has survived of the first Byzantine basilical-church except for the foundation slabs (stylobates) which supported the colonnades and patches of decorative floor mosaics, one of which has a fragmentary Greek dedicatory inscription (*illustration 9.3*). Crowfoot dated it to the sixth century but wrote that it 'is too fragmentary to give an intelligible meaning'. My colleague, Dr Leah Di Segni, however, thinks she is up to the task. In a letter to me she wrote: 'I believe something can be made of the text: on the first line you can see very clearly the word *euch]aristo[n*, "giving thanks" (or perhaps *eucharistontes* in the plural, if the participle is continued in line 2). It is a common term in dedicatory inscriptions: somebody built this or that in thanksgiving. The letters in line 2 suggest very strongly *tēn st[oan*, which goes quite well with the fact, that you mention, that the inscription was found in the southern aisle of the church. *Stoa* is one of the terms for aisle in late antiquity. The last N may be the ending of the word "Amen".' Leah would date the inscription a little earlier to the fifth century or to the beginning of the sixth at the latest.

What happened to this early church, whether it was eventually destroyed in an earthquake or dismantled by human hands, we simply do not know. However, it did have quite a long history, surviving into Abbasid times, even after the main Byzantine church (in the area of the village) had long been a heap of ruins. The *Commemoratorium de Casis Dei* (*c.* 808) mentions the church 'where the prison was and [where] he [John] was beheaded' and that ceremonies were still conducted there by Bishop Basil and twenty-five presbyters, monks and clergy. One scholar, Denys Pringle, has suggested that the destruction of this church was the work of Caliph Hakim (1009–1114) [note 9.8]. The church was substantially rebuilt sometime at the end of the eleventh century, with the use of all sorts of architectural bits and pieces taken from ancient buildings at the site. The four columns that support the domed ceiling of the church date from this time, as well as the oldest visible portions of the walls, and column shafts with red-painted graffiti and crosses. A badly weathered wall painting of a row of saints (?), dated on stylistic grounds to *c.* 1080, was visible in the north-west corner of the church. The church was restored and rebuilt, probably during the Crusader period (twelfth century), and it was during this stage that the Chapel of the Invention of the Head was constructed in the north-east corner of the church with the restoration of an underground crypt below it. Two steps led up to the floor of the chapel from the aisle of the church and it was here that some writers noticed a marble circle in the floor.

Unlike the large Cathedral of St John in the village, travellers and pilgrims visiting Sebaste hardly mentioned this small church and many perhaps passed by without even knowing of its existence. There is an excellent description of the church and its crypt in the writings of the Cretan pilgrim John Phocas (AD 1185): 'In the midst of the upper part of the city stands a hill, upon which in ancient times stood Herod's palace, where the feast took place, and where that wicked damsel danced and received the sacred head of the Baptist as the reward for her dancing. At the present day, however, the place has become a Roman [sic. should be Greek] monastery. The church of this monastery is covered with a vault [or is domed]. On the left side of the altar is a little chapel [κελλίον], in the midst of which is a medallion [or circle] of marble, lying at the bottom of a very deep excavation, wherein was made the discovery of the sacred head of the Forerunner, revered by angels, which had been buried in that place by Herodias' [note 9.9]. Another visitor, Burchard of Sion (1283), refers to the fact that there were two churches dedicated to John at Sebaste. The small church he described as follows: 'The other church stands on the brow of the hill, where the King's palace once stood. Therein dwell Greek monks, Christians, who received me kindly and gave me food. In that church these same Greeks show the place where they say that John was imprisoned and beheaded by Herod; which I say is a vain thing because . . . all agree in saying that he was beheaded at Macherunta [i.e. Machaerus], which is now called Haylon' [note 9.10]. Burchard rightly treated this claim with scepticism because of the Machaerus location specified by Josephus that he was well aware of, and also because, as he pointed out, Herod Antipas clearly could not have had jurisdiction in Samaria at the time of John the Baptist.

A flight of eight steps led from the north aisle of the church down to the crypt (only 2.3 m high from floor to ceiling) and there were crosses cut by pilgrims in the walls. A hole was visible in the ceiling of the crypt and it must have extended down from the floor of the chapel above it. Perhaps holy effluences ascended through this hole to the worshippers above. Crowfoot, the excavator, described the moment when he first entered the crypt in a very dry and matter-of-fact fashion, which is quite disappointing: 'The crypt was quite empty when we entered it except for insignificant accumulations of dust below the hole in the roof and at the foot of the steps; the painting on the east wall was all that had survived of its former decoration, and this had been mutilated' [note 9.11]. Under the floor of the crypt, beneath the plaster bedding of a robbed-out flagstone pavement, Crowfoot found (at a depth of about 0.5 m) what he described simply as 'a rifled grave cut in the rock in the middle of it'. For some unknown reason, the exact shape of the grave was left out of his plan of the crypt, but on the basis of some section drawings one may reconstruct it as having been oblong (2 metres in length and 1 metre wide) with shelves cut into the side walls to accommodate four covering slabs of stones. It was positioned towards the east and in form resembles many simple graves known from the Byzantine period in different parts of the country. Although Crowfoot did not seem to think that the grave was of any significance (to such an extent that he did not even bother publishing a photograph of it), I think that this may very well be the place where a skull was found, identified by some as that of John the Baptist, and that this was clearly referred to by John Phocas (1185) when he wrote that the head was found beneath the chapel 'at the bottom of a very deep excavation'. The subject of the Crusader-period painting in the east crypt wall reinforces this suggestion.

9.4

The paintings were in a very bad state of preservation when Crowfoot first entered the crypt, and, subsequently, after the discovery, some unknown person broke the lock on the door and slashed the faces of the two monks. The paintings can hardly be made out in the photographs from the 1930s and so we are lucky that a crayon rendering was made by Muriel Bentwich at the time of the excavation, otherwise it would be almost impossible to discuss this unique painting. New photographs taken in the 1980s and published in a massive book by Kühnel on Crusader-period paintings are also useful in the reconstruction of the original appearance of the painting (see the drawing which I have prepared for this book: *illustration 9.4*).

The niche in the east wall was subdivided by a stone shelf into two areas, with representations of kneeling angels on either side. The painting in the top register shows the first martyrdom of John the Baptist that is the scene of his decapitation. On the left is the figure of a soldier, wearing a red tunic and a blue cloak billowing down from his shoulders, with his right arm stretched out above the bent figure of John. Presumably he is holding in his hand a sword, or at least a dagger. His left hand is also visible on the neck of John the Baptist. John is not kneeling but is represented as a bent standing figure wearing long robes with a girdle around his waist. The colour of the robe is unclear but Crowfoot describes it as a 'sombre' colour (brown, grey?), whatever he means by that. The head of John has been destroyed but the edges of the *nimbus* can just be made out. John's arms are extended forward in an act of supplication. To his right is an unclear mass of colour which is said to have been of the same sombre colours as John's robes. This was identified by Crowfoot as possibly representing a seated or kneeling Salome, which seems unlikely. The suggestion by Kühnel that this might represent the fallen John a moment after decapitation had taken place is certainly likely. However, I would suggest that this is actually a representation of the doorway of John's prison. The background colour for the entire scene was probably green, similar to the background colour of the flanking angels. These adoring angels, symbolising victory over death, are probably the ones referred to by John Phocas in his description of the place from 1185, in effect providing a good latest date for the wall painting. The angels are depicted kneeling with raised arms, wearing mauve robes, and with outstretched wings, one painted upwards and the other down. The feathers of the wings were painted in alternating green and black stripes and the edges were highlighted in red. The entire upper scene was surrounded by a red-painted frame.

The painting in the lower register of the niche represents the second martyrdom of John the Baptist that is the scene of the desecration of his tomb. Against the background of a large rounded hill, painted in yellow with scattered red and blue flowers, which must represent the actual hill of Samaria/Sebaste, are two men wearing red jerkins and holding tools (presumably spades) in their hands and digging up the large head of

John the Baptist (destroyed except for the outline of the *nimbus*) from within a pyramid-like tomb cavity painted in black. It is unlikely that they are stoking a fire because smoke is not depicted. Two sets of figures are shown looking on against the blue background of the sky. The figures on the right, both beardless and one wearing a distinctive white cap, were identified by Crowfoot as possibly representing a young woman and man who gave the money for the building of the chapel. Alternatively, Kühnel has proposed that they symbolise the pagans who instigated the desecration of the tomb at the time of Julian the Apostate (I shall discuss this further below) and I think this fits very well the understanding of the scene as a whole. Hence, the bearded men on the opposite side are ecclesiastics or monks witnessing the event and perhaps symbolising the same pilgrims who, according to tradition, gathered up the relics of John's bones after the desecration. It is interesting to note that the width and position of the black pyramid-shaped area, in which the head of John the Baptist is being dug up in the painting, actually corresponds exactly to the physical width and position of the rock-grave located in front of it, and in my mind this cannot be coincidental.

Who made these paintings and when? The paintings have been attributed by Kühnel to a local school of Byzantine artists because of their typical Middle Byzantine style, and he dated them to the third quarter of the twelfth century at the latest. However, not all scholars agree: Folda believes that they are the work of Western artists instead, suggesting that they predate 1160; and another investigator, L.-A Hunt, has dated them a little earlier to AD 1150 [note 9.12]

The Greek church and monastery continued to survive following the capture of Sebaste by Saladin in 1187. In the church various changes were made to the altar and to the various structural parts of the building, including the narthex which was walled up. Crowfoot also uncovered evidence of cooking. This phase must be Mamluke in date (i.e. thirteenth to fifteenth centuries). Nicolas of Poggibonsi (1346–50) reports seeing Greek monks there and heard about this being the reputed place of the beheading. The church he described as 'made with two naves [aisles?], completely vaulted above, with an altar raised above ground on four columns; and beneath the altar there is a marble slab, and in the middle of the stone there is a round hole; and in that place his head was cut off. But the original stone of the place was translated to Alexandria. And above this altar there is a dome, raised above every other building, with a large window in the top. Within this church there are five altars.' In 1479 we are informed by Count Johannes Tuchern that the Greeks had only just abandoned their church and monastery. Slightly later, Francesco Suriano (1485) mentions the church as the place of the beheading, but does not mention any monks there. Finally, a Muslim traveller, Evliya Çelebi (1648–50), expresses knowledge about a monastery on a hilltop nearby that had been abandoned since the days of Caliph al-Ma'mun (AD 813–33).

As a result of all the information presented above, I think we are now in the position to propose a tentative history of this church and its changing traditions. In the Byzantine period, in the fifth or sixth centuries, a monastery was built at this location and it included a small church in the form of a three-aisled basilica which was very typical of that period. This church was founded on the spot of the traditional palace and prison of John the Baptist. Theodosius (518) must have had this place in mind when he wrote that Sebaste was the place of John's beheading but ignored the tomb. The monks living here would have accepted that the large Byzantine church, located more than half a kilometre away (now within the village), had the actual Tomb of John beneath its floors. The tomb in this crypt was probably only that of a local saint or one of the abbots of the monastery, but it had nothing whatsoever to do with John. In the eleventh century, however, during the reconstruction of the church, one may speculate that the tomb was discovered and opened, revealing skeletal remains inside. It is possible that as a result of decomposition only the skull had survived and it was this that was thereafter regarded as the relic skull of John with the crypt now being adapted to a new tradition, that of the Invention of the Head of John the Baptist. This tradition was then maintained until the Crusader period and, judging by the exact alignment of the lower scene of the painting – showing the discovery of the head – with the physical position of the grave below the floor, it must also have been visible to pilgrims visiting the crypt.

I found it quite exciting looking at all the extant information regarding this church, and there is no doubt in my mind that this building deserves to be resurveyed and, if possible, re-excavated. I think there is still a lot of information that could be extracted about this site, particularly in regard to the earlier Byzantine church. Indeed, Crowfoot mentions that while he did clear a good part of the Byzantine monastery to the west of the church and a portion of its cemetery to the east, he did not in fact insert a spade into the ground either to the north or south of the church and so these areas remain *terra incognita* for the time being and await new archaeological investigation.

It was crazy to even attempt it. But it had to be done. I needed a modern plan of the Tomb of John the Baptist located beneath the large Crusader cathedral within the village of Sabastiyeh. I contacted my friend and colleague Mahmud Huwari, who in recent years has been conducting an important architectural survey of ancient buildings in that village, but it transpired that, because of the outbreak of the *al-Aqsa intifada* (the latest Palestinian uprising), he had not got round to measuring the tomb. In the past two years the West Bank has seen some of the worst violence between the Israeli army and the indigenous Palestinian population since the occupation began there in 1967. An almost total disregard for human dignity has characterised the conflict. Palestinians have had to suffer curfews, expropriation of land, economic hardship, random killings and unjust imprisonment. Every family has a story to tell of an injustice that has been meted out to themselves or to relatives; there is an enormous feeling of despair and anger. On the other hand, the persistent and devastating attacks of Palestinian suicide bombers in Israel has crippled those Israelis with left-wing tendencies, among them intellectuals and academics, and very few have spoken out against the recent heavy-handed treatment of Palestinians in the occupied territories. Israel has drifted far to the right and its citizens now believe in hitting the Palestinians hard and where it hurts, with the bull-dozing of the family homes of those connected to violence, imprison-ment of suspects without trial and collective punishment dealt out to entire communities. This cycle of violence continues with hardly any interruption and the greatest tragedy of all is that many Palestinians and Israelis have become so hardened by events that they now see violence as an inevitable part of their daily lives.

Nowadays it is extremely difficult for any European to travel without hindrance in the territories. There are too many dangers, even for researchers and journalists. I really wanted to go to see the tomb of John the Baptist but at the same time I knew that this was not possible in the circumstances. Knowing the risks, Fadi Amirah, the Palestinian archae-ological surveyor who works with me, offered to make the trip to Sebaste by himself to take measurements and photographs. It would be a bit of an adventure, he said. I kept my fingers crossed fearing that there might be some mishap along the way. The following is based on his account of the precarious journey he made to Sebaste to measure the Tomb of John the Baptist.

Ordinarily a trip by car from Ramallah to Nablus should not take more than two hours, but the direct route is no longer possible and one can only travel by service-taxis in relays from place to place, and so the time needed for travelling is doubled or even quadrupled. A further hindrance along the way are the numerous army checkpoints, manned by nervous and sometimes insolent soldiers. As a Jerusalemite Palestinian, Fadi was treated quite differently from his fellow travellers of the territories: he was regarded with a great amount of suspicion. The Israeli authorities could not understand why Fadi should want to do archaeological work in a war zone; why did he have measuring equipment, millimetre paper, pencils, a camera and film in his bag, they wanted to know. At one checkpoint, Fadi was not even allowed back on the taxi and when the investigator had tired of interrogating him, he let Fadi go on foot to the nearest village where he then caught another taxi onwards. Since this was the first day of the Ramadan fast, Fadi as a good Muslim was not even drinking water and by the time he reached Nablus he was feeling completely parched and quite exhausted by the ordeal.

Fadi was supposed to have met up with Zahra Zawari, an architect of the Sebaste municipality, but because of the delay he missed her and she had already set out from Nablus. To get to Sebaste, Fadi took a service-taxi for the first relay to Et-Tell but when he got there found that there was no matching vehicle to take him on to the next village of Ain-Nakoura, so Fadi began walking and continued walking the distance along a path leading through a wadi full of rubbish dumps, known locally as the 'el-mazballe'. Hours later he reached the *beladiya* (municipality) of Sebaste where he finally met up with Zahra, who provided him with their own schematic maps of the mosque and *maqam* (holy Muslim place) of Yahya (John the Baptist) and the keys to the place as well. The tomb itself, located beneath the *maqam*, had clearly not been opened for quite a while and when Zahra opened the door a mouse jumped out. Like a perfect gentleman, Fadi suggested to Zahra that he should first go in by himself on the off chance that there might be more mice lurking about below. The door led to a steep flight of steps in a narrow sloping corridor descending down into the dusty darkness in a southerly direction. Fadi flicked a switch and the entire rectangular subterranean chamber below was flooded with electrical lighting.

The tomb of John the Baptist that was once such a major attraction for pilgrims and travellers throughout the ages is hardly visited by anyone nowadays, even by local Muslims. En route to Sebaste, Fadi met up with a villager who exclaimed with surprise that anybody should have even the slightest interest in the tomb, even though they themselves use the adjacent mosque on a daily basis. This villager could not remember when he had last seen someone give the *fatiha* prayer from the Quran at the entrance to the tomb (this is usually done with outstretched hands and is intended to give honour to the saint), let alone venture inside. The rubbish and dust on the floor of the chamber confirmed that the place had hardly been visited and perhaps cleaned only once a year. Fadi took quite a few photographs of the interior and began measuring. The only plan of the tomb that I am aware of was made by the British explorers of the Palestine Exploration Fund led by Charles Wilson in March 1866. Wilson wrote: 'a plan was made of the church, and the grotto, which seems to be of masonry of a much older date than the church' [note 9.13]. Fadi found that Wilson's plan was on the whole fairly reliable, although he was of course able to improve it considerably.

The present-day access to the tomb chamber is via a covered flight of eighteen steps descending from the north (from a small domed oblong

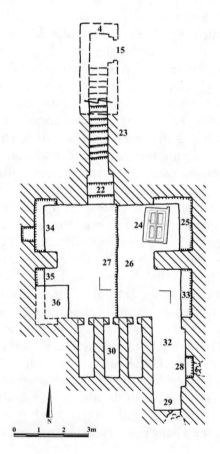

9.5

room on the north side of the nave), and these steps must date back either to the time of the Crusader cathedral or perhaps even to the time of the earlier Byzantine church at the spot (*illustration 9.5, plate 14a*). In any case, the original tomb entrance was at the bottom of this flight of steps and in front of it there would have been some sort of forecourt which is now buried about four metres below the pavement of the church. On entering, the first thing that one notices, dead ahead, is the south wall pierced with two rows of three tunnel-like burial spaces (*loculi* or *kokhim*) which are of body-length, and these would have been used for primary burials, i.e. shrouded bodies would have been inserted into these spaces and laid to rest there. At the top of the wall is a row of shorter recesses (0.9 m deep) which would have been very suitable for storing stone bone-boxes (ossuaries) (*plate 14b*). If this is correct then it would lend a particular Judaean or Jerusalemite flavour to this tomb since ossuaries are not at all typical of the other tombs of this period that have been excavated in the Samaria region. The arched openings to these *loculi* have been blocked up and small rectangular windows have been left so that one might still look inside (these are the 'small pigeon-holes' referred to by Wilson). Fadi did not have a torch with him so he took photographs in each one of the *loculi* and these show that they are all empty. The main chamber has a barrel-vaulted ceiling. On opposite sides of the main chamber there are two pairs of burial spaces located beneath arched recesses (*arcosolia*). In the south-eastern corner of the main chamber is an elongated, rectangular space that by comparison with other tombs of this sort was probably originally used as a bone-collecting chamber. A blocked-up niche on the east side of this chamber suggests that there may be a hidden *loculus* (*kokh*) at this location. The original tomb was clearly not rock-cut, judging by the excellent-quality masonry seen inside the two rows of *kokhim* and by the descriptions of earlier explorers who managed to probe the masonry behind the plaster.

The general plan of the tomb which has a combination of *loculi* and *arcosolia* burial recesses is typical of the first century AD [note 9.14] and so we need not hesitate to ascribe the initial use of the tomb to that period (*illustration 9.6*). It was clearly a family tomb and by that I mean that it served for the burial of numerous individuals linked by kinship and that some of them must have undergone secondary burial (i.e. their bones were gathered into ossuaries or placed into the bone-collecting chamber). It seems quite likely that the tomb continued to be used during the course of the second and third centuries, as Hamilton suggested in his *Guide to Samaria–Sebaste* [note 9.15]. It was at this stage

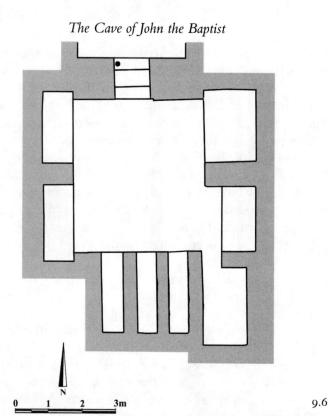

9.6

that the original tomb entrance was enlarged and a large pivoted door made of black basalt was inserted instead. This door may still be seen fallen on the floor on the left side of the chamber. The surface of this massive door had a decorative panelled exterior and the door swung inward from left to right. A hole in the panelled surface of the door once held a metal ring with which the door could be pulled shut (remember nobody could close the heavy door from inside by pushing, unless of course they planned to stay inside for ever!). A similar panelled door with a ring has been found in a tomb uncovered at Askar near Nablus, not too far away from Sebastia. Fadi tried to lift the fallen door so that he could draw the other side but it was just too heavy even to budge. Since later descriptions mention the existence of stone coffins within the chamber, it is quite possible that sarcophagi were indeed brought into the chamber during the second to third centuries. This may have entailed cutting back the *arcosolia* in the side walls to accommodate the sarcophagi. Tombs that went through similar stages of use between the first and third centuries are known in the Samaria–Nablus region, with barrel-vaulted and domed ceilings, sarcophagi and heavy panelled doors.

It is not surprising that it was at this location that the tomb of John the Baptist was identified in the Byzantine period, since this area was originally just *outside* the ancient city of Samaria/Sebaste and was being used as a cemetery during the Roman period, if not earlier. In fact, the tomb is located only seventeen metres to the east of the Roman city wall. The builders of the Byzantine church of St John knew perfectly well where to begin construction – it had to be at a location outside the area of the city and at a place where ancient tombs were known. We cannot know for certain why the Byzantine builders chose this specific tomb to sanctify beneath their church but perhaps some oral tradition existed regarding the spot, and it was still known to the people of Sebaste at the beginning of the Byzantine period. Indeed, as early as the fourth century a tomb (or tombs) linked to Elisha and Obadiah was also being pointed out in the area. Another interesting Roman tomb in this cemetery, which has a domed ceiling with a very early use of spherical pendentives, was investigated by Hamilton in the 1930s to the south of the area. It had a pivoted door, sarcophagi, and was dated to the second to third centuries. Additional tombs were investigated about 150 metres to the east on the other side of the valley. These too had pivoted doors and contained sarcophagi.

What happened to the tomb in the centuries following its use as a burial vault is not entirely clear in archaeological terms, and this is because the masonry walls are now completely covered with a very heavy coat of plaster (up to 3 cms thick in places) and so it is difficult to be absolutely certain about the various stages of its use. However, there can be no doubt that during the Byzantine period the tomb was converted into an underground chapel or grotto in honour of John the Baptist. The steps leading down to the entrance possibly date from this time. The two burial recesses to the west were cancelled out. The eastern half of the floor was raised (and probably separated from the rest of the chamber with a screen), and the focus of prayer was directed towards the burial recesses on the east side of the chamber. These two burial recesses are probably the ones which were thought to have contained the bones or ashes of John the Baptist (most likely this was the one to the north-east: *plate 14b*) and the other of Obadiah and Elisha. The openings to the *loculi* in the southern wall were blocked up leaving small windows to allow pilgrims to peer inside. The single *loculus* in the east wall of the bone-collecting chamber was probably also blocked up at this time. A small circular hole was let into the barrel-vaulted ceiling for ventilation purposes, or perhaps (as in the crypt of the small Greek church, elsewhere at the site) effluences rising through the hole were thought to have had some beneficial healing powers for the worshippers in the chapel above.

The early Christian tradition of the tomb of John the Baptist at Sebaste (together with those of Elisha and Obadiah) can be traced back to the fourth century. While there is no mention of the tomb in Eusebius' *Onomasticon*, this is not surprising because he was only concerned with preparing a list of places mentioned in the Old Testament and their identifications, and Christian holy places were of secondary interest to him. The tradition of the tomb being located at Sebaste also appears in Theodoret (393–457) but the tomb itself is not described. The tombs of John, Obadiah and Elisha were first witnessed by Egeria *c.* 384 during her visit to Sebaste but nothing concrete is said about the place [note 9.16]. However, we do have the writings of Jerome, and in his account of the travels of Paula (404), he wrote that she arrived at the site and 'in it lie buried Elisha and Obadiah the prophets, and John the Baptist, greater than all the sons of women. Here there were strange sights which startled and frightened her: in front of the saints' tombs she watched demons crying out in every kind of torment, and men making sounds like beasts, howling, barking, roaring, hissing or lowing. Some shook their heads from side to side, others leaned back to touch the ground behind them with the crown of their head, and women were hanging up by one foot, but their clothes did not fall down over their faces. On all of them she [Paula] had compassion. She shed tears over each one, and prayed Christ to show mercy. Then, despite her weakness, she climbed up the mountain to see the two caves where the prophet Obadiah kept the hundred prophets alive with bread and water in time of famine and persecution' [note 9.17].

At first glance, it looks like Paula had some kind of hysterical fit while visiting John's tomb and so her description, quoted by Jerome, of 'strange sights' there should perhaps be seen as a total fantasy. However, this is not necessarily the case because, setting aside the element of exaggeration in this passage, there was a belief at that time that by bringing possessed individuals to such a tomb they would regain their sanity and the demons would be scared away. This is probably what Paula saw. Indeed, John Chrysostom (*Catechesis* VII, 1–8), wrote in the late fourth century about the phenomenon in general: 'I myself might threaten you, flatter, frighten or urge you without effect. But when you enter a martyr's chapel, and just look at the sainted man's grave, your eyes stream with tears, and your heart warms with fervent prayer. Why is this? Because you envisage the figure of the martyr, and that evokes the thought of his achievement. Face to face with his grandeur, you become conscious of your beggarly poverty; you realise how great is the gulf between yourself and him: the martyrs are in a position to speak freely in God's presence, and to rejoice in His honour and glory' [note 9.18]. What we do not have in these early descriptions of the tomb in Jerome's writings is information regarding its exact position, and one cannot help but wonder whether the traditional tomb pointed out at Sebaste since the Crusader period is the same as the one mentioned by Jerome. This has to remain an open question. However, at the same time *absence of evidence is not evidence of absence* and by that I mean that until we have contrary evidence regarding the location of the tomb, we must assume that the ancients got it right.

During the Crusader period the chapel was renovated and reused at the time of the construction of the enormous cathedral above. A large block of masonry was inserted into the south-west corner of the tomb chamber to take the weight of one of the piers separating the nave from the southern aisle of the overlying cathedral. The chamber was paved with slabs of stone, one of which had a couple of mason's marks in its surface, and with a pavement of smaller fitted black-and-red stones in patterns in front of the two traditional tombs which had been built up with raised walls to protect their contents. Two pairs of windows were let into the corners of the ceiling to the east and west, to provide lighting and ventilation. When the place began to be used by Muslims (after 1187) a *mihrab* (prayer niche) was inserted into the southern end of the bone-collecting chamber.

Above the tomb is a domed rectangular building, the *maqam* (holy place), dedicated to Yahya (John the Baptist). Fadi began measuring here after he found himself plunged into darkness in the tomb below as a result of a sudden electrical power cut. Very little has survived of the original Byzantine-period building except for the tops of low walls to the north and east which are now used as benches within the present building. The original floor of the building is 0.6 m above the vaulted ceiling of the tomb below. Sunken in the floor is the line of the marble edging for a chancel, with slots for screen panels, indicating that the direction of prayer was to the east, and it corresponds exactly to the line of the raised floor in the tomb below, suggesting that they were built at the same time. At least three white marble screen panels from the Byzantine period, decorated with two crosses each (now somewhat defaced), were later incorporated into the western interior wall of the building. These were already noticed by Buckingham in 1822 and Robinson in 1838 [note 9.19]. A chancel post with moulded decoration is also used as the threshold of the northern door of the building. Another marble screen with very fine fluting along one edge was built into the side of the *mihrab* (prayer niche) in the next room of the building. This small chapel– forming a kind of *edicule* above the tomb of John – was already being used as a cult place from the fourth century, and we hear of a bishop of Sebaste participating in the Nicaea Council of 325. This cult place was later incorporated within the fifth-century Byzantine church but then, at the time of the construction of the Crusader cathedral, it was dismantled and reconstructed using the original stones but with its walls now abutting the new piers of the church. This is the building that one can see today, except for its upper parts and the dome which are clearly much later in date. The building had two entrances from the north and south. At a later date, the building was expanded to the south to accommodate the space between the original building and the south wall of the cathedral, with the insertion of a *mihrab* as well [note 9.20]. Sculpted stones taken from the ruins of the Crusader cathedral, including the 'bull's head' and 'man tearing his beard' carvings, are now kept inside the building. A few additional carvings are stored in Jerusalem, but many of the sculpted capitals, including one depicting 'Herod's feast' and another one of the 'dance of Salome', were taken to Istanbul in 1894 [note 9.21]. The *maqam* is used today by the inhabitants of Sebaste as a place for washing the dead before they are taken out for burial to the local cemetery. A wooden table and a stretcher for this purpose are kept on one side of the building. Just as Fadi had completed his measurements inside the building, a number of villagers appeared at the door bearing a dead body on a stretcher.

In the writings of the medieval period which mention the Tomb of John, it is sometimes difficult to ascertain whether the writers were referring to the small structure capping the tomb or to the actual subterranean vaulted tomb chamber below. Daniel the Abbot (AD 1106–1108), for example, wrote that 'there is a small enclosed space here which was the prison of Saint John the Baptiser of Christ and in this prison John the Precursor of Christ was beheaded by King Herod.' This must be a reference to the chapel above the tomb. He then proceeds: 'the Tomb of John the Precursor is here and there is a fine church dedicated to him, and there is a very rich Frankish monastery' [note 9.22]. Writing in the 1170s, a Muslim writer, al-Harawi, mentions seeing the tombs of John and Elisha, but, unusually, there is also a mention of the Tomb of

Elizabeth (John's mother). According to a report from before 1184 written by the Secretary of Saladin, the Tomb of John was ornamented with silver and gold objects and veils, and pilgrimages were made to this place once a year on a fixed date. A fairly detailed description of the tomb, chapel and church was provided by John Phocas (AD 1185):

A day's journey away is the city Sebaste . . . In it is the venerable head of him who was the greatest of men born of woman, John the Baptist . . . In the middle of this city is the prison into which he was thrown because of his accusations against Herodias, and there also his head was cut off. This prison was underground, and has twenty steps leading down to it. In the centre of it is an altar containing the spot where he was beheaded by the guard. On the right of the altar is a coffin in which is preserved the body of Saint Zacharias, the father of the Forerunner. And on the left side is a second coffin in which lies the body of Saint Elisabeth his mother. And in the walls on either side of the Prison rest the remains of several other saints and of the disciples of the Forerunner. Above the Prison is a church in which lie two coffins carved in white marble. The one on the right contains the dust of the venerable Forerunner after it was burned, and the other the body of the Prophet Elisha. Above this, in the church, the left hand of the Forerunner is displayed in a gold vessel, and this itself is completely encased in gold' [note 9.23].

By circa 1225, Yaqût mentions that the chamber below still included the tomb of Zacharias (John's father) and other prophets. Burchard of Sion (1283) describes the tomb of John the Baptist as 'made of marble after the fashion of the Lord's sepulchre, where the same saint had been buried between Elisha and Obadiah.'

Fadi's journey back from Sebaste was just as eventful as his journey to Sebaste. Having stayed the night in an (almost empty) hotel in Nablus, Fadi attempted to return to Sebaste to do another day's work of recording and measuring. Little did he know but a curfew had been placed by the Israeli army on Nablus the previous night and he could be shot on sight. Setting out very early in the morning, he thought it a bit strange that the streets were totally empty and that the taxi-service office was closed, but decided to start walking instead, hoping that he would flag down a passing taxi at some stage. Eventually, he reached Ain-Nakoura and was just about to start down the path leading through the rubbish dumps of 'al-mizballeh' towards Sebaste, when an Israeli army patrol passed by and called him to halt. They first made him stand to one side of the road in the sun for forty minutes while they deliberated what to do. After a brief interrogation it became clear to them that he was totally unaware of the curfew and so luckily they decided to let him go, provided that he returned immediately to Nablus. Fadi had had enough. This encounter with the Israeli army was just too much for him and so, as soon as he got back to Nablus, he quickly negotiated with a taxi driver to take him back towards Jerusalem and set off as quickly as he could go.

Originally there was a large Byzantine church at Sebaste which was in the form of a basilica (a long building with columns separating the nave from the aisles), which preserved within it the earlier Chapel or *edicule* above the Tomb of John. In archaeological terms very little of the Byzantine church has been preserved. It would seem that the later Crusader workmen did a good job in demolishing the earlier building before they got on with their own building work. Wilson, who did some excavations in the area of the building in 1866, did note that the 'northern side and north-west tower are of older date than the Crusades; I think early Saracenic; in the latter there is a peculiarly arched passage. The church is on the site of an old city gate, from which the "street of columns" started and ran round the hill eastwards' [note 9.24]. Hamilton, in the work he did at the site in the British Mandate period, was able to establish that the medieval building followed more or less the ground plan of the original Byzantine church. He noted, however, that the 'only part of the Byzantine cathedral still in position is the lower portion of its north wall. If you walk round outside the north wall of the mosque you can see that the lower courses are of older and more weather-worn masonry than that which surrounds the windows above; except for several obvious bits of modern patchwork all that older masonry belongs to the early cathedral. The best preserved piece is at the north-east corner of the building.' He was also able to locate five capitals that belonged to the columns of the church [note 9.25].

There is actually an excellent pictorial representation of this church – marked in Greek letters as 'Sebastis' – in an eighth-century mosaic floor uncovered by the Franciscan archaeologist, Michelle Piccirillo at the Church of St Stephan at Umm al-Rasas in modern Jordan (*illustration 9.7*) [note 9.26]. It depicts the church as a large building with a single doorway in the façade, large side windows and two rows of smaller windows in the clerestory, and a gabled tiled roof. The two side towers are an artistic device intending to indicate that the building was located within a city – other town sites in the Umm al-Rasas mosaic are shown

9.7

in the same manner. However, it may not be a coincidence but the Sebaste church was in fact incorporated within the line of the Roman city wall and Crowfoot was able to trace remnants of it on either side of the church. Moreover, the actual thickness of the present façade of this building matches the thickness of the Roman city wall below it. The recent demolition of a structure (in 2002) immediately north of the entrance to the church has revealed the south-west corner of a defence tower of Roman date built of courses of marginal-drafted stones. According to the mosaic depiction, there used to be a large rectangular area with an arcade close to the church. I would suggest that this was a large open square (or piazza) with porticoes that existed immediately west of the church. In fact, the outline of this square is still visible in the layout of this part of the village. Perhaps Wilson was right and the well-known columned street led to this area and the city wall was pierced by a gate. At the bottom right of the mosaic floor is a solitary tower which marked the fountain of the city that was fed with water brought by aqueduct from Ain Nakoura [note 9.27].

Like many other Byzantine churches in the Holy Land, popular tradition attributed the founding of this church to Helena, mother of Constantine [note 9.28]. However, the Byzantine church must have been built by the mid-fifth century, by which time Sebaste had become a well-established bishopric, with a dependence on the archbishop of Caesarea. John Rufus, writing in 512, at the time of the Council of Chalcedon, does not appear to have visited the actual tomb but only the

277

chapel above it and the church itself: 'This place was in effect a particular chapel of the church [temple], enclosed by grilles, because there are two caskets covered with gold and silver, in front of which lamps are always burning; one is that of St John the Baptist and the other that of the prophet Elisha; a throne, covered by a cloth, on which nobody used to sit, is also placed in that spot' [note 9.29]. The Piacenza Pilgrim (570) describes the church as the 'basilica' of St John and in a separate passage refers to this place as the 'resting-place' of the prophet Elisha. The tradition of the tomb being located at Sebaste also appears in the *Chronicle Paschale* (629) but further details are absent. The 'village' of Sebaste was visited by Williband in 726 but he does not mention the church, only the tombs of John, Obadiah and Elisha. As I suggested easrlier, Theodosius (518) may have had this place in mind when he wrote that Sebaste was the place of John's beheading and ignores the tomb. The *Commemoratorium de Casis Dei* (*c.* 808) mentions that 'at Sebastia, where the body of St John lies buried, there used to be a great church, but it has now fallen to the ground. All that is left is the place of the glorious Baptist's tomb, which has not been entirely destroyed . . .' [note 9.30]. There are a number of possible dates for the destruction of the church. Usually scholars have suggested this occurred at the time of the Persian invasion of AD 614. My own view is that this took place as a result of the earthquake of AD 749. The latter seems more reasonable when taking into account that the words 'fallen to the ground', mentioned in the *Commemoratorium,* sounds like a collapse that was the result of an act of nature and not a purposeful destruction. In any case, the building was still shown standing in the mid-eighth-century mosaic depiction at Umm al-Rasas.

Only the shell of the medieval Cathedral of St John has survived but it is still impressive even in its ruined state and originally it must have been a magnificent building. Was it ever completed? One scholar suggests that, at the time of its capture by the Muslims in 1187, the building was still in an unfinished state. We shall perhaps never know. When Tancred first captured the place for the Franks in 1099, Sebaste was nothing more than a small provincial village that had gradually diminished in size since the Byzantine period, followed by the destructive activities of Caliph Hakim and years of unrest. The reason why a diocese was set up in the first place at Sebaste, as a suffragan see of Caesarea, was not because it had any particular military or administrative significance, but because it was recognised to be a major Christian pilgrimage centre, even though at that time there were plenty of holy sites around, some of them located at much better locations and closer to pilgrim routes. Sebaste was served by a number of bishops and some of their names are known. Baldwin is the first Bishop of Sebaste we know of and is mentioned in a Charter dated to March 1129. Bishop Rainer and later Bishop Randuph were the ones who authenticated the relics of John the Baptist and supervised the building operations of the cathedral. The bishops of Samaria had their own distinctive seals: on one side was depicted the figure of the bishop with a crozier and mitre, and on the other a depiction of Jesus being baptised by John. What would it have been like being a bishop at Sebastia? A counterpart in Acre, James of Vitry, described his own daily activities as follows: 'I have

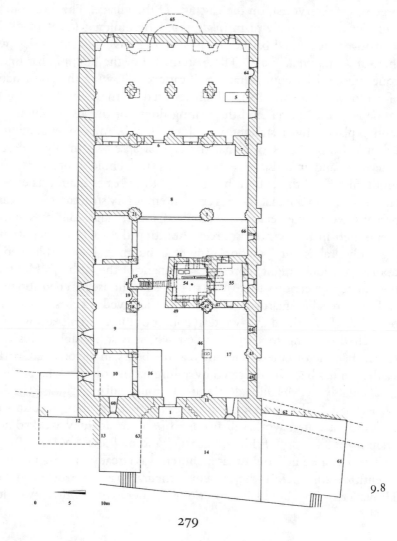

9.8

arranged my day in the following way . . . Having celebrated Mass at dawn, I hear confessions until midday, and then, having with great difficulty forced down some food – for I have lost my appetite . . . since I came overseas – I visit the sick in the city until the hour of nones or vespers. After this I hear cases relating to widows and orphans and other people . . . with the result that I have no pleasant time left for reading, except at Mass or matins, or when I can hide myself away for some brief space of time. I have kept the quiet time of night for prayer and recollection' [note 9.31].

To gain access to the cathedral, one is obliged to descend a staircase from either the north or south to a sunken courtyard (beneath which are large water reservoirs), on the east side of the village. The façade of the building is surprisingly plain (*plate 15c*). The building (25 × 50 m) is a west-to-east-oriented basilica divided into a nave and side aisles, with three apses (*illustration 9.8*). The eastern end of the building has undergone substantial architectural modifications following the construction of a mosque here in 1889, which resulted in the remodelling of the transept of the church and the tearing down of the apses which were then replaced by a straight wall [note 9.32]. An old engraving by Laborde from 1847 shows that the central apse was highly decorated externally and it must have been a joy to behold [note 9.33]. The southern wall of the church has a series of buttresses against its external face. It seems to me that there were contemporary structures in this area, perhaps even the elusive Canon's Cloister and Bishop's House mentioned in the written sources. Abutting the south-west corner of the cathedral is the exterior wall of a building with a blocked up doorway, which might represent a remnant of the Bishop's House. In the nineteenth century there used to be a small house perched above this wall where the guardian of the mosque lived (it has since been demolished). At the north-western corner of the church is a tower with an arched opening towards the west which is still visible. This is the tower that Victor Guérin identified as the belfry in 1870. The Crusader Cathedral has been investigated by a number of eminent scholars in the past, notably by Melchior de Vogüé, Camille Enlart, R. W. Hamilton, N. Kenaan-Kedar and Denys Pringle, but reading their accounts one realises that much work still needs to be done to fully work out the architectural history of this fascinating building [note 9.34].

There can be no doubt that a church was already in existence in the twelfth century before the present cathedral was constructed in 1145. However, there should be no confusion here, this church was not a rebuilding of the old Byzantine church, but comprised only the small chapel (the present-day *maqam* building) overlying the tomb of John. At the time of the visit of Abbot Daniel (1106–1108) to 'Sebastopolis', as he called it, this chapel was being used by a Latin religious community. They were receiving endowments and, as Abbot Daniel himself emphasises, the attached monastery itself was quite rich. The existence of a functioning church at the site is also clear from the writings of the Syrian Usama Ibn Munqidh, who has also provided us with an interesting description of Frankish devout behaviour relating to the cult of John the Baptist. An account of his visit (1140–1143) appears in his *Kitab al-'Asa* (Book of Staffs or Walking Sticks – the shepherd's staff, called *assayah* in colloquial Arabic and *'asa* in literary Arabic – not 'rods' or 'sticks' as some have translated it). He wrote: 'I paid a visit to the tomb of John the son of Zacharias [Yahya Ibn Zakariyya] – God's blessing on both of them! – in the village of Sebastiya in the province of Nablus. After saying my prayers, I came out into an enclosed space in front of the place where the tomb is. I found a half-closed gate, opened it and entered a church. Inside were about ten old men, their bare heads as white as combed cotton. They were facing the east, and had on their chests staffs ending with cross-bars turned up like the rear end of a saddle, on which they were leaning. And with them one receives hospitality. The sight of their piety touched my heart, but at the same time it displeased and saddened me, for I had never seen such zeal and devotion among Muslims' [note 9.35].

Following the decision to establish Sebaste as the seat of a Latin bishop and as a major Frankish administrative and religious centre, work began (at some point in time just *before* 1145) on the construction of one of the most sumptuous and grandiose churches that had ever been known in this region (*plate 15a*). It was second only in size to the Church of the Holy Sepulchre and was modelled along the lines of similar churches existing in France (one scholar believes that the Cathedral at Sens in France served as its model). Its sculpted work was equal to the best stone craftsmanship known in medieval Europe. Everything had to be built of the best quality of stone and to the best possible standards. The problem is that they quickly ran out of money and construction was temporarily suspended. It is perhaps not too much of a coincidence that this occurred at the same time (in 1145) as a 'discovery' was made of a silver casket packed to the brim with relics of John the Baptist, fellow prophets and other saintly notables. This discovery was extremely news-worthy and knowledge of the find spread throughout Europe and beyond (even a pilgrim from Iceland, Nicolas Bergsson of Thverá, wrote about this find). The Patriarch of Jerusalem (William) put out an appeal for funds, but there was a catch. Those willing to provide donations also wanted something in return, a relic or two. This is where the Sebaste 'workshop', if one can call it that, went into full swing and craftsmen began churning out relics according to demand. Relics appear to have been available to some pilgrims who visited the site to commemorate the Birth or Beheading of John, or the date of the Invention of his remains. One of the most illustrious donors, King Louis VII, also went away with a relic. Since some of the relics were provided to donors who were closely related (such as to members of the House of Champagne), one has to assume that some record was kept at Sebaste listing who had received what, otherwise it would have been terribly embarrassing if two members of the same family received the same type of relic (such as an identical fragment of skull); one can just imagine the explaining the bishop back in Sebaste would have had if this had happened. Donations began pouring in and relics continued to be supplied. Gifts were also received not only from Christians but also by Muslims wishing to visit the Tomb of the Baptist. A considerable wealth was amassed and the bishop had an extremely rich lifestyle, much more so than even his contemporaries, such as the archbishop of Caesarea.

In 1184 Saladin threatened the safety of Sebaste but the bishop (probably Radulph) managed to negotiate the safety of the church and village. But not for long. The allure of the riches of Sebaste was simply too much of a temptation and immediately following the famous Battle of Hattin, Saladin's nephew (Husam al-Din Muhammad) ransacked the church (in July 1187), stealing its rich fittings and objects ('images', 'hangings' and 'ornaments of silver and gold'), leaving only that which was necessary for establishing a mosque there. 'Imad al-Din tells us (there are two versions of his account) that since Husam was a 'pious Muslim' he had a *mihrab* (niche for direction of prayer) established in the south wall and set up a *minbar* (pulpit) there as well, and then had the whole building transferred lock stock and barrel to Muslim control. Husam also had the bishop – it is said of him that he was 'a gentle and distinguished man' – scourged and tortured until he finally gave up and revealed the whereabouts of certain hidden treasures. Following the passing of the church into Muslim hands, Christians were still on occasion given access to the Cathedral, particularly to see the grotto in which the tomb of John the Baptist was located (see for instance the testimony of Burchard of Sion from 1283).

By 1333 the church lay in ruins. In 1485, the Franciscan Francesco Suriano visited the site and, after praying at the Tomb of John the Baptist, he says that he saw (probably in the chapel above the tomb) 'two tombs of the finest marble, the most beautiful, I believe, in the world. One is where was buried Eliseus and the other the prophet Joel; although the martyrology says Abdias [i.e. Obadiah], yet on the tomb is incised Joel. The church is built like a fortress similar to that of Bethlehem, and in it lives the *Machademo*, that is the Governor.' Pringle has already pointed out that the inscription *Ioel* must have been *Io[hann]es* and must have been misread [note 9.36]. Another traveller, Morosini (AD 1514), also mentions what sound like Roman sarcophagi: 'two very fine square tombs of marble, very white with festoons and leaves'.

Travellers and explorers who reached Sabastiyeh in the nineteenth century were occasionally given a difficult time by the locals who were said to be sometimes 'very restless and given to uprisings'. Some of the archaeological features connected with the Crusader Cathedral and its vicinity that were shown to the visitors have long since disappeared. Edward Robinson was one of the first to provide a proper factual description of the building and its features, as a result of his visit there in 1838. John Wilson attempted to enter the church in 1843 without success but he did notice ruins to the south of the church in the presumed area of the Bishop's House in the Crusader period [note 9.37]. Victor Guérin also recorded the building in some detail and mentions some interesting features: the tower at the north-west corner of the church (still visible today), which he suggested was the belfry of the church, and enormous water cisterns and remains of large buildings to the south of the church which he identified as parts of the monastery and Bishop's House [note 9.38]. Officers of the British Survey of Western Palestine reached the site in July 1872 and later in June 1875 [note 9.39]. Some visitors were not as impressed by the site as the explorers. Mark Twain, for example, described the place as 'hot and dusty' when he reached the village in 1867: 'There was nothing for us to do in Samaria but buy handfuls of old Roman coins at a franc a dozen, and look at a dilapidated church of the Crusaders and a vault in it which once contained the body of John the Baptist. This relic was long ago carried away to Genoa' [note 9.40].

Entering the mosque today you would not know that you were located at the eastern end of a very large Crusader church: nothing ancient can be seen and nothing remains of the three apses that were once in the eastern wall. A new mosque was constructed here at the

9.9

time of Abd el-Hamid's reign in 1889 (see the Arabic inscription above the main entrance) and it replaced an older mosque that had been at this location. This new construction resulted in the destruction of the ruined apse and some parts of the original vaulting. The upper part of the minaret (*mithaneh*) at the south-west corner of the mosque was also rebuilt. Comparing a photograph taken from exactly the same angle as in a painting by John Fulleylove in 1902, I can see that very few changes have taken place and those that have been made are only cosmetic (*illustration 9.9*) [note 9.41]. The interior of the mosque looks very much like any other modern religious building of this sort: a *mihrab* (prayer niche) and a *minbar* (pulpit) lit up with fluorescent lighting, black and brown marble-encased walls, a well-plastered and painted ceiling, carpets on the floors, and electrical lighting and ceiling fans. Betty Murray, back in 1933, described how she and the rest of the excavators attended a social activity inside the Church of St John and in front of the mosque:

> We had supper early in order to attend an educational film in the mosque. It was an amusing and romantic scene, but an atrocious film. By the light of a very few lanterns and a young moon we assembled in front of the mosque inside what was once the nave of the ruined Crusader church. Not only all Sabustia, but also people from the

surrounding villages came. We were escorted up to the top of the walls. Women and children lined the roof of the mosque, and we sat along one of the side walls – which ran up sheer to the height of the mosque roof. People had even climbed along the narrow wall connecting the ruined walls with one of the few piers still standing and two boys squatted right out there. Far below the crowds were gathered in widening rings round the table with the projector on it and the school teacher conducted the ceremonies.

It came to me in the middle of the night as I lay in bed, tossing and turning, pondering the enigma of why the followers of John should have wanted to bury him in Samaria/Sebaste of all places. It was not the most likely spot, representing neither the place where he had died nor the place where he was born – as far as I could see he did not have relatives there, nor was there any other particular link that I could make out with some event in John's life. I scrambled out of bed and made myself a cup of coffee. It seemed to me that the only way of finding a solution was to try and work out the significance of John's death for his disciples. Was his death an unexpected blow to all their hopes? What did they now want to do? If John had seen himself in the role of Elisha preparing for the return of Elijah, then how could John be beheaded without any sign of the return of Elijah? If the followers had thought of him as Elijah incarnate, then undoubtedly John's death would have been even more uncomfortable for them, a situation that would have been difficult to explain to his general followers, let alone to outsiders. He could ascend to heaven in a fiery chariot (like Elijah) – that was fine – but to have one's head cut off was just too messy and ignoble, and not at all in keeping with the strength of their expectations. For the Elijah/Messiah to arrive, then John the Precursor as Elisha/Elijah would have had to be active as the 'Voice in the Wilderness' (Isaiah 40:3), not dead. If some of the disciples regarded John as their Messiah, which seems likely, then his death must have been even more of a disaster in regard to all their hopes and dreams. They were now caught up in an impossible situation: should they continue to follow the teachings of John or perhaps, because of their disappointment, they should now join Jesus and his disciples? And so, they eventually gave John his final burial rites in Sebaste in a city that was almost exclusively pagan by all accounts. True, this would have meant that his burial could go unnoticed; the inhabitants of Sebaste probably would not have known who he was and others perhaps would not have cared. But out of all the possible places, why there at Sebaste? One scholar suggested that Sebaste was chosen as the place, in preference to say Judaea or elsewhere, precisely because it was well out of Antipas' jurisdiction, but surely this was unnecessary because Antipas could easily have prevented the body being taken away from Machaerus in the first place [note 9.42]. There had to be some other link, even the smallest of links, between John and Sebaste. And why was the place of his burial kept such a secret in the Gospels?

Ordinarily, a person was buried at the place where he had met his death, or near the place of his residence or hometown, or at a location connected with some family tradition. Clearly, Josephus' evidence indicates that the actual beheading of John took place at Machaerus, so we may eliminate the possibility that John was executed in Sebaste. In any case, Herod Antipas had no jurisdiction there. I think also that there is an underlying assumption in both Matthew (14:12) and Mark (6:29) that John was ultimately buried elsewhere, otherwise why did John's disciples have to make their way to Machaerus to bury him if he had already been buried there in a tomb or, as was the common practice with the bodies of criminals in those days, in a general pit? Herod Antipas must have given specific orders to allow for John's body to be released to his disciples for burial so that they could take it away. Nothing of course is said about the head, but I think one must assume that John's head and body would have been kept together for burial, unless Herod Antipas wished to further denigrate John's memory, which I find unlikely because of Herod Antipas' pathological fear of an uprising erupting against him at any time. There is also the matter of Herod Antipas later hearing about Jesus and thinking that he was possibly John resurrected: 'But when Herod heard thereof, he said, It is John, whom I beheaded: he is risen from the dead' (Mark 6:16). If indeed John had been buried at Machaerus, surely Herod Antipas would have had all the means available to him to have the tomb checked out to see if his corpse was still there. Regarding his hometown, there can be no doubt, as we have seen in previous chapters, that this was in Ain Karim or its vicinity, close to Jerusalem and quite far away from Sebaste and indeed also from Machaerus. Hence, we are left with the possibility that John's ultimate resting place was at Sebaste because of some family tradition. But what could this be? Elizabeth, we are told by Luke (1:5), was a descendant of the highly respected House of Aaron (see Chapter One of this book). Is there a link between the House of Aaron and the region of Sebaste? The actual tomb of Aaron, the first priest of the Israelites, is not known, and according to Jewish tradition its place was

+ΧΕ ΑΝΑϚ ΚΟϹΜΟΙΟ ΜΕΓΑϹΘΕΝ℞ ΒΟΗΘΗϹϾΕΦΑΝ
ΟϹ ΤΟΥΠΡΟΔΡΟΜΟΥϹΟΥΘΡΟΝΟΝΙΘΥΝΙΝΛΑΧΩΝΥΠΟϹΟ
+ΑΓΛΑΟΝΔΟΜΟΝΗΛΙΑΠΡΟΦΗΤΗ Τ Ω ϹΩ ΕΤΕΨϚΕΤΟΝΔ

9.10

intentionally kept hidden so that it might not turn into a holy place.

While we cannot pinpoint any specific Jewish traditions linking the House of Aaron with Sebaste, it is perhaps no coincidence that there were two later Byzantine-period chapels dedicated to Aaron and Elijah, which were constructed not too far away from each other, at Ain Haroun ('the spring of Aaron') and Boberiyeh (the Arabic name is derived from the French word *boverie* = stable of byre), almost two kilometres to the south-east of the city of Sebaste, close to the aqueduct that brought water from Ain Nakoura to Sebaste (only a ten-minute horse-ride). The subterranean chapel at Ain Haroun had, from its last stage of use, Christian grafitti indicating that the place was dedicated to Aaron [note 9.43]. Di Segni has suggested that this chapel of Aaron, together with the nearby chapel of Elijah at Boberiyeh, were dedicated to 'a cult of spring-and rain-spirits intended to guarantee the water-supply of Samaria'. The 'church' of Boberiyeh is located on a hill to the east of Ain Haroun, and an inscribed lintel, of the fifth or first half of the sixth century, was found here by Alt bearing a metric dedication to Elijah the prophet, and mentioning a bishop of Sebaste, called Stephanus, and ´referring to John the Baptist by his title 'prodromus' (Πρόδρομος) (*illustration 9.10*) [note 9.44].

I should now like to propose a reconstruction of the events that took place in the aftermath of John's execution. There are a lot of 'unknowns' here so we must step carefully forward in this attempt to work out the secret of why John came to be buried in Samaria. On hearing of John's death, his disciples, who cannot have been too far away, hurried to Machaerus and, in the absence of John's relatives (possibly his immediate family were dead at that time), made a claim on his body (and head) from Herod Antipas. Because of what they perceived to be the shameful manner of his death and because of their utter disappointment at the unexpected turn of events, I think his disciples would first have concentrated on making the necessary arrangements for an immediate burial. But where to exactly? It is unlikely to have occurred at the place of execution itself – the scene of his shame – but further away, and I suggest this must have been near one of John's previous centres of activity, such as at Bethabara, east of the Jordan. In any case, John's body could not have been transported for any great distance in any direction, especially in a hot climate, and the burial itself could not be delayed for more than eight hours. The exact place of burial was clearly kept a secret, perhaps because John's disciples feared that people would flock to see the tomb and this was not in keeping with the ideas that they wished to disseminate about him, i.e. that John as the Elijah-type of figure was to be resurrected yet again. The Gospels do indicate that stories of John's possible return were flourishing not long after his death, and this would have been impossible had the exact whereabouts of John's tomb been common knowledge. There is of course the story that Herod Antipas feared that Jesus might be John resurrected (Mark 6:16). Elsewhere, when Jesus reached Caesarea Phillipi (Banias) there were those who thought he might be John (Matthew 16: 13–14). It is also interesting to note that adulation of the tombs of prophets and holy men was frowned upon at that time by the followers of Jesus and this might also have been the case with the followers of John: 'Woe unto you, scribes and Pharisees, hypocrites! Because ye build the tombs of the prophets, and garnish the sepulchers of the righteous' (Matthew 23:29). In the normal course of events, John's body laid out in a cave burial would have eventually decomposed and then, as in normal Jewish practice of the first century, his bones would have been gathered up by his followers into a bone-box (ossuary) for the purpose of storage or transportation elsewhere – perhaps in this case to Sebaste. I should like to think that, in keeping with Jewish custom, John's disciples would eventually have made sure that he was given the honour due to him, by receiving his final burial rites at a location where his parents would have been born or buried, or where he had close relatives. This may very well have been at Sebaste or in its immediate region.

10

Relics, Souvenirs and Cults of John

One would probably think that relic-collecting is a quaint, albeit 'primitive' and forgotten custom of a bygone Christian age, when communication of religious ideas among certain people was sometimes only achieved successfully through the medium of physical objects of worship and devotion, such as a piece of the wooden cross of Jesus, some camel hair from the tunic of John the Baptist, the fingernail of Francis of Assisi, an icon bearing the painted image of Mary, and so forth. People would gaze upon these articles of devotion, touch them, and feel a direct connection to the holiness that they perceived as imbued in them. This close proximity that was established between worshippers and their 'holy' artefacts provided an enormous sustenance for their beliefs, helping them through difficult times and serving as a bridge between their daily lives and an appreciation of the essence of the Bible and its messages, even though the devotees themselves might be placed at great geographical distances from the places where the saints and holy men, of whom they had relics, actually lived and operated.

In an age of intellectualism and with the possibility of rational thinking available for all and sundry, with access to diverse printed literature and the opening up of worldwide communications via television and the internet, you would think that extreme cultic behaviour such as the devotion of relics would cease altogether. Strange as it may seem, however, not only has this phenomenon of relic-collecting not disappeared in Western society but it is still going strong, with the focus having now shifted dramatically away from the cult of holy or saintly persons to that of the cult of celebrities and television personalities.

Although I am sure that there are probably one or two people out there who would like to possess a few hairs from the head of the present Pope or a hand-cloth with which Mother Teresa wiped her hands, these Christian relic-hunters have now been replaced almost totally by a new breed of religious devotees altogether – hundreds of thousands of them actually – who would much prefer to possess a dress that once belonged to Marilyn Monroe, a handkerchief that was once used by Frank Sinatra, or a 'Dirty Harry' firearm used by Clint Eastwood. For many fans the search for relics and mementoes of their favourite television and film personalities, pop stars and sports persons, whether dead or alive (John Lennon and Elvis Presley are prime examples of dead celebrities whose relics are constantly sought after), is undertaken with a great deal of religious intensity and fervour. Consequently, the industry of relics connected with these celebrities grows from day to day, and a wide variety of mementoes and paraphernalia are now readily available, and signed photographs of film and television personalities are common-place (there are even shops that specialise in the sale of the autographs of famous people – many of which I suspect cannot be authentic). More unique items are constantly sought after, such as the sweat-laden shirts of footballers who at the end of matches take them off and throw them into the crowds, or bizarre personal items, such as the underpants of singers of well-known boy-bands. Although one is perhaps repelled by the idea of someone worshipping worn underpants, how different is this from someone who worshipped a withered brown finger or a curled piece of skin said to be that of John the Baptist?

Many of those who collected relics in antiquity were devout Christian pilgrims who, returning from their travels to the Holy Land, donated the relics to local churches or private chapels. Pilgrimage is about a passionate and focused frame of mind, a means of cementing a bridge between the Christian believer, on the one hand, and the words of the Bible on the other. The late Sir Steven Runciman, historian and storyteller, once wrote that 'the desire to be a pilgrim is deeply rooted in human nature' [note 10.1]. The pilgrim has the burning desire to stand and see with his own eyes the landscapes of the Holy Land, to bend his knees at the threshold of the numerous sites associated with the great figures of the Old and New Testaments, and, finally, to see the place of the Jewish Temple in Jerusalem where God chose to live, and the places which saw the passion and resurrection of Jesus. Early pilgrimage was rare in the first few centuries after the death of Jesus because Christians at that time were much more interested in emphasising the divine nature of Jesus and the universality of his message. However, this does not mean that pilgrimages did not exist – some of our earliest references to them date back to the third century – it was just that it was not formalised in any way. This only occurred at the time of Constantine the Great in the early fourth century, when churches were first built at some of the pivotal holy sites in Palestine, notably the place of the Nativity of Jesus in Bethlehem and the Tomb of Jesus in Jerusalem. Indeed, Constantine's mother is sometimes regarded as the world's first Christian 'pilgrim–archaeologist' since, according to tradition, she was the one who supervised the digging up of fragments of the wooden cross of Jesus in a cistern/cave not far from the Rock of Golgotha in Jerusalem where the crucifixion was believed to have taken place [note 10.2].

The ultimate purpose of the pilgrim at the holy locations was to gain access, to pray, to achieve spiritual edification through a process of meditation; and, by the reading of holy scripture, to receive blessings and guidance from the guardians of these holy spots, and then, before going away, to leave alms. To accommodate the ever-growing number of pilgrims, numerous hospices with beds, kitchens and stables were set up close to the holy sites; monasteries also opened their doors to pilgrims. As with tourists nowadays, these pilgrims wanted to take away with them mementoes of their visits: phials of holy oil and water (*ampullae*), pendant-crosses, oil lamps, religious trinkets of one sort or another, and, of course, if possible, also reliquaries. The need for relics and souvenirs of saints and holy persons definitely fulfilled a dual purpose, as proof that the pilgrims had indeed visited the Holy Land and also as gifts for those who were not able to make the trip and stayed behind. The collection of relics that began fairly innocently with the early development of Christian pilgrimage to the Holy Land in the fourth century rapidly led to the blooming of a hunger for mementoes and souvenirs among visitors in the fifth to seventh centuries and this, ultimately, led to an unbridled passion for relic-collecting in the eighth century, especially when the Holy Land was no longer in Christian hands and access to the holy sites became more difficult. From the ninth century the need for a constant source of relics for pilgrims was catered for by a professional class of relic-makers and the peak of their activities took place from the time of the Crusaders onwards.

In the late 1990s the White Fathers in Jerusalem asked me to make an investigation of the structural history of the ancient buildings uncovered in and around the Bethesda Pool, the same pool where Jesus is said to have cured a paralytic man in Jerusalem (John 5). While measuring the large subterranean reservoir beneath the Crusader Chapel of the *Probatica*, which had recently been cleared of rotting rubbish and a few dead pigeons, the place was invaded by a flock of Russian female pilgrims with rounded faces and flowery-patterned dresses. They seemed to be immediately overcome by the odour of sanctity in the place, they were almost in ecstasy, but there were so many of them that they had a hard time balancing on the narrow and slippery steps. They began filling scores of small bottles with the water, cupping their hands into the water so that they could drink and splash their faces as well. I stood on the lower step with the pressure from their heaving breasts, throbbing with religious intensity, at a horizontal level with my eyes. I clapped my hands and tried to draw their attention, to suggest that they should desist from drinking or bottling the water: 'The authorities have put poison into the water to prevent bacteria and vermin from breeding here,' I said. When I did not elicit the expected response, I thought I would simplify matters: 'This water, no good,' I said and gestured with my hands. Of course, they did not seem at all perturbed and this was perhaps not surprising since none of them seemed to know English. They probably thought I was a bit crazy. A friend of mine subsequently arrived who does speak Russian but after first listening to her explanations with appropriate courtesy, they then waved their hands to the sky and laughed and continued filling their bottles with the contaminated water to take back to their friends in their homeland.

This fascination with possessing the actual water, soil or rocks of the Holy Land as 'holy souvenirs' is quite amazing. Back in the 1970s there were even those who catered for this fascination, setting up extremely profitable businesses in that part of the world. For a fee, you could acquire any number of well-labelled small bottles of 'holy' water from the Jordan River or sardine-type tins full of 'holy' soil. On my visit to examine the archaeological remains being uncovered at the baptism sites in Jordan, the archaeologist in charge, Mohammed Waheeb, provided us with bottles of water from the Jordan River left over from the Pope's visit to the site in March 2000. The bottles were labelled 'To commemorate the apostolic visit of his holiness Pope John Paul II to the baptism site. Holy water – John the Baptist spring – Bethany beyond the Jordan.' Naturally, we were encouraged to drink of this 'holy water'.

Returning in the early 1980s to Crouch End, a neighbourhood in north London where I had grown up as a boy, I walked down the street to visit a devout Catholic Irish lady, whom I always remembered fondly as smiling and saying good morning. Since I had with me a fragment of a Roman cooking pot which had been dug up not too far away from the actual Tomb of Jesus in Jerusalem, I thought she might like it as a present, that she might have some fascination for this object. I was right, she nearly fainted when I explained the age of the potsherd and was totally overcome by the idea that she was actually touching an artefact that had come from the proximity of a holy site that meant so much to her. Her enjoyment was such a marvel that I did not have the heart to tell her that thousands of such potsherds dating from the time of Jesus had been uncovered over the years in and around the Church of the Holy Sepulchre in Jerusalem; this potsherd was not in any way a unique discovery. Since pilgrimage began, a variety of different kinds of items and souvenirs were brought back to England and Europe from the Near East and, from the mid-nineteenth century onwards, mounted albumen photographic prints of the Holy Land were particularly popular and in many instances replaced painted icons, engravings and watercolours. Some pilgrims and visitors were known to come back home with dried flowers pressed between the pages of their books, as well as twigs and leaves and pebbles from the holy sites. The seventeenth-century traveller Henry Maundrell wrote about pilgrims collecting the fruit of the carob tree from the traditional site of the Wilderness of John the Baptist:

> After a good hours travel in this wilderness, we came to the cave and fountain, where, as they say, the Baptist excers'd those sever austerities related of him, Matt. 3.4. Near this cell there still grow some old locust trees, the monuments of the ignorance of the middle times. These the fryars aver to be the very same that yielded substance to the Baptist; and the popish pilgrims, who dare not be wiser than such blind guides, gather the fruit of them, and carry it away with great devotion.

But of all the objects that pilgrims brought back with them from the Holy Land, relics were perhaps the most interesting and every church worth its salt in England and Europe had to boast a relic or two. The American writer Mark Twain undoubtedly had a fascination for relics and these were frequently mentioned in his *The Innocents Abroad*, a book written in 1867 that takes one on a humorous trail through Europe to the Holy Land. Some of the relics Twain described were quite recent, including the bullet and two vertebrae of the archbishop of Paris who had been shot dead by insurgents in 1848. On arriving in Milan, Twain went to see the Cathedral there:

> The priests showed us two of St Paul's fingers and one of St Peter's; a bone of Judas Iscariot (it was black) and also bones of all the other disciples; a handkerchief in which the Saviour had left the impression of his face. Among the most precious of relics were a stone from the Holy Sepulchre, part of the crown of thorns (they have a whole one at Notre Dame), a fragment of the purple robe worn by the Saviour, a nail from the cross, and a picture of the Virgin and Child painted by the veritable hand of St Luke. This is the second of St Luke's Virgins we have seen. Once a year all these holy relics are carried in procession through the streets of Milan.

On arriving in Rome: 'They have twelve small pillars in St Peter's, which came from Solomon's Temple. They have also – which was far more interesting to me – a piece of the true Cross, and some nails, and a part of the crown of thorns.'

Eventually, Twain reached the Holy Land. He did not see the head of John the Baptist in Damascus, but he did get to go to Samaria and see John's tomb and he mentioned that his relic head had been sent off to Genoa long ago. In the Church of the Holy Sepulchre, Twain was greatly impressed with all of Helena's digging operations in the fourth century in the attempt to locate the True Cross: 'She had a laborious piece of work here, but it was richly rewarded. Out of this place she got the crown of thorns, the nails of the Cross, the true Cross itself, and the cross of the penitent thief' [note 10.3].

The veneration of relics from the Holy Land began very early on in the Byzantine period and by the fifth century there are numerous archaeological indications that the cult of relics was extremely wide-spread. Many examples of Byzantine-period relic-boxes have been found in excavations in Israel/Palestine [note 10.4]. The idea that was prevalent at that time was that by touching the relic (or its container) the sanctity of the holy person or saint would immediately be transferred to the worshipper himself. Some relics were placed beneath the paving stones of the chancel and others were placed in niches cut into the sides of walls or columns for the purposes of veneration. Those relics that were visible became an important focus of the liturgy and ceremony practised within churches. Relics could include bones, hair and pieces of clothing, but bits of wood purportedly from the 'True Cross' of Jesus and chips of stone taken from the place of the Crucifixion ('Golgotha') were the most popular. Naturally, pilgrims wished to touch the relics with their own hands but it was quickly realised that this would be quite detrimental to their preservation. Hence, relics were placed within containers (reliquaries) where they could be protected for posterity.

Originally, reliquaries were small stone or metal boxes resembling sarcophagi in appearance. Later medieval reliquaries came in all shapes and sizes, and some were wonderfully crafted containers. They were made of different materials: metals (silver or gilding), bone or shell. Semi-precious stones, pearls and various ornaments were frequently attached to reliquaries and some of these had incised Greek or Latin inscriptions identifying the relic or bearing the name of its donor. The rule is that the greater the decoration on a reliquary box, the more recent its craftsmanship. The general shape is usually rectangular, similar to jewellery boxes, but there are also examples crafted superbly in the shape of churches, and others where the box assumes the shape of the relic itself and this is true of those containing various segments of human anatomy, notably heads, arms, hands and feet. There are also examples of reliquaries in the shape of a cross or a crown embedded with various bone relics: one example of a crown of this kind comes from the Church of John the Baptist in Jerusalem (*plate 15b*).

On 20 June in the year 336 articles of clothing purported to have belonged to the Evangelist Luke and the Apostle Andrew were placed with considerable pomp and ceremony in the Church of the Apostles in Constantinople [note 10.5]. Hitherto, the city had possessed very few Christian relics, but this was to change dramatically from the second half of the fourth century onwards, and eventually it came to have one of the largest collections of relics in the East. Fragments of the Holy Cross were widely distributed and this was followed by relics of the ashes of the saints, drops of blood, bone fragments and so forth. More relics were brought over to Constantinople from the Near East and as these relics became much more 'biblical', so too were doubts expressed about their origins. The empress Eudocia appears to have had a passion for relic-collecting and in the mid-fifth century she is reported to have transported from Jerusalem to Constantinople a portrait of Mary made by St Luke [note 10.6].

It seems unlikely that important relics, especially those relating to Jesus, John the Baptist and the Apostles, could have been acquired by pilgrims, except for rank forgeries and minor items, and so the important relics must have remained in the East at least until the time of the Muslim invasion of the Levant in the mid-seventh century when some of them were brought to Constantinople. The remains of early Christian saints and martyrs became highly collectible items but it was not always possible to obtain their relics. Instead, pilgrims would frequent their tombs and acquire bottles of oil that had been passed through their bones; reliquary-tombs of this sort are known in Palestine from the Byzantine basilica at the coastal town of Dor and at a place to the south-west of Maresha in the foothills region. A reliquary-sarcophagus for a saint is also known from the basilica-church of St Titus at Gortyn in Crete [note 10.7]. In some of the textual sources, we hear about the virtues that were perceived to exist in relics (Saint Ambrose and Saint Victricius, for example) but there were also those (Saint Basil) who expressed some doubts about their authenticity. Runciman says that in the eleventh century there was 'an endless stream' of travellers to the East and particularly to Constantinople where pilgrims would gawp at the rich relics located there: the Crown of Thorns, the Seamless Garment, the Edessa Cloth with the face of Christ, St Luke's portrait of Mary, the hair of John the Baptist, the mantle of Elijah, and so forth [note 10.8].

During archaeological excavations along the western Old City wall of Jerusalem during the mid-1970s, a group of youngsters from various Israeli farming villages (*moshavim*) volunteered to excavate alongside the counterscarp of the moat surrounding the area of the Citadel, where it met up with the city wall. There were tons of rubbish in this area that had to be removed, and these fills were found to contain a myriad of artefacts: potsherds, figurines and coins. One of the unusual finds made by these youngsters was that of a rusty cross-shaped reliquary, and when it was cleaned it could be seen to have engraved Christian drawings on its front and back [note 10.9]. Within this reliquary were carbonised wooden fragments which we eventually had analysed, but they turned out to be of twigs rather than the bits of tree trunk that we had been expecting. Clearly, the person who bought this reliquary in the Fatimid period was hoodwinked into believing that it contained an actual relic of the 'Holy Cross' of Jesus. Instead, it was a blatant forgery. Perhaps the person who bought it had a look inside and this is the reason why the reliquary was chucked into the dumps outside the city walls of Jerusalem.

The collection, dissemination and trade in relics and reliquaries became big business in the twelfth century, following the capture of Jerusalem by the Crusaders in 1099. A number of production centres for relics in the Holy Land were established at this time, among them those at Jerusalem and Samaria; and because there was such an abundance of available relics, of which many were forgeries, the suppliers had to ensure that the relics they dealt with came from reputable sources. Hence, Letters of Authenticity accompanying the relics became very fashionable, and if it was possible to have these letters signed by religious figures in attendance at one of the holy sites in the Near East, then this was even better. Once the industry had been firmly established the West could be supplied with an unlimited number of relics and the artisans concentrated their efforts at producing the best possible reliquaries that they could manufacture and market [note 10.10]. Many of these contained fragments of wood purporting to be from the Holy Cross of Jesus. Some of the major relics of the cross in the possession of the Crusaders appear to have been lost to the Muslims during the major Battle of Hattin fought in 1187. Queen Thamar of Georgia (1184–1212) is said to have asked for their return but Saladin refused [note 10.11]. There were also other biblical relics which passed around, including the bones of the Maccabees said to have been found at Modi'in, which at that time was identified with the hill of Suba (Belmont) [note 10.12].

The year 1204 saw the pillage of Constantinople by the Crusaders. The Fourth Crusade had set out for the Holy Land the year before but was diverted through Venetian greed to Constantinople. When a riot broke out in the city in 1204 this was taken as a signal for the Crusaders to capture and plunder the city. Runciman wrote: 'It is hard to exaggerate the harm done to European civilization by the sack of Constantinople. The treasures of the City, the books and works of art preserved from distant centuries, were all dispersed and most destroyed' [note 10.13]. The church of Saint Sophia was utterly despoiled and plundered for its treasures, including the relics, and the body of the emperor Justinian was chucked into the gutter, like that of a common thief. Comte Riant made detailed records of the ecclesiastical plunder taken by the Crusaders at that time and these were later published in his *Exuviae Sacre Constantinopolitanae*. Most of the stolen relics later turned up in the West. The typical recipient of these relics, as described by Hutton, displayed 'the passion of a collector of antiquities combined with the business instincts of a dealer of curiosities and the piety of a hagiologist' [note 10.14]. What exactly was stolen and from where is something that is now difficult to determine. Before the thirteenth century there were very few relics in Europe and most of these were only of local saints. This changed following the pillage of Constantinople, with a flood of what were believed to be 'authentic' relics appearing in the West, including those of Jesus himself, of Mary and of the Apostles. The relics were transported with or without their reliquaries, and they included fragments of the Holy Cross (supposedly found by Helena), drops of Jesus' blood, one of his teeth, some of his hair, the purple robe, some of the bread from the Last Supper, etc. The heads of John the Baptist and the Apostles also found their way to the West [note 10.15].

The extent of the devastation that occurred during the sack of Constantinople in 1204 is very clear from the contemporary chronicle of Robert of Clari, a French knight who participated in the events. Robert described a variety of relics that he observed in the 'Holy Chapel' (i.e. in the Church of the Blessed Virgin of the Pharos) after the capture of the city. Robert's description reads a bit like a child listing the contents of a sweetshop and I can imagine him standing there with his mouth wide open: 'Within this chapel', wrote Robert:

> were found many rich relics. One found there two pieces of the True Cross as large as the leg of a man and as long as half a *toise*, and one found there also the iron of the lance with which Our Lord had His side pierced and two of the nails which were driven through His hands and feet, and one found there in a crystal phial quite a little of His blood, and one found there the tunic which He wore and which was taken from Him when they led Him to the Mount of Calvary, and one found there the blessed crown with which He was crowned, which was made of reeds with thorns as sharp as the points of daggers. And one found there a part of the robe of Our Lady and *the head of my lord St John the Baptist* and so many other rich relics that I could not recount them to you or tell you all the truth. [Italics: S.G.]

Robert brought back to France his own collection of relics and these are listed among other relics, such as 'half the girdle of the Blessed Virgin, the arm of St Mark the Evangelist, the finger of St Helena', in a manuscript inventory of the Treasure of Corbie drawn up in 1283 [note 10.16].

Visitors to Rome are able to look at local relics as well as some of the relics that originated in Constantinople and other parts of the Levant. At the Church of St John Lateran, which is a basilica dedicated to both John the Baptist and to St John the Evangelist, and is the main cathedral now used by the Pope, there are relic heads of St Peter and St Paul contained in reliquaries of gold and silver that were shaped as portrait heads of the two apostles. In the Lateran Palace, not far away from the flight of twenty-eight marble stairs (*Scala Sancta*) said by tradition to be the same as those descended by Jesus in Pontius Pilate's palace in Jerusalem, traditionally thought to have been brought to Rome by St Helena, are further relics: a piece of the True Cross, a portion of the lance of Longinus that was used to strike Jesus, a part of the sponge used to offer Jesus vinegar during the crucifixion, and one of the thorns from the crown of thorns. At the Church of St Praxedes on the Esquiline Hill in Rome, one could see the column of the scourging of Jesus, made of jasper. It was brought to Rome about seven hundred years ago by Cardinal John Colanna (Pontifical Legate in Palestine). Another relic kept in the Vatican is the head of St Lawrence which is stored within a jewelled reliquary of crystal and bronze.

As we saw in the previous chapter, the traditional place of the tomb of John the Baptist was situated at Sebaste in the northern central highlands of Palestine. In 1145, during the construction there of the large Cathedral of St John, a 'discovery' was made of a silver casket said to contain relics of John the Baptist himself. This seems unlikely. In fact, the traditional tombs, including those of Obadiah and Elisha, had already been ransacked by pagans as early as *c.* AD 363, with the bones of John the Baptist having been taken out, burnt and then scattered in the fields. Who were these pagans who did this dastardly deed?

Paganism in Palestine during the Hellenistic and Roman periods was deeply rooted in the considerably older Syro-Canaanite cults, but in the case of Sebaste it would appear that no such syncretism of this kind existed, suggesting that the population at Sebaste at that time was not as mixed and heterogeneous as it was once assumed [note 10.17]. It is unclear who these pagans were who participated in the desecration of the tomb of John the Baptist (except that they were inhabitants of the town of Sebaste), and it is also not known to what extent they were acting with the direct encouragement and approval of Julian the Apostate (AD 361–363). Less than forty years after the institution of Christianity as an official religion of the Roman empire, Julian the Apostate, who may best be described as an 'ascetic revolutionary', did his utmost to reverse this process and to reinstate paganism, but with little success [note 10.18]. At this time there was an outbreak of anti-Christian disturbances in Palestine, notably at Gaza and Ashkelon with the burning of churches there, and this fits in well with what traditional Christian tradition relates regarding the pagan desecration of the tomb of John the Baptist at Sebaste in *c.* 363. Even if Julian had not actually instigated the desecration of the tomb, he undoubtedly would have given his blessing after the event.

According to Theodoret (AD 393–457), a theologian born at Cyrrhus (north of Aleppo) in Syria, the heathen inhabitants of Sebaste opened the chest (θήκη) of John and then, on taking out the bones, burnt them [note 10.19]. An account of the desecration of the tomb and the burning of the bones of the Baptist is also provided by Philostorgius [note 10.20]. However, from Rufinus of Aquileia we hear that the cult of John the Baptist was rapidly restored and a good proportion of the bones were carefully collected by visiting monks from the Monastery of Philip in Jerusalem and then taken away to Alexandria in Egypt where Bishop Athanasius temporarily took care of them until some of the relics were taken to Jerusalem and placed in a new church on the Mount of Olives in 370. According to Rufinus, the pagans

> frenziedly attacked the tomb of John the Baptist with murderous hands and set about scattering the bones, gathering them again, burning them, mixing the holy ashes with dust, and scattering them throughout the fields and countryside. But by God's providence it happened that some men from Jerusalem, from the Monastery of Philip, the man of God, arrived there at the same time in order to pray. When they saw the enormity being perpetrated by human hands at the service of bestial spirits, they mixed with those gathering the bones for burning, since they considered dying preferable to being polluted by such a sin, carefully and reverently collected them, as far as they could in the circumstances, then slipped away from the others, to their amazement or fury, and brought the sacred relics to the pious father Philip. He in turn, thinking it beyond him to guard such a treasure by his own vigilance, sent the relics to Athanasius, then supreme pontiff, in the care of his deacon Julian, who later became bishop of Parentium. Athanasius received them and closed them up within a hollowed-out place in the sacristy wall in the presence of a few witnesses, preserving them in prophetic spirit for the benefit of the next generation, so that now the remnants of idolatry had been thrown down flat, golden roofs might rise for them on temples once unholy [note 10.21]

The earlier tradition regarding the desecration of John's tomb at the time of Julian the Apostate was maintained by writers even until medieval times. An anonymous pilgrim's text from the twelfth century records that John's body was dug up, burnt and his ashes were scattered to the wind, 'save the head, which had before this been translated to Alexandria, whence it was afterwards translated to Poitou in France; and save also the forefinger wherewith he had pointed to Jesus as He came to be baptised . . . The blessed virgin Thekla brought the forefinger with her into the Alps and there it is kept with the greatest in the church of St Jean de Maurienne' [note 10.22]. A rather garbled account – the existing translation is clearly not the best in the world – was later provided by the French writer Ernoul (AD 1220), who substituted Herod's wife for Julian the Apostate and referred to Sebaste as Sabat: 'Thither his disciples brought him [John], when Herod had had his head cut off. A little after, when Herod's wife heard that he was buried, she sent thither and had his bones taken from the earth and burnt, and the powder sold, and for this reason children still on St John's night might make a fire of bones, because his bones were burnt [this is a reference to one of the customs for making bonfires on St John's eve]' [note 10.23].

I stepped out of the car and the freezing cold air hit me directly in the face. The car had been overheated and it was like going from the heat of the African jungle to the cold of the Antarctic within seconds. I was in Germany, in the town of Marburg on the Lahn, and there was dry, powdery snow everywhere in sight. I was with family and friends and the first thing we did was have lunch to provide ourselves with some fuel to heat our bodies, then we climbed up to the castle to look at the breathtaking view of the snowy rooftops of the town, and then, finally, we reached the Church of St Elizabeth, which is the earliest purely Gothic church in Germany.

Hidden away and overlooking the Chapel of the Counts is the Altar of St John the Baptist with a magnificent painting of the destruction of the grave of John and the desecration of the relics, made by Johann von der Leyten and dating from 1512 [note 10.24]. The pagans are seen in the centre of the picture, hammering away at John's sarcophagus-like tomb, and collecting his bones in a basket ready to be carried away (*illustration 10.1*). In the background, behind the arches, one can see the digging, collecting and burning of the bones. Herodias or Salome is shown as an observer, insane and haunted by her crime. John's head is on a platter held by one man and in front of him is a lone figure digging with a mattock in the ground, perhaps symbolising the invention of the relic head of John the Baptist. I looked again and was surprised – the stance of the figure of the digger is almost identical to that of the figure of the digger in the twelfth-century wall painting in the crypt of the

10.1

Church of the Invention of the Head of John at Sebaste (see previous chapter). Perhaps the painter had seen the Sebaste painting or had seen a reproduction of it somewhere?

Back in the Old City of Jerusalem, the light glints and scatters across the rooftops and alleyways, sharpening the shadows in the pointed windows and doorways. There is always at least one cat basking in the sun on top of the domed roofs of the city, seemingly uninterested in the pungent smells and the din of voices wafting up from the narrow alleys below; a soldier lounges in a doorway, one of the shopkeepers peers across the road and picks his nose; two small children chase each other down the road with bulging schoolbags on their backs. The shortest way to get to the Church of Saint John the Baptist is through the Jaffa Gate along the western wall of the Old City. One plunges down through the bustling *suq* (market-place), humming with the frenetic activities of all those buying and selling. Manoeuvring carefully past piles of hand-painted ceramic cups and glass trinkets against the evil eye, you enter

Christian Street (originally known as Patriarch's Street) which has incorporated within it a wonderful patch of ancient stone pavement that resonates with the footsteps of time.

Arriving at a small iron gate (No.113 on Christian Street), we entered and found ourselves in a paved courtyard in front of a small church with a silver dome (*plate 15d*). This is the Church of St John the Baptist in the Muristan and it is under the direct custody of the Greek Orthodox Patriarchate. On the right is a slippery flight of steps leading up to a series of rooms, from which a nun emerged who had been visibly suffering from a very bad bout of influenza, with bright beady eyes and a red pulsating nose. She gestured towards the church and we followed her. To the right of the courtyard was a boundary wall with blocked-up doorways. Entering the church, which is evidently ancient, the walls are gaudily covered with paintings depicting numerous scenes from the life of John the Baptist and Jesus. The plan of the church is cruciform, with one apse to the east separated by an impressive iconostasis with the altar behind. I asked the nun if she knew anything about relics of John the Baptist and straight away she indicated in front of me a wooden stand, highly decorated on all sides, on top of which there was a painting of John the Baptist's head placed on a charger (*plate 16c*). In the sunken receptacle next to it, covered with glass, one could see a number of skull fragments, which the nun said were those of John the Baptist. According to the nun the best example of a relic of the arm of John the Baptist was to be found in one of the monasteries of Mount Athos in Greece.

Until the late nineteenth century, the Church of St John stood in the midst of a field of ruins of Crusader date extending all the way to the Church of the Holy Sepulchre [note 10.25]. At a depth of 7.5 metres below the present church is an older one of identical plan dating back to the fifth century. The lower church was first properly measured by Archibald Dickie by 'candle-light' in the late nineteenth century. His survey indicated that the walls had two stages of construction, the lower Byzantine and the upper medieval. A tradition says that the Byzantine church was erected over the ruins of the original house of Zacharias, father of John the Baptist. Another tradition says this is where the remains of John the Baptist were brought for safekeeping after the desecration of the tomb at Sebaste, but this seems unlikely because the church does not predate the mid-fifth century at the earliest.

At the time of the Persian conquest of Jerusalem in 614 many thousands of Christians found refuge in this church and its outbuildings, and at some point during the seventh century it was in the hands of the Georgians. The upper church was apparently built by Italian traders in the eleventh century and the lower church was turned into a crypt; the entire church was substantially rebuilt at the time of the Crusaders [note 10.26].

To confuse matters there was apparently another Crusader-period church dedicated to John the Baptist with a large hospital in the Muristan quarter of Jerusalem, and it too had relics of the saint. The impetus to the worship of John the Baptist and the construction of churches in his honour in Jerusalem and elsewhere was provided when the order of the Crusader Hospitallers was established. According to an anonymous pilgrim from the twelfth century, 'The Church of St John the Baptist stands almost opposite, facing the great church [i.e. the Church of the Holy Sepulchre], and is worthy of honour both because of its most holy relics and its exceeding famous charities.' This source indicates that this church was 'near' the Church of St Mary the Latin [note 10.27].

An elaborate story about John the Baptist was told by Jacobus de Voragine (*c.* 1230–1298) in his *Legenda Aurea Sanctorum* (The Golden Legend). Apparently, John's head had been taken from Machaerus to Jerusalem by Herodias and it was buried there as a precaution to prevent John's resurrection. Later, at the time of the emperor Marcian (*c.* 453), two monks had a revelation and went to Jerusalem to search for John's head: 'They hurried to the palace that had been Herod's, and found the head rolled up in haircloth sacks – the cloth, I suppose, that he wore in the desert' [note 10.28].

After the conquest by Saladin the church continued to be used by Christian pilgrims but an area adjacent to the church served as a Muslim hospital after 1192. It was at this time that the original name of the church was forgotten and it came to be referred to by some travellers as the 'House of Zebedee' (as well as that of the evangelist St John). When Süleyman the Magnificent began building the fortifications of Jerusalem in the mid-sixteenth century, he apparently used quite a few stones taken from the Muristan area and from the church itself. In the late sixteenth century the Franciscan Bernardino Amico published a plan and elevation drawing of the church but although the drawings look good they must be schematic because at that time (1596) the church was being used as a mosque and access to Christians was not permitted [note 10.29]. Another visitor, Alcarotti (1597), was also not able to enter the mosque and feared even raising the suspicions of the locals by looking at it from outside.

Amico was told (incorrectly) that this was the Church of James and John the Evangelist. This incorrect identification had been put about since the fourteenth century, but before that, judging by the sources, the church had been properly identified as the one dedicated to John the Baptist. In 1600 the Greek Orthodox acquired the place from the Muslims. The ancient church itself was forgotten and filled up with soil. A description by Horn from 1725 refers to this church as being of cruciform plan, built of squared stones, having a domed ceiling pierced with eight windows. Inside the church was a painting of John's head in a silver frame that pilgrims would kiss. Next to the church there was a garden and the ruins of a monastery which were said to be quite impressive.

According to the sources there were at least two other churches dedicated to John the Baptist in the Byzantine and Early Islamic periods at various locations in the immediate vicinity of the city. One of these was located in the area of the present-day Russian Monastery on the Mount of Olives. From the Byzantine sources we hear of a presbyter named Innocent, who was of Italian origin and had once been a married man, serving in an administrative position under Constantine the Great, but later deciding to become a monk and subsequently relocating to the Mount of Olives. It was here (in 370) that he built a *Martyrium* to house some of the relics of John the Baptist, as well as an adjacent monastery. These relics Innocent apparently received from Athanasius, Bishop of Alexandria, who had held them there since the desecration of the tomb of John at Sebaste *c.* 363. It is indeed quite possible that Innocent was one of the group of monks who helped collect the scattered bones of John the Baptist at the time of the desecration of the tomb at Sebaste and this may explain why he instigated their return to Jerusalem on the event of the construction of the new church on the Mount of Olives [note 10.30]. Perhaps not all of the relics were returned from Alexandria since there is also mention in the sources that another Bishop of Alexandria, Theophilus, kept the bones in a shrine of Serapis that had been consecrated as a church. The remains of a Byzantine-period church on the Mount of Olives, with exquisite decorated mosaic floors of the fifth-century, were found during the construction work for the foundations of the Russian church, undertaken there between 1870 and 1887. According to the monk Anastas Vardapet (seventh century), this Armenian Church of the Precursor (*Prodromos*) belonged to the Monastery of Pantaleon and was maintained by 'Albanians' monks. This church is also mentioned in the *Commemoratorium de Casis Dei* dated to around 808 [note 10.31].

There was apparently yet another Byzantine Church of John the Baptist to the east of the Church of St Stephen, mentioned by John Rufus and by Anastas as the 'Monastery of the Mamikoneans' named after St John, and it would appear to have been close to the area of Karm el-Sheikh (the present-day Rockefeller Museum). Nothing more is known about it [note 10.32]. Anastas also mentioned another church dedicated to John on Mount Zion. In addition, travellers in the twelfth century were shown a spot on the Haram al-Sharif (Temple Mount) in Jerusalem where, according to tradition, it was believed that the birth of John the Baptist was announced, but whether or not there was a shrine at this location is not known [note 10.33].

There are so many heads of John the Baptist in churches and monasteries at different locations in the Near East, as well as in Mediterranean countries and in Europe, that one loses track of them all after a while. Since it is obvious that John the Baptist could not have possessed more than one head, it naturally means that all but one must be forgeries.

Relics of John the Baptist were kept in the churches of Jerusalem during the Byzantine period but we are not told whether or not this included his head. Clearly the relics that Innocent brought back with him from Alexandria and that were placed in his Church on the Mount of Olives in 370 did not include the head, which had already been transferred on to Emessa or Damascus. However, in the Byzantine period (*c.* 530) there is mention of the charger (*discus*) on 'which the head of St John was carried', which was shown among other relics and artefacts kept in the Golgotha area of the *martyrium* of the Church of the Holy Sepulchre in Jerusalem [note 10.34]. In the twelfth century there is a reference to an altar of John the Baptist that was situated on the left-hand side of the entrance to the Church of the Holy Sepulchre, but there is no mention of a head [note 10.35]. Fragments of a relic-head of John were being shown at one of the two churches dedicated to John the Baptist located in the Muristan, and Burchard of Sion wrote (1280) that while his body had been buried at Sebaste, his head was 'buried' in Jerusalem: 'But after he had been beheaded, in Macherunta [=Machaerus] as aforesaid, his body was buried in Samaria by his disciples between the aforesaid prophets, but his head was buried at Jerusalem' [note 10.36]. It should be pointed out that it seems highly unlikely that in the first century the disciples of John would have buried his body in one place and his head in another.

Many of the sources agree that the head of John the Baptist reached Alexandria in Egypt, together with other remains of his body, following the desecration of his tomb at Sebaste in AD 363. But these relics were apparently not the same as those that were reported in Alexandria after the twelfth century. Marino Sanuto (1321) referred to a chest (*scrinium*) of relics of John the Baptist (perhaps also the head) that was kept in an unnamed monastery in Egypt: 'Every year they carry the aforesaid chest some five leagues down the Nile to another church of monks, which is also built in his honour. After Mass they place the chest in the river, to try in which place the saint wishes his relics to rest – that is, whether in this place or the former; and presently, before the eyes of all, the chest moves up against the stream of the river exceeding fast, so that men riding at full speed on horseback cannot outrun it.' Nicolas of Poggibonsi (1346–1350) wrote that John's head, with the stone on which the beheading took place, were taken to Alexandria and that he (Nicolas) reported seeing it there at the Church of St John; this was repeated by Frescobaldi in 1384.

There are quite a few sources that indicate that a head of John the Baptist eventually ended up in Constantinople (modern Istanbul) in Turkey. There are various accounts as to how it got there. According to Sozomen, the head was first taken from Jerusalem to Cilicia and only from there to Constantinople [note 10.37]. Theodoric (AD 1169–1172), however, has a different story: 'his [John's] head, however, was first carried to Alexandria, and was translated thence to an island called Rhodes, and was thereafter removed to Constantinople by the Emperor Theodosius' [note 10.38]. At the time of the sack of Constantinople in 1204, the French knight Robert of Clari describes having seen one head of John the Baptist in the Church of the Blessed Virgin of the Pharos before it was ransacked [note 10.39].

Another head was believed to have been housed in the Church of St John of Studius and it too was lost when the church was pillaged in 1204. This church is one of Istanbul's oldest – built before AD 463 by the Roman patrician Studius (consul during the reign of Emperor Marcian, AD 450–457). It became part of a monastery under the rule of Abbot Theodore in the late eighth century, but very little has survived except for some external walls. The destruction of the church appears to have been done in recent centuries, because Richard Pococke in his book on his travels (published in 1745) visited it and said that it was 'the finest mosque next after Saint Sophia'. It was to this church that the emperor of Byzantium was said to have come on the 29 August to mark the beheading of the precursor [note 10.40].

Even though it is now regarded as a questionable source (at least in

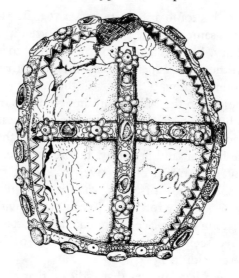

10.2

regard to the description of lands beyond the Holy Land), John Mandeville (*c.*1356) had the following garbled information about the head of John the Baptist: 'The head was enclosed in a wall at Sebastiyeh but the Emperor Theodosius had it taken out, and found it wrapped in a bloody cloth.' He goes on to say that half the head was transported to Constantinople and the other half was sent to the Church of St Silvester in Rome [note 10.41].

There is another fragment of the skull of John the Baptist which I have examined myself – bejewelled and encased in gold with Greek inscriptions – in the Treasury of the Topkapi Palace (*illustration 10.2*). Originally a Byzantine relic, it was presented by Mehmed II (1451–81) to Mara Despina, daughter of the Serbian king. Subsequently, it became the property of Cezayirli Hasan Paşa and after his death it was deposited in the Topkapi palace somewhere around 1790. The skull fragment was kept in a beautiful eight-sided crystal case, of a type dating to around the late sixteenth century.

A head of John is reported from Emesa (modern Homs) in Syria. The pilgrim Williband (AD 754), sailing from Cyprus, arrived on the coast of Lebanon and then made his way to Emesa which was conquered by the Muslims in 636: 'they walked to a city which is called Emesa, twelve miles distance. There is a large church, which St Helena built in honour of St John the Baptist, and his head, which is now in Syria, was there for a long time.' The implication from this passage is that by Williband's time the head of John the Baptist was no longer there; perhaps by the

308

eighth century it had been transferred to another location in Syria [note 10.42]. According to Jacobus de Voragine (*c.* 1230–1298) the head of John had been taken in the fifth century to Emessa by a local potter after having taken it from the monks who had dug it up in Jerusalem. There it was venerated outside the city in a cave by the potter and his successors. At a later date a monk, St Marcellus, who inhabited the cave discovered it as a result of a revelation. John came to him with two others and gave him the 'kiss of peace'. When Marcellus asked John where he had come from, John said: 'I have come from Sebaste!' Marcellus subsequently did some digging, found the head in an urn beneath the floor of the cave and then took it to Bishop Julian where it was finally displayed in the church within the city of Emessa. According to de Voragine, this same head was eventually transported first to Chalcedon (kept in the village of Cosilaos in Pantichium) and then on to Constantinople where it was displayed in a church built by Theodosius.

Another head of John the Baptist was revered in Damascus. It was apparently shown in the fourth-century church of Theodosius, a building that was later destroyed at the time of the construction of the Umayyad Mosque that was built there in AD 708 [note 10.43]. But the head itself did survive (unless, of course, this was another one) and it is now kept in a shrine with a marble dome at the east end of a large prayer hall in the mosque. Nothing much is to be seen today and this is because the head is kept within a reliquary which in turn is hidden beneath a green cloth (with Arabic calligraphy on it) and this is protected by an iron and glass screen that fends off all the devout pilgrims who would like to touch the reliquary. A wonderful anecdote about the head of John the Baptist in Damascus used to be told by Peter Dorrell, a British archaeologist and photographer who used to travel up and down the Near East and even worked with Kathleen Kenyon on her excavations at Jericho in the 1950s. The story went that a friend of his, while visiting the Great Umayyad Mosque in Damascus, struck up a conversation with the elderly Muslim guardian who had the job of looking after the small shrine of the Head of John the Baptist. Finding him to be a friendly and mild-mannered man, Peter's friend said to him, 'You do know that there are at least two other places which claim to have the head of John the Baptist?' to which the custodian coolly replied, 'Ah yes, but *ours* is the head of John the Baptist *as a young man.*'

One head of John the Baptist and a separate jawbone are reported as coming from the amazing Mount Athos which is located in the

Macedonia region in Greece, and is the abode of some 30,000 monks belonging to the Orthodox Russian, Balkan and Byzantine churches. There are twenty monasteries at Mount Athos and most of them possess Byzantine treasures of one sort or another, including numerous reliquaries containing the bones of saints and also box-like crosses holding fragments of the 'Holy Cross'. Indeed, there are so many relics there of the 'Holy Cross' scattered throughout the monasteries of Mount Athos that, if they could somehow all be combined together, I think there would be sufficient wood for at least two crosses if not more. A large chunk of wood said to be that of the 'Holy Cross' – apparently the largest fragment in the world – is located in the Monastery of Xeropotamou [note 10.44]. The jawbone was seen by one traveller in the Monastery of Stavronikita.

In the Monastery of Dionysiou, perched precariously on a cliff edge (seemingly about to topple down into the sea) on the south-western end of the peninsula, founded in the fourteenth century, the relic head of John the Baptist was seen there between 1755 and 1759 by Timothy Gabashvili: 'and we venerated the altar and the fearsome head of John the Baptist. It was most to be revered and had been lavishly adorned by some ancient kings. In the midst of his forehead there was a jacinth as big as a dove's egg, and also some great rubies and pearls.' The same head was also described by Curzon who visited Mount Athos in 1833: 'I was taken, as a pilgrim, to the church, and we stood in the middle of the floor . . . whilst the monks brought out an old-fashioned low wooden table, upon which they placed the relics of the saints which they presumed we had come to adore . . . Then there was an invaluable shrine for the head of St John the Baptist, whose bones and another of his heads are in the cathedral at Genoa. St John Lateran also boasts a head of St John, but that may have belonged to St John the Evangelist.' Curzon does not seem to have been particularly interested in the head, but he did go into raptures about the reliquary box itself:

This shrine was the gift of Neagulus, Waywode or Hospodar of Wallachia: it is about two feet long and two feet high, and is in the shape of a Byzantine church; the material is silver-gilt, but the admirable and singular style of the workmanship gives it a value far surpassing its intrinsic worth. The roof is covered with five domes of gold; on each side it has sixteen recesses, in which are portraits of the saints in *niello*, and at each end there are eight others. All the windows are enriched in open-work tracery, of a strange sort of Gothic pattern, unlike anything in Europe. It is altogether a wonderful and precious monument of ancient art, the production of an almost unknown country, rich, quaint, and original in its design and execution, and is indeed one of the most curious objects on Mount Athos . . . [note 10.45].

There are a few relic cranium fragments, teeth and jawbones to be found at various locations in Italy. A relic-tooth of John the Baptist, for example, is located in the Museo Serpero in the Duomo in the town centre of Monza, a satellite town of Milan in northern Italy. According to de Voragine, a church dedicated to John the Baptist was built in the fourth century at Monza, perhaps to house this or other relics. During a visit to Florence, I had a look at a number of relics of John the Baptist that were once exhibited in the Baptistry of San Giovanni, next to the Duomo, but which are now kept in glass cabinets in the adjacent Museo dell' Opera del Duomo. I looked at four relics while I was there, including a jaw-bone fragment (with one preserved tooth) in a hexagonal sided container and stand, of gilded silver and copper, that was made in 1564 by Pietro Cerluzi (or Cambiuzi as it was recently suggested). Surmounting the stand is a small cast statuette of John the Baptist shown holding a staff in one arm. The relic was given to the Baptistery in 1394 by a Venetian noblewoman named Nicoletta Grioni, and placed within a relic box in 1397 or 1398 by Matteo di Lorenzo. It was heavily damaged in the floods of 1557 together with other objects located in the area of the main altar of the Baptistery. In 1564 the Grand Duke Cosimo I commissioned the goldsmith Pietro Cerluzi to make the present reliquary [note 10.46].

Some medieval sources suggest that two of the heads of John the Baptist eventually ended up in France. An anonymous source dating from the twelfth century indicates that while the body of John the Baptist had been desecrated at the time of Julian the Apostate (363), this was 'save the head, which had before this been translated to Alexandria, whence it was afterwards translated to Poitou in France . . .' [note 10.47]. Another source, Fettellus (1130), wrote that 'His [John's] head had long before been taken to Alexandria by Marcellus, a priest; it was afterwards carried to Aquitaine, along with the Three Innocents, by Felicius [or Felix], a monk, in the reign of Pipin [i.e. Pippin I who reigned as King of Aquitaine from 797–838]. He was then returning from the slaughter of the Vandals, and twenty of his soldiers who had fallen in the war were restored to life by the merits of the blessed John' [note 10.48]. This head of John the Baptist is the same as the one that was mentioned by Ademar of Chabannes as having been 'discovered' in 1016 by monks in the Monastery of St Jean d'Angély in a village on the border of the regions of Poitou and northern Aquitaine. It was originally contained within a stone reliquary in the shape of a pyramid, but the duke of Aquitaine, William V, had the head transferred to a silver vessel on which was written: 'Here lies the head of the herald of the Lord.' Later, the head was returned to the original stone reliquary and the head was suspended on silver chains. The Monastery of St Jean d'Angély was eventually destroyed in the 1560s by the Calvinists and one has to assume that at that time the head was finally lost [note 10.49]. Another head of John the Baptist – or at least parts of his skull – was deposited in 1170 in a newly built church at Nemours, well-known for its twelfth- to seventeenth-century château, located some fifteen kilometres to the south of Fontainebleau. This relic had been entrusted to the church of Nemours by King Louis VII of France after having received it as a gift from Bishop Randulph of Sebaste, and it must have come from the cache of relics of 1145. Another head said to have been brought back from Constantinople following the sack of that city was deposited in 1206 in the Cathedral of Amiens, north of Paris.

I enjoyed having a hot bath and drinking apple tea in Istanbul. The hot bath entailed my being pummelled and manhandled in an ancient bath-house (the *hammam*): the body is first slowly tenderised in a hot steam-room and then it is flayed rapidly with bags filled with flakes of soap. The masseur's fingers dug into my flesh relentlessly, leaving weals and red puffy patches. Buckets of water were subsequently chucked all over my body. The *hammam* is an impressive building: streaked marble on the floors and walls, a roof built of brick, and a fountain in the octagonal central room. I could close my eyes and imagine myself in a Roman bath-house two thousand years ago. I opened my eyes; the man was gesturing towards the door. Clearly I had overstayed my welcome. Outside, I met up with my companion, Anna de Vincenz, who had been to the female part of the bath-house, and then together we set off to a nearby tea house where a handsome student of engineering smiled at me and did his best to chat me up.

I had never been to the Topkapi Palace in Istanbul before and so was naturally curious to see as much of it as I could. However, I did have a strong desire to lay my eyes first on the relic arm of John the Baptist, said to be housed somewhere in the palace. Eventually, I tracked it down to one of the chambers of the Inner Treasury building (the fourth room)

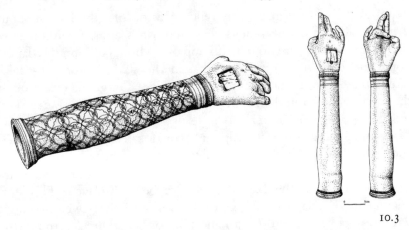

10.3

where it was shown with other relics in a sunken display cabinet, barely visible in the subdued lighting [note 10.50] (*illustration 10.3*). The right arm (hand and occipital bone) was entirely encased in gold, even the fingers of the hand (with the thumb touching the tip of the third ring-finger in the 'Greek' form of benediction), and it was highly decorated in parts. To make sure that the observer should know that there was indeed a human arm beneath all that gold, a little window with hinges had been cut in the area of the golden hand clearly showing the bones beneath. There were Greek letters on the areas of the wrist and hand but I could not make out the inscription clearly. The guard scowled as I approached the cabinet as best as I could, steaming up the glass with my breath in the process.

This relic was well-travelled. It would appear that the golden arm was first a relic of Eastern Christians. It seems unlikely, however, that this was the same relic hand/arm encased in gold seen at Sebaste (the burial place of John the Baptist) by John Phocas in 1185, since he says that it was the *left* not the right arm that was preserved there. It was subsequently venerated in the Church of St John of Pera in Constantinople (Istanbul). Eventually it fell into Ottoman hands at the time of the conquest (1453). In 1484 it was sent as a gift by the ruler Bayezid II (1481–1512) to the Knights of Rhodes, probably to curry favour. The person who received it was the grandmaster of the Hospital in Rhodes, Pierre d'Aubusson. It was subsequently discovered in Lefkoşe Castle in Cyprus and returned home to Istanbul in 1585. I now turned my attention to the relic skull of John the Baptist located in the same glass cabinet, but not before managing to upset a tourist with pouting lips who clearly was of the opinion (and she was right of course) that I had been monopolising this particular cabinet of relics for too long.

Just as there are a great many relic-heads of John the Baptist about, there are also numerous relics fingers and hands/arms. Interestingly, as far as I know, there are no relic rib, hip or leg bones of John the Baptist. Some medieval traditions relate that in the sixth century St Thecla returned to Europe bearing a prize: 'The blessed virgin Thecla brought the forefinger [of John] with her into the Alps and there it is kept with the greatest in the church of St Jean de Maurienne' [note 10.51]. Maurienne is a region of the Alps in Savoy, located between Chambéry and the Italian border, and the small town has a cathedral dating back to the twelfth to fifteenth centuries; possibly this was the church where the forefinger of John the Baptist had once been displayed. This story relating to Thecla was also given by various other twelfth-century writers, notably Fettellus (1130) and John of Würzburg (c.1160–1165). Fettulus mistakenly called Thecla 'Tygris' and indicates that the finger was the one 'with which he [John] pointed out Jesus coming to his baptism' [note 10.52].

There can be no doubt that from the twelfth century an arm was venerated at the Tomb of John the Baptist at Sebaste, or exhibited in the chapel immediately above it (see the previous chapter). According to Theodoric (1169–1172): 'a piece of his *arm* is preserved there, and is held most sacred' (italics: S.G.) [note 10.53]. John Phocas (1185) says that: 'above this [the tomb], in the church, the *left hand of the Forerunner* is displayed in a gold vessel, and this itself is completely encased in gold' (italics: S.G.) [note 10.54]. It would appear that at some point following the capture of Sebaste by the Muslims in 1187, the arm of John the Baptist was transferred elsewhere. Nicolas of Poggibonsi (1346–1350) in his brief history of the relics of John at Sebaste says that the 'left hand' was originally shown there but was eventually taken to a Greek monastery (Qasr el-Yehud) in the lower Jordan Valley, all except for a finger that was kept in the collection of King Hugh IV of Cyprus. However, contrary to Nicolas of Poggibonsi, it seems unlikely that the two relic left hands/arms of John at Sebaste and Qasr el-Yehud were the same because the former was encased in gold and the latter in silver.

The earliest known pilgrim to describe in detail (and to touch) the relic hand and arm of John at Qasr el-Yehud was James of Verona (1335). 'It is', he says, 'in a wooden box of modest value, but the hand and arm are covered in silver, except for the fingers and hand, which can be touched by all, and there are still finger-nails and flesh on the bones.' Ludolph Von Sudheim (or Suchem) (1336–41) confirms that the Greek monks of Qasr el-Yehud possessed a relic 'arm' of John the

Baptist [note 10.55]. An anonymous English pilgrim from around the same time (1344–1345) adds that it was indeed the left hand and that it was contained 'in a little chest, wrapped up in a covering of byssus'. An excellent description of the relic was provided by Nicolas of Poggibonsi (1346–1350): 'And the Greek monks who live in the said monastery [of Qasr el-Yehud] show at the gate a box of cypress, in which they display the hand of St John the Baptist; and the hand is withered, with the fist open.' In 1384 we have various accounts of the relic by Italian pilgrims, one describing a hand with a missing thumb and the other a silver hand-reliquary containing only one finger. Later, Nicolas de Martoni (1395) speaks of the relic left hand as well.

Additional relic hands/arms/fingers of John the Baptist are known from numerous locations in different Mediterranean and European countries. Caesar of Heisterbach (*c.* 1180–1250) refers to an arm of John the Baptist 'covered in skin and flesh' that was brought to Gröningen in Germany and subsequently it was encased in 'a receptacle in the form of an arm, of silver and gilt, adorned with precious stones'. Preserved in the parish church of the town of St Jean-du-Doigt ('St John of the Finger') in Finestère, the westernmost region of Brittany in France, is a small silver coffer in which is preserved one of the index fingerbones of John the Baptist. It is claimed that the finger was miraculously transported from Lô during the Hundred Years War in the mid-fifteenth century. In Greece at Mount Athos, in the Monastery of Dionysiou, there is a golden hand-shaped reliquary (said to have been crafted in 1810), bejewelled with precious stones and pearls, covering the supposed right arm of John the Baptist and the monks commemorate it on the 7 January, i.e. according to them on the day after the Baptism of Jesus. The thumb of John the Baptist was kept in the Monastery of Aiamon on the Island of Chios and it was seen there between 1755 and 1759 by Timothy Gabashvili [note 10.56].

I myself was able to examine in Florence three fingers of John which are displayed within highly decorated reliquaries in the Museo dell' Opera del Duomo [note 10.57] (*plate 16a*). The first is that of an index finger and it is said to be the most important of the saint's relics in Florence, but I am sceptical whether it really is a human finger – to me it looks more like a modelled piece of grey clay with the fingernail delineated (*plate 16b*). The relic is kept in a reliquary stand made of cast silver and semi-precious stones; it was made in 1698 by an unknown Florentine artist. On top of the *aedicule* containing the relic is a small cast figure of a lamb (Agnus Dei) with the cross and flag. Originally belonging to Pope Urban V, who had been given it by the Patriarch of Constantinople in 1363, it was lost and then recovered in 1386. The relic was donated to the Florentine republic in the will of Baldassarre Cossa (Antipope John XXIII) who died in Florence in 1419 and was buried in the Baptistery. Giovanni del Chiaro commissioned the original reliquary but it got damaged in the flood of 1557 and the present reliquary was made in 1698 (according to the inscription on the base of the reliquary) and was paid for by the local nobleman Francesco Maria Sergrifi.

The second Florentine relic is also that of a fingerbone, with stamped sealing wax on its side, and it is kept in a cast and polished reliquary stand made by an unidentified local artist. The reliquary has gilded silver and embossed decorations, and is surmounted by a small gilded figure of John the Baptist holding a staff (*plate 16d*). According to Bishop Antonino, the relic was brought to Florence from Constantinople in 1392 by Pepo di Arnoldo di Lapo Ruspi, who had bought it from a palace official (*domestikós*) of the Eastern emperor. The stand was made in the second half of the fifteenth century. The reliquary was refurbished in the eighteenth century. It was originally placed in the Baptistery.

The third Florentine relic came from the Duomo itself (as opposed to the others coming from the Baptistery) and it too is of a fingerbone. The reliquary is kept in a different glass cabinet from the other two, against a reddish carpet background. The *aedicule*-reliquary was made of silver, partly gilded, and with transparent enamel, by a Florentine artist (Matteo di Giovanni), and it dates from the first half of the fifteenth century. The relic was donated in 1391 by the Emperor of Byzantium to Giovanni Corsini during his travels in that part of the world. He later gave it to his brother, Pietro, the Cardinal of Florence, who, in turn, placed it in the safekeeping of the Chapel of San Lorenzo within the Corsini family chapel located in the Duomo. The reliquary was begun between 1416 to 1419, completed in 1426, and finally restored in 1707 by Bernardo Holzman.

Apart from relic-bones, there were also other relic materials associated with John the Baptist that circulated in the ancient world, namely his ashes, hair, bits of clothing and so forth. Naturally, there was always a constant supply of ashes of the saint and according to twelfth century sources his 'dust' was said to be present in his tomb at Sebaste [note 10.58]. The hair of John the Baptist was displayed in Constantinople in the eleventh century [note 10.59]. A relic of John's clothing was obtained from the abbot of the Monastery of St Catherine at Mount Sinai and is mentioned among other relics in a Letter of Authentification, written by Guy of Blond, a monk of Grandmont, between 1128 and 1152. This same Guy was also able to receive further relics of John the Baptist from various people in Nablus [note 10.60]. The Bishop of Sidon, Amalrich, is known to have supplied Godefroid de Huy with relics of John the Baptist in return for silver vessels.

Many of the smaller relics – especially the cranium fragments and fingerbones – probably originated in the Holy Land, and one of the major sources of these was the Sebaste workshop following the supposed miraculous 'discovery' there of relics of John the Baptist in 1145. Some bones eventually even reached as far as England – such as the relics that were kept from the mid-twelfth century in the Benedictine Abbey at Abingdon, Berkshire. In 1148 or 1153 a request was made to the Bishop Frederick of Acre that some of the recently discovered relics at Sebaste might be presented to the Canons of the Church of St John the Evangelist in Liège and to the abbey of Florennes. Bishop Rainer of Sebaste was persuaded to part with some of the relics and through an intermediary, an envoy by the name of Bovo, they were delivered to their destinations [note 10.61]. In 1169 Bishop Rainer and Prior Randulph were called upon to authenticate relics of the Baptist that were given to Maurice II of Craon. In 1170 (at the latest), the rebuilding of the Sebaste Cathedral was stopped owing to a lack of funds, and Randulph (now a bishop) sent further relics to the West so that the necessary funds could be obtained. It is amazing to think how so many people were hoodwinked into believing that the relics they were receiving were real, whereas they were actually being churned out by the crafty monks of Sebaste. Relics of John at (or from) Sebaste are frequently mentioned in the sources dating between 1160 and 1265. It seems highly likely that the bishops of Sebaste or their subordinates, who were regulating the production of the John the Baptist relics until 1187 (see the previous chapter), must have kept a detailed record of their relic forgeries and the names of all the recipients (individuals, churches and monasteries), otherwise confusion would have set in and the scam would quickly have come to light. Such records would probably have been kept within the bishop's house which was located either to the south or east of the main cathedral. I would love to excavate there and find out if any of these records have survived, or, better still, if one could uncover the actual workshop where the relics were manufactured . . .

The car climbed slowly up the winding road leading to the Golan Heights. It was very early in the morning and we were the only ones on the road. We were heading for the site of er-Ramthaniyyeh located not too far away from Katzrin, the central modern town of the Golan (ancient Gaulanitis), to conduct an archaeological survey. The basalt landscapes of the Golan are quite awe-inspiring and they are dotted with numerous well-preserved Roman and Byzantine villages. The fact that since 1967 the Golan Heights have been disputed territory between Syria and Israel has in some ways meant the preservation of the landscapes from modern development, though admittedly quite a lot of destruction has been caused to ancient sites and field systems within the closed military zones. During the 1980s four of the ancient villages were the focus of an in-depth research project led by French archaeologist Professor Claudine Dauphin, and assisted by myself [note 10.62]. The expedition worked on mapping the layout of each village, looking at its houses, public buildings, shrines, water sources and animal pens, as well as the surrounding landscapes with their fields and roads, cemeteries and stone quarries. The ancient houses were very well preserved, sometimes to the height of a second storey, with ceiling beams made not out of tree trunks but out of long slabs of basalt stone in corbelled fashion. It was not unusual to stumble across beautiful carvings, totally unknown Greek inscriptions, lintels with incised Christian crosses and Jewish candelabra, all just lying amid the ruined houses. The project was a very exciting one and we all felt like pioneering explorers. There were, of course, some dangers, with many wild animals lurking among the ruins, such as wild boar, dogs, foxes and hyenas. A swarm of hornets chased after one of our team members, attracted to his glossy black curly hair. The villages were also overrun with snakes and on one occasion a snake with a head the size of a cat popped out of a crack in a wall and gave me a fright. There were other dangers. One site we were working on was situated quite close to military minefields. The commander of the local Israeli army unit kindly provided us with a map showing the boundaries of their minefields. 'We are pretty sure where we have laid our mines,' said the army commander, 'but I am not sure where the Syrian ones are.' He smiled and added: 'If you find any of the Syrian ones, please let us know.'

The site of er-Ramthaniyyeh is located off the main road and a rutted track leads up to the village which was built on a volcanic plug. The area is used by the military as a firing zone and it is not accessible without permission. As a result, the ground surface of this ancient site, particularly in the fields round about, are littered not only with potsherds but also with half-exploded mortars, spent shells, trip-wires and other

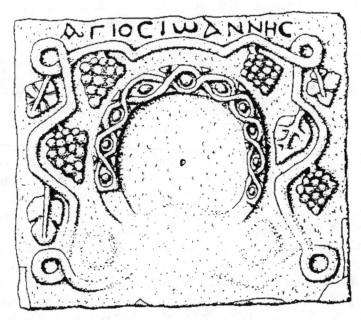

10.4

modern army paraphernalia. We had to be very careful how we walked around. On one occasion we had the shock of our lives when tanks began firing shells roughly in our direction, and so we ran to the car and made a hasty retreat. It transpired later that the Israeli archaeological officer for the region had 'forgotten' to inform the army authorities that we were entering the firing zone. At the top of the hill is a large ancient building that dominates the area; this was the building used in 1895 by the Jewish Bene-Yehuda colonists when they tried (unsuccessfully) to live as farmers at the site, with the support of the British philanthropist Laurence Oliphant. In the early Byzantine period, this building served as a large *martyrium* dedicated to John the Baptist, according to an inscription on a squared block that was found built into one of the arches at the site. The decipherment of this eleven-line inscription indicated that the church had been built or enlarged in AD 377 by a high-ranking military man by the name of Flavius Na'aman. Another carved stone also bore the name of Saint John above a vine trellis (*illustration 10.4*). A relic of John would appear to have been attached to the central surface of this stone, perhaps inserted within a metal cross reliquary, but it is now lost. This relic may very well have come from Sebaste some ten years or so after the desecration of John's tomb in 363. The church must have been an impressive building judging by the carvings and the size of the ruins; it was surrounded by various outbuildings, a chapel, caves, all of which were enclosed by a wall. At the foot of the hill, to the east, was a fairly large expanse of water; rough stones were set in the form of steps to facilitate a descent to the water, and its eastern wall was roughly apse-ended. Clearly the pool had been used by people who wished to bathe in the water for ritual purposes. In the fields around the pool, we came across areas used as tent encampments, processional routes, standing stones and outdoor prayer-niches.

The ancient name of the site is unknown but in the Byzantine period it appears to have been used as a major regional pilgrimage centre by the Bene Ghassan tribesmen, who gathered there to mark the calendar dates of the birth or death of John the Baptist. Having encamped in the areas allocated for that purpose round about the site, the Ghassanid worshippers would then have set off along the prescribed ceremonial routes, with prayers and invocations being made at various places on the way, next to specific markers, such as standing stones and makeshift altars. Having reached the large pool, the worshippers would have stripped and entered the waters to participate in collective baptism rites, similar to those that were undertaken in the Jordan River, and under the watchful eye of the local priest. From the pool, the worshippers would have climbed the hill to the large church at the top to participate in a ceremony there that might well have included the relic of John the Baptist as its focal point.

The princes of Bene Ghassan were the rulers of a satellite state of the Byzantine Empire, an area that extended from Syria and Damascus as far south as the Golan and Hauran and northern Transjordan. This buffer state served to protect the settled area of Byzantium to the west from the threat of the Lakhimids in the east, with whom they were in a perpetual state of warfare; many desert raids occurred and continual looting took place within each other's territories. The Ghassanids were pagan nomads and camel-breeders from southern Arabia – perhaps they were originally a clan of the tribe of Azd – who arrived in the Syrian Desert before the fifth century and were eventually converted to Christianity. Prior to becoming Christians they worshipped idols and spirits at sites of standing stones and sacred trees, springs and wells. In AD 529 Justinian recognised Harith ibn Jabala IV of the Bene Ghassan as a phylarch, with the rank of patrician. The Ghassanids possessed Christian Monophysite beliefs (i.e. they believed that Jesus only had one Divine nature, as opposed to the Nestorians who affirmed that the Divinity and Humanity of Christ were separate natures) and this was deemed heretical by the official orthodox church of the Byzantine Empire. Persecution subsequently ensued, with the condemnation of Monophysite beliefs at the Council of Chalcedon. In 581 the prince of the Bene Ghassan was even captured and taken to Constantinople to answer charges of heresy. As a result of this, the Christians of the Gaulanitis region and especially those located in the Hauran further to the east, remained in a situation of semi-rebellion. One may speculate that, because of their nomadic lifestyle, the Christian Bene Ghassan were particularly fascinated by John the Baptist, and this is the reason why more than one regional pilgrimage centre dedicated to this saint was established within their territory. Proof of this is provided by an inscription published back in 1865 by the explorer Ewing, which indicates that a memorial to the martyrdom of Saint John was also established in the Hauran by a 'head of a tribe' (of the Bene Ghassan) on the 22 March or 31 April in the year 568 [note 10.63].

It was inevitable that with the advent of Christianity in the fourth century the cult of John the Baptist would naturally spring up at locations in the Holy Land and subsequently in the countries around the

Mediterranean and throughout the Old World. John the Baptist was worshipped *through* Christianity as the Precursor and as the Baptiser of Jesus Christ, and numerous churches, chapels and holy places dedicated to him thus came into existence. In some places John was held in great reverence and regarded as the patron of entire Christian communities, in other places his relics were kept in prominent places within churches as articles of devotion and as a focus for prayer for the general worshippers and pilgrims. There are many churches named for John the Baptist in the Holy Land itself and the most important of these are undoubtedly those connected with his traditional birthplace (Ain Karim), baptism activities (Jordan River) and death (Sebaste). We have discussed these places in some detail in previous chapters [note 10.64]. However, there are also quite a few smaller and lesser-known churches and chapels in Palestine and beyond, and a number of these are only known to have been dedicated to John through the chance discovery of inscriptions [note 10.65].

Churches of St John from the Byzantine period are also known in Transjordan and Syria at the sites of Jerash, Madaba, Damascus and Bostra. The church of St John at Jerash is one of a group of three churches sharing a common atrium, all of which were completed between AD 529 and 533. The Church of John is actually the largest of the three. According to the excavator, Kraeling, the Church of St John the Baptist has a plan that could be regarded as 'a reduced edition of the cathedral at Bostra which was built some twenty years earlier, 512–513 AD.' The Greek inscription within a *tabula ansata* in the mosaic floor indicates that the founders (Bishop Paul and the donor Theodore) dedicated the church in AD 531 to John the 'forerunner' = Prodromus (Πρόδρομος) [note 10.66]. A church dedicated to the memory of the martyrdom of John the Baptist was also established at Madaba in the sixth century. At Damascus a church was built in honour of John the Baptist in the fifth century and it was referred to by Adomnan in 685 as a 'great church'; the building was later torn down and transformed into a mosque by Caliph Walid in 708 [note 10.67]. A church of St John, probably the Baptist rather than the Evangelist, is also mentioned in an inscription from a stone quarry near Qasr el-Hallabat, Bostra.

In the Crusader-period Kingdom of Jerusalem, quite a few churches dedicated to John the Baptist were built, at new locations or in places which originally had Byzantine churches, notably those at Acre, Mount Carmel, Haifa, Caesarea, Sebaste, Ain Karim, and at Qasr el-Yehud at the Jordan River. The impetus for the worship of John the Baptist and the construction of churches in his honour was provided with the establishing of the order of the Hospitallers which was recognised by the pope in 1113. An important church of St John existed at Acre and the upper walls of this church were still visible as late as the 1680s in an engraving made for Louis XIV of France. The crypt of the Crusader church continued to be used in the early twentieth century by local Christians celebrating the feast of St John [note 10.68]. A church of St John was also built at al-Tira on the south-west slope of Mount Carmel; the reason for the connection made between John the Baptist and Mount Carmel was because of the traditional association that Christians made linking the saint and Elijah who was thought to have spent some time on this mountain [note 10.69]. According to the available sources churches are known to have existed at Haifa and Caesarea but their remains have not yet been found [note 10.70]. Apart from the official churches there were apparently also a few hermitages in the Holy Land during the twelfth century, inhabited by Orthodox monks who adopted a way of life using John the Baptist as their model. One impressionable English pilgrim by the name of Godric visited Palestine and, upon returning to England, decided to seek out the wilderness there, eating grass and wild honey 'after the example of John the Baptist', living first in caves and then in the woods [note 10.71].

In the Christian calendar, John the Baptist is the only figure – together with Jesus and Mary – who had days set aside to commemorate both his birth and death [note 10.72]. In the West the traditional birthday of John is celebrated on 24 June and his death by beheading is marked on 29 August; both traditions may be traced back to the fifth century, to the time of Saint Augustine. In addition, the annunciation to Zacharias was celebrated in the West on 24 September (until 1472). John the Baptist is regarded as the Patron Saint of Turin, Genoa and Florence and 24 of June is St John's day, which is celebrated in these places today as a local holiday with fireworks. In Florence the celebrations take place at the Piazzale Michelangelo. First celebrated in 1084 in the open ground next to the Baptistery building, a few centuries later the feast became a significant event with a three-day holiday starting on 23 June, with processions and feasting [note 10.73]. Some of the relics of John the Baptist were then displayed to the festive crowds. On the following day gifts were received from representatives of the territories that were under Florentine rule. In the fifteenth century St John's day was marked by the lighting of bonfires, with the idea that fires represented a purifying force in much the same way as John used water. It is interesting to note that in France there was also a custom for making bonfires on St John's eve and Ernoul (1220) linked it to the remembrance of the burning of the bones of John at the time of the desecration of his tomb: '. . . and for this reason children still on St John's night might make a fire of bones, because his bones were burnt' [note 10.74]. The traditional Breton pilgrimage on 24 June at St Jean-du-Doigt ('St John of the Finger') in France includes a small boy dressed as John the Baptist and leading a lamb on a ribbon at the head of a procession from the church. Later there is a huge bonfire and the attending pilgrims subsequently dance and feast.

In the East a general festival day for John the Baptist was marked on 7 January, one day following Epiphany, and this tradition may be traced back to the fourth century. The annunciation to Zacharias was celebrated on 23 September. In Palestine in the 1860s, the following Latin prayer was made in churches to mark the holiday of John the Baptist: *Antra deserti teneris sub annis, civium turmas fugiens, petisti, ne levi posses maculare vitam crimine linguae* (roughly meaning: In the years of my childhood I looked to the caves of the desert, in addition to the face of the masses, so that I would not blemish my life in sin even a small one of the tongue) [note 10.75]. To mark the day of remembrance of the beheading of John, there was a custom in some parts of Greece to conduct a strict fast and then subsequently to avoid anything that resembled the blood of the saint's head, such as berries, black grapes and so forth. Walnuts were also avoided because the Greek word for walnut is the same as the English 'Adam's apple' in a man's throat. In Lemnos, there used to be a belief, rife amongst the peasantry, attributing all fevers and shaking fits suffered by people during the month of August to the memory of the beheading of John. A person coming down with this kind of ailment was obliged to go immediately to church and to bring St John some oil, incense or candles. There was a popular belief in Cyprus that at dawn on 29 August one could make out the outline of the severed head of John on the disk of the sun [note 10.76].

John the Baptist was regarded as an important prophet in Islam. His tomb was venerated at Sebaste and his relic-head was kept in the Great Mosque in Damascus. He was known in Arabic as Nebi Yahya which is a derivation from Yohannah (John) [note 10.77]. In 1384 the pilgrim Frescobaldi wrote: 'And know you that the Saracens [Arabs] pay reverence to the Virgin Mary, and to St John the Baptist and to St Catherine and to all the patriarchs of the Old Testament; and they hold Christ to be, after Mohammed, the greatest prophet.' John the Baptist (as the prophet Yahya) was briefly referred to on a number of occasions in the Quran, in the petition to God made by his father Zacharias (Zakariyya) who wishes a child in his old age (21:89; cf. 6:85). The following excerpt is from 19:14–15: ' "O John, take the Book forcefully", and We gave him judgement, yet a little child, and a tenderness from Us, and purity; and he was god-fearing, and cherishing his parents, not arrogant, rebellious. "Peace be upon him, the day he was born, and the day he dies, and the day he is raised up alive!" ' [note 10.78]. John also appeared in local Palestinian folklore, in a short passage translated from the Arabic by Canaan as follows: 'We journeyed and went down to the tomb of Christ, [where] we found St John sitting down to rest. He spread for us his carpet [his cloak], and said, "Sit down!" He opened for us his gospel and said, "Listen!" We heard reading, we heard voices, we heard reading which revives the spirit. We ascended the mountain, and found three doves, one prays, one fasts and one waves the censer to and fro.' Canaan suggested that the three doves symbolised Peter, Paul and John [note 10.79].

In the southern marshlands of Iraq is a small religious sect known as the Mandaeans and scholars have shown a particular interest in them because the central figure of their beliefs was John the Baptist (named Yohannah) and an important feature of their rituals included repeated washings in the running water of a symbolic Jordan. Could these Mandaeans be the descendants of the original followers of John the Baptist? And would it be possible to reconstruct the writings of the first followers of John based on an analysis of Mandaean literature?

Unfortunately, the answer is a negative one: they are definitely not the descendants of the original baptists. The name of the sect is derived from the Aramaic *Manda d'Haiye*, which means 'the knowledge of life'. In the 1980s it was estimated that there were still some 15,000 living in southern Iraq, with a few living in neighbouring Iran; a number of Mandaeans were even working as silversmiths in Baghdad. Although it was once thought that the Mandaeans were a heretical sect of Judaism, their beliefs are actually a mixture derived from many different Semitic sources. They are sometimes linked with the Sabians (the 'Sabi'ah') mentioned in the Quran, as well as with the 'Mughtasilah' (the 'washing sect') mentioned by Ibn an-Nadim (d.385 AH/995 AD). Incidentally, an-Nadim may also have referred to them as the 'Sabat al-Batha'ih' (the 'Sabians of the Lowlands') in a text from AD 988. They are also sometimes linked with the Elchasaites, a baptising sect, but this is disputed by scholars [note 10.80].

The excitement of early researchers suggesting possible links between disciples of John, who had in some fashion preserved his heritage, and Mandaean religious writings was quickly dashed by the scholar F. C. Burkitt who was able to show that there is nothing in the Mandaean literature that could actually predate the fifth to seventh centuries AD. Moreover, those Mandaean writings pertaining specifically to John the Baptist must reflect adaptations from the Gospels and are not alternative writings on John. The Mandaean writings may be divided into three main sources: the Great Book (the *Ginza*, i.e. 'the treasure'); the Book of John; and the book of One Thousand and Twelve Questions. Some of the Mandaean writings are notably hostile towards Christianity and Jesus, who is described as the 'prophet of lies', as well as towards Judaism [note 10.81].

Although I have tried to be as thorough as possible while researching the fascinating story of the relic heads and bones of John the Baptist, I have to say that never ever did I entertain the thought of tabulating comprehensively every known relic of John the Baptist in existence – happily I leave that most difficult of tasks to someone else. However, I can report that during my most recent count of relic bits and pieces of John, I did come up with the figure of some nineteen heads (or parts of heads, notably cranium fragments, jawbones and teeth) and something in the order of fifteen hands or arms (including fingers). Of course, one must also not forget the scores of bones of John existing as well. Someone somewhere is having a good chuckle . . .

Appendix:
The Description of John the Baptist in Josephus

Since most people have copies of the New Testament and can easily look up the relevant passages about John the Baptist, they may find it difficult to obtain access to a proper translation of Josephus' *Jewish Antiquities*.* Hence, I have quoted here the whole passage about John the Baptist from the two translations from Greek by Thackeray and Feldman:

(a) Thackeray's translation:

> . . . but some of the Jews believed that Herod's army was destroyed by God, God punishing him very justly for John called the Baptist, whom Herod had put to death. For John was a pious man, and he was bidding the Jews who practiced virtue and exercised righteousness towards each other and piety towards God, to come together for baptism. For thus, it seemed to him, would baptismal ablution be acceptable, if it were used not to beg off from sins committed, but for the purification of the body when the soul had previously been cleansed by righteous conduct. And when everybody turned to John – for they were profoundly stirred by what he said – Herod feared that John's so extensive influence over the people might lead to an uprising (for the people seemed likely to do everything he might

*The Jewish historian Josephus Flavius wrote a number of works of which the most important are *Jewish War* (*Bellum Judaicum*) and *Antiquities* (*Antiquitates Judaicae*). For more information on Josephus see: Tessa Rajak, 1983. *Josephus: The Historian and his Society*. Duckworth: London; Uriel Rappaport (ed.). *Josephus Flavius: Historian of Eretz-Israel in the Hellenistic–Roman Period*. Yad Ben Zvi: Jerusalem (Hebrew with English summaries).

counsel). He thought it much better, under the circumstances, to get John out of the way in advance, before any insurrection might develop, than for himself to get into trouble and be sorry not to have acted, once an insurrection had begun. So because of Herod's suspicion, John was sent as a prisoner to Machaerus, the fortress already mentioned, and there put to death. But the Jews believed that the destruction which overtook the army came as a punishment for Herod, God wishing to do him harm. [Josephus, *The Antiquities of the Jews*, XVIII, 5, 2 = 116–19; translation by H. St John Thackeray, Loeb Classical Library edition.]

(b) Feldman's translation:

But to some of the Jews the destruction of Herod's army [by the Nabataean ruler Aretas] seemed to be divine vengeance, and certainly a just vengeance, for his treatment of John, surnamed the Baptist (βαπτιστοῦ). For Herod had put him to death, though he was a good man and had exhorted the Jews to lead righteous lives, to practice justice towards their fellows and piety towards God, and so doing to join in baptism (βάπτισμα). In his view this was a necessary preliminary if baptism was to be acceptable to God. They must not employ it to gain pardon for whatever sins they committed, but as a consecration of the body implying that the soul was already thoroughly cleansed by right behaviour. When others too joined the crowds about him, because they were aroused to the highest degree by his sermons, Herod became alarmed. Eloquence that had so great an effect on mankind might lead to some form of sedition [or revolt]. For it looked as if they would be guided by John in everything that they did. Herod decided therefore that it would be much better to strike first and be rid of him before his work led to an uprising, than to wait for an upheaval, get involved in a difficult situation and see his mistake. Though John, because of Herod's suspicions, was brought in chains to Machaerus, the stronghold that we have previously mentioned, and there put to death, yet the verdict of the Jews was that the destruction visited upon Herod's army was a vindication of John, since God saw fit to inflict such a blow on Herod. [Josephus, *Jewish Antiquities* XVIII, 116–19; translation by Louis H. Feldman, Loeb Classical Library edition.]

Select Bibliography and Notes

INTRODUCTION AND CHAPTER ONE

The following is a select bibliography of essential books and articles on the subject of John the Baptist, arranged alphabetically: Baldi, D., 1982. *Enchiridion Locorum Sanctorum: Documenta S. Evangelii Loca Respicientia.* Jerusalem; Baldi, D., and Bagatti, B., 1980. *Saint Jean-Baptiste: dans les souvenirs de sa Patrie.* Studium Biblicum Franciscanum. Collectio Minor No. 27. Franciscan Printing Press. Jerusalem; Cullman, O., 1950. *Baptism in the New Testament.* Studies in Biblical Theology. London; Farmer, W. R., 1962. 'John the Baptist'. Pp. 955–62 in Buttrick, G. A., *The Interpreter's Dictionary of the Bible.* Nashville and New York; Hollenbach, P. W., 1992. 'John the Baptist'. Pp. 887–99 in Freedman, D. N., *Anchor Bible Dictionary.* Vol. 3. New York and London; Kraeling, C. H., 1951. *John the Baptist.* New York and London; Leclercq, H., 1927. 'Jean-Baptiste (Saint)'. Pp. 2167–84 in Cabrol, F., and Leclercq, H., *Dictionnaire d'archéologie Chrétienne et de liturgie.* Vol. 7. Paris; Murphy-O'Connor, J., 1990. 'John the Baptist and Jesus: History and Hypotheses'. *New Testament Studies* 36: 359–74; Scobie, C. H., 1964. *John the Baptist.* London; Tatum, W. B., 1994. *John the Baptist and Jesus: A Report of the Jesus Seminar.* Sonoma; Taylor, J. E., 1997. *John the Baptist Within Second Temple Judaism.* London; Webb, R. L., 1991. *John the Baptiser and Prophet: A Socio-Historical Study.* Sheffield; Wink, W., 1968 (reprinted in 2000). *John the Baptist in the Gospel Tradition.* Cambridge.

CHAPTER TWO

2.1: Suba was also mentioned by the writer Yāqūt as a village in the Jerusalem district in the thirteenth century: ed. Wüstenfeld, iii, p. 431.

2.2: Harper, R. P., and Pringle, R. D., 2000. *Belmont Castle: The Excavation of a Crusader Stronghold in the Kingdom of Jerusalem*. CBRL: Oxford.

2.3: Guérin, V., 1868. *Description géographique, historique et archéologique de la Palestine*. Judée. Vol. I. Paris; Gibson, S., Dar, S., and Clarke, J., The Archaeological Setting and the Surrounding Landscape' in Harper, R. P., and Pringle, R.D. (see note 2.2).

2.4: Robinson, E., 1860, *Biblical Researches in Palestine*. Vol.I, pp. 215, 333, Vol.II, pp. 10, 11; pp. 234–235 in Ritter, C. *The Comparative Geography of Palestine and the Sinaitic Peninsula*. Vol. IV, translated by W.L. Gage. Edinburgh: Clark; Guérin, V., 1868. *Description géographique, historique et archéologique de la Palestine*. Judée. Vol. I. Paris.

2.5: Tosefta, *yebamoth* 1:10–241, 25. P. 54 in Dalman, G., 1935. *Sacred Sites and Ways: Studies in the Topography of the Gospels*. New York. The identification of Sobah with Seboim was made on p. 149 by Avi-Yonah, M., 1936. Map of Roman Palestine, Quarterly of the Department of Antiquities of Palestine V: 139–93; idem 1976. *Gazetteer of Roman Palestine* (Qedem 5), IES: Jerusalem, p. 94; see also Abel, F.-M., *Géographie de la Palestine*. Vol. II, p. 452, Paris; pp. 114–15 in Press, Y., 1961. *mehkarim beyediat haaretz vetopographia miqra'it*. (*Studies in the Knowledge of the Land and Biblical Topography*). Jerusalem (Hebrew).

2.6: Papyrus No. 18, (see *illustration* 2.1 in this book), pp. 84–89 and note 3 on p. 84 in Naveh, 1992. *On Sherd and Papyrus: Aramaic and Hebrew Inscriptions from the Second Temple, Mishnaic and Talmudic Periods*. Pp. 84–89 and note 3 on p. 84. Magness Press: Jerusalem (Hebrew).

2.7: Kesalon (Chasalon; Χασαλών) was mentioned by Eusebius, *Onomasticon*, 172:16, in the territory of Aelia (i.e. Jerusalem): Avi-Yonah, M., 1976. *Gazetteer of Roman Palestine* (Qedem 5). P. 49; IES: Jerusalem. Tsafrir, Y., Di Segni, L. and Green, J., 1994. *Tabula Imperii Romani Iudea, Palestina. Eretz Israel in the Hellenistic, Roman and Byzantine Periods. Maps and Gazetteer*. p. 103. Jerusalem: Israel Academy of Sciences and Humanities.

2.8: P. 61 in Flusser, D., 1963. *The Beginnings of Christianity*. Written down and edited by Ziona and Israel Katz. Hebrew University: Jerusalem (Hebrew).

2.9: Pp. 52–3 in Dalman, G., 1935. *Sacred Sites and Ways: Studies in the Topography of the Gospels*. New York.

2.10: Schneemelcher, W. (ed.), 1991. *New Testament Apocrypha. Volume I: Gospels and Related Writings*. P.421–39. Revised Edition. Translation by R. McL. Wilson. Cambridge and Westminster.

2.11: p. 95 in Avi-Yonah, M., 1966. *The Holy Land From the Persian to the Arab Conquests (536 BC to AD 640): A Historical Geography*. Grand Rapids; p. 191 in Schürer, E., 1979. *The History of the Jewish People in the Age of Jesus Christ (175 BC – AD 135)*. Revised and edited by G. Vermes, F. Millar and M. Black. Vol. II. Edinburgh.

2.12: Horowitz, Israel S., 1923. *Palestine and the Adjacent Countries*. pp. 240–41. Vol. I. Vienna (Hebrew).

2.13: P. 215 in Ritter, C., 1866. *The Comparative Geography of Palestine and the Sinaitic Peninsula*. Vol. IV. Translated by W.L. Gage. Edinburgh: Clark.

2.14: P. 28 in Petrozzi, M. T., 1971. *Ain Karim*. Jerusalem.

2.15: Guérin, V., 1868. *Description géographique, historique et archéologique de la Palestine*. Judée. Vol. I. Paris; pp. 121–2 in Gibson, S., 2003. *Jerusalem in Original Photographs, 1850–1920*. London.

2.16: P. 81 in Press, I., 1951. *A Topographical-Historical Encyclopedia of Palestine*. Mass: Jerusalem (Hebrew). For an early twentieth-century photograph showing an inhabitant of Ain Karim filling her jars at the spring: plate opposite p. 64 in Finley, J., 1927. *A Pilgrim in Palestine. Being an Account of Journeys on Foot by the First American Pilgrim After General Allenby's Recovery of the Holy Land*. Scribner: New York.

2.17: Pp. 392–3 in Kallai, Z., 1986. *Historical Geography of the Bible: The Tribal Territories of Israel*. Jerusalem, Leiden.

2.18: Schick, *Zeitschrift des Deutschen Palästina-Vereins* 13, 1890. P. 92. See also Dalman, *ZDPV* 37, 1914, p. 351 who locates it at the village Beth Ta'amir north of Herodium. Alt thought it at el-Hatchar near Bir Ayyub, *PJB* 24, 1928, P. 19 ff.; *PJB* 26, 1930, p. 26.

2.19: Aharoni, Y., 1967. 'Beth-Haccherem', Pp. 171–184 in: Winton Thomas, D. (ed.). *Archaeology and Old Testament Study. Jubilee Volume of the Society for Old Testament Study 1917–1967*. Clarendon Press: Oxford.

2.20: P. 38 in Avi Yonah, M. 1976. *Gazetteer of Roman Palestine* (Qedem 5), IES: Jerusalem; p. 82 in Tsafrir, Y., Di Segni, L., and Green, J., 1994. *Tabula Imperii Romani Iudea, Palaestina. Eretz Israel in the Hellenistic, Roman and Byzantine Periods. Maps and Gazetteer*. Jerusalem: Israel Academy of Sciences and Humanities. See also pp. 295–6 in Abel, F.-M. *Géographie de la Palestine*. Vol. II, Paris, 1938.

2.21: Some scholars have suggested that the *middoth* and *niddah* in the Mischna passages refer to two different Beth Haccerem valleys, the one at Ain Karim near Jerusalem and the other in the Lower Galilee (in the area of Majd el-Krum): p. 38 in Avi-Yonah, M., 1976. *Gazetteer of Roman Palestine* (Qedem 5), IES: Jerusalem; p. 82 in Tsafrir, Y., Di

Segni, L., and Green, J., 1994. *Tabula Imperii Romani Iudea, Palaestina. Eretz Israel in the Hellenistic, Roman and Byzantine Periods. Maps and Gazetteer.* Jerusalem: Israel Academy of Sciences and Humanities. Avi-Yonah (and Tsafrir et al.) follow Klein's view from 1939 when he pointed out that some later rabbinic sources do refer to a valley by this name in the Galilee.

2.22: Allegro, J.M., 1960. *The Treasure of the Copper Scroll.* Routledge and Kegan Paul: London. See recently: Goranson, S., 1992. 'Sectarianism, Geography, and the Copper Scroll'. *Journal of Jewish Studies* XLIII (2): 282–7; Lefkovits, J. K., 1993. *The Copper Scroll 3Q15: A Reevaluation. A New Reading, Translation and Commentary.* Leiden; Wolters, A., 1996. *The Copper Scroll: Overview, Text and Translation.* Sheffield.

2.23: Allegro, J. M., 1960. *The Treasure of the Copper Scroll.* Routledge and Kegan Paul: London, drawing on p. 50 with transcription on p. 51: Column X, Lines 5–7, Item 48. Allegro's attempt (pp. 101–2, 161, note 235) to place Beth Haccerem at Bethphage, on the western slope of the Mount of Olives, seems highly unlikely. Lefkovitz, J. K. 1993. *The Copper Scroll 315: A Reevaluation. A New Reading, Translation and Commentary.* Leiden, pp. 331–4, Item 46, Lines 10.5–10.7. Lefkovitz similarly discusses (p.333 and note 11) the suggestion to identify Beth Haccerem in the Kidron Valley east of Jerusalem and rightly points out the weaknesses of Aharoni's argument. Wolters, A., 1996. *The Copper Scroll: Overview, Text and Translation.* Sheffield, pp. 50–1, Column Ten, Lines 5–6.

2.24: Mignana, A., 1927. *Woodbrooke Studies. Edition and translation of Christian Documents in Syriac and Garshuni.* With Introduction by R. Harris. *BJRL* 11, Manchester. 329 ff, passage on pp. 446–9.

2.25: P. 459 and passage quoted between pp. 467–8 in Schneemelcher, W. (ed.), 1991. *New Testament Apocrypha. Volume I: Gospels and Related Writings.* Revised Edition. Translation by R. McL. Wilson. Cambridge and Westminster. Serapion's work was also the source for the later writings of Isho'dad of Merv and Cedrenus: see p. 21 in Schonfield, H. J., 1929. *The Lost Book of the Nativity of John.* Edinburgh.

2.26: Pp. 65, 77, 119, 137 and 156 in Wilkinson, J., 1977. *Jerusalem Pilgrims Before the Crusades.* Jerusalem.

2.27: Avi-Yonah, M., 1964. *The Madaba Mosaic Map. With Introduction and Commentary.* Jerusalem; Donner, H., 1992. *The Mosaic Map of Madaba: An Introductory Guide.* Kampen.

2.28: Guérin, V., 1868. *Description géographique, historique et archéologique de la Palestine. Judée.* Vol. I. Paris; Piccirillo, M., 1994. Aïn Karim: les sanctuaries de l'enfance de Jean'. *Le Monde de la Bible* 89: 24–5.

2.29: Schick, C., 1899. 'Ancient Rock-cut Wine-presses at 'Ain Karim, *Palestine Exploration Fund Quarterly Statement*: 41–2.

2.30: P. 174 in Baedeker, K., 1876 (p. 94 of revised 1912 edition). *Palestine and Syria. Handbook for Travellers*. Leipzig.

2.31: P. 370 ff. in Tobler, T. 1853. *Topographie von Jerusalem und seinen Umgebungen*. Vol. II; see also Guérin, V., 1868. *Description géographique, historique et archéologique de la Palestine*. Judée. Vol. I. Paris.

2.32: Pp. 30–38 in Pringle, R. D., 1993. *The Churches of the Kingdom of Jerusalem: A Corpus. Volume I: A-K (excluding Acre and Jerusalem)*. Cambridge University Press: Cambridge.

2.33: Pp. 16–17, 20 in Bagatti, B., 1983. *Antichi villaggi Cristiani della Giudea e del Neghev*. Jerusalem; pp. 65–69 in Petrozzi, M. T., 1971. *Ain Karim*. Jerusalem; p. 66, note 158 in Di Segni, L., 2002. *The Aqueducts of Israel* (ed. Amit, Patrich and Hirschfeld).

2.34: Pp. 38–47 in Pringle, R. D., 1993. *The Churches of the Kingdom of Jerusalem: A Corpus. Volume I: A-K (excluding Acre and Jerusalem)*. Cambridge University Press: Cambridge.

2.35: Vatasso, M., 1906. *Frammenti d'un Livio del V secolo (Cod. Vat. Lat. 10696)*. Rome; pp. 98–9 in Petrozzi, M. T., 1971. *Ain Karim*. Jerusalem.

2.36: P. 407 in Meisterman, B., 1923. *Guide to the Holy Land*. London.

2.37: Guérin, V., 1868. *Description géographique, historique et archéologique de la Palestine*. Judée. Vol. I. Paris.

2.38: Schick, C., 1905. 'The Birthplace of St John the Baptist'. *Palestine Exploration Fund Quarterly Statement*. January: 61–9. In addition to this article, there are also a number of unpublished articles by Schick on Ain Karim in the archives of the Palestine Exploration Fund: 'Carriage Road to "Ain Karim"' and 'Ain Karim or St Johan [John]' (dated February 1897) (PEF/Schick/125/4), and 'Mar Zacharias near Ain Karim' (dated March 1897) which has a plan, two sections and a photograph (reproduced here as *plate 4b*) (PEF/Schick/126/2).

CHAPTER THREE

3.1: Taylor, J., 1993. *Christians and the Holy Places. The Myth of Jewish–Christian Origins*. Oxford.

3.2: Gibson, S., and Taylor, J. E., 1994. *Beneath the Church of the Holy Sepulchre: The Archaeology and Early History of Traditional Golgotha*. PEF: London; Biddle, M., 1999. *The Tomb of Jesus*. Sutton: London.

3.3: Dauphin, C., 1998. *La Palestine byzantine: Peuplement et Populations*. Vols 1–3. BAR International Series 726, Oxford; Tsafrir, Y., 2000. 'The

Spread of Christianity in the Holy Land', pp. 29–37 in Israeli, Y. and Mevorah, D. (eds). *Cradle of Christianity*. Israel Museum Catalogue No. 438: Jerusalem.

3.4: Wilkinson, J., 1981. *Egeria's Travels to the Holy Land*. Revised edition. Jerusalem and London.

3.5: Hunt, E. D., 1984. *Holy Land Pilgrimage in the Later Roman Empire AD 312–460*. Clarendon Press: Oxford.

3.6: P. 14 in Donner, H., 1992. *The Mosaic Map of Madaba: An Introductory Guide*. Kampen.

3.7: Safrai, Z., 1998. 'The Institutionalization of the Cult of Saints in Christian Society', in Houtman, A., Poorthuis, M., and Schwartz, J. (eds). *Sanctity of Time and Space*. Leiden.

3.8: Jung, C.G. (ed.), 1964. *Man and His Symbols*. Picador: London.

3.9: Israeli, Y., 2000. 'Christian Images and Symbols'. Pp.117–65 in Israeli, Y., and Mevorah, D. (eds), *Cradle of Christianity*. Israel Museum Catalogue No. 438: Jerusalem.

3.10: P. 74 and Fig. 27 in Bulliet, R.W., 1975. *The Camel and the Wheel*. Harvard University Press: Cambridge, Massachusetts.

3.11: Plate 19: photo 37 in Negev, A., 1978. 'The Greek Inscriptions from "Avdat". *Liber Annuus* XXVIII: 87–126; Fig. 32:4, 35:1 in Bagatti, B., 1983. *Antichi villagi Cristiani della Giudea e del Neghev*. Jerusalem.

3.12: Masterman, E.W.G., c.1920. *Hygiene and Disease in Palestine in Modern and Biblical Times*. PEF: London.

3.13: Pp. 13–14 in Ferguson, G., 1961. *Signs and Symbols in Christian Art*. Oxford University Press: London, Oxford and New York.

3.14: Pp. 49–50 in Baldock, J., 1990. *The Elements of Christian Symbolism*. Dorset.

3.15: Sukenik, E. L., 'Jewish Tombs in the Kedron Valley', *Kedem* II: 23–31, discussion on page 24 and Fig. A.

3.16: Fig.120 and pages 270–4 in Testa, E., 1981. *Il Simbolismo dei Giudeo-Cristiani*. Studium Biblicum Franciscanum Collectio Maior No. 14. Jerusalem.

3.17: For examples of full-face representations of a male or female in an *orans* position: pp. 24–5 in du Bourguet, P. 1965. *Early Christian Painting*. London; figures in a depiction of Daniel in the Lion's Den on the wall of a burial cave in western Galilee, dated to the fourth to fifth centuries: Foerster, G., 1986. 'A Painted Christian Burial Cave Near Kibbutz Lochmei HaGetu'ot'. Pp. 416–31 in Yedaya, M. (ed.), *The Western Galilee Antiquities*. Tel Aviv (Hebrew); saints on part of a wall painting unearthed in a vault below a palace in Caesarea, dating from the sixth to seventh centuries: pp. 82–3 in Israeli, Y., and Mevorah, D. (eds). *Cradle of Christianity*. The Israel Museum Catalogue No. 438: Jerusalem.

3.18: At Bawit: see Walters, C. C., 1974. *Monastic Archaeology in Egypt*. Warminster. Fig.xxxi on p. 257.

3.19: for similar facial features – curled hair, eyes and nose – see the figures represented on sixth-century metal *ampullae*: see for example, pp. 200–201 in Israeli, Y., and Mevorah, D. (eds), *Cradle of Christianity*. Israel Museum Catalogue No. 438: Jerusalem; see also the sixth-century representation of St Sergius on a silver basin from a site on the northern coast of Cyprus: p. 173 and Plate IX in Dalton, O. M., 1921. *A Guide to the Early Christian and Byzantine Antiquities in the Department of British and Medieval Antiquities*. Second edition. British Museum: London.

3.20: Fig. 32: 2–3 (Nessana) and Fig. 35:1 (Avdat) in Bagatti, B., 1983. *Antichi villaggi Cristiani della Giudea e del Neghev*. Jerusalem; Photo 37 (Avdat) in Negev, A., 1978. 'The Greek Inscriptions from "Avdat"'. *Liber Annuus* 28, 87–126; an incised drawing of a figure on a roof tile from Umm al-Rasas (late Byzantine–Umayyad): p. 392, Fig. 7 in Piccirillo, M., 1997. 'La chiesa di San Paola a Umm al-Rasas – Kastron Mefaa', *Liber Annuus* 47, 375–94; this type of Christian graffiti of standing figures is also known from Egypt: a Coptic drawing scrawled on the wall of an Egyptian tomb at el Amarna, p. 16 in Reeves, N., 2001. *Egypt's False Prophet: Akhenaten*. London; the naïve style resembles those known from Byzantine synagogue art of the sixth century, for example the figure holding the reigns of a donkey in the 'Sacrifice of Isaac' mosaic panel at Beth Alpha: Plate XIX in Sukenik, E. L., 1932. *The Ancient Synagogue of Beth Alpha*. Jerusalem and Oxford.

3.21: pp. 47–48 in Ferguson, G., 1961. *Signs and Symbols in Christian Art*. Oxford University Press: London, Oxford and New York.

3.22: Gregory Thaumaturgus (X, 1184–8), quoted in Dale, 1898: 404–5. (see below, note 6.5) 3.23: Struckmann, R., 1990. 'Asklepios in Epidauros'. Pp. 19–36. In Kasas, S., and Struckmann, R. *Important Medical Centres in Antiquity: Epidaurus and Corinth*. Athens.

3.24: Friedlander, Walter J. 1992. *The Golden Wand of Medicine. A History of the Caduceus Symbol in Medicine*. Contributions in Medical Studies No. 35. Greewood Press: Westport, Conn.

3.25: Winzen, D., 1957. *Symbols of Christ*. Longmans Green: London, New York, Toronto.

3.26: The T-shaped staff was often found in Eastern art of the twelfth century, as opposed to representations of the shepherd's crook in the

West: p. 51 in Kühnel, G., 1988. *Wall Painting in the Latin Kingdom of Jerusalem.* Berlin.

3.27: P. 152 in Neil, J., 1907. *Palestine Explored. With a View to its Present Natural Features, and to the Prevailing Manners, Customs, Rites and Colloqual Expressions of its People, Which Throw Light on the Figurative Language of the Bible.* London: James Nisbet.

3.28: For examples of the cross-and-serpent symbol see pp. 278–82 and Figure 125, and for the staff-cross: see pp. 317–21 and Fig. 133 in Testa, E., 1981. *Il Simbolismo dei Giudeo-Cristiani.* Studium Biblicum Franciscanum Collectio Maior No. 14. Jerusalem; p. 48 in Baldock, J., 1990. *The Elements of Christian Symbolism.* Dorset; pp. 41–2 in Winzen, D., 1957. *Symbols of Christ.* Longmans Green: London, New York, Toronto.

3.29: P. 72 in Israeli, Y., and Mevorah, D. (eds). *Cradle of Christianity.* Israel Museum Catalogue No. 438: Jerusalem.

3.30: P. 88 in Dalton, O. M., 1921. *A Guide to the Early Christian and Byzantine Antiquities in the Department of British and Medieval Antiquities.* Second edition. British Museum: London.

3.31: Pp. 412–16 and Fig. 152 in Testa, E., 1981. *Il Simbolismo dei Giudeo-Cristiani.* Studium Biblicum Franciscanum Collectio Maior No. 14. Jerusalem; pp. 15–16 in Ferguson, G., 1961. *Signs and Symbols in Christian Art.* Oxford University Press: London, Oxford and New York; Baldock, J., 1990. *The Elements of Christian Symbolism.* Dorset.

3.32: Book IV Chapter 141 page 737 in Schmidt, C. (text editor) and Macdermot, V. (translator), 1978. *Pistis Sophia.* The Coptic Gnostic Library, Nag Hammadi Studies Vol. IX. Leiden: Brill.

3.33: P.109* in Ziffer, I., 1998. *O My Dove, That Art in the Clefts of the Rock: The Dove-allegory in Antiquity.* Eretz Israel Museum Catalogue: Tel Aviv.

3.34: P. 186 in Schick, C., 1894. 'The Jerusalem Cross'. *Palestine Exploration Fund Quarterly Statement:* 183–9; Plate XVI in Desreumaux, A., and Humbert, J. B., 1981. 'Hirbet Es-Samra', *Annual of the Department of Antiquities of Jordan* XXV: 33–84.

3.35: Tzaferis, V., no date. 'When and Why the Sign of the Cross Became the Official Symbol of Christianity'. Unpublished manuscript; Baudler, G., 1997. *Das Kreuz: Geschichte und Bedeutung.* Dusseldorf; Laliberte, N., and West, E. N., 1960. *The History of the Cross.* New York and London; p. 121 in Israeli, Y. and Mevorah, D. (eds). *Cradle of Christianity.* Israel Museum Catalogue No. 438: Jerusalem; Brock, M., 1879. *The Cross: Heathen and Christian.* London.

3.36: P.283 in Chadwick, H., 1967. *The Early Church*. Harmondsworth; p. 216 in Runciman, S., 1956. *Byzantine Civilization*. Meridian: Cleveland and New York; pp. 24–6 in James, L., 2000. 'Dry Bones and Painted Pictures: Relics and Icons in Byzantium', in Lidov, A. (ed.). *Relics in the Art and Culture of the Eastern Christian World*. Moscow.

3.37: Baldi, D., and Bagatti, B., 1980. *Saint Jean-Baptiste: dans les souvenirs de sa Patrie*. Studium Biblicum Franciscanum. Collectio Minor No. 27. Franciscan Printing Press. Jerusalem; plate 31:5 in Testa, E., 1981. *Il Simbolismo dei Giudeo-Cristiani*. Studium Biblicum Franciscanum Collectio Maior No. 14. Jerusalem; Taylor, J. E., 1987. 'A Graffito Depicting John the Baptist in Nazareth?', *Palestine Exploration Quarterly* 119: 142–8.

3.38: See examples on p. 200 and 212 in Israeli, Y., and Mevorah, D. (eds), *Cradle of Christianity*. Israel Museum Catalogue No. 438: Jerusalem).

3.39: P. 30 (and illustration) in Forsyth, G. H., and Weitzmann, K., 1978. 'Saving the Mount Sinai Mosaics. *Biblical Archaeology Review* 4: 16–31. Main publication: p. 13 face of John the Baptist showing great pathos giving rise to the impression of John as a tragic prophet. Plates CLXXVI and CLXXX in Forsyth, G. H., and Weitzmann, K., 1973. *The Monastery of Saint Catherine at Mount Sinai. The Church and Fortress of Justinian*. Ann Arbor.

3.40: No. B.11. Pp. 32–5 and Plate XIV in Weitzmann, K., 1976. *The Monastery of Saint Catherine at Mount Sinai. The Icons. Vol. I: From the Sixth to the Tenth Century*. Princeton.

3.41: No. B.55, pp. 88–91 and Plate XXXIV in Weitzmann, K., 1976. *The Monastery of Saint Catherine at Mount Sinai. The Icons. Vol. I: From the Sixth to the Tenth Century*. Princeton.

3.42: Original watercolour by C. R. Conder, signed and dated 17 December 1873. Middle chapel Kuruntul (frescos) Sheet 18 No. 3. Scale 1/48 Niche in north wall; p. 202 in Conder, C. R., and Kitchener, H. H., 1882. *The Survey of Western Palestine. Volume III*. London; letter (WS/CON/79) sent from Jerusalem 17 December 1873; pp. 255–6 in Pringle, R.D., 1993. *The Churches of the Kingdom of Jerusalem: A Corpus. Volume I: A-K (excluding Acre and Jerusalem)*. Cambridge University Press: Cambridge.

3.43: Pp. 36–48, Pl.XII in Kühnel, G., 1988. *Wall Painting in the Latin Kingdom of Jerusalem*. Berlin.

3.44: Pp. 63–4 in Meinardus, O., 1980. *Notes on the Laurae and Monasteries of the Wilderness of Judaea*. Jerusalem.

3.45: Walters, C. C., 1974. *Monastic Archaeology in Egypt*. Warminster;

Plate 4.3 in Gabra, G., 2002. *Coptic Monasteries: Egypt's Monastic Art and Architecture*. Cairo and New York; for further representations of John the Baptist from Egypt and Ethiopia: Plates I-II in Clédat, J., 1902. 'Notes archéologiques et philologiques'. *Bulletin de l'Institut Français d'archéologie orientale* II: 41–70; colour plate on p. 404 in Playne, B., 1950. 'In Search of Early Christian Paintings in Ethiopia.' *Geographical Magazine* 22 (10): 400–11.

3.46: Pp. 16, 31 and Plates 9, 102 in du Bourguet, P. 1965. *Early Christian Painting*. London; Thiede, C. P. and D'Ancona, M., 2000. *The Quest for the True Cross*. P. 190, note 40. Disputed fresco in the Callisto Catacomb (second quarter of the third century) said to represent John the Baptist 'marking' Christ (reference to Matthew 3: 13–17).

3.47: Kostof, S., 1965. *The Orthodox Baptistery of Ravenna*; Bovini, G., 1957. *The Ravenna Mosaics*; p. 18 (the reproduction is back to front) in de Borchgrave, H. 1999. *A Journey into Christian Art*. Oxford.

3.48: P. 169 and Plate III opposite page 34 in: Dalton, O. M., 1921. *A Guide to the Early Christian and Byzantine Antiquities in the Department of British and Medieval Antiquities*. Second edition. British Museum: London.

3.49: P. 40 and Illustration 29 in Talbot Rice, D., 1963. *Art of the Byzantine Era*. London.

3.50: Pp. 69–71 in Ferguson, G., 1961. *Signs and Symbols in Christian Art*. Oxford University Press: London, Oxford and New York.

3.51: Contrary to the view expressed by Calvesi. See p. 14 in: Calvesi, M., 1998. *Caravaggio*. Prato.

CHAPTER FOUR

4.1: Pp. 60–2 in Webb, R. L., 1991. *John the Baptiser and Prophet: A Socio-Historical Study*. Sheffield.

4.2: Winter, P., 1956. 'The Proto-Source of Luke I', *Novum Testamentum* I: 184–99; Oliver, H. H., 1963–64. 'The Lucan Birth Stories and the Purpose of Luke-Acts', *New Testament Studies* X: 202–26; p. 49 ff. in Scobie, H. H. C., 1964. *John the Baptist*. London; pp. 60–72 in Wink, W., 1968 (reprinted in 2000). *John the Baptist in the Gospel Tradition*. Cambridge; Brown, R. E., 1977. *The Birth of the Messiah: A Commentary on the Infancy Narratives in Matthew and Luke*. London; pp. 22–3 in Tatum, W. B., 1994. *John the Baptist and Jesus: A Report of the Jesus Seminar*. Sonoma.

4.3: P. 9 and note 18 in Taylor, J. E., 1997. *John the Baptist Within Second Temple Judaism*. London.

4.4: P. 19 in Kraeling, C. H., 1951. *John the Baptist*. New York and London.

4.5: Winter, P., 1956. 'The Proto-Source of Luke I', *Novum Testamentum* I: 184–99.

4.6: Pp. 421–439 in Schneemelcher, W. (ed.), 1991. *New Testament Apocrypha. Volume I: Gospels and Related Writings*. Revised Edition. Translation by R. McL. Wilson. Cambridge and Westminster.

4.7: Section 22.3 on p. 436 in Schneemelcher, W. (ed.), 1991. *New Testament Apocrypha. Volume I: Gospels and Related Writings*. Revised Edition. Translated by R. McL. Wilson. Cambridge and Westminster.

4.8: Plate LVI in Grabar, A., 1958. *Ampoules de Terre Sainte (Monza – Bobbio)*, Paris; p. 86 and Pl.XVI:1 in Baldi, D., and Bagatti, B., 1980. *Saint Jean-Baptiste: dans les souvenirs de sa Patrie*. Studium Biblicum Franciscanum. Collectio Minor No. 27. Franciscan Printing Press. Jerusalem. On whether the *eulogia* had mosaic or wall-painting prototypes, see p. 107 in Rahmani, L. Y., 1970. 'A *Eulogia* Stamp from the Gaza Region', *Israel Exploration Journal* 20: 106–8. The idea that the *eulogia* may have been made at their point of origin is a line of enquiry that should be pursued by experts through methods of petrography or Neutron Activation Analysis. Tokens depicting the baptism scene are assumed to have been made at the Church of St John at the Jordan River, and the ones with Elizabeth and John at Ain Karim.

4.9: My thanks to Leah Di Segni who is preparing an article on this find from the Temple Mount (e-mail of 23 August 2002). For a photograph see p. 43 in Mazar, E., 1999. *The Monastery of the Virgins. Byzantine Period. Temple Mount Excavations in Jerusalem*. Jerusalem.

4.10: Barnett, P. W., 1981. 'The Jewish Sign Prophets – AD 40–70: Their Intentions and Origin'. *New Testament Studies* 27: 679–97.

4.11: P. 114 in Rajak, T., 1983. *Josephus: The Historian and His Society*. London; p. 80 in Goodman, 1987. *The Ruling Class of Judea: The Origins of the Jewish Revolt Against Rome AD 66–70*. Cambridge University Press: Cambridge.

4.12: P. 570 in Davies, S. L., 1983. 'John the Baptist and Essene Kashrut'. *New Testament Studies* 29: 569–71.

4.13: P. 209 in Funk, R. W., 1959. 'The Wilderness', *Journal of Biblical Literature* LXXVIII: 205–14; pp. 362–3 in Webb, R. L., 1991. *John the Baptiser and Prophet: A Socio-Historical Study*. Sheffield.

4.14: See the entry ἔρημος' on p. 313 in Liddell, H. G., and Scott, R., 1964. *Intermediate Greek–English Lexicon*. Oxford. 1964.

4.15: pp. 25–9 in Taylor, J. E., 1997. *John the Baptist Within Second*

Temple Judaism. London; p. 357 in Charlesworth, J. H., 1999. 'John the Baptiser and Qumran Barriers' in *Light of the Rule of the Community.* Pp. 353–75 in Parry, D. W., and Ulrich, E. (eds), *The Provo International Conference on the Dead Sea Scrolls: Technological Innovations, New Texts, and Reformulated Issues.* Leiden, Boston.

4.16: P. 30 in Ginzberg, L., 1968. *The Legends of the Jews.* Vol.VI. Philadelphia.

4.17: The first stanza of a poem by the German writer Hermann Hesse, who won the Nobel Prize for Literature in 1946, entitled 'The Wanderer Speaking to Death', in *Wandering: Notes and Sketches by Hermann Hesse.* Translated by J. Wright, 1972. London.

4.18: Pp. 34–5 and photograph on p. 36 in Taylor, J. E., 1997. *John the Baptist Within Second Temple Judaism.* London.

4.19: P. 255 in Neil, James, 1907. *Palestine Explored. With a View to its Present Natural Features, and to the Prevailing Manners, Customs, Rites and Colloqual Expressions of its People, Which Throw Light on the Figurative Language of the Bible.* London.

4.20: P. 570 in Davies, S. L., 1983. 'John the Baptist and Essere Kashrut'. *New Testament Studies* 29; see also Anderson, F. I., 1961–1962. 'The Diet of John the Baptist'. *Abr-Nahrain* 3: 60–74.

4.21: Leviticus 11:21–3: 'Yet these may ye eat of every flying thing creeping thing that goeth upon all four, which have legs above their feet, to leap withal upon the earth. 22: Even these of them ye may eat; the locust after his kind 23, and the beetle after his kind, and the grasshopper after his kind. But all other flying creeping things, which have four feet, shall be an abomination unto you.'

4.22: P. 367 in Charlesworth, J. H., 1999. 'John the Baptizer and Qumran Barriers in *Light of the Rule of Community'.* Pp. 353–75 in Parry, D. W., and Ulrich, E. (eds). *The Provo International Conference on the Dead Sea Scrolls:* Technological Innovations, New Texts, and Reformulated Issues. Leiden, Boston.

4.23: Pp 33–41 in Feliks, Y., 1994. *Fruit Trees in the Bible and Talmudic Literature.* Rubin Mass: Jerusalem (Hebrew); p. 51 in Broshi, M., 1986. 'The Diet of Palestine in the Roman Period – Introductory Notes'. *The Israel Museum Journal* 5: 41–56.

4.24: P. 325 in Tristram, H. B., 1898. *The Natural History of the Bible.* London.

4.25: Pp. 164–5 in Layard, A. H., 1897. *Nineveh and Babylon. A Narrative of a Second Expedition to Assyria During the Years 1849, 1850, & 1851.* London.

4.26: P 85, note 2 in Farrar, F. W., 1879. *The Life of Jesus.* Cassell Petter

& Galpin: London.

4.27: P. 318 quoted in Tristram, H. B. 1898. *The Natural History of the Bible*. London.

4.28: P. 547 in Whiting, J. D., 1915. 'Jerusalem's Locust Plague'. *National Geographic* 28 (December): 511–50.

4.29: P. 153 in Chichester Hart, H., 1888. *Scripture Natural History. II. The Animals Mentioned in the Bible*. London.

4.30: P. 318 quoted in Tristram, H. B., 1898. *The Natural History of the Bible*. London.

4.31: Bodenheimer, F.S., 1950. 'Note on Invasions of Palestine by Rare Locusts'. *Israel Exploration Journal* 1:146–8.

4.32: P. 317 quoted in Tristram, H. B., 1898. *The Natural History of the Bible*. London.

4.33: P. 513 in Whiting, J. D., 1915. 'Jerusalem's Locust Plague'. *National Geographic* 28 (December): 511–50; see also p. 144, note 39 in Jeremias, J., 1969. *Jerusalem in the Time of Jesus*. London.

4.34: P. 237 in Jarvis, C. S., 1941. *Yesterday and Today in Sinai*. Edinburgh and London.

4.35: Pp. 167, 169: 2 in Schneemelcher, W. (ed.), 1991. *New Testament Apocrypha. Volume I: Gospels and Related Writings*. Revised Edition. Translation by R. McL. Wilson. Cambridge and Westminster.

4.36: *Historia Hierosolymitana* 53, 1075; p. 72 in Jotischky, A., 1995. *The Perfection of Solitude. Hermits and Monks in the Crusader States*. Pennsylvania.

4.37: P. 31 in Fabri, Felix, Vol. II (part I), *Palestine Pilgrims' Text Society*. London 1893; p. 210 in Amar, Z., 2002. 'The "Sacred Botany" of Eretz Israel in Christian Tradition'. *Ariel* 155–6: 206–14.

4.38: P. 96 in Western, A. C., 1961. 'The Identity of Some Trees Mentioned in the Bible'. *Palestine Exploration Quarterly* Vol. 93, July–December: 89–100.

4.39: P. 92 and pp. 237–8 in Sperber, D., 1974. *Roman Palestine 200–400: Money and Prices*. Bar-Ilan University: Ramat Gan.

4.40: P. 154 in Liphshitz, N., 1987–1989. 'The Carob (*Ceratonia siliqua*) in Israel – a Young or Ancient Cultivation?' *Israel – People and Country* (Annual of the Eretz-Israel Museum, Tel Aviv) 5–6: 151–4 (Hebrew); pp. 148–51 in Liphshitz, N., and Biger, G., 1998. *Trees of Eretz-Israel: Characteristics, History and Uses*. Ariel 124–5: Jerusalem (Hebrew).

4.41: Pp. 202–9 in Amar, Z., 2000. *Agricultural Produce in the Land of Israel in the Middle Ages*. Yad Ben Zvi: Jerusalem (Hebrew).

4.42: Pp. 203–14 in Feliks, Y., 1994. *Fruit Trees in the Bible and Talmudic Literature*. Rubin Mass: Jerusalem (Hebrew).

4.43: Pp. 45 in Broshi, M., 1986. 'The Diet of Palestine in the Roman Period – Introductory Notes'. *Israel Museum Journal* 5: 41–56.

4.44: P. 7 in Kempe, D., 1988. *Living Underground. A History of Cave and Cliff Dwelling*. London.

4.45: Havakook, Y., 1985. *Cave-dwellers of the Hebron Mountains*. Tel Aviv. (Hebrew).

4.46: Letter from B. Murray to her mother, Palestine Exploration Fund Archives, London.

4.47: Lidror, R, 1990. 'Cave Disease in Israel'. *Niqrot Zurim* 16: 147–57, Appendix 1 (Hebrew).

4.48: Pp. 67–8 in Schick, C., 1905. 'The Birthplace of St John the Baptist'. *PEFQS*: January: 61–9.

4.49: P. 58 in Conder, C. R., 1874. 'XX. Gezer, Modin, Gibeah, and Ai', *PEFQS* April: 55–64; p. 93 in Conder, C. R., and Kitchener, H. H., 1883. *The Survey of Western Palestine*. Vol. III. *Judaea*. London.

4.50: Pp. 140–8 in Petrozzi, M. T., 1971. *Ain Karim*. Jerusalem.

4.51: Twite, R., 1990. 'Saint John in the Desert'. *Ariel: A Review of Arts and Letters in Israel* 79: 77–86.

4.52: Previous explorers exhibit some confusion as to the number of steps leading up to the cave (Guérin has six, Conder and Meistermann both have twelve, and Petrozzi nine) but this may be because the area around the pool has been elevated and some of the lower steps may no longer be visible.

4.53: P. 125 in Vilnay, Z., 1965. *The Holy Land in Old Prints and Maps*. Jerusalem; p. 657 in Sepp, J.N., 1873. *Jerusalem und das heilige Land*. Schaffhausen.

4.54: Translation by J. E. Taylor of p. 221 of Zuallardo, G. 1587, *Il devotissimo viaggio di Gerusalemme* (published in various editions and languages). See also p. 103 in Conder C. R. 1902, 'Zuallardo's Travels', *PEFQS*, pp. 96–105.

4.55: Davis, R. B., 1955. *George Sandys: Poet-Adventurer. A Study in Anglo-American Culture in the Seventeenth Century*. Bodley Head: London.

4.56: Sandys, *Travels, Containing an History of Original and Present State of the Turkish Empire, etc. With Fifty Graven Maps and Figures*. First edition 1615 but numerous editions exist with varying titles. Quotations taken from 1673 edition. John Williams: London.

4.57: Pococke, R., 1745. *A Description of the East and Some Other Countries*. Vol. II (Part I). London.

4.58: Water systems dating back to the Roman and Byzantine periods have been studied at Sataf, on the slope opposite Ain el-Habis: Gibson, S., Ibbs, B., and Kloner, A., 1991. 'The Sataf Project of Landscape Archaeology in the Judaean Hills: A Preliminary Report on Four Seasons of Survey and Excavation (1987–89)', *Levant*, 23 (1991): 29–54.

4.59: P.103 in Ben-Yosef, S., 1982. 'Rainmakers in the Judean Mountains'. *Israel – Land and Nature* 7: 100–103.

4.60: Pp. 171–2 in Ellenblum, R., 1992. 'Construction Methods in Frankish Rural Settlements', in B.Z. Kedar (ed.), *The Horns of Hattin*. London; p. 18 in Pringle, R. D., 1997. *Secular Buildings in the Crusader Kingdom of Jerusalem: an Archaeological Gazetteer*. Cambridge.

4.61: Pp. 24–6 in Pringle, R.D., 1993. *The Churches of the Kingdom of Jerusalem: A Corpus. Volume I: A-K (excluding Acre and Jerusalem)*. Cambridge University Press: Cambridge.

4.62: Kopp, C., and Stève, A.-M, 'Le désert de Saint Jean près d'Hébron', *Revue Biblique* 53 (1946): 559–75. See Fig. 6 for plan and Fig. 7 for elevation drawing through building. For further discussion of this site see p. 505 in Ben-Pechat, M., 1990. 'Baptism and Monasticism in the Holy Land: Archaeological and Literary Evidence'. Pp.501–22 in Bottini, G. C., Di Segni, L., and Alliata, E. (eds), 1990. *Christian Archaeology in the Holy Land: New Discoveries. Essays in Honour of Virgilio C. Corbo, OFM*. Jerusalem.

4.63: *Frescobaldi, Gucci and Sigoli's Visit to the Holy Places of Egypt, Sinai, Palestine and Syria in 1384*. Bellorini, Th., and Hoade, E. (transl.), and Bagatti, B. (ed.), 1948. Jerusalem.

4.64: Site No. 6. Pp. 29–30 in Pringle, R. D., 1993. *The Churches of the Kingdom of Jerusalem: A Corpus. Volume I: A-K (excluding Acre and Jerusalem)*. Cambridge University Press: Cambridge.

4.65: P. 242 in Wilkinson, J., Hill, J., and Ryan, W.F., 1988. *Jerusalem Pilgrimage 1099–1185*. London.

4.66: Magen, I., and Baruch, Y., 1997. 'Khirbet Abu Rish (Beit 'Anun)', *Liber Annuus* 47: 339–58; Baruch, Y., 1998. 'Khirbet Beit 'Anun in the Hebron Hills – a Site Connected to the Activities of John the Baptist'. In Y. Eshel (ed.), *Judea and Samaria Research Studies – Proceedings of the Seventh Annual Meeting 1997*. Pp. 169–79. Ariel (Hebrew).

CHAPTER FIVE

5.1: Sanders, E. P., 1993. *The Historical Figure of Jesus*. London.

5.2: Thompson, P., 2000. *The Voice of the Past: Oral History*. Oxford.

5.3: Pp. 47–77 in Webb, R. L., 1991. *John the Baptiser and Prophet: A*

Socio-Historical Study. Sheffield; Tatum, W. B., 1994. *John the Baptist and Jesus: A Report of the Jesus Seminar.* Sonoma. Regarding the overall purpose of the gospels, see: Aune, D. E., 1990. 'The Gospels – Biography or Theology', *Bible Review* VI (1): 14–21, 37.

5.4: For the overall credibility of Josephus, in historical and archaeological terms, see the articles collected in Rappaport, U. (ed.), 1982. *Josephus Flavius: Historian of Eretz-Israel in the Hellenistic-Roman Period.* Yad Ben-Zvi: Jerusalem (Hebrew).

5.5: P. 290 in Sanders, E. P., 1993. *The Historical Figure of Jesus.* London.

5.6: P. 34 in Kokkinos, N., 2002. 'Herod's Horrid Death', *Biblical Archaeology Review* 28 (2): 28–35.

5.7: P. 467 in Schneemelcher, W. (ed.), 1991. *New Testament Apocrypha. Volume I: Gospels and Related Writings.* Revised Edition. Translation by R. McL. Wilson. Cambridge and Westminster.

5.8: P. 176 in Kasher, A., 1988. *Jews, Idumeans and Ancient Arabs.* Tübingen.

5.9: For a summary of some of these opinions: Vermes, G. and Millar, F., 1973. 'Excursus I: The Census of Quirinius'. Pp. 420–7 in E. Schürer, *The History of the Jewish People in the Age of Jesus Christ (175 BC – AD 135).* Revised and edited by G. Vermes and F. Millar. Vol. I. Edinburgh. See also the remarks on pp. 86–7 in Sanders, E. P., 1993. *The Historical Figure of Jesus.* London. For an alternative view, see pp. 374–5 in Kokkinos, N., 1998. *The Herodian Dynasty. Origins, Role in Society and Eclipse.* Sheffield.

5.10: *Biblical Archaeology Review* 28 (1): 24–33. For a balanced critical response to this discovery, see Puech, E., 2003. 'James the Just, or Just James? The Epigrapher's Trail', *Minerva* 14 (1): 4–5.

5.11: Rahmani, L. Y., 1994. *A Catalogue of Jewish Ossuaries in the Collections of the State of Israel.* IAA: Jerusalem. For the ossuary of Theophilis: p. 41 in Barag, D. and Flusser, D., 1986. 'The Ossuary of Yehohanah Granddaughter of the High Priest Theophilis', *Israel Exploration Journal* 36: 39–44.

5.12: P. 40 and illus. 20 in Naveh, J., 1992. *On Sherd and Papyrus: Aramaic and Hebrew Inscriptions from the Second Temple, Mishnaic and Talmudic Periods.* Magness Press: Jerusalem (Hebrew).

5.13: P. 62 and Illus. 36 in Naveh, J., 1992. (See above, note 5.12.)

5.14: P. 130, illus. 85 in Naveh, J. 1992. (See above, note 5.12.)

5.15: P. 42 in Stern, M., 1991. *Studies in Jewish History: The Second Temple Period.* Yad Ben-Zvi: Jerusalem (Hebrew).

5.16: P. 64 in Naveh, J., 1992. *On Sherd and Papyrus: Aramaic and Hebrew*

Inscriptions from the Second Temple, Mishnaic and Talmudic Periods. Magness Press: Jerusalem (Hebrew).

5.17: P. 74 in Morton, H. V., 1937. *In the Footsteps of St Paul.* London.

5.18: Tarphon is also the name of a rabbi on a later Byzantine period burial epitaph found at Jaffa: iIllus. 141 in Naveh, J. 1992. *On Sherd and Papyrus: Aramaic and Hebrew Inscriptions from the Second Temple, Mishnaic and Talmudic Periods.* Magness Press: Jerusalem (Hebrew).

5.19: Institute of Archaeology Inventory No. 1522; *SEG* 8, No. 202; Spoer, H., *Journal of the American Oriental Society* 28, 1907: 355–9; Thomsen, *Zeitschrift des Deutschen Pälastina–Vereins* 44, 1921, 115, No. 192b; p. 14 and Tafel 2 in Sukenik, E.L., 1931. *Jüdische Gräber Jerusalems um Christi Geburt,* Jerusalem; pp. 239, 308 in Ilan, T., 2002. *Lexicon of Jewish Names in Late Antiquity. Part One: Palestine 330 BCE – 200 CE.* Tübingen. I am grateful to Dr Jonathan Price for the information about the 'Yohanan son of Yosef son of Elisheva' ossuary which is in a private collection and remains unpublished: e-mail message of 19 September 2002.

5.20: Pp. 236–239 in Naveh, J., 1992. *On Sherd and Papyrus: Aramaic and Hebrew Inscriptions from the Second Temple, Mishnaic and Talmudic Periods.* Magness Press: Jerusalem (Hebrew).

5.21: P. 362 and note 13 and the bibliography in Murphy-O'Connor, J., 1990. 'John the Baptist and Jesus: History and Hypotheses'. *New Testament Studies* 36: 359–74.

5.22: P. 65 in Schonfield, H. J., 1969. *The Passover Plot. New Light on the History of Jesus.* New York.

5.23: De Vaux, R., 1965. *Ancient Israel: Its Life and Institutions.* Second edition. London.

5.24: P. 101 in Meimaris, Y. E., 1986. *Sacred Names, Saints, Martyrs and Church Officials in the Greek Inscriptions and Papyri Pertaining to the Christian Church of Palestine.* (ΜΕΛΕΤΗΜΑΤΑ 2). Research Centre for Greek and Roman Antiquity: Athens. The six inscriptions he lists are on pp. 100–2: Nos. 593–8. It should be noted that it seems unlikely – contrary to Meimaris – that Inscription No. 597 from Khirbet Umm er Rus (Judaean Hills, 20 km SW of Jerusalem) refers to John the Baptist. It is more likely to have been the name of a holy man of that time. Hence the list includes only five inscriptions mentioning John the Baptist: Auja Hafir / Nessana (No. 593); Boberiyeh / Samaria (No. 594); Jerash (No. 595); Jerash (No. 596); Madaba (No. 598).

5.25: *SEG* 8, Inscription No. 238; Avi-Yonah, M., 1932. 'Mosaic Pavements in Palestine', *Quaterly of the Department of Antiquities of Palestine* 2: 136–81.

5.26: Vincent, H., 1903. 'Les ruines de Beit Cha'ar', *Revue Biblique*, pp. 612–14.

5.27: Document No. 89 in Kraemer, C J., 1958. *Excavations at Nessana. Volume 3: Non-Literary Papyri*. Princeton University Press: Princeton.

5.28: *SEG* VIII, 1937, No. 119; Meimaris (see above, note 5.24). No. 594.

5.29: Kraeling, C. H., 1938. *Gerasa: City of the Decapolis*. ASOR: New Haven. Inscription No. 306 on pp. 242, 479–80, Pl.XLVI:b; Inscription No. 314 on p. 482, Pl. LXXIII: top of picture.

5.30: Frösén, Jaakko, and Fiema, Zbigniew T. (eds), 2002. *Petra – A City Forgotten and Rediscovered*. Amos Anderson Museum. Publications No. 40, Helsinki.

5.31: P. 146, Inscription No. 81 in Ewing, W., 1895. 'Greek and Other Inscriptions Collected in the Hauran'. *Palestine Exloration and Quaterly Statement* 1895: 131–60. I am grateful to Leah Di Segni for her comments on the date of this inscription.

5.32: Meimaris (see above, note 5.24) No. 598; Avi-Yonah, M., 1964. *The Madaba Mosaic Map. With Introduction and Commentary*. Jerusalem.

5.33: I am grateful to Joe Zias and Emile Puech for this information.

5.34: Barnett, P. W., 1981. 'The Jewish Sign Prophets – A.D. 40–70: Their Intentions and Origin'. *New Testament Studies* 27: 679–97; Horsley, R. A., 1984. 'Popular Messianic Movements Around the Time of Jesus'. *Catholic Biblical Quarterly* 46: 471–95; p. 80 in Martin Goodman, 1987. *The Ruling Class of Judea: The Origins of the Jewish Revolt Against Rome A.D. 66–70*. Cambridge University Press: Cambridge.

5.35: P. 79 in Rowley, H. H., 1963. *The Growth of the Old Testament*. New York.

5.36: Compare with the conventional wisdom on p. 28 in Wink, W., 1968 (reprinted in 2000). *John the Baptist in the Gospel Tradition*. Cambridge. On the matter of Elijah as the forerunner of the Messiah: Faierstein, M. M., 1981, 'Why do the Scribes Say that Elijah Must Come First'. *Journal of Biblical Literature* 100 (1): 75–86; Fitzmeyer, J. A., 1985. 'More About Elijah Coming First', *Journal of Biblical Literature* 104 (1): 295–6.

5.37: Pp. 64–5 in Albright, W. F., 1963. *The Biblical Period from Abraham to Ezra*. New York.

5.38: P. 97 in Dorrell, P., 1993. 'The Spring at Jericho From Early Photographs', *Palestine Exploration Quarterly* 125: 95–114.

5.39: Brownlee, W. H., 1958. 'John the Baptist in the Light of Ancient Scrolls'. Pp. 33–53 in K. Stendahl (ed.), *The Scrolls and the New*

Testament. London; pp. 207–8 in Scobie, C. H., 1964. *John the Baptist*. London; p. 570 in Davies, S. L., 1983. 'John the Baptist and Essene Kashrut'. *New Testament Studies* 29: 569–71; Lichtenberger, H., 1992. 'The Dead Sea Scrolls and John the Baptist: Reflections on Josephus' Account of John the Baptist'. Pp. 340–6 in Dimant, D., and Rappaport, U. (eds), *The Dead Sea Scrolls: Forty Years of Research*. Leiden and Jerusalem; Puech, E., 1994. 'Jean Baptiste était-il essénien?' *Le Monde de la Bible* 89: 7–8; Betz, O., 1992. 'Was John the Baptist an Essene?' Pp. 205–14 in Shanks, H. (ed.), *Understanding the Dead Sea Scrolls*. New York; p. 48 in Taylor, J. E., 1997. *John the Baptist Within Second Temple Judaism*. London; Stegeman, H., 1998. *The Library of Qumran. On the Essenes, Qumran, John the Baptist, and Jesus*. Grand Rapids, Cambridge and Leiden; Charlesworth, J. H., 1999. 'John the Baptiser and Qumran Barriers in Light of the Rule of the Community.' Pp. 353–75 and further bibliography in notes 7–10, in Parry, D. W., and Ulrich. E. (eds), *The Provo International Conference on the Dead Sea Scrolls: Technological Innovations, New Texts, and Reformulated Issues*. Leiden, Boston. A revised version of Charlesworth's paper was sent to me by the author.

5.40: P. 114 in Broshi, M., 1992. 'The Archeology of Qumran – A Reconsideration'. Pp. 103–5 in Dimant, D., and Rappaport, U. (eds), *The Dead Sea Scrolls: Forty Years of Research*. Leiden and Jerusalem; Broshi, M., 2001. 'Qumran and its Scrolls: Stocktaking'. *Cathedra* 100: 165–82 (Hebrew).

5.41: Broshi, M., and Eshel, H., 1999. 'Residential Caves at Qumran'. *Dead Sea Discoveries* 6 (3): 328–47.

5.42: Flusser, D., 1963. *The Beginnings of Christianity*. Written down and edited by Ziona and Israel Katz. Hebrew University: Jerusalem (Hebrew).

5.43: E-mail message from Magen Broshi, 5 August 2002.

5.44: The suggestion that the 'Teacher of Righteousness' should be identified with John the Baptist – a view few scholars accept – was already made many years ago: pp. 208–12 in Thiering, B. E., 1979. *Redating the Teacher of Righteousness*. Australian and New Zealand Studies in Theology and Religion.

5.45: Broshi, M., and Eshel, H., 2003. 'Whose Bones? New Qumran Excavation, New Debates'. *Biblical Archaeology Review* 29: 26–33, 71.

CHAPTER SIX

6.1: Gibson, S., and Jacobson, D. M., 1996. *Below the Temple Mount in Jerusalem: A Sourcebook on the Cisterns, Subterranean Chambers and Conduits of the Haram al-Sharif.* BAR International Series 637, Oxford; Kloner, A., 2001–2002. 'Water Cisterns in Idumea, Judaea and Nabatea in the Hellenistic and Early Roman periods'. *ARAM* 13–14: 461–485.

6.2: Mishna *Abodah* Zarah 3:2. Although this would have applied to votive model legs and hands, such as those known from the Bethesda Pools in Jerusalem and from Caesarea, it could also apply to footprint stones as well.

6.3: According to the Mishna *Yadaim* 4:1: footbaths could hold between two *logs* and nine *kabs* of water and the ceramic types would become unclean if they cracked. Footbaths hewn into the ground in the close proximity to Jewish ritual cleansing pools have also been found in excavations near Beth Shemesh conducted by Emanuel Eisenberg from the IAA.

6.4: Gibson, S., 2003., Stone Vessels of the Early Roman Period from Jerusalem and Palestine. A Reassessment. Pp. 287–308 in Bottini, G. C., Di Segni, L., and Chrupcala, L. D. (eds). *One Land – Many Cultures: Archaeological Studies in Honour of S. Loffreda.* Jerusalem.

6.5: P. 125 in Dale, J.W., 1898. *Johannic Baptism* ΒΑΠΤΙΖΩ: *An Inquiry into the Meaning of the Word as Determined by the Usage of the Holy Scriptures.* 1993 reprint. Wauconda, Phillipsburg and Toney.

6.6: P. 69 in Baldock, J., 1990. *The Elements of Christian Symbolism.* Dorset; Ferguson, G., 1961. *Signs and Symbols in Christian Art.* Oxford University Press: London, Oxford and New York; p. 56 in Walters, C. C., 1974. *Monastic Archaeology in Egypt.* Warminster.

6.7: See engraving on p. 14 of Macalister, R. A. S., 1912. *A History of Civilization in Palestine.* Cambridge University Press: London.

6.8: Dunbabin, K. M. D., 1990. '*Ipsa deae vestigial . . .* Footprints Divine and Human on Graeco-Roman Monuments', *Journal of Roman Archaeology* 3: 85–109.

6.9: Pp. 313–14 in Buckingham, J. S., 1822. *Travels in Palestine, Through the Countries of Bashan and Gilead, East of the Jordan: Including a Visit to the Cities of Geraza and Gamala, in the Decapolis.* Vol. I. London.

6.10: P. 198 in Twain, M., 1869. *The Innocents Abroad or the New Pilgrim's Progress.* New edition 1966. New York, Ontario.

6.11: P. 108 in Pringle, R. D., 1990–1991. 'Crusader Jerusalem', *Bulletin of the Anglo-Israel Archaeological Society* 10: 105–13.

6.12: P.106 in Baedeker, K., 1876. *Jerusalem and its Surroundings. Handbook for Travellers.* Leipzig and London.

6.13: P. 112 and note 2 and plan on page 117 of Bagatti, B., 1997. *Bernardino Amico: Plans of the Sacred Edifices of the Holy Land.* Jerusalem.

6.14: P. 112 and note 2 in Bagatti, B., 1997. (See above, note 6.13), p. 256 in Prag, K., 1989. *Blue Guide: Jerusalem*. Black, Norton: London, New York. Canaan (see above, note 6.13: p. 293) mistakenly seems to think that the imprints of the two feet from the Chapel of the Ascension are unrelated to the one kept at the Aqsa Mosque (below the Aqsa Srir 'Isa).

6.15: Topkapi Palace, Istanbul. The first footprint stone is kept in a black box-like stand surrounded with gold and is labelled Env. No. 21/195. The second footprint stone is labelled Env. No. 21/466.

6.16: Pp. 241–3, and 296 in Canaan, T., 1927. *Mohammedan Saints and Sanctuaries in Palestine*. Jerusalem.

6.17: Reich, R., 1990. *Miqwa'ot (Jewish Ritual Immersion Baths) in Eretz Israel in the Second Temple Period and the Period of the Mishna and Talmud*. Unpublished Ph.D., dissertation. Hebrew University, Jerusalem (Hebrew); Reich, R., 2002. 'They are Ritual Pools'. *Biblical Archaeology Review* 28(2): 50–5.

6.18: Amit, D., 1996. *Ritual Pools From the Second Temple Period in the Hebron Hills*. M.A. Thesis, Hebrew University; Amit, D., 1999. 'A Miqveh Complex Near Alon Shevut'. *'Atiqot* 38: 75–84; Fig. 42 on p. 56 in Strus, A., 2000. *Bet Gemal: Pathway to the Tradition of Saints Stephen and Gamliel*. Rome.

6.19: Pp. 171–84 in Grossberg, A. 2001. 'A Miqveh in the Bathhouse'. *Cathedra* 99 (Hebrew).

6.20: Humbert, J.-B, and Chambon, A., 1994. *Fouilles de Khirbet Qumran et de Ain Feshka*. Göttingen; p. 728 in Reich, R., 2000. 'Miqwa'ot at Khirbet Qumran and the Jerusalem Connection. In Schiffman, L. H., Tov, E., and VanderKam, J. C., *The Dead Sea Scrolls. Fifty Years After Their Discovery*. Jerusalem; Galor, K., no date. 'Qumran's Plastered Pools: A New Perspective'. Unpublished paper.

6.21: P. 42 and illustrations 60–61 and Plate V in Netzer, E., 2001. *Hasmonean and Herodian Palaces at Jericho. Final Reports of the 1973–1987 Excavations. Volume I: Stratigraphy and Architecture*. Jerusalem.

6.22: Pp. 88–90 and photo 2.78 in Reich, R., 2000. 'IIc. Hellenistic to Medieval Strata 6–1'. In H. Geva, *Jewish Quarter Excavations in the Old City of Jerusalem Conducted by Nahman Avigad, 1969–1982. Volume I: Architecture and Stratigraphy: Areas A, W and X-2. Final Report*. IES: Jerusalem.

6.23: Pp. 75–76 in Dale, J.W., 1898. *Johannic Baptism* ΒΑΠΤΙΖΩ: *An Inquiry into the Meaning of the Word as Determined by the Usage of the Holy Scriptures*. 1993 reprint. Wauconda, Phillipsburg and Toney; pp. 90–116 in Scobie, C. H., 1964. *John the Baptist*. London; pp. 49–100 in Taylor,

J. E., 1997. *John the Baptist Within Second Temple Judaism*. London; pp. 95–216 in Webb, R. L., 1991. *John the Baptiser and Prophet: A Socio-Historical Study*. Sheffield; pp. 115–44 in Tatum, W. B., 1994. *John the Baptist and Jesus: A Report of the Jesus Seminar*. Sonoma; pp. 95–122 in Kraeling, C. H., 1951. *John the Baptist*. New York and London.

6.24: Pp. 261–262 in Schiffman, L.H., 1982. 'Proselytism in the writings of Josephus: Izates of Adiabene in light of the Halakhah', in: Rappaport, U. (ed.), *Josephus Flavius: Historian of Eretz-Israel in the Hellenistic-Roman Period*. Yad Ben-Zvi: Jerusalem (Hebrew); Rowley, H. H., 1940. 'Jewish Proselyte Baptism and the Baptism of John', *Hebrew Union College Annual* 15: 313–34; pp. 319–20 in Samet, M., 1993. 'Conversion in the First Centuries C.E.', in Gafni, I., Oppenheimer, A., and Stern, M. (eds), *Jews and Judaism in the Second Temple, Mishna and Talmud Periods*. Yad Ben-Zvi: Jerusalem (Hebrew).

6.25: Pfann, S. J., 1999. 'The Essene Yearly Renewal Ceremony and the Baptism of Repentance'. Pp. 337–52 in Parry, D. W. and Ulrich, E. (eds), *The Provo International Conference on the Dead Sea Scrolls: Technological Innovations, New Texts, and Reformulated Issues*. Leiden, Boston.

6.26: Baumgarten, J. M., 2000. 'The use of "*mei niddah*" for General Purification'. Pp. 481–5 in Schiffman, L. H., Tov, E., and VanderKam, J. C., 2000. *The Dead Sea Scrolls. Fifty Years After Their Discovery*. Jerusalem.

6.27: Keck, L. E., 1970–1971. 'The Spirit and the Dove'. *New Testament Studies* 17: 41–67; Ziffer, I., 1998. *O My Dove, That Art in the Clefts of the Rock: The Dove-allegory in Antiquity*. Eretz Israel Museum Catalogue: Tel Aviv; pp. 90–7 in Stratton-Porter, G., 1916. *Birds of the Bible*. London; pp. 106–23 in Wood, J. G., 1887. *Bird Life of the Bible*. London.

6.28: P. 9 in Cullman, O., 1950. *Baptism in the New Testament*. Studies in Biblical Theology. London.

6.29: Taylor, J., 1993. *Christians and the Holy Places. The Myth of Jewish-Christian Origins*. Oxford.

6.30: P. 32 in Tsafrir, Y., 2000. 'The Spread of Christianity in the Holy Land', in Israeli, Y., and Mevorah, D. (eds), *Cradle of Christianity*. Israel Museum Catalogue No. 438: Jerusalem.

6.31: P. 500 in Stern, M., 1991. *Studies in Jewish History: The Second Temple Period*. Jerusalem (Hebrew).

6.32: Pp. 31–3 in Vermes, G., 1976. *Jesus the Jew*. London.

6.33: P. 160 in Schneemelcher, W. (ed.), 1991. *New Testament Apocrypha. Volume I: Gospels and Related Writings*. Revised Edition. Translation by R. McL. Wilson. Cambridge and Westminster.

6.34: P. 361 in Murphy O'Connor, J., 1990. 'John the Baptist and Jesus: History and Hypotheses. *New Testament Studies* 36: 359–74.

6.35: Kloner, A., and Tepper, Y., 1987. *The Hiding Complexes in the Judean Shephelah*. Tel Aviv (Hebrew).

6.36: Eshel, H., and Amit, D. (eds), 1998. *Refuge Caves of the Bar Kokhba Revolt*. Tel Aviv (Hebrew).

6.37: Thompson, P. 2000. *The Voice of the Past: Oral History*. Oxford.

6.38: P. 108: Wilkinson, J. 1977. *Jerusalem Pilgrims Before the Crusades*. Jerusalem.

6.39: P. 154: Farrar, F. W., 1879. *The Life of Christ*. London.

CHAPTER SEVEN

7.1: Mishna *middoth* 3:4 (Herbert Danby edition. 1933 Oxford University Press: Oxford); in keeping with Exodus 20: 25 and Deuteronomy 27:5.

7.2: P. 140. Horowitz, I. S., 1923. *Palestine and the Adjacent Countries*. Vol. I. Vienna (Hebrew).

7.3: Most of the limekiln installations that have been investigated by archaeologists date from later periods, but one Late Iron Age kiln was excavated to the north-east of Jerusalem: S. Gibson, 'Lime Kilns in North-East Jerusalem', *Palestine Exploration Quarterly*, 116 (1984): 94–102.

7.4: Ron, Z. Y. D., 1985. 'Development and Management of Irrigation Systems in Mountain Regions of the Holy Land'. *Transactions of the Institute of British Geographers*. NS. 10: 149–69.

7.5: Early Bronze Age (third millennium BC) terracing has been found at nearby Sataf: Gibson, S., Ibbs, B., and Kloner, A. 1991. 'The Sataf Project of Landscape Archaeology in the Judaean Hills: A Preliminary Report on Four Seasons of Survey and Excavation (1987–89)'. *Levant* 23: 29–54.

7.6: Source: *Atmospheric Chemistry Glossary*, 2002 version, Chemistry Department, Sam Houston State University.

7.7: Shiloh, S., 1992. 'Underground Water Systems in the Land of Israel in the Iron Age'. Pp. 275–93 in Kempinsky, A., and Reich, R. (eds), *The Architecture of Ancient Israel From the Prehistoric to the Persian Periods*. Jerusalem.

7.8: Tsuk believes that the reason why water systems did not exist in the Early Iron Age is because large cities from this period are lacking in the highland regions: p. 13* in Tsuk, T., 2000. *Ancient Water Systems in Settlements in Eretz-Israel (from the Neolithic Period to the End of the Iron*

Age). Ph.D. thesis, Tel Aviv University. (Hebrew with English summary.)

7.9: For the Beth Shemesh reservoir, see Tsuk 2000, (see above, note 7.8). Pp. 144–6 and illustration in Fig. 204. See also: Tsuk, T., 2001–2002. 'Urban Water Reservoirs in the Land of the Bible During the Bronze and Iron Ages (3000 BC – 586 BC)', *ARAM* 13–14: 377–401, Figs. 11–12 (Beth Shemesh); 15 (Amman); 16–17 (Beer Sheba).

7.10: Shiloh, S., 1992. 'Underground Water Systems in the Land of Israel in the Iron Age'. Pp. 275–93 in Kempinsky, A., and Reich, R. (eds), *The Architecture of Ancient Israel From the Prehistoric to the Persian Periods.* Jerusalem).

7.11: De Geus, C.H.J., 1975. 'The Importance of Archaeological Research into the Palestinian Agricultural Terraces, with an Excursus on the Hebrew Word *gbi*', *Palestine Exploration Quarterly* 117: 65–74.

7.12: For a discussion regarding the concept of 'sacred' sites and what constitutes a place of special significance within the natural landscape, see: Carmichael, D. L., Hubert, J., Reeves, B., Schanche, A. (eds), 1994. *Sacred Sites, Sacred Places.* One World Archaeology No. 23. Routledge: London and New York.

7.13: For an investigation of the meaning and significance of ritual places in the natural landscape, see: Bradley, R., 2000. *An Archaeology of Natural Places.* Routledge: London.

7.14: P. 257 in Jaffé, A., 1964. 'Symbolism in the Visual Arts'. Pp. 257 in Jung, C.G. (ed.), *Man and His Symbols.* Picador: London.

7.15: Masterman, E.W.G., c.1920. *Hygiene and Disease in Palestine in Modern and Biblical Times.* PEF: London.

CHAPTER EIGHT

8.1: Pp. 427: Twain, M., 1869. *The Innocents Abroad or the New Pilgrim's Progress.* New edition 1966. New York, Ontario.

8.2: Pp. 194–5 in Kinglake, A.W., 1845. *Eothen, or Traces of Travel Brought Home from the East.* London.

8.3: There is absolutely no need to seek the location of this site at AbaraH, one of the fords on the Jordan a little north of Beth Shean: pp. 319–21 in Conder, F. R., and Conder C. R., 1882. *A Handbook to the Bible.* London.

8.4: Pp. 38–9: Avi-Yonah, M., 1964. *The Madaba Mosaic Map. With Introduction and Commentary.* Jerusalem; p. 14 in Donner, H., 1992. *The Mosaic Map of Madaba: An Introductory Guide.* Kampen.

8.5: Parker, P., 1955. 'Bethany Beyond Jordan', *Journal of Biblical*

Literature LXXIV: 257–61. Parker suggests that the event did take place at the Bethany near Jerusalem, which is across or opposite (πέραν) the place where John had been baptising. His arguments are not very convincing.

8.6: Sion, O., 1996. 'The Monasteries of the "Desert of the Jordan"'. *Liber Annuus* 46: 245–64.

8.7: Piccirillo, M., no date. 'The Sanctuaries Visited by the Pilgrims on the East Bank of the Jordan'. (I am grateful to Father Piccirillo for providing me with a draft of his unpublished paper); Hirschfeld, Y., 2002, *The Desert of the Holy City: The Judean Desert Monasteries in the Byzantine Period.* Jerusalem (Hebrew).

8.8: P. 161 in Wilkinson, J., 1981. *Egeria's Travels to the Holy Land.* Jerusalem and Warminster.

8.9: P. 69 in Wilkinson, J. 1977. *Jerusalem Pilgrims Before the Crusades.* Jerusalem.

8.10: P. 81 in Wilkinson, J. 1977. (See above, note 8.9.) Jerusalem.

8.11: Sophronius, *Vita Mariae Aegyptiae* chs. 26, 32, *PG* 87, cols. 3716, 3720 in Greek, chs. 18, 20, *PL* 73, cols. 683, 685 in the Latin version of the *Vitae Patrum* (English translation in B. Ward, 1987. *Harlots of the Desert*, Kalamazoo, pp. 26–56.)

8.12: Pp. 4–5 in John Moschus, *The Spiritual Meadow* (*Pratum Spirituale*). Transl. John Wortley 1992. Cistercian Studies Series No.139. Michigan; pp. 186–191 in Waddell, H., 1962. *The Desert Fathers.* London and Glasgow.

8.13: P. 107 in Wilkinson, J. 1977. *Jerusalem Pilgrims Before the Crusades.* Jerusalem.

8.14: Pp. 120–1 in Wilkinson, J. 1977. *Jerusalem Pilgrims Before the Crusades.* Jerusalem; H. Donner, 1971. 'Die Palästinabeschreibung des Epiphanius Monachus Hagiopolita', *Zeitschrift des Deutschen Pälastina–Vereins* 87:78.

8.15: P. 129: Wilkinson, J. 1977. *Jerusalem Pilgrims Before the Crusades.* Jerusalem.

8.16: P. 138 in Wilkinson, J. 1977. (See above, note 8.15.) Jerusalem.

8.17: Pp. 136–7 in Wilkinson, J, Hill, J., and Ryan, W.F. (eds), 1988. *Jerusalem Pilgrimage 1099–1185.* London.

8.18: Site 209: pp. 242–3 in Pringle, R. D., 1998. *The Churches of the Kingdom of Jerusalem: A Corpus. Volume II: L-Z (excluding Tyre).* Cambridge University Press: Cambridge.

8.19: P. 153 in Pringle. R.D., 1994. 'Templar Castles on the Road to the Jordan'. In M. Barber (ed.), *The Military Orders: Fighting for the faith and caring for the Sick.* Aldershot.

8.20: P. 11 in Piccirillo, M., no date. 'The Sanctuaries Visited by the Pilgrims on the East Bank of the Jordan'.

8.21: Pp. 244–8 in Abel, F. M., 1932. 'Exploration du sud-est de la vallée du Jourdain (suite)'. *Revue Biblique* 41: 237–57.

8.22: Waheeb, M., 1998. 'Wadi al-Kharrar Archaeological Project (Al-Maghtas)'. *Annual of the Department of Antiquities of Jordan* XLII: 635–38; Waheeb, M., 1998. 'New Discoveries Near the Baptism Site (Jordan River) (al-Maghtas Project)'. *Occident & Orient* 3 (1): 19–20; Waheeb, M., and Doleh, Y., 1999. *Occident & Orient* 4 (1–2): 10–11; Waheeb, M., no date. 'Recent Discoveries east of Jordan River. Wadi al-Kharrar Archaeological project – Preliminary Report'. (I am grateful to Dr Waheeb for providing me with a draft of his unpublished paper); Khouri, R. G., 2000. 'Fourth Church Discovered at Byzantine Complex Near the Jordan River –Parts I and II' (Jordan Antiquity, Nos. 171–172); Khouri, R. G., 2001. 'Intriguing Staircase Discovered At Jordan River Byzantine Church Complex' (Jordan Antiquity, No. 177).

8.23: Khouri, R. G., 2001. 'Department of Antiquities Denies Discovery of the Skull of John the Baptist at Ancient Cave-Church at Wadi el-Kharrar Baptism Site' (Jordan Antiquity, No. 173).

8.24: Waheeb, M., 1998. 'Wadi al-Kharrar Archaeological Project' (Al-Maghtas). *Annual of the Department of Antiquities of Jordan* XLII: 635–8; Waheeb, M., 1998. 'New Discoveries Near the Baptism Site (Jordan River) (al-Maghtas Project)'. *Occident & Orient* 3 (1): 19–20; Waheeb, M., and Doleh, Y., 1999. *Occident & Orient* 4 (1–2): 10–11; Waheeb, M., 1999. 'Wadi al-Kharrar Archaeological Project: The Monastery'. *ADAJ* XLII: 549–57; Waheeb, M., no date. 'Recent Discoveries east of Jordan River. Wadi al-Kharrar Archaeological project – Preliminary Report'.

8.25: pp. 115–16 in Liphshitz, N., and Biger, G., 1998. *Trees of Eretz-Israel: Characteristics, History and Uses.* (Ariel 124–5) Jerusalem (Hebrew).

8.26: pp. 37–8, No.6 in Avi-Yonah, M., 1964. *The Madaba Mosaic Map. With Introduction and Commentary.* Jerusalem; p. 38 in Donner, H., 1992. *The Mosaic Map of Madaba: An Introductory Guide.* Kampen. pp. 37–8; p. 167 in Patrich, J., 1995. *The Judean Desert Monasticism in the Byzantine Period: The Institutions of Sabas and his Disciples.* Yad Ben-Zvi; Jerusalem (Hebrew).

8.27: The inscription was published on p. 636 and fig. 2 in Waheeb, M., 1998. 'Wadi al-Kharrar Archaeological Project (Al-Maghtas)'. *ADAJ* XLII: 635–8. The reading of the Greek inscription published here was provided by Dr Leah Di Segni (e-mail message of 20 November 2002), who pointed out that the great number and variety of abbreviations in the inscription point to a date in the sixth century (or late fifth century at the earliest).

8.28: Pp. 558–70 in Barclay, J.T., 1858. *The City of the Great King; or, Jerusalem as it was, as it is, and as it is to be.* Philadelphia.

8.29: Quoted on pp. 321–2 in Dale, J. W., 1898. *Johannic Baptism* ΒΑΠΤΙΖΩ: *An Inquiry into the Meaning of the Word as Determined by the Usage of the Holy Scriptures.* 1993 reprint. Wauconda, Phillipsburg and Toney.

8.30: Guérin, V., 1868. *Description géographique, historique et archéologique de la Palestine.* Samarie. Vol. I. Paris; p. 364–5 in Murphy O'Connor, J., 1990. 'John the Baptist and Jesus: History and Hypotheses'. *New Testament Studies* 36: 359–74.

8.31: Pp. 350–1 in Ritter, C., 1866. *The Comparative Geography of Palestine and the Sinaitic Peninsula.* Vol. II. Translated by W.L. Gage. Edinburgh: Clark; p. 320 in Conder, F. R., and Conder C. R., 1882. *A Handbook to the Bible.* London; p. 159 in Albright, W. F., 1956. 'Recent Discoveries in Palestine and the Gospel of John', in Davies, W. D., and Daube, D. (eds), *The Background of the New Testament and its Eschatology.* Cambridge.

8.32: Pp. 108–12 in Wilkinson, J., 1981. *Egeria's Travels to the Holy Land.* Jerusalem and Warminster.

8.33: Avi-Yonah, M., 1964. *The Madaba Mosaic Map. With Introduction and Commentary.* Jerusalem; pp. 14, 37 in Donner, H., 1992. *The Mosaic Map of Madaba: An Introductory Guide.* Kampen.

8.34: Abel, F.-M., 1913. 'Mélange I, exploration de la vallée du Jourdain', *Revue Biblique* 10: 218.

8.35: P. 110 ff. in Hoehner, H. W., 1972. *Herod Antipas.* Cambridge; pp. 174–83 in Kasher, A., 1988. *Jews, Idumeans and Ancient Arabs.* Tübingen.

8.36: Haldeman, C., 1973 'The Feverish Head on the Disk of the Sun: Salome Through the Ages'. *International History Magazine* 10:64–79.

8.37: Farrar 1879 (see above, note 6.39): 301, note 1.

8.38: Kokkinos, N., 1986. 'Which Salome did Aristobulus Marry?' *Palestine Exploration Quarterly* 118: 33–50.

8.39: Jacobus de Voragine, *Legenda Aurea Sanctorum* [The Golden Legend]. 138–9 in Vol. II. Transl. Ryan, W. G. Princeton.

8.40: Pp. 119–28 and plate opposite p. 80 in Ilton, P., 1959. *Digging in the Holy Land.* London.

8.41: P. 48 and Fig.4 in Kokkinos, N., 1986. 'Which Salome did Aristobulus Marry?', *Palestine Exploration Quarterly* 118: 33–50.

8.42: Pp. 145, 147 in Conder, C. R., 1883. *Heth and Moab. Explorations in Syria in 1881 and 1882*. London.

8.43: Pp. 30–41 of Abel, F. M., 1911. *Une Croisière autour de La Mer Morte*. Paris.

8.44: Vardaman, J., 1968. 'The Excavations of Machaerus'. Unpublished manuscript. Institute of Archaeology Library, Hebrew University.

8.45: Letter by e-mail dated 16 July 2002.

8.46: Strobel, A., 1974. 'Observations about the Roman Installations at Mukawer'. *Annual of the Department of Antiquities of Jordan* XIX: 101–27; Strobel, A., 1974. 'Das römische Belagerungswerk um Machärus Topographische Untersuchungen'. *Zeitschrift des Deutschen Pälastina–Vereins* 90: 128–84.

8.47: Piccirillo, M., 1979. 'First Excavation Campaign at Qal'at el-Mishnaqa-Meqwer (Madaba)'. *ADAJ* XXIII: 177–83; Corbo, V., 1978. 'La Fortezza di Macheronte'. *Liber Annuus* XXVIII: 217–31; Loffreda, S., 1981. 'Preliminary Report on the Second Season of Excavations at Qal'at el-Mishnaqa Machaerus'. *ADAJ* XXV: 85–94; Corbo, V., 1979. 'Macheronte: La Reggia-Fortezza Erodiana'. *Liber Annuus* XXIX: 315–26.

8.48: P. 293 in Schneemelcher, W. (ed.), 1991. *New Testament Apocrypha. Volume I: Gospels and Related Writings*. Revised Edition. Translation by R. McL. Wilson. Cambridge and Westminster.

8.49: P. 56 in Warren, C., 1868. Letter XXI. In *PEF Proceedings and Notes: 1865–1869*. London.

8.50: P. 35 in Moore, C. A., 1990. 'Judith: The Case of the Pious Killer', *Bible Review* VI: 26–36.

8.51: Chapman, R., 1986–1987. 'Executions or Atrocities?: A Note on Tomb P19 at Jericho'. *Bulletin of the Anglo-Israel Archaeological Society* 6: 29–33.

8.52: Wood-Jones, F., 1908. 'The Examination of the Bodies of 100 men executed in Nubia in Roman times'. *British Medical Journal* 1:736; Boylston, A., Knüsel, C. J., Roberts, C. A., and Dawson, M., 2000. 'Investigation of a Romano-British Rural Ritual in Bedford, England'. *Journal of Archaeological Science* 27: 241–54; Hengel, M., 1977. *Crucifixion in the Ancient World and the Folly of the Message of the Cross*. Philadelphia.

8.53: My thanks to the excavator, Boaz Zissu, for providing me with a photograph of this find. For a short report on this discovery: Nagar, Y., and Shteibel, G., 2001. 'Beheadings in the Early Roman Period – Anthropological and Historical Evidence', *Proceedings of the Twenty-Seventh Archaeological Conference in Israel (2–3 April)*, p. 17, Bar-Ilan: Ramat Gan (Hebrew).

CHAPTER NINE

9.1: Betty Murray's letters and photo albums are located in the archives of the Palestine Exploration Fund, London.

9.2: Gibson, S., 1999. 'British Archaeological Institutions in Mandatory Palestine 1917–1948'. *Palestine Exploration Quarterly* 131: 115–43.

9.3: P. 49 in Finkielsztejn, G., 1998. 'More Evidence on John Hyrcanus I's Conquests: Lead Weights and Rhodian Amphora Stamps'. *Bulletin of the Anglo-Israel Archaeological Society* 16: 33–63)

9.4: Josephus, *The Jewish War* (II: 232). Translation by H. St J., Thackeray. Loeb Classical Library, London, 1927.

9.5: Murphy O'Connor, J., 1992. *The Holy Land: An Archaeological Guide From Earliest Times to 1700*. Pp. 405–6. Revised edition. Oxford: Oxford University Press.

9.6: Their survey took place in July 1872 and June 1875: p. 211 in Conder, C. R., and Kitchener, H. H., 1882. *The Survey of Western Palestine. Volume II. Sheets VII-XVI. Samaria*. London.

9.7: P. 324 in Ritter, C., 1866. *The Comparative Geography of Palestine and the Sinaitic Peninsula*. Vol. IV. Translated by W.L. Gage. Edinburgh: Clark.

9.8: Pp. 297–301: Site No. 226 in Pringle, R.D., 1998. *The Churches of the Kingdom of Jerusalem: A Corpus. Volume II: L-Z (excluding Tyre)*. Cambridge University Press: Cambridge.

9.9: *The Pilgrimage of Joannes Phocas in the Holy Land*. Transl. A. Stewart, *Palestine Pilgrims' Text Society*, 1889, London; p. 322: 12.10–12 in Wilkinson, J, Hill, J., and Ryan, W.F. (eds), 1988. *Jerusalem Pilgrimage 1099–1185*. London.

9.10: *Burchard of Mount Sion*. Transl. A. Stewart, *Palestine Pilgrims' Text Society*, 1896, London. Burchard's text seems to have been later copied by John Poloner (1422), Juan Perera (1553) and Bernardino Surius (1666).

9.11: P. 36 in Crowfoot, J. W., 1937. *Churches at Bosra and Samaria-Sebaste*. British School of Archaeology Supplementary Paper No. 4. London.

9.12: Pp. 195–204 and Plates LXXII-LXXV in Kühnel, G., 1988. *Wall Painting in the Latin Kingdom of Jerusalem*. Berlin; pp. 313–315, Plates 8B.16 b-e in Folda, J., 1995. *The Art of the Crusaders in the Holy Land*. Cambridge.

9.13: Letter No. V sent to the Palestine Exploration Fund from Nablus on 17 March 1866: *PEF Proceedings and Notes, 1865–1869*; see Alliata, E., and Piccirillo, M., 1994. 'La tombe de Jean Baptiste.' *Le Monde de la Bible* 89: 35–6.

9.14: Kloner, A. 1980. *The Necropolis of Jerusalem in the Second Temple Period*. Ph.D. thesis, Hebrew University, Jerusalem (Hebrew).

9.15: P. 40 in Hamilton, R.W., 1961. *Guide to Samaria-Sebaste*. Amman.

9.16: P. 201 in Wilkinson, J., 1981. *Egeria's Travels to the Holy Land*. Jerusalem and Warminster.

9.17: Pp. 51–52 in Wilkinson, J. 1977. *Jerusalem Pilgrims Before the Crusades*. Jerusalem. In the *Letter of Paula and Eustochium*, Jerome refers to the ashes of John the Baptist, Elisha and Obadiah at Sebaste. In Jerome's *Commentary on the Book of Obadiah*, Chapter 1, he mentions the tomb of this prophet Obadiah at Sebaste together with those of John the Baptist and Elisha. It should be noted, however, that this Obadiah is not necessarily the same as King Ahab's steward mentioned in 1 Kings 18:3. In the additions made by Jerome to the *Onomasticon* he also mentions the tomb of John the Baptist as the place where his remains were still resting, but not those of Elisha and Obadiah.

9.18: Quoted on p. 122 in Lietzmann, H., 1961b. *A History of the Early Church. Vol.IV: The Era of the Church Fathers*. London.

9.19: P. 419 in Buckingham, J. S., 1822. *Travels in Palestine*. London; Robinson, E., 1860. *Biblical Researches in Palestine and in the Adjacent Regions. A Journal of Travels in the Year 1838*. Boston.

9.20: Buckingham describes this area as follows: 'the mosque itself is a small oblong room, with steps ascending to an oratory, and its only furniture is a few simple lamps and some clean straw mats for prayer, the recess of the Caaba [i.e. the *mihrab*] being in the southern wall.' P. 419 in Buckingham, J. S. 1822. *Travels in Palestine*. London.

9.21: Boas, A. J., 1999. *Crusader Archaeology. The Material Culture of the Latin East*. Routledge: London and New York. Walsh suggested that these 'historiated' capitals were part of a cycle of scenes from the life of John the Baptist and that they came from the decoration of the single western portal of the church: p. 20 in Walsh, D. A., 1969. 'Crusader Sculpture from the Holy Land in Istanbul'. *Gesta* 8:20–9. Kenaan-Kedar, however, thinks these same capitals might have come from the *edicule* above the crypt of the tomb of John the Baptist. She also believes the sculptures were produced by artistic centres located in northern France: p. 113 in Kenaan-Kedar, N., 1992. 'The Cathedral of Sebaste: Its Western Donors and Models'. In Kedar, B.Z. (ed.), 1992. *The Horns of Hattin*. Yad Ben-Zvi, Israel Exploration Society and Variorum: Jerusalem and London. Contrary to these scholars, I would suggest that they may all have come from the transept at the eastern end of the cathedral, judging by Buckingham's description of the interior and exterior of the central apse:

'among other things seen there, are the representations of scaly armour, an owl, an eagle, a human figure, and an angel, all occupying separate compartments, and all are distinct from each other.' The exterior of the apse was also similarly decorated: 'In the lower cornice are human heads, perhaps in allusion to the severed head of the Baptist; and there are here as fantastic figures as on the inside [of the apse], the whole presenting a strange assemblage of incongruous ornaments in the most wretched taste.' P. 418 in Buckingham, J. S., 1822. *Travels in Palestine*. London.

9.22: P. 156 in Wilkinson, J., Hill, J., and Ryan, W.F. (eds), 1988. *Jerusalem Pilgrimage 1099–1185*. London.

9.23: P. 322 in Wilkinson, J., Hill, J., and Ryan, W.F. (eds), 1988. (See above, note 9.22.)

9.24: Letter No. V sent to the PEF from Nablus on 17 March 1866: *PEF Proceedings and Notes, 1865–1869*. See Alliata, E., and Piccirillo, M., 1994. 'La tombe de Jean Baptiste'. *Le Monde de la Bible* 89: 35–6.

9.25: p. 35 in Hamilton, R. W., 1961. *Guide to Samaria-Sebaste*. Amman.

9.26: This exceptional mosaic floor was located in the nave of the church at Umm al-Rasas and the depiction of the towns appear in sequence along its border. Other places represented there include Jerusalem, Nablus, Caesarea, Lod, Beth Guvrin, Ashkelon and Gaza. An adjoining dedicatory inscription dates apparently to AD 718, with another inscription in the apse area dating to AD 756. Plate XII and page 180 in Piccirillo, M., and Alliata, E., 1994. *Umm al-Rasas Mayfa'ah I. Gli scavi del complesso di Santo Stefano*. Jerusalem: SBF.

9.27: An aqueduct extended from the spring of Ain Nakoura for a distance of almost two kilometres from the south-east to the circular water tower at Sabastiyeh, which then diverted water to the different parts of the city with a major channel extending to the Forum. This water system has been dated to the third to fourth centuries AD, see Frumkin, A., 1989. 'The Water Supply System of Sebastia'. Pp. 157–67 in Amit, D. and Hirschfeld, Y. (eds), *The Aqueducts of Ancient Palestine* (Hebrew). Barth refers to a great arch for water (an aqueduct?) close to the Crusader church which had a visible length of 140 feet and a breadth of 30 feet: quoted on p. 322 and note 2 in Ritter, C., 1866. *The Comparative Geography of Palestine and the Sinaitic Peninsula*. Vol. IV. Translated by W. L. Gage. Edinburgh: Clark.

9.28: P. 416 in Buckingham, J. S., 1822. *Travels in Palestine*, London.

9.29: P. 283 in Pringle, R. D., 1998. *The Churches of the Kingdom of Jerusalem: A Corpus. Volume II: L-Z (excluding Tyre)*. Cambridge University Press: Cambridge.

9.30: P. 138 in Wilkinson, J. 1977. *Jerusalem Pilgrims Before the Crusades.* Jerusalem

9.31: Quoted in Hamilton, B., 1980. *The Latin Church in the Crusader States: The Secular Church.* Variorum: London.

9.32: An exact plan of the apses may be reconstructed based on plans published by Condor and Kitchener, and by Hamilton, see p. 211 in Conder, C. R., and Kitchener, H. H., 1882. *The Survey of Western Palestine. Volume II. Sheets VII–XVI.* Samaria. London; p. 36 in Hamilton, R. W., 1961. *Guide to Samaria–Sebaste.* Amman. Photographs of the foundations of the central apse taken by Hamilton in the 1930s are now kept in the archives of the Israel Antiquities Authority: File ATQ 164.

9.33: Buckingham described the exterior and interior of the central apse in some detail, but his description seems to have been ignored by modern scholars, which is a pity: pp. 417–18 in Buckingham, J. S. *Travels in Palestine.* London.

9.34: Pp. 358–62 in De Vogüé, 1860. *Les Eglises de la Terre Sainte*, Paris; Kenaan-Kedar N., 1992. 'The Cathedral of Sebaste: Its Western Donors and Models'. In Kedar, B. Z. (ed.), *The Horns of Hattin.* Yad Ben-Zvi, Israel Exploration Society and Variorum: Jerusalem and London; Site No. 225: pp. 283–97 in Pringle, R. D., 1998. *The Churches of the Kingdom of Jerusalem: A Corpus. Volume II: L-Z (excluding Tyre).* Cambridge University Press: Cambridge.

9.35: Wild, S., 1994. 'Open Questions, New Light. Usama Ibn Munqidh's Account of His Battles Against Muslims and Franks'. Pp. 9–29 in Athamina, K., and Heacock, R., 1994. *The Frankish Wars and Their Influence on Palestine.* Birzeit University: Al-Ram; pp. 283–97 in Pringle, R. D., 1998. *The Churches of the Kingdom of Jerusalem: A Corpus. Volume II: L-Z (excluding Tyre).* Cambridge University Press: Cambridge.

9.36: P. 287 in Pringle, R. D., 1998. *The Churches of the Kingdom of Jerusalem: A Corpus. Volume II: L-Z (excluding Tyre).* Cambridge University Press: Cambridge.

9.37: Pp. 82, 301 in Volume 2 of Wilson, J., 1847. *The Lands of the Bible Visited and Described.* London.

9.38: Pp. 189–209 in Guérin, V., 1874. *Description géographique, historique et archéologique de la Palestine.* Vol. II (part 2): *Samarie.* Paris.

9.39: Pp. 212–13 in Conder, C. R., and Kitchener, H. H., 1882. *The Survey of Western Palestine. Volume II. Sheets VII–XVI. Samaria.* London.

9.40: P. 397 in Twain, M., 1869. *The Innocents Abroad or the New Pilgrims Progress.* New edition 1966. New York, Ontario.

9.41: Opposite page 166 in Kelman, J., 1912. *The Holy Land*. London.

9.42: P. 126 in Parrot, A., 1958. *Samaria: The Capital of the Kingdom of Israel*. Studies in Biblical Archaeology No.7. SCM: London.

9.43: Pp. 69–70 in Bagatti, B., 1979. *Antichi villaggi cristiani di Samaria*. Jerusalem; p. 66 in Di Segni, L., 2002. 'The Water Supply of Roman-Byzantine Palestine in Literary and Epigraphic Sources'. Pp. 37–67 in: Amit, D., Hirschfeld, Y., and Patrich, J. (eds), *The Aqueducts of Israel* (Journal of Roman Archaeology Supplementary Series No. 42). Portsmouth.

9.44: Alt, A. 1925. 'Ein vergessenes Heiligtum des Propheten Elias', *Zeitschrift des Deutschen Palästina-Vereins* 48: 393–7; *SEG* VIII, 1937, No. 119; No. 594 in Meimaris, Y.E., 1986. *Sacred Names, Saints, Martyrs and Church Officials in the Greek Inscriptions and Papyri Pertaining to the Christian Church of Palestine*. (ΜΕΛΕΤΗΜΑΤΑ 2). Research Centre for Greek and Roman Antiquity: Athens.

CHAPTER TEN

10.1: P. 38 in Runciman, S., 1951. *A History of the Crusades*. Volume I: *The First Crusade and the Foundation of the Kingdom of Jerusalem*. Cambridge University Press: Camridge.

10.2: On the Helena traditions relating to the discovery of the cross: Taylor, J. E., 1993. *Christians and the Holy Places*. Oxford. On the Constantinian edifice: Gibson, S., and Taylor, J. E., 1994. *Beneath the Church of the Holy Sepulchre: The Archaeology and Early History of Traditional Golgotha*. PEF: London.

10.3: Pp. 97, 129, 196, 411 in Twain, M., 1869. *The Innocents Abroad or the New Pilgrim's Progress*. New edition 1966. New York, Ontario.

10.4: Pp. 76–7 in Israeli, Y., and Mevorah, D. (eds), *Cradle of Christianity*. Israel Museum Catalogue No. 438: Jerusalem; pp 23–4 in Teteriatnikova, N., 2000. 'Relics in the Foundations of Byzantine Churches', in Lidov, A. (ed.) *Relics in the Art and Culture of the Eastern Christian World*. Moscow.

10.5: P. 50 in Delehaye, H., 1933. *Les origins du culte des martyrs*. Second edition. Paris.

10.6: Nicephorus Callistus, *Historia Ecclesiastica*, in M.P.G. Vol. CXLVI, Col. 10161, which also deals with Eudocia's relic-collecting habits; pp. 24–26 in James, L., 2000. 'Dry Bones and Painted Pictures: Relics and Icons in Byzantium', in Lidov, A. (ed.), *Relics in the Art and Culture of the Eastern World*. Moscow.

10.7: Pp. 26–7 and note 11 in Dauphin, C., and Gibson, S., 1994–95. 'The Byzantine City at Dor/Dora Discovered'. *Bulletin of the Anglo-Israel Archaeological Society* 14: 9–38.

10.8: Pp. 49–50 in Runciman, S., 1951. *A History of the Crusades.* Volume I: *The First Crusade and the Foundation of the Kingdom of Jerusalem.* Cambridge University Press. Cambridge.

10.9: This reliquary is the subject of a detailed research paper by Dr Claudine Dauphin which has not yet been published.

10.10: Boas, A. J., 1999. Pp. 160–2. *Crusader Archaeology. The Material Culture of the Latin East.* Routledge: London and New York.

10.11: Frolow, A., 1961. *La rélique de la vraie croix.* Paris; Thiede, C. P., and D'Ancona, M., 2000. *The Quest for the True Cross.* London.

10.12: Pp. 234–5 in Ritter, C., 1866. *The Comparative Geography of Palestine and the Sinaitic Peninsula.* Vol. IV Translated by W.L. Gage. Edinburgh: Clark; also Harper, R. P., and Pringle, R. D., 2000. *Belmont Castle: The Excavation of a Crusader Stronghold in the Kingdom of Jerusalem.* CBRL: Oxford.

10.13: P. 46 in Runciman, S., 1956. *Byzantine Civilization.* Meridian: Cleveland and New York.

10.14: P. 115 in Hutton, W. H., 1925. *Constantinople: The Story of the Old Capital of the Empire.* London: Dent.

10.15: Pp. 114–17 in Hutton, W. H. 1925. (See above, note 10.14.)

10.16: Pp. 6, 103 in McNeal, E.H., 1969. *The Conquest of Constantinople. Robert of Clari. Translation with Introduction and Notes.* Norton and Co.: New York.

10.17: P. 165 in Friedheim, E., 1996. 'The Pagan Cults of Samaria-Sebaste in the Hellenistic and Roman Periods and the Ethnical Composition of the Local Population'. Pp. 157–70 in Eshel, Y. (ed.). *Judea and Samaria Research Studies.* Kedumim-Ariel (Hebrew).

10.18: Bowersock, G. W., 1978. *Julian the Apostate.* Harvard University Press: Cambridge; Brock, S. P., 1976. 'The Rebuilding of the Temple Under Julian: A New Source', *Palestine Exploration Quarterly* 108.

10.19: *Eccles.Histor.* 1.3, c.vii. Theodoret also relates how one monk of Syria had visions relating to John the Baptist and his relics: p. 141 in *A History of the Monks of Syria.* Transl. R. M. Price, 1985, Kalamazoo.

10.20: *Eccles. Histor.* 7.4, p. 80. Edited by Bidez. Series: *Die griechischen christlichen Schriftsteller der ersten drei Jahrhunderte.* Leipzig and Berlin. 1913.

10.21: *Eccles. Histor.* II.28, col. 1034. Edited by D. Vallarsi. Series: *Patrologia Cursus Completus, Series Latina* (PL) XXI: 536–7. General Series editor: J.P.Migne. Paris 1844; *The Church History of Rufinus of Aquileia,* Books 10 and 11. Transl. Amidon, P. R., 1997, Oxford; Lietzmann, H., 1961b. *A History of the Early Church. Vol.III: From Constantine to Julian.* London; Hunt, E.D., 1984. *Holy Land Pilgrimage in the Later Roman Empire, AD 312–460.* Clarendon Press: Oxford. The exact location of the Monastery of St Philip in Jerusalem (founded c. 340) is unknown: see No.96 on pp. 54–5 of Vailhé, S., 1900. 'Répertoire alphabétique des monastères de Palestine'. *Revue de l'Orient Chrétien* 5: 19–48.

10.22: Anonymous Pilgrim VI; *Palestine Pilgrims' Text Society* 1894. Transl. A. Stewart.

10.23: City of Jerusalem, *Palestine Pilgrims' Text Society* 1888. Transl. C.R. Conder. London.

10.24: P. 53–4 in Leppin, E., 2001. *The Elizabeth Church in Marburg.* Marburg.

10.25: Pp. 78–80 in Bahat, D., 1981. 'The Small Churches in Jerusalem', *Kardom* 16–17: 74–80 (Hebrew). A reliquary-crown (*see plate 15b*) in this book) also comes from the Church of John the Baptist and is now found in the museum of the Greek Orthodox Patriarchate. It has multiple relics of many saints, including those of John the Baptist, the apostles as well as a piece of the Holy Cross. It was apparently made in Jerusalem in the 1150s: pp. 297–9 in Folda, J., 1995. *The Art of the Crusaders in the Holy Land, 1098–1187.* Cambridge.

10.26: Dickie, A. C., 1899. 'The Lower Church of St John, Jerusalem'. *Palestine Exploration Fund Quarterly Statement* January-March: 43–5; pp. 642–8 and Plates LXIII-LXIV in Vincent, H., and Abel, F.-M., 1922. *Jérusalem: recherches de topographie, d'archéologie et d'histoire. II: Jérusalem nouvelle,* Paris. Additional excavations were made below the present floor of the crypt by the Rev. Archimandrite Kallistos in 1923 (Palestine Department of Antiquities Archives Vol. 101; IAA, Jerusalem). The crypt of the church was restored in 1926 and is now only open to the public on special occasions. Kendall, H., 1948. *Jerusalem. The City Plan. Preservation and Development During the British Mandate 1918–1948.* London: HM Stationary Office. Plate 163 shows the crypt of the church and the clear Frankish construction work of the ceiling: cross-vaulting with arches built of ashlars and vaults made of narrow oblong stones set in mortar. For a discussion relating to the whereabouts of the Hospital: pp. 73–4 in Richards, D. S., 1994. 'Saladin's Hospital in Jerusalem: Its Foundation and Some Later Archival Material'. Pp. 70–83 in Athamina, K., and Heacock, R., (eds). *The Frankish Wars and Their Influence on Palestine.* Birzeit.

10.27: Anonymous Pilgrim II, *Palestine Pilgrim's Text Society* 1894. Transl. A. Stewart.

10.28: *Palestine Pilgrim's Text Society* 1896. Transl. A. Stewart; Jacobus de Voragine, *Legenda Aurea Sanctorum [The Golden Legend]*. Transl. Ryan, W. G., Princeton.

10.29: Bagatti, B., 1997. *Bernardino Amico: Plans of the Sacred Edifices of the Holy Land*. Jerusalem.

10.30: Hunt, E.D., 1984. *Holy Land Pilgrimage in the Later Roman Empire, AD 312–460*. Clarendon Press: Oxford; p. 4, note 2 in Patrich, J., 1995. *The Judean Desert Monasticism in the Byzantine Period: The Institutions of Sabas and his Disciples*. Yad Ben-Zvi; Jerusalem (Hebrew).

10.31: No. 1 on p. 276 in Sanjian, A. K., 1969. 'Anastas Vardapet's List of Armenian Monasteries in Seventh-Century Jerusalem: A Critical Examination'. *Le Muséon* 82: 265–92; p. 24 in Narkiss, B., 1979. 'Mosaic Pavements'. Pp. 21–8 in Narkiss, B. (ed.), *Armenian Art Treasures of Jerusalem*. Jerusalem. See also page 92, notes 310–11 in Bahat, D., 1996. 'The Physical Infrastructure'. Pp. 38–100 in Prawer, J., and Ben-Shammai, H. (eds). *The History of Jerusalem: The Early Muslim Period, 638–1099*. Yad Ben-Zvi, New York University Press: Jerusalem.

10.32: John Rufus (*Plerophoriae*, ch. 79); see Vincent H., and Abel, F.M., 1922 (see above, note 10.26): P. 920 and note 5; Also Marshall, *Bulletin of the American Schools of Oriental Research* 159 (1959): 9–15; No. 11 on p. 276 in Sanjian, A, K., 1969. 'Anastas Vardapet's List of Armenian Monasteries in Seventh-Century Jerusalem: A Critical Examination'. *Le Muséon* 82: 265–92. See page 92, notes 310–311 in Bahat, D., 1996. 'The Physical Infrastructure'. Pp. 38–100 in Prawer, J., and Ben-Shammai, H. (eds). *The History of Jerusalem: The Early Muslim Period, 638–1099*. Yad Ben-Zvi, New York University Press: Jerusalem.

10.33: Anonymous Pilgrim VII, *Palestine Pilgrims' Text Society* 1894. Transl. A. Stewart.

10.34: Brevarius of Jerusalem, sixth century; p. 59 in Wilkinson, J. 1977. *Jerusalem Pilgrims Before the Crusades*. Jerusalem.

10.35: Anonymous Pilgrim VII, *Palestine Pilgrims' Text Society* 1894. Transl. A. Stewart.

10.36: *Palestine Pilgrims' Text Society* 1896. Transl. A. Stewart.

10.37: *Histor. Eccles.* 7.21.

10.38: Theodoric, *Palestine Pilgrims' Text Society* 1891. Transl. A. Stewart.

10.39: P. 6 in McNeal, E.H., 1969. *The Conquest of Constantinople. Robert of Clari. Translation with Introduction and Notes*. Norton and Co.: New York.

10.40: P. 190 in Hutton, W. H., 1925. *Constantinople: The Story of the Old Capital of the Empire.* London: Dent.

10.41: P. 268 in Milton, G., 1996. *The Riddle and the Knight. In Search of Sir John Mandeville.* London.

10.42: *Palestine Pilgrims' Text Society* 1891. Transl. Brownlow.

10.43: P. 41 in Runciman, S., 1951. *A History of the Crusades.* Volume I: *The First Crusade and the Foundation of the Kingdom of Jerusalem.* Cambridge: Cambridge University Press; see also p. 99 in Delehaye, H., 1933. *Les origines du culte des martyres.* Second edition. Paris.

10.44: P. 87 in Provatakis, T. M., 2001. *Mount Athos: A Brief History of Mount Athos and a Description of its Monuments.* Thessaloniki.

10.45: P. 102 in Gabashvili, T., *Pilgrimage to Mount Athos, Constantinople and Jerusalem 1755–1759.* Transl. by M. Ebanoidze and J. Wilkinson (see also p. 110 for the relic-jaw of John the Baptist in the Monastery of Stavronikita at Mount Athos); pp. 382–3 in Curzon, R., 1849. *Visits to the Monasteries of the Levant.* London.

10.46: Pp. 130–1 in Montrésor, C., 2000. *The Opera del Duomo Museum in Florence.* Florence; pp. 120–1 in Giusti, A., 2000 *The Baptistery of San Giovanni in Florence.* Florence.

10.47: Anonymous Pilgrim VI, *Palestine Pilgrims' Text Society* 1894. Transl. A. Stewart; p. 366 in Benvenisti, M., 1970. *The Crusaders in the Holy Land.* Israel Universities Press: Jerusalem; pp. 284–5 in Pringle, R.D., 1998. *The Churches of the Kingdom of Jerusalem: A Corpus.* Volume II: *L-Z (excluding Tyre).* Cambridge University Press: Cambridge.

10.48: Fettellus, *Palestine Pilgrims' Text Society,* 1892. Transl. J. R. MacPherson.

10.49: P. 215 in Domke, H., 1987. *Aquitanien.* Munich; Landes, R., 1995. *Relics, Apocalypse, and the Deceits of History; Ademar of Chabannes, 989–1034.* Cambridge. A translation of the passage from Ademar by Thomas Head has also been posted on the internet: *http://urban.hunter.cuny.edu.*

10.50: Pp. 51, 55 – photographs of the arm and the skull relics in Can, T., 1998. *Topkapi Palace.* Orient Publications: Istanbul; see also p. 287 in Pringle, R. D., 1998. *The Churches of the Kingdom of Jerusalem: A Corpus.* Volume II: *L-Z (excluding Tyre).* Cambridge University Press: Cambridge. This arm may have been the same as the one mentioned in the eleventh century in the monastery of St Mary Peribleptos: p. 218 in Mango, C., 1972. *The Art of the Byzantine Empire, 312–1453. Sources and Documents.* New Jersey.

10.51: Anonymous Pilgrim VI, twelfth century, *Palestine Pilgrims' Text*

Society 1894. Transl. A. Stewart; p. 99 in Delehaye, H., 1933. *Les origines du culte des martyres;* p. 41 in Runciman, S., 1951. *A History of the Crusades.* Volume I: *The First Crusade and the Foundation of the Kingdom of Jerusalem.* Cambridge: Cambridge University Press.

10.52: *Palestine Pilgrims' Text Society,* 1892. Transl. J. R. MacPherson.

10.53: *Palestine Pilgrims' Text Society* 1891. Transl. A. Stewart.

10.54: P. 322 in Wilkinson, J., Hill, J., and Ryan, W.F., 1988. *Jerusalem Pilgrimage 1099–1185.* London; see also *Palestine Pilgrims' Text Society* 1889. Transl. A. Stewart.

10.55: Description of the Holy Land, *Palestine Pilgrims' Text Society* 1895. Transl. A. Stewart.

10.56: P. 75 and photograph on p. 154 in Provatakis, T. M., 2001. *Mount Athos: A Brief History of Mount Athos and a Description of its Monuments.* Thessaloniki.

10.57: Pp. 64, 131, 134 in Montrésor, C., 2000. *The Opera del Duomo Museum in Florence.* Florence; pp. 119, 121 in Giusti, A., 2000. *The Baptistery of San Giovanni in Florence.* Florence.

10.58: Anonymous Pilgrim VII, *Palestine Pilgrims' Text Society* 1894. Transl. A. Stewart.

10.59: Pp. 49–50 in Runciman, S., 1951. *A History of the Crusades.* Volume I: *The First Crusade and the Foundation of the Kingdom of Jerusalem.* Cambridge: Cambridge University Press; p. 51 Arutiunova, V., 2000. 'Relics in the Armenian-Byzantine Relationship: Political and Religious Aspects', in Lidov, A. (ed.), *Relics in the Art and Culture of the Eastern Christian World.* Moscow.

10.60: Pp. 52, 104 in Pringle, R.D., 1998. *The Churches of the Kingdom of Jerusalem: A Corpus. Volume II: L-Z (excluding Tyre).* Cambridge University Press: Cambridge.

10.61: For the full story of these specific relics, see: Berlière, U., 1908. 'Fréderic de Laroche, évêque d'Acre et archevêque de Tyr. Envoi de reliques à l'abbaye de Florennes (1153–1161)', *Annales de l'Institut archéologique du Luxembourg* 43: 67–79; see also Kenaan-Kedar, N., 1992. 'The Cathedral of Sebaste: Its Western Donors and Models'. Pp.99–120. In Kedar, B.Z. (ed.), 1992. *The Horns of Hattin.* Yad Ben-Zvi, Israel Exploration Society and Variorum: Jerusalem and London.

10.62: Gibson, S., and Dauphin, C., 1990. 'Landscape Archaeology at Er-Ramthaniyye in the Golan Heights', in Fiches, J.-L., and Van Der Leeuw, E. E. (eds), *Archéologie et Espaces. Actes des Xes Rencontres Internationales d'Archéologie et d'Histoire, Antibes, Octobre 1989.* Juan-Les-Pins; pp. 325–7 (Inscriptions 25, 27) in Dauphin, C., Brock, S., Gregg,

R. C., and Beeston, A. F. L., 1996. 'Païens, Juifs, Judéo-Chrétiens, Chrétiens et Musulmans en Gaulanitide: Les inscriptions de Na'ran, Kafr Naffakh, Farj et Er-Ramthaniyye'. *Proche-Orient Chrétien* 46: 305–40.

10.63: P. 146, Inscription No. 81 in the list provided in Ewing, W., 1895. 'Greek and Other Inscriptions Collected in the Havran.' Palestine Exploration Fund Quarterly Statement 131–60.

10.64: Baldi, D., 1955–56. 'Santuari di S. Giovanni Battista in Terrasanta'. *Liber Annuus* 6: 196–239.

10.65: P. 101 in Meimaris, Y.E., 1986. *Sacred Names, Saints, Martyrs and Church Officials in the Greek Inscriptions and Papyri Pertaining to the Christian Church of Palestine*. (ΜΕΛΕΤΗΜΑΤΑ 2). Research Centre for Greek and Roman Antiquity: Athens.

10.66: Inscription No. 306; pp. 242–3, 479–80, Pl.XLVI:b. in Kraeling, C. H., 1938. *Gerasa: City of the Decapolis*. ASOR: New Haven.

10.67: Kelman, J., 1912. *The Holy Land*. London.

10.68: Pp. 372–3 in Pringle, R.D., 2000. Book Review in: *Medieval Archaeology* 44; see also p. 306 in Folda, J., 1995. *The Art of the Crusaders in the Holy Land, 1098–1187*. Cambridge.

10.69: Pp. 369–70 in Pringle, R.D., 1998. *The Churches of the Kingdom of Jerusalem: A Corpus. Volume II: L-Z (excluding Tyre)*. Cambridge University Press: Cambridge.

10.70: Pp. 223 and 180 in Pringle, R.D., 1993. *The Churches of the Kingdom of Jerusalem: A Corpus. Volume I: A-K (excluding Acre and Jerusalem)*. Cambridge University Press: Cambridge.

10.71: Pp. 72–3 in Jotischky, A., 1995. *The Perfection of Solitude. Hermits and Monks in the Crusader States*. Pennsylvania.

10.72: P. 38 in Kühnel, G., 1988. *Wall Painting in the Latin Kingdom of Jerusalem*. Berlin.

10.73: Pp. 13–14, Giusti, A., 2000. *The Baptistery of San Giovanni in Florence*. Florence.

10.74: *City of Jerusalem, Palestine Pilgrims' Text Society* 1888, London, transl. C.R. Conder.

12.75: Guérin, V., 1868. *Description géographique, historique et archéologique de la Palestine*. Judée. Vol. I. Paris.

10.76: Haldeman, C., 1973. 'The Feverish Head on the Disk of the Sun: Salome Through the Ages'. *International History Magazine* No. 10: 64–79.

10.77: Canaan, T., 1927. *Mohammadan Saints and Sanctuaries in Palestine*. Jerusalem.

10.78: P. 481 in Glassé, C., 2001. *The Concise Encyclopedia of Islam.* Revised Edition. Stacey International: London.

10.79: P. 243, note 3 in Canaan, T., 1927. *Mohammedan Saints and Sanctuaries in Palestine.* Jerusalem.

10.80: P. 287 in Glassé, C., 2001. *The Concise Encyclopedia of Islam.* Revised Edition. Stacey International: London.

10.81: For the early history of research into the Mandaean literature and their origins, see: pp. 281–2 in Albright, W. F., 1940. *From the Stone Age to Christianity. Monotheism and the Historical Process.* Baltimore; pp. 43–4 in Lietzmann, H., 1961. *A History of the Early Church. Vol.I: The Beginnings of the Christian Church.* London.

Index

369

Index

Index